Understanding Human Agency

Our self-understanding as human agents includes a commitment to three crucial claims about human agency: that agents must be active, that our actions are part of the natural order, and that intentional actions can be explained by the agent's reasons for acting. While all of these claims are indispensable elements of our self-conception as human agents, they are in continuous conflict and tension with one another, especially once one adopts the predominant view of what the natural order must be like. One of the central tasks of the philosophy of action consists in showing how, despite appearances, these conflicts can be resolved and our self-understanding as agents be vindicated. The mainstream of contemporary philosophy of action holds that this task can only be fulfilled by an event-causal reductive view of human agency, paradigmatically embodied in the so-called standard model developed by Donald Davidson. Erasmus Mayr, in contrast, develops a new agent-causal solution to these conflicts and shows why this solution is superior both to event-causalist accounts and to Von Wright's intentionalism about agency. He offers a comprehensive theory of substance-causation on the basis of a realist conception of powers, which allows one to see how the widespread rejection of agent-causation rests on an unfounded 'Humean' prejudice about nature and causal processes. At the same time, Mayr addresses the question of the nature of reasons for acting and complements his substance-causal account of activity with a non-causal account of acting for reasons in terms of following a standard of success.

Erasmus Mayr is Professor of Philosophy at the Universität Erlangen-Nürnberg. He studied philosophy and law in Munich and Oxford, and received the Wolfgang-Stegmüller Award of the German Society for Analytical Philosophy (GAP) in 2009 for his PhD thesis.

Understanding Human Agency

Erasmus Mayr

Great Clarendon Street, Oxford, OX2 6DP,
United Kingdom

Oxford University Press is a department of the University of Oxford.
It furthers the University's objective of excellence in research, scholarship,
and education by publishing worldwide. Oxford is a registered trade mark of
Oxford University Press in the UK and in certain other countries

© Erasmus Mayr 2011

The moral rights of the author have been asserted

First published 2011
First published in paperback 2018

All rights reserved. No part of this publication may be reproduced, stored in
a retrieval system, or transmitted, in any form or by any means, without the
prior permission in writing of Oxford University Press, or as expressly permitted
by law, by licence or under terms agreed with the appropriate reprographics
rights organization. Enquiries concerning reproduction outside the scope of the
above should be sent to the Rights Department, Oxford University Press, at the
address above

You must not circulate this work in any other form
and you must impose this same condition on any acquirer

Published in the United States of America by Oxford University Press
198 Madison Avenue, New York, NY 10016, United States of America

British Library Cataloguing in Publication Data
Data available

Library of Congress Cataloging in Publication Data
Data available

ISBN 978–0–19–960621–4 (Hbk.)
ISBN 978–0–19–882585–2 (Pbk.)

Links to third party websites are provided by Oxford in good faith and
for information only. Oxford disclaims any responsibility for the materials
contained in any third party website referenced in this work.

For my parents

Acknowledgements

This book developed out of my D.Phil. thesis, of which it is a fundamentally modified and revised version. The thesis was written at the Ludwigs-Maximilians-Universität in Munich throughout 2005–7, during which time I spent one academic year at the University of Oxford, supported by a scholarship from the German Academic Exchange Service (DAAD), for whose support I want to express my gratitude. I also wish to express my thanks to the German National Academic Foundation (Studienstiftung des Deutschen Volkes) for supporting me with a scholarship and to the German Society for Analytic Philosophy (GAP) for awarding the thesis with the Wolfgang-Stegmüller-Preis.

In addition, there are many people who have helped and supported me during the writing of this book. Special thanks are due to my thesis supervisor, Wilhelm Vossenkuhl, for his continuous encouragement and good advice. I also want to express my gratitude to Peter Hacker, John Hyman, and Joseph Raz, who were kind enough to supervise my work during my stay at Oxford, and from whose comments I have profited enormously. Of the great number of people to whom I owe thanks for support, helpful advice, or stimulating discussions, I can name but a few here: Thomas Buchheim, Gerhard Ernst, Johannes Hübner, Florian Leiss, Angela Matthies, Martin Rechenauer, Ulrich Schroth, Stephan Sellmaier, Thomas Splett, and Till Vierkant. Jay Wallace very kindly read the last part of the manuscript, and his advice greatly helped me to see—and hopefully to say—more clearly what I wanted to express. In addition, two anonymous referees for OUP provided very helpful comments, and Peter Momtchiloff, Sarah Parker, and Jennifer Lunsford deserve great thanks for their editorial work and their great patience. Thanks are also due to my copy-editor, Bob Marriott, and to Mary Morton, for the proof-reading.

I am, however, particularly indebted to Erich Ammereller and Franz Knappik, who patiently and heroically read through earlier and later versions of the manuscript and offered excellent suggestions both on the content and on the formulations. Their comments greatly helped me to avoid errors and close gaps in my arguments, as well as to make the text less tedious to read than it otherwise might have been. Any remaining errors are due entirely to my stubborn resistance to accept the rest of the good advice and criticism that was offered.

Erasmus Mayr
München

Contents

Introduction	1
1 The problem of human agency	5
1.1. Three harmless theses and a problem	6
1.2. Reacting to the problem: the 'privileging' reaction	14
2 The agenda for finding a solution	23
2.1. What kind of solution is required?	23
2.2. Performances, agential control, and intentionalism	27
2.3. Event-causalism versus agent-causalism	36
3 Alien desires and Frankfurt's problem of identification	46
3.1. The challenge from Frankfurt's cases of alienation	47
3.2. Frankfurt's hierarchical model	52
3.3. Responses to the three problems: the later Frankfurt, Watson, and Velleman	58
4 Identification, desires, and practical reasoning	69
4.1. Identification as 'treating a desire as reason-giving'	70
4.2. The authority of practical reasoning and the nature of motivating reasons	80
4.3. Three objections	91
4.4. Conclusion	102
5 Deviant causal chains	104
5.1. The problem of antecedential waywardness	104
5.2. The standard of adequacy for a causalist analysis	109
5.3. The 'immediate causation' strategy	114
5.4. Sensitivity strategies	117
5.5. Sustaining causation	121
5.6. The new 'manifestation' or 'well-functioning' analyses of action	130
5.7. Conclusion	140
6 How agent-causation works I: the problem, and a brief theory of powers	142
6.1. The classical argument against the possibility of agent-causation	146
6.2. Powers as genuine properties	159
7 How agent-causation works II: the irreducibility of powers	169
7.1. The irreducibility of power-ascriptions	170
7.2. The ontological irreducibility of powers	181

7.3. Powers without 'natural necessity' and essentialism	188
7.4. Conclusion	196

8 How agent-causation works III: from causal powers to agent-causation ... 198
   8.1. Substance-causation among inanimate substances ... 198
   8.2. Agent-causation by human beings ... 219
   8.3. The proposed account and the standard objections against agent-causation ... 226

9 Are agent-causal powers reducible to microproperties? ... 233
   9.1. Five degrees of dependence of the properties of composites ... 234
   9.2. The dependence of human powers on microproperties ... 239
   9.3. Human powers and 'downward causation' ... 240
   9.4. Summary ... 247

10 Intentional agency and acting for reasons ... 249
   10.1. Davidson's challenge and the purported causal element in reasons-explanations ... 251
   10.2. Reacting to the challenge—why (surprisingly) causalism itself does not provide an answer ... 254
   10.3. Some unsuccessful non-causal answers to Davidson's challenge ... 259

11 Understanding human agency ... 268
   11.1. Acting for a reason as following a standard of success ... 268
   11.2. Putting it all together ... 291

References ... 297
Index ... 311

Introduction

It is one of the truisms about our life that there are things that we do and other things that happen to us. Persons eat their lunch, go to work, walk their dogs, or write books, but they also get hungry, are fired, are bitten by dogs on the street, or fall asleep. It is equally a truism about our life that there is a difference between doing something and having something happen to one, that it is not the same, whether one is fired or gives notice oneself, or whether one drives to work or is driven by a chauffeur. We are accustomed to describe this difference in terms of the oppositions between acting and suffering, or activity and passivity.

The paradigm case of activity, as found in nature, seems to be human agency. Even if we are passive with regard to natural processes around us or with regard to what other people do to us, even though we may be overcome by desires or stuck with beliefs that we cannot get rid of, we must be active with regard to the actions we perform, for otherwise they could not be actions—or so it seems. But when we start to reflect on the nature of those actions and about our supposedly active role in performing them, we begin to be puzzled by the question of how the picture of us as active beings can be reconciled with another picture of the world to which we have grown accustomed since the eighteenth century—an image of the world as a flux of events, following upon each other, where one event can be explained by appeal to prior events and to natural laws discovered by natural science, if it can be explained at all. As we are part of the world, it seems that we must also fit ourselves in this latter, 'scientific', picture of the world—and this latter picture seems to have no room for activity, but only for happenings that befall the inhabitants of this world.

At the same time, our understanding of human actions is intimately tied to a characteristic kind of explanation: namely, explanation in terms of the agent's reasons for acting. When we ask why John booked a trip to Madagascar, we typically want to know what his reasons were for doing so; e.g., what aim he was pursuing in booking the trip; and when we have learned about his aim—that he intended to impress his girlfriend, for example—we feel that we have understood why this action was performed. So far, so good. But again, when we start to think about the relation between this kind and other kinds of explanation, a tension begins to appear with the kind of explanation characteristic to the 'scientific' image of the world. For as our actions are part of the world, it seems that they can be explained either by appeal to prior events and natural laws, or cannot be explained at all. How does this leave space for reasons-explanations as genuine explanations of action in their own right? Must we not assume that reasons-explanations are, contrary to appearance, just a sub-type of explanation of the other kind in order to avoid a problematic form of 'explanatory over-determination'?

The interconnections and mutual tensions between these three fundamental elements in our self-understanding as agents—activity, our place in the natural order, and reasons-explanations of actions—give rise to what I call the problem of human agency. This is, basically, the problem of how these three elements could be reconciled in a unified account of the nature of human agency. The aim of the present work is to present this problem and to develop a solution for it.

I begin by showing that there are three basic kinds of reaction to the perceived tensions between the three elements, each of which consists in elevating one of these elements to the centrepiece of human agency, at the expense of the others. The results of these reactions are agent-causalist, naturalist event-causalist, and intentionalist theories of action. While the first theory claims that what is crucial to agency is a causal role of the agent himself which is not reducible to causal contributions of events involving the agent, the second models human agency on the flux-of-events model and reduces it to the causation of behaviour by mental states. The intentionalist model rejects both causalist approaches, and claims that what is crucial for human agency is only the applicability of a certain kind of explanation: namely, reasons-explanation, or teleological explanation.

My own preferred solution to the problem is an agent-causal theory which recognizes the intrinsic connection between activity and reasons-explanations. The apparent tension with the second element is dissolved by arguing that this tension stems only from a misconceived and overly restrictive view of the 'natural order'. The route towards establishing this solution will be the following.

In Chapter 2 I show that purely intentionalist accounts of action are bound to fail, because they cannot deal with the required control of the agent over the results of his actions in the case of actions consisting in peripheral bodily movements. With regard to such actions, the issue therefore reduces to one between an event-causal and an agent-causal account. This issue must be decided by enquiring how well each of these accounts is able to deal with the crucial elements of our notion of agency—and the one crucial element which I take as a touchstone is the idea of 'control' over his bodily motions which an agent must exert when he performs a bodily movement.

In Chapters 3–5 I criticize the event-causal model of causation and show that the account it offers of the agent's 'control' is inadequate. For the event-causal account in its most influential form—the 'standard model'—the control of the agent is constituted by causation of the bodily motions by the agent's mental states that constitute his will. I argue that both the proposed 'bearers' of control—mental states such as desires—and the proposed 'mode' of control—event-causation—cannot play the role that would be required for a success of the standard model.

In Chapter 3 I begin with the proposed 'bearers' of control, focusing especially on the agent's desires, and addressing the 'problem of identification' developed by Harry Frankfurt. This problem throws grave doubts on the idea that the agent's control can be made intelligible in terms of the causal role of his desires, because it shows that his own desires may be obstacles to the realization of the agent's will. As I argue in Chapter 4, on the most convincing solution to the problem of identification, an agent identifies with a desire if he is prepared to treat the desire as reason-giving in his practical reasoning. This analysis implies that desires themselves cannot determine what an agent 'really wants', because they are not reasons themselves, and identification presupposes an activity of the agent, expressed in his capacity for practical reasoning, that cannot itself be reduced to the causal role of those desires.

In Chapter 5 I turn to the proposed mode of control and try to show that the event-causalist account is faced with the intractable problem of deviant causal chains, which excludes that actions might be reduced to the causings of bodily movements by the right mental antecedents. This problem arises from the possibility that bodily motions are caused by the agent's desires or intentions 'in the wrong way'—in a way that prevents, rather than ensures, the agent's control over his motions—for example, via uncontrollable nervousness causing spastic motions. Consequently, the resulting effect may either not be the result of any action at all, or not a result that was intentionally brought about. A variety of proposed solutions to this problem are discussed, and shown to fail.

Having rejected the event-causalist standard model of human agency, we are left with the constructive task of developing an agent-causal account of human agency. Though the idea of control is easily captured by the notion of agent-causation itself, there are widespread misgivings about the possibility of agent-causation, which concern both the coherence of the notion and the possibility of its instantiation 'in the natural order'.

Chapters 6–9 are dedicated to the task of showing how these misgivings can be answered, and how the first two fundamental elements of human agency—activity and 'our place in the natural order'—can be reconciled. I develop a wider notion of substance-causation, based on a model of powers as genuine properties of objects, of which agent-causation will be a special instance in those cases where the substance involved is a human person. In this way it becomes apparent how agent-causation can and should be accepted 'in the natural order', and the apparent incompatibility of the first and second element turns out to rest solely on a mistaken prejudice that 'the natural order' must be purely event-causal.

The account of agential control will be incomplete as long as we have not explained how the agent, in his actions, can respond to perceived reasons for action. In Chapters 10 and 11, I therefore try to show how the agent-causal account can do justice to the third element of our self-understanding as human agents: that intentional actions can be explained by the agent's reasons. Adherents of the standard model regularly claim that only an event-causal connection between reason and action can explain the difference between those reasons an agent has without acting on them, and those reasons for which an agent acts. Against this claim, I develop an account of what it is to act for a reason which construes acting for a reason as following a standard of success. This account allows us to explain the connection between the claim that the agent has acted for one reason rather than another, and the essential feature of reasons-explanations that they not only show why an action was performed, but also make this action rationally intelligible, thus playing a justificatory role. The model which emerges finally provides the solution to the problem of human agency, because it shows how the three core elements of agency are to be integrated into a unified account which does justice to all of them.

The model of human agency which I develop is deeply rooted in what may be called the Aristotelian–Wittgensteinian tradition in the philosophy of action. It is therefore—both with regard to its overall approach and with regard to more particular aspects—much indebted to philosophers from this tradition, such as Elizabeth Anscombe, Georg Hendrik von Wright, Anthony Kenny, and, more recently, Joseph Raz, Maria Alvarez, John Hyman, and Peter Hacker. This is true even at those points where I openly find myself in disagreement with these philosophers. The points of disagreement should therefore not disguise the underlying fundamental consensus, and should not make it appear that my aim is to develop a completely novel or rival account to this tradition. My main motivation is, rather, to develop what I consider has been lacking so far: a workable comprehensive account of agency within the agent-causalist strand of the Aristotelian–Wittgensteinian tradition.

1
The problem of human agency

Our self-understanding as human agents brings with it three central commitments which appear trivial in themselves, but which easily come into conflict with one another: the commitments to an active role of the agent, to his 'place in the natural order', and to reasons-explanations of actions. The tensions among these commitments give rise to what I call the problem of human agency—the problem of how these commitments can be reconciled within a unified account of human agency (Section 1.1).

The overwhelming majority of present-day philosophers believe that at least one of the commitments must be abandoned or fundamentally modified. Their common reaction to the problem consists in privileging one of the commitments while admitting the other two only insofar as they can be made to fit with it. In its extreme form, this reaction leads to abandoning two of the commitments in favour of the third. The resulting positions are radical agent-causalism with 'ultimate control of the self', naturalist eliminativism, and 'pure' intentionalism. Most of the present-day accounts of human agency are not radical to this degree, but practically all current theories of action can be seen as results of privileging one of the commitments over the others. According to which commitment is favoured, this reaction leads to an agent-causalist, naturalist event-causalist, or intentionalist view of agency (Section 1.2).

However, no solution to the problem of human action which rests on privileging one of the core commitments to the detriment of the others can be completely satisfactory, for it would imply that our self-conception as human agents is deeply flawed because not all three commitments can be honoured. To avoid this result, we must try to show how the three commitments can be reconciled without loss to any of them; and an element can only be 'privileged' in the sense that we take it as the starting-point, not in the sense that the others are 'subordinated' to it. We therefore have to examine which of the three main directions in action theory provides the best starting-point for an account which integrates all three elements. Developing such an account is the task to which the rest of this book will be dedicated.

1.1. Three harmless theses and a problem

Let us begin with the following three innocuous statements about human agency:[1]

Thesis 1 Human actions are instances of activity: the agent is active with regard to what he is doing and not a merely passive sufferer.
Thesis 2 Human actions are natural phenomena—part of the 'natural order'.
Thesis 3 Human actions, insofar as they are intentional, can be explained by citing the reasons for which they have been performed.

Theses 1, 2, and 3 express central parts of our self-understanding as human agents, to which we are strongly committed. Thesis 1 expresses a conceptual truth about agency: if an agent does not actively do something, then he does not act. This is the crucial difference between actions and things that just 'befall' us, and with regard to which we can be purely passive—such as toothaches. Thesis 2 is a reflection of the trivial fact that human beings are not divine or supernatural beings, but part of nature.[2] And Thesis 3 describes the characteristic kind of explanation by which we typically try to understand why a human being has acted in a certain way. Intentional actions are those actions which are performed for reasons, and which can therefore be explained successfully by citing those reasons. This kind of action is the paradigmatic or 'central' kind of human actions in general.[3] Giving up either of Theses 1, 2, or 3 seems absurd, for this would imply either that actions are no different from the things that we suffer—such as toothaches—or that we stand outside the natural order, or that we never act for reasons—and none of these are possibilities that we can seriously consider as long as we see ourselves as human agents at all.

There is a fourth claim which many philosophers consider as equally essential to our self-understanding as human agents, but which I have neither mentioned separately nor intend to treat as a separate Thesis. This is the claim that we are autonomous agents who freely choose for ourselves our courses of action. To a large extent, this commitment to autonomy is already contained in Theses 1 and 3, as autonomy is—crucially—an instance of being active for reasons. But this does not exhaust autonomy, which also contains an additional element: freedom of choice.[4] This element connects the notion of autonomy to the problem of free will. As we will not be dealing with the latter topic

---

[1] For the sake of convenience I will call these statements 'Theses'—though considered as constitutive parts of our pre-theoretical self-understanding as human agents they are not theses that we could accept or reject, but truisms. It is only in philosophical reflection—when we realize the tensions between them and ask ourselves whether one or two of them have to be given up—that they properly become theses.

[2] Some philosophers would want to argue that strictly speaking, not actions themselves, but only the events intrinsically connected to actions, are part of the 'natural order'. For our following arguments, however, the difference between this view and Thesis 2 is mostly irrelevant, for the problems I will present also arise, *mutatis mutandis*, on the former view.

[3] Cf. Anscombe (1957), 9 ff.; Raz (1999), 23.

[4] At least on one common understanding of autonomy, where it includes that the agent's decision is not determined by factors outside his will. Cf. Wolf (1990), 10 ff., who contrasts autonomy with (mere) 'determination by the self'.

here—because we are only concerned with agency simpliciter, and not with *free* agency in particular—we will leave out the additional element of free choice, and will only deal, implicitly, with the notion of autonomy insofar as it is contained in Theses 1 and 3.

Though we regard each of Theses 1, 2, and 3 as expressing obvious truths, the Theses and their underlying commitments pull us into different directions. And once we try to take one of the individual commitments seriously, and thoroughly spell out its implications, this inexorably leads to conflict with the other two commitments—or, at least, so it seems. To illustrate this, let us begin with Thesis 2 and examine how spelling out the implications of this Thesis leads to tensions with Theses 1 and 3.

Since the rise of the natural sciences from the seventeenth century onward, we have become accustomed to regard natural phenomena as amenable to scientific explanation—at least insofar as they are not in principle unexplainable, such as results of pure chance, or due to miracles. In one way, actions are clearly amenable to scientific explanation: namely, to the explanations offered by psychology or the social sciences. But the claim of scientific explainability is traditionally focused on explainability by the *natural* sciences: Natural phenomena must either 'already' be explainable by these sciences, or at least must fit into the general picture of nature that these sciences suggest—the 'emerging scientific image' of the world, as self-declared 'naturalist' philosophers like to call it. On this view, the following claim is simply the 'updated' version of Thesis 2:

Thesis 2★: Human agency must fit within the 'emerging scientific image of the world' (insofar as it is not miraculous).

What Thesis 2★ commits one to depends on what is taken to be the 'emerging scientific image'. If we take the 'picture of reality' offered or suggested by the present-day natural sciences as a guideline, the claim is not overly demanding. For these sciences do not present us with a *uniform* picture of this kind at all, but their conjunction provides a highly multi-faceted and multi-layered image of nature, which does not claim to be complete, but is open for the addition of yet new facets which have hitherto escaped the 'network' of established facts. So, if compatibility of a purported phenomenon with the 'emergent scientific image' just means that the phenomenon is not at odds with what is suggested by the natural sciences, this condition is easily fulfilled. Due to the lack of uniformity or closure of the picture suggested by the sciences, it requires only that the phenomenon is not positively in conflict with established scientific findings.

If Thesis 2★ is understood in this way, it is hard to see how it could come into conflict with Theses 1 or 3. Only 'miraculous' human actions that positively 'break' the natural laws are directly at odds with the established findings of science—and these cases, for which we have already made an exception in Thesis 2★, do not really fall within the purview of a theory explaining *human* agency at all. But how could the presently established findings of physics, chemistry, biology, or neurophysiology rule out the possibility of human activity or agency for reasons in general? Either they do not even talk about those phenomena as such—as far as physics or chemistry are concerned—or what they tell us about what happens when we act is, so far, much too sketchy to provide us with even a complete picture of what neurophysiological processes must occur when we act.

Nonetheless, it is sometimes claimed that the possibility of human activity or agency for reasons—in particular for *free* human agency—has already been 'empirically refuted' by the findings of neurophysiology.[5] I cannot discuss these alleged experimental refutations in any detail here. Suffice it to say that none of them can be considered as a compelling refutation of the possibility of human activity or of agency for reasons. The experimental results are either open to quite different interpretations, according to the background philosophical theory of action to which one subscribes,[6] or they are based on particular cases of errors which do not warrant a general scepticism about agency.[7] But beyond the failure of these particular 'refutations', the more general point can be made that no such refutation of the possibility of human activity or agency for reasons can be expected from the findings of natural science alone—for the simple reason that the empirical sciences by themselves do not tell us what the nature of human activity or agency for reasons consists in. The latter is not an empirical but a conceptual question of how to understand the commitments integral to our self-understanding as human agents. Therefore, any interpretation of experimental results as providing a refutation of the possibility of agency will necessarily be a philosophical interpretation of these results on the basis of a *particular* theory of human action; and so, at most, *this particular* theory could be refuted by the experimental findings,[8] but the findings cannot show that the commitments expressed by Theses 1 and 3 are, as such, untenable.

Thus, no direct conflict between Thesis 2★, on the one hand, and Theses 1 and 3, on the other, is to be expected if the 'scientific image of the world' is taken to be the picture suggested by the actual findings of the present-day natural sciences. The conflict with Theses 1 and 3 arises, however, once we spell out some widespread philosophical preconceptions of what the 'emerging scientific image of nature' must be like—preconceptions which have been enormously influential because since the eighteenth century they have shaped, to a large degree, the understanding of what

---

[5] The most influential experiments on which claims of this kind are usually based are Libet's experiments about unconscious initiation of actions; cf. Libet (1985). Other influential experiments concern the misattribution of authorship, Wegner and Wheatley (1999), and automatic unconscious control of movements, Jeannerod (2003). Wegner (2002) provides what is probably the best-known exposition of the general conclusion that conscious will plays no role in the initiation or control of action, but is a mere epiphenomenon.

[6] For the Libet experiments this is convincingly shown, for example, by Bennett and Hacker (2003), 229 ff.

[7] This applies to Wegner's argument; for a more detailed discussion, cf. Walde (2006), 116 ff.

[8] For instance, Libet's argument might have been successful in refuting one particular theory of free action, on which it required initiation by a conscious volitional act without any physical causes.

the natural sciences are doing. For our purposes, the two most important preconceptions are the 'event-causal view' of nature and the 'bottom-up'[9] picture of the world.

On the event-causal view—which has its origin in David Hume's discussion of causation in his *Treatise*—nature is seen as a flux of events or happenings, wherein substances only appear as objects which undergo changes. The events are partly connected amongst each other, it is assumed, by natural laws—deterministic or indeterministic—which empirical science must discover. The only form of causation within this course of events is event-causation, which depends on the existence of those connecting natural laws; and if a happening in this flux of events can be explained at all, it can be explained by prior happenings in conjunction with the connecting laws. This event-causal view—which is widely considered to be an obvious part of 'our scientific view of the world'[10]—clearly has no place for any genuine activity of human agents, nor of any other natural substances. It implies that all human actions, as natural phenomena, must also be part of the flux of events and, as such, 'happenings'; and the only way in which it allows that this happening can essentially involve the agent, as actions do, is as something that happens *to* the agent or is connected to other events that happen *to* him, but not as something of which he is the active source.[11] So, if the event-causal view is part of the 'emerging scientific image of nature', Thesis 2★ and Thesis 1 are clearly in conflict.

The event-causal view also gives rise to difficulties for an adequate understanding of reasons-explanations of actions, and thus creates tensions with Thesis 3. Reasons-explanations of actions have a distinctive way of making intelligible why an action has been performed. They show what was the 'point' of the chosen course of action for the agent, and thus make the action intelligible as something that was, to a degree 'the rational thing to do'; thus, they are 'rationalizations' of actions.[12] At the same time, however, they are not *mere* rationalizations, but genuine explanations of why actions have been performed. Mere rationalizations are 'sham' explanations which only point out features that *could* have made the action rational in some respect, but which *have* not, in fact, motivated the agent. The best-known instances of this kind are self-deceptive *ex post* rationalizations, by which persons who have acted for reasons which they do not want to admit to themselves try to construct some new reason *ex post factum*, which makes the action appear in a better light. Reasons-explanations have a rationalizing function, but are also proper explanations and, as such, different from such mere self-justificatory practices; and the event-causal view creates difficulties for accounting for both these characteristics at the same time.

---

[9] This term is taken from Searle (1984), 94.
[10] Velleman (1992), 467.
[11] This implication has been worked out especially vividly by Thomas Nagel (1986), 111 ff. For Nagel, the 'event-causal picture' is part of the external perspective, which is at odds with the internal view of action, on which at least free actions 'originate with us'; op. cit., 117.
[12] Cf. Davidson (1963), 3; Dancy (2000), 94 ff.

For, on the event-causal view, actions are events, which must be explainable by earlier events and relating causal laws—if they are explainable at all. Assume that such an explanation can be found for an intentional action: for example, in terms of earlier neurophysiological or mental events. Then the question arises as to how this explanation relates to the reasons-explanation, which, according to Thesis 3, is also possible and which concerns the same explanandum. With regard to this question, we seem to face the following dilemma.

The first alternative is that the two explanations are distinct from each other, and we cannot reduce one to the other. Then we seem to have a case of 'explanatory overdetermination', in which one and the same phenomenon is given two different and independent explanations. Cases of 'explanatory overdetermination', however, are viewed with suspicion by many philosophers, who think that once an event has been given one successful explanation, any other independent explanation must be otiose—because no event could 'be given more than one *complete* and *independent* explanation',[13] except for cases of genuine causal overdetermination. These worries have some *prima facie* plausibility: As long as we do not understand the relation between two kinds of explanation which are both applicable, the two kinds of explanation appear to 'compete' with each other, and this unstable 'parallelism' of explanations can be satisfactorily dissolved only by rejecting or reducing one of them. At the same time, assuming genuine causal overdetermination is implausible with regard to the relation between reasons and neurophysiological causes, because we normally assume that with one of the two factors missing, the action would not have been performed.

So, if one shares the worries about 'explanatory overdetermination', it seems that one will have to accept that one of the two explanations is not genuine. As the standing of the neurophysiological explanation as an explanation is not in doubt, the explanation that will be considered as 'sham' is the reasons-explanation, which will be 'downgraded' to a mere rationalization. But, as we have seen, this is at odds with Thesis 3.

If one is sceptical about the possibility of 'explanatory overdetermination', but wants to maintain that reasons-explanations have genuine explanatory force, one seems forced to accept the second alternative: namely, to assume that reasons-explanations are instances of causal explanations of events in terms of antecedent events. This view, however, is faced with the difficulty that the rationalizing function of reasons-explanations distinguishes them from ordinary event-causal explanations. The latter do not explain events by presenting them as what 'rationally ought to happen', but by presenting them as instances of what 'generally happens', in conformity to the natural laws.[14] This difference in the distinctive ways in which reasons-explanations and ordinary event-causal explanations make things intelligible presents a major obstacle

---

[13] Kim (1989b), 258 (emphasis in the original). The principle of explanatory exclusion goes back to Malcolm (1968).

[14] Cf. McDowell's characterization of the difference between the two types of explanation in (1985), 389.

to considering the former as a sub-type of the latter.[15] And it is not the only difference between the two sorts of explanation. While the explanans in an ordinary event-causal explanation always mentions an event which was the explanandum's cause, this is not the case in reasons-explanations, where the explanans often either mentions no event at all or no event which could have been the action's cause. Thus, the following are perfectly good reasons-explanations: 'I told him the way because one should be polite' and 'He precipitately left for the station because his train was leaving five minutes later'—though the first does not cite an event as the explanatory factor, but a normative fact, and the second cites an event temporally subsequent to the action.

So, none of the two alternative understandings of reasons-explanations on the basis of the event-causal view seems to be satisfactory, because the problem of 'explanatory overdetermination' threatens to turn reasons-explanations either into mere rationalizations or into event-causal explanations which are no rationalizations at all. In this way, the event-causal view brings Thesis 2★ in conflict with Thesis 3 as well as with Thesis 1.

The conflicts raised by the event-causal view are further aggravated by the second preconception about what the 'emerging scientific image' must be like: namely, by the bottom-up picture of reality. On this picture, reality is constituted by a hierarchy of different levels of phenomena, starting from fundamental microphysical levels and advancing to continuously more complex macrolevels. The higher levels are thought to 'arise from' and 'depend on' the lower levels. While this 'hierarchical' picture of reality is, in itself, compatible with very weak forms of dependence, often the dependence is considered to go so far that the phenomena on the higher levels and their causal relations can be reduced to lower-level phenomena, or are 'realized' by the latter.

But the dependence of the higher-level phenomena on the lower-level phenomena need only be so strong as to amount to causal determination of the macrolevel phenomena by the lower-level phenomena, in order for the bottom-up view to threaten Theses 1 and 3. For consider the macrolevel phenomenon of a human action, which will then depend on lower-level phenomena—supposedly on neurophysiological processes which lead to the agent's bodily motions. If all the macrolevel phenomena are causally determined by microlevel phenomena, this seems to imply that all the 'causal work' is done on the neurophysiological level and that no real causal activity is left for the higher level, 'on which' the agent himself, his actions, and his perceptions of reasons are situated. So, on the one hand, the agent himself would be left without any active role. On the other hand, reasons-explanations, as higher-level explanations, could not be genuine causal explanations either, as no real causal work is done on the higher level. Given the worries about 'explanatory overdetermination' mentioned earlier, this would undermine their claim to being proper explanations, in general,

---

[15] This problem traditionally confronted adherents of the old causal-nomological account of reasons-explanations—for example, Hempel (1965) and P. M. Churchland (1970)—who were forced to claim that there were general natural regularities corresponding to rational principles, or that rationality was an empirical concept.

because for all the relevant higher-level phenomena there will be causal neurophysiological explanations.[16]

In this way, once we start to spell out the implications of Thesis 2★, some widely held preconceptions about the 'emerging scientific image of the world'—especially the event-causal view and the bottom-up view of nature—produce severe conflicts with both Theses 1 and 3.

Conflicts between the two latter Theses arise once we attempt to spell out certain ideas naturally seen as connected with Thesis 1, or if we try to explain how reasons-explanations work (even though these conflicts are not as severe as the conflicts arising with Thesis 2★). I will mention just two of those conflicts, which can be directly linked to some of the agent-causal theories which attempt to account for a 'substantial' form of agential activity.

The first kind of conflict arises when we try to respond to the worries, discussed earlier, that reasons-explanations might not be proper *explanations*, but mere rationalizations. To be able to distinguish the former from the latter, an extra element seems to be needed whose presence separates cases where an agent acted for a particular reason from cases where he could have acted from this consideration, but did not do so. The overwhelming majority of present-day philosophers believes, since Donald Davidson's *Actions, Reasons, and Causes*, that this extra element must be an event-causal one.[17] When the performance of an action can truly be explained by appeal to a reason, they think, this reason, or some mental state or event suitably related to it, must be an event-cause of the action. If one follows them in making this assumption, it becomes difficult to see how the agent's own activity can itself be explained by the reasons for his action. For, as we have seen, the agent's active role cannot be captured by mere event-causal processes, and so presumably will not be part of the event-causal process connecting reason and action. Therefore, it will not itself be caused by the reason, or some mental state which 'embodies' the acceptance of the reason. But if the activity can only be explained by appeal to the agent's reason when the latter—or some related mental state—causes the activity, as the above assumption about the agent's reason would imply, this means that the agent's activity cannot itself be explained by appeal to the agent's reason. This result would be patently absurd, because the agential activity is a constitutive feature of the action and therefore must also be explainable by the agent's reasons when the action itself can be so explained.[18] Therefore, genuine agential activity as a constituent feature of agency which is amenable to reasons-explanations

---

[16] Bracketing the fact that for Kim the dependence of the higher-order phenomena is of a non-causal kind, this is, *in nuce*, Kim's argument for the epiphenomenalism of the mental; cf. Kim (1998), passim.

[17] Cf. Davidson (1963), 10 f.

[18] This criticism applies, for example, to Clarke's agent-causal theory in his (1993), which takes over the event-causal standard model of human action, according to which the agent's reasons—understood as mental states—cause the bodily motion, and combines it with the view that the agent causes 'her performing that action for that ordering of reasons or another action for different reasons'; op. cit. 205. If Clarke is right, the agent-causing itself will not be explicable by the agent's reasons, but only the result of this causing.

seems to be incompatible with the currently standard view of how reasons-explanations work.

The second kind of conflict is the result of trying to spell out possible implications suggested by talk of 'the agent's activity' in Thesis 1 for the case of *free* actions. When one takes the idea of agential activity seriously, it is tempting to understand free agency primarily in terms of unconstrained activity of the agent. Talk of unconstrained 'activity' suggests that it must be completely 'up to the agent', whether or not he acts, and that he must be free to decide without determination by other factors. True activity, it appears, implies free self-determination. This idea quickly creates a conflict between the commitments to agential activity and agency for reasons; for it presents the agent's active role and the influencing role of his reasons—either as causal determinants, or as 'rational' determinants in the form that he can rationally only choose one course of action—as competing with each other, for the agent's reasons seem to belong to those other factors which stand in the way of true self-determination.[19] On this view we can only be truly active insofar as our choices are not determined by reasons and, to this degree, arbitrary; and if this is right, reasons-explanations of free agential activity are impossible because the activity can only fill up the space left open by the underdetermining reasons.[20] Even worse, once this picture of the agent's active role and the influence of reasons as 'competing' is accepted for free actions, it seems plausible to adopt this picture for actions in general, because the notions of agential activity and acting for reasons involved in both cases are the same. Therefore, Thesis 1 and Thesis 3 will generally be in conflict.

These potential conflicts will suffice to show, in an exemplary manner, the tensions between Theses 1 and 3 that are manifested in them, once we try to develop either of the two Theses. Together with the conflicts which arise between Thesis 2 and Theses 1 and 3, once we attempt to spell out what are widely regarded to be the consequences of Thesis 2★, they illustrate the potential tensions between the three basic commitments integral to our self-understanding as human agents.

The existence of these tensions gives rise to a fundamental worry that these commitments are, ultimately, at odds with each other, and that our self-understanding as human agents, which includes all of them, is somehow irremediably flawed and inconsistent. If this were true, we could not really be what we believe ourselves to be: human agents. The difficulty of how these commitments can be reconciled despite these tensions, and how our self-understanding as human agents can be vindicated in this way, is what I call the 'problem of human agency'.

This problem is connected to, but different from, the second fundamental problem in the philosophy of action: the problem of free will. This latter problem arises from the

---

[19] This impression becomes even stronger when we recognize that most reasons for which we act have 'sources external to ourselves' or are themselves such external stimuli. Cf. Wolf (1990), 11.

[20] This was, as I understand him, Chisholm's unfortunate view about the relation between an agent and his reasons, which becomes particularly clear in his discussion of the example in (1978), 629 f., and (1995), 99.

worry that the commitments underlying our self-understanding as *moral* natural beings—our view of ourselves as both morally responsible for our actions and as natural beings—are ultimately irreconcilable. Any solution to this problem presupposes a solution to the problem of human agency; for if our self-understanding as natural agents must be given up, the problem of free will—at least as it is traditionally conceived as concerning free *actions* and not merely free thoughts or intentions—loses its basis. The problem of human agency, however, can be treated independently of the problem of free will,[21] and is thus more basic. Agency need not be free agency, and although—as I will argue—there is an essential connection between intentional action and *normative* practices, these normative practices need not be moral ones.

1.2. Reacting to the problem: the 'privileging' reaction

As all of Theses 1, 2, and 3 express central commitments of our self-understanding as human agents, we cannot resolve this problem by simply renouncing one of them—for if we did, we would cease to talk about human agency altogether. But because the tensions which have given rise to the problem of human agency make it seem unlikely that we can do full justice to all the Theses, it appears to be a promising strategy to take one of the three commitments as fundamental for one's account of agency, to which one subordinates the other two elements. This means that one gives full weight to the 'privileged' element and fully elaborates its 'implications', and that conflicts arising from this elaboration are resolved at the expense of the other two elements. That is, they are only accepted within the account of agency insofar as they are compatible with the elaboration of the 'privileged' commitment, which means that they can be modified or, in the extreme case, be completely omitted.

This neatly describes, in abstract terms, the general reaction of the overwhelming majority of present-day philosophers of action to the problem of human agency. As they do not believe that an account of human agency can fully do justice to all three commitments, they 'privilege' one of them at the expense of the others. According to which of the three commitments is taken as fundamental—the agent's activity, the place of human agency 'within the natural order', or the explainability of intentional actions in terms of the agent's reasons—this kind of reaction produces one of the three mainstream types of action theory in contemporary philosophy: agent-causalist, naturalist event-causalist, or intentionalist.

In the following, I shall present a brief overview of these general 'families' of action theory. Within these 'families' there is, of course, much room for further differentiation, and they will be more or less successful in accommodating the subordinated elements, depending especially on two factors: first, on the degree to which they

---

[21] The connecting link between the two is the idea that we are autonomous agents, which 'cuts across' both problems. One part of this idea—activity for reasons—already concerns the problem of human agency, while another part—*free* choice—only becomes relevant for the problem of free will.

privilege the fundamental elements over the others—that is, to what extent they allow conflicts between 'implications' of the former and the subordinated elements to be resolved, exceptionally, in favour of the latter—and second, on what they regard as the 'implications' of the fundamental element. In the extreme case they will simply reject the other two elements, because they consider them to be fully incompatible with the fundamental element and its 'implications'. But even action theories that are not extreme in this way cannot be expected to do full justice to the subordinated elements, and their shortcomings in dealing with them are likely to reflect the tensions between Theses 1, 2, and 3, that we have discussed previously.

a) Agent-causalists try to take seriously the idea that agents are genuinely active when they act. As we have already seen, a 'substantive' activity of the agent is incompatible with the event-causal view of reality. If actions, or the events that are constitutive of actions, are part of a flux of events where only event-causation occurs, agents play purely passive roles, being, at best, 'vehicles' of the changes that cause their bodily motions, but not doing anything themselves. In order to 'upgrade' agents from mere loci of changes to active sources of their actions, agent-causalists have appealed to the notion of agent-causation, which is a causation of events by the agent himself, *qua* substance. Agents are claimed either to cause their actions, or to cause events which are constitutive parts of the actions—for example, their bodily motions.[22]

The appeal to agent-causation enables agent-causalists to fully maintain Thesis 1 in ascribing a 'robust activity'[23] to the agent. At the same time, however, it tends to bring them into conflict with Theses 2 and 3, in the ways already sketched in Section 1.1. In view of these tensions, the extreme form of agent-causalism is quite happy to accept that human agents 'transcend' the natural order and have a 'God-like' capacity of self-determination which they exercise when they act (or, at least, when they act freely). This view—or something very close to it—has been defended by Roderick Chisholm, who claimed that free agents possess 'a prerogative which some would attribute only to God: each of us, when we act, is a prime mover unmoved'.[24] At the same time, the extreme form of agent-causalism tends to consider (free) human activity as not determined by reasons, but as rationally arbitrary—at least to a degree. For when activity is seen as radical self-determination, it is easily viewed as competing with the influence of reasons, on the basis of the argument discussed in Section 1.1.

Present-day agent-causal theories are far removed from this 'extreme' version, and go to some lengths to show the compatibility of agent-causation with both naturalism and the explainability of actions by the agent's reasons. Timothy O'Connor, for instance, tries to show that agent-causation can be reconciled with naturalism by

---

[22] The first view was held by Taylor (1966), 122 f., the second by Bishop (1983), 77, and Alvarez and Hyman (1998), 224.
[23] Cuypers (1998), 271.
[24] Chisholm (1966), 23.

appealing to emergent properties of the agent, which are not reducible to microproperties and could invest the agent with an agent-causal power. He also argues that actions that are agent-caused can still be explained by reasons, because the agents cause intentions whose content specifies the reason for which the action is performed.[25] But these proposals do not fully avoid the objections which reflect the tensions between Theses 1, 2, and 3. In particular, if the applicability of reasons-explanations to actions is ensured only by the content of a mental state that the agent causes, his causal activity itself seems to remain outside the scope of the reasons-explanation—which, as we saw in Section 1.1, would be an unacceptable result.

b) For naturalist event-causalists, the key desideratum of a theory of human behaviour is its compatibility with the 'emerging scientific image'. This, it is thought, requires especially two things. First, since agent-causation is incompatible with the event-causal view of nature, human agency must be construed in terms of event-causation of bodily behaviour by mental states of the agent or changes within him. Within this general approach, actions are identified either with the bodily motions caused by those mental events, or by states within the agent, so that these motions are extrinsically qualified as actions by their causal origin,[26] or else are identified with the whole complex process consisting of the mental antecedents causing the bodily motion.[27] Second, naturalist event-causalists usually consider causation by mental states as incompatible with the 'emerging scientific image', and the bottom-up picture of the world, in particular, so long as this form of causation cannot be reduced to causation by physical events.[28] Consequently, they usually subscribe to at least token–token identity between physical and mental states and events, so that, on their view, mental events cause effects in virtue of their physical characteristics.[29]

While the naturalist event-causalist approach, by its own standards, fits into the 'emerging scientific picture of the world', it directly inherits the conflicts between Thesis 2 and Theses 1 and 3 discussed in Section 1.1, and consequently tends to have problems in accounting for the latter Theses. In its extreme form—eliminative materialism—it eschews both human activity and reasons-explanation, claiming that 'folk psychology' which ascribes mental states and explains the agents' behaviour on their

---

[25] O'Connor (2000), ch. 5 and 6.
[26] Cf. Davidson (1971a), 49.
[27] For example, Thalberg (1969) and Searle (1983), 94. With the revival of volitionalism, there has also been a re-emergence of views which identify the action with the crucial causal antecedent of the bodily motion, such as the willing or the trying; for example, Hornsby (1980).
[28] An important argument for this is the alleged causal closure of the physical realm; cf. Kim (1993). But there are also philosophers who reject mental causation without physical causation for quite different reasons—for example, Davidson (1970a), who rejects this possibility due to his nomic theory of causality and his thesis of the anomalousness of the mental.
[29] The *locus classicus* is Davidson (1970a). Although he has tried to resist the claim that events cause effects only 'in virtue' of their physical properties, (1993a), the above formulation is an apt characterization of his position, because he thinks that causal relations presuppose strict law-like connections, which can only relate physical characterizations of events, not mental ones.

basis should be altogether abandoned as an empirical theory which has been refuted and made obsolete by the advance of the neurosciences. In present-day philosophy of mind, this view is defended by P. S. and P. M. Churchland.[30] As agential activity is, conceptually, part of human agency, eliminative materialism is no longer a recognizable account of human agency, and its truth would imply that we must renounce the view that we are human agents. While I fail to see how any argument could convincingly establish such a conclusion—rather than amounting to a *reductio* of its premises—I cannot discuss the position of eliminative materialism in more detail here, and will leave it aside, because it does not make any attempt to offer a solution to the problem of human agency.

Eliminative materialism is a minority position among naturalists, who generally try to integrate Theses 1 and 3, in some form, in their theories of action, and have also been partly successful in this respect. Thus, the conflict between event-causal naturalism and Thesis 3, discussed earlier, has apparently been resolved by the most influential event-causal theory of action—the 'standard model' inspired by Donald Davidson, which we will consider in more detail later. This theory construes the explanans of a complete reasons-explanation of an action to be a belief–desire pair which both rationalizes the action and causes it. What accounts for the rationalizing function is the fact that the contents of the belief–desire pair form the premises of a practical syllogism which has as its conclusion the verdict that an action of this kind should be performed.[31] As the causal relation between the belief–desire pair—or an event suitably related to it—and the action rests on underlying physical mechanisms, this account makes agency for reasons compatible with the naturalistic preconceptions about the 'emergent scientific image' of the world. At the same time, it allows that reasons-explanations have a further 'rationalizing' element which is not reducible to a purely event-causal explanation.

However, even if a reconciliation between the 'standard model' and Thesis 3 should be possible in this way, Thesis 1 remains to be accommodated. This is attempted by a reductive account of the agent's active role in terms of the causal contribution of his mental states (or changes in those states). As the agent is not active with regard to those states themselves—or not in the same way as he is active with regard to his actions[32]—such an analysis escapes a vicious regress.[33] But for the very same reason, the event-

---

[30] Cf. P. M. Churchland (1981) and P. S. Churchland (1986). Myles Brand's project of a 'naturalized action theory' also proceeds in the same direction, though Brand himself believes that this project leads not to a wholesale rejection of folk-psychological concepts, but only to less severe transformations; (1984), 168 f.

[31] Cf. Davidson (1963)—with the peculiarity, however, that he takes the conclusion of the syllogism to be that the *particular* action performed has a desirability characteristic; *vide* his characterization of the contents of the belief–desire pair in (1963), 5. It is only in (1970b), 31, that he moves towards the above formulation; cf. also (1978), 84.

[32] Philosophers such as Raz—see his (1999), ch.1—argue that the activity of persons consists in their responding to reasons, and in this sense agents can be active with regard to propositional attitudes as well as to actions. But this is clearly a different sense of activity than the one necessarily involved in human agency.

[33] Davidson (1973a), 72.

causal account cannot completely capture the idea of agential activity expressed by Thesis 1. There remains the mystery of how a truly active role of the agent could arise from the causal function of states which he non-actively possesses, or changes which he (passively) undergoes.[34]

c) Finally, intentionalists[35] consider the possibility of reasons-explanations or teleological explanations as the distinguishing feature of human actions. Teleological explanations explain something in terms of its *aim*, or what it is *for*—the typical conjunctive between explanans and explanandum being 'in order to'. The logical inference scheme underlying teleological explanations is the Practical Inference (which is a transformation of the first-person practical syllogism into the third-person form):

(P1) He intends to F.
(P2) He believes that he cannot F unless he Gs.[36]
(C) Therefore, he Gs.

I consider teleological explanations of actions to be a sub-kind of reasons-explanations; for whenever an agent pursues an aim by his action, he has a corresponding reason for which he acts. For example, when he runs to the station in order to get the bus, his reason is that he must get the bus or wants to get the bus. We can therefore assume that each teleological explanation is equivalent to a reasons-explanation. But not the other way round, for teleological explanations explain actions in terms of aims that lie beyond the actions themselves. When no such aim is pursued and the agent performs an action purely 'for its own sake', he may have a reason to do so—for example, to do his duty—but there will be no further aim that he pursues which corresponds to this reason.

For intentionalists, a piece of observable behaviour qualifies as an intentional action in virtue of having a certain recognizable 'physiognomy':[37] namely, that of being *aimed* at an end that the agent is pursuing. Intentionalists believe that recognizing something as an intentional action is not to recognize its causal source, but normally means 'to *understand* [the meaning of] the agent's conduct, i.e. to see that by certain changes in his body…the agent is *aiming* at this result'.[38] (In the following, this kind of understanding will be called 'intentionalistic'.) Recognizing something as an action thus generally includes both understanding what kind of action it is and identifying an aim that the agent pursues in performing this action—which implies being able to provide a teleological explanation of his behaviour. There are, however, exceptions to this

---

[34] Cuypers (1998), 276 f.
[35] The most important intentionalist is von Wright, together with his pupils—particularly Stoutland. Also Anscombe had some affinities with this view, while there are also agent-causalist elements in her work.
[36] For von Wright, at least, the second premiss of the practical inference must state a belief about necessary means to the intended end; cf. von Wright (1971), 96.
[37] The term is von Wright's (1969), 32.
[38] Von Wright (1969), 31.

general connection between teleological explanation and understanding behaviour as an action. For instance, as previously mentioned, teleological explanation of an intentional action is not possible when the action is performed for its own sake. Even then, however, a 'mutilated' practical inference of the form 'A intended to F, therefore he Fd' will be available, which suffices for understanding the behaviour as an action.[39]

According to intentionalism, applicability of a certain kind of understanding is therefore the decisive factor distinguishing intentional actions from other kinds of behaviour. This, however, threatens to circumvent agential activity as an essential feature of agency, which brings intentionalism into conflict with Thesis 1. When Theses 1 and 2 are altogether ignored, the result is a 'pure intentionalism', which is antirealist or 'fictionalist' about agency. This view would divorce agency from both agential activity and the presence of neurophysiological preconditions for actions, claiming that actions are simply those phenomena in human life to which the Practical Inference scheme of explanation is *de facto* applied; and this application would be considered as ultimately arbitrary, because it is not constrained by objective preconditions. Such 'fictionalism' about agency is, however, not normally advocated by contemporary intentionalists.

When they examine the relation of intentionalism to the commitments expressed by Theses 1 and 2, intentionalists are mainly concerned about the compatibility with Thesis 2—particularly with respect to the question of whether different forms of understanding and explanation can be simultaneously applicable to one and the same item of bodily behaviour. For if intentionalism is right, the same item of bodily behaviour that is understood intentionalistically will, according to Thesis 2, also be causally explainable by its antecedent neurophysiological processes—which raises the question of whether these two kinds of understanding and explanation[40] are compatible with each other. Georg Henrik von Wright has tried to show how they can be compatible;[41] and if he is right, then at least the bodily behaviour can be completely part of the natural order, even though the action itself is not subject to a purely naturalistic explanation.

The much greater difficulty for intentionalists lies in accommodating agential activity. At this point I will discuss one 'radical' intentionalist response to this difficulty in more detail, because it puts in question the whole set-up of the problem of human agency which we have presented. While this set-up has treated Theses 1 and 3 as

---

[39] Von Wright (1971), 123 f.
[40] For von Wright, the item of behaviour which can be explained in physiological terms cannot itself be explained teleologically, for this requires, as an intermediate step, its being understood intentionalistically. So for him there are not, strictly speaking, two potentially competing explanations, but a potential conflict between being understood as an action and being amenable to causal explanation; (1971), 124. But von Wright's distinction seems unnecessarily refined, because understanding behaviour as an action already involves an implicit application of the Practical Inference scheme.
[41] Von Wright (1971), 125 ff.

separate claims, an intentionalist might try to equate these claims by reducing the element of agential activity to the intelligibility of actions in terms of the reasons for which they have been performed. According to this proposal, an agent would be active just insofar as his behaviour can be seen as a response to reasons.[42]

Even though there is a connection between Theses 1 and 3—which will concern us at some points of the following investigation—the proposed equation of Theses 1 and 3 is mistaken. For activity is, conceptually, a feature of *all* human actions, while agency and reasons-explanations of behaviour can come apart. The most important kinds of case in which they do so are completely unintentional actions; and as the existence of such actions is far from undisputed, I need to discuss their case in more detail.

Reasons-explanations of actions fail when actions are performed unintentionally. And not all actions are intentional, though this has been claimed by several philosophers—most famously by Davidson, for whom action is bodily behaviour of a person that is performed intentionally 'under one description'.[43] According to the latter view, an agent does something unintentionally only when he does something else intentionally and is not aware of certain aspects of what he is doing. Unintentional actions are, so to speak, the aspects of intentional actions of which the agent is not aware.[44] For example, when James intentionally throws away the old copy of 'Essays on Actions and Events' which he has found on his doorstep, without knowing that this is Peter's copy that Peter has promised to lend him, he unintentionally throws away Peter's copy. But on this view there are no 'purely' unintentional actions.

Insofar as this claim is resisted in the philosophical discussion, it is mostly resisted, because Davidson's view that all unintentional actions are intentional under one description rests on his conviction that when we do A by doing B, doing A and doing B are one and same action,[45] and the latter view about the identity-conditions for particular actions is rejected by many philosophers.[46] If one subscribes to a more fine-grained view about the identity of particular actions than Davidson's, and believes that when Michael poisons his neighbour's dog by feeding him with arsenic, poisoning the dog and feeding him with arsenic are two distinct actions, not one, it will be admitted that there are actions which are completely unintentional. For example, if Michael is unaware of feeding poison to the dog, the action of poisoning is deemed unintentional. Admitting this, however, is not tantamount to accepting that agents can

---

[42] Cf. Raz's proposal for understanding human activity in terms of responding to reasons, (1999), ch.1. Raz, however, is not an intentionalist.

[43] Davidson (1971a), 46: 'a man is the agent of an act if what he does can be described under an aspect that makes it intentional'. Intentionalists agree—for example, Stoutland (1976b), 273: 'whenever an agent acts, he also acts intentionally.'

[44] At least, with regard to those aspects of which one is unaware, the action is unintentional. Whether there can be aspects of the action of which one is aware, but with regard to which the action is still unintentional, is disputed; cf. Bratman (1984), 199.

[45] Davidson (1971a), 59; this thesis was originally proposed by Anscombe (1957), 45 f.

[46] More 'fine-grained' individuations of actions are defended, for example, by Goldman (1970), ch. 1 and 2, and Alvarez and Hyman (1998), 234 ff.

be active without doing *anything* intentionally at all, because one may still consider it as a necessary condition for unintentional action that the agent also performs an intentional action at the same time.

So, deciding the issue of identity-conditions for human actions does not really help us to answer the question of whether agential activity and intentionality can be separated. Instead, we must show directly that an agent can perform an action without doing anything intentionally. This happens when we perform actions completely absent-mindedly—especially due to force of habit. Among these cases we can distinguish two different types. First, when one's attention is completely occupied by something else—a tricky philosophical problem, for example—one sometimes performs trivial activities such as drumming one's fingers on the table, without paying any heed to this activity. Though drumming one's fingers is something one actively does, it is not an intentional action. Second, we sometimes make 'double-capture errors'. In these cases one has formed an intention to do F, but due to absent-mindedness, does something else, G, which one is habituated to do under the circumstances.[47] Consider the following case. You decide to go into the bathroom in order to change your shirt; but when you arrive there, deeply absorbed in thoughts about Davidson's philosophy of action, you begin to brush your teeth instead—out of habit, because this is what you normally do when you go into the bathroom. The action of brushing your teeth is completely unintentional and not performed for any reason, because you neither intentionally brush your teeth nor do something else intentionally, of which the teeth-brushing is an unintentional by-product.[48]

These cases show that agential activity and intentional action can become separated,[49] which means that intentionalists cannot analyse agential activity simply in terms of amenability to reasons-explanations, but must provide some independent account of this element.

This concludes our overview of the three mainstream theories of action in the current philosophical debate. We have seen how each of them is the result of 'privileging' one particular commitment of the three commitments embodied in Theses 1, 2, and 3—even at the risk of not doing full justice to the other two. And we have seen how, for this reason, the theories continue to be haunted by the conflicts between the

---

[47] Roessler/Eilan (2003b), 4.

[48] Mele (2006a) claims that practical mistakes—such as forgetting that one intends to go to the supermarket, and driving home instead—do not make the action of driving home (completely) unintentional. For some practical mistakes, this may be right. There may still be some description under which the action is intentional. But generally this claim is implausible; and Mele's argument for the presence of a proximate intention—that the action is produced in the same way as in cases where the agent does what he earlier intended to do (2006a), 250—is simply question-begging in the context of a dispute about the nature of action.

[49] When we consider reasons-explanations in general, and not just of human behaviour, it is also clear that reasons-explanations and agential activity can come apart in the opposite way. Propositional attitudes, for instance, are normally amenable to reasons-explanations, though they are not themselves actions, nor usually the results of actions.

three Theses encountered in Section 1.1. As, in general, their answer to those tensions is to partly or wholly 'sacrifice' one or two of the elements, in approaching more or less the doctrines of the transcendence of agency over the natural order, of reductivism about agential activity, or of antirealism about human agency, none of them is likely to reconcile the three Theses without loss to one of them. Therefore, each of these main approaches leaves us, so far, with a feeling of dissatisfaction.

2
The agenda for finding a solution

The result of Chapter 1 leaves us in an unenviable position. If our self-understanding as human agents is not to turn out to be deeply flawed, we must be able to reconcile the three Theses. At the same time, however, none of the standard approaches in philosophy of action, which result from 'privileging' one of the Theses over the others, are likely to satisfactorily accommodate all three of them. We must therefore seek another way to reconcile the three Theses. In this chapter I will take some preliminary steps towards developing such a theory—sketching the road, so to speak, which we will have to travel.

In order to acquire a better grip on the task before us, we must first become clear about what kind of solution to the problem is required (Section 2.1). I will then restrict the focus of our investigation to 'performances'—actions which have results—for, as I believe, key points at issue can be best illustrated in their case. I will go on to show that an intentionalist account of agency is unpromising with regard to performances because it is unable to do justice to the requirement that the agent must be in control of the bodily motions that are results of his actions (Section 2.2). This will set the stage for opposing the agent-causal and the event-causal approaches against one another. I will argue that the chief touchstone for the event-causal approach is whether it can satisfactorily capture the idea that the agent is in control of his motions when he performs physical actions, for this idea is part and parcel of the key claim that agency involves the activity of agents (Section 2.3). This will set the agenda for our future quest for a theory which can provide an answer to the problem of human agency.

2.1. What kind of solution is required?

Before we can properly set out on our task of solving the problem of human agency, we must become clearer about what this task will be. What kind of answer to the problem of human agency is needed, and what would a fully satisfactory solution to this problem look like? In the face of a real or apparent clash between certain commitments none of which we can well give up there are, in principle, three different kinds of response, whose adequacy depends on the nature of the problem with which we are faced.

The 'minimal' response consists in just refuting the particular arguments that purport to show specific incompatibilities and in demonstrating that they are inconclusive, without addressing the question of how the different commitments can be *positively* reconciled. The rationale behind the 'minimal' response is the specific dialectical situation between someone holding each commitment jointly and the 'sceptic' who claims that the commitments are at odds. As each of the commitments, taken separately, is part of something that we cannot well give up—in our particular case, of our self-understanding as human agents—we are entitled to maintain them jointly, as long as no inconsistency between them is positively established, even if it may be mysterious how the commitments can be conjoined.

In the discussion about the problem of free will, this kind of 'minimal' response has had some prominence, because historically this discussion was less influenced by a *general* feeling that our self-understanding as morally responsible agents must be at odds with our place within the natural order, but much more by *specific* arguments purporting to show that the two are incompatible.[1] This is not the case with the problem of human agency, which arises from deep-running tensions—especially between Theses 1 and 2—which manifest themselves in a variety of conflicts and give rise to a general impression that these commitments must somehow be at odds.[2] For this reason, I assume, a 'minimal' response to this latter problem is insufficient because a general feeling of incompatibility has to be removed, and not just a particular way in which this feeling manifests itself.

The second kind of response to a perceived clash consists in 'dissolving' this conflict by showing that the commitments are not related in such a way that they could possibly ever come into conflict. This is achieved by showing that a conflict between them could not even be coherently or sensibly formulated. For instance, if the commitments belonged to totally unrelated different stances or areas of discourse, the apparent tensions between these commitments would have to rest on misunderstandings of their status or on the illicit transfer of claims that express these commitments to areas of discourse to which they do not belong.[3] If the problem of human agency is dissolved in this way, no unified account of human agency which integrates Theses 1, 2, and 3 is offered, but instead, the ground for the quest for such a unified account is removed, because the apparent need for such an account is shown to rest on the very same mistake as the apparent conflict itself.

The third kind of response lies in providing a unified account of the commitments in question and showing, in this way, either how they can be reconciled despite their

---

[1] Especially in the discussion about particular arguments for incompatibilism, such as Van Inwagen's (1983) argument, this has been, I take it, the general dialectical position. Refuting these arguments was taken to suffice for solving the free will problem, even though it would not positively show how free actions could be part of a purely deterministic world.

[2] More recently, this feeling has become more widespread in the discussion about the free will problem—especially since the view that free will cannot be realized in an indeterministic world either has begun to be combined with classical incompatibilism. If both these views are accepted, there will be a general feeling that responsibility *must* be at odds with the place of agents in the natural order.

[3] Such a solution is proposed by Sellars for the apparent conflicts between the 'manifest' and the 'scientific image' of the world, (1962).

tensions, or how these apparent tensions rest on a mistaken conception of one or more of the commitments. This kind of response is not as different from the second kind as it may appear, as showing how two commitments can be reconciled can consist in showing that they belong to two different kinds of discourse. The main difference to the second kind of response is that a unified account cannot leave these two levels 'standing side by side', so to speak, but must include an account of how these levels are related and interconnected, thus showing how both kinds of discourse concern the same basic phenomenon.

I think that if there is an adequate response to the problem of human agency at all, it must be of the third kind. The reasons for this are mainly the following two. First, *merely* dissolving the problem by demonstrating that Theses 1, 2, and 3 belong to unrelated different levels of discourse or stances would not be completely satisfactory, because it would not vindicate our basic conviction that there is one single phenomenon of agency with which they are all concerned.

Thus, suppose that the problem of agency can be completely 'dissolved' in the following way (which I consider the most promising attempt at a 'dissolution'). Theses 1, 2, and 3 are expressions of two different stances: an essentially 'subjective' or 'first-person' view of reality, and an essentially 'objective' or 'third-person' view. These are stances that we adopt on different occasions, but as no person can adopt both stances simultaneously, none of them can fault the other and they cannot be incompatible— like the claims made from an aesthetic stance towards a phenomenon and from a purely natural-science standpoint, which cannot come into mutual conflict. Now, we do believe that all the stances putatively expressed by Theses 1, 2, and 3 can be taken with regard to *one and the same* individual action: that is, we believe that the same action which I actively perform for certain reasons can be explained by you by citing those reasons, and can be seen by a third person as a part of the natural order. For example, when I raise my arm on seeing a squirrel, you can explain this action by pointing out that I wanted to scare the animal away, while someone else can explain my raising my arm as a manifestation of my pathological fear of squirrels. Furthermore, we believe that the view of the phenomenon which can be taken from one stance constrains what views can rightly be taken from other stances. For example, if I do not act at all, but my arm is raised by you, a third person cannot understand the motion of my arm as a manifestation of my pathological fear of squirrels; only if I raise my arm myself can this be interpreted as a gesture of fear or evasion. These two facts—the possible identity of the object of the different stances, and the mutual constraints between their contents— will remain mysterious as long as the systematic relations between the two stances are not explained; and to this extent, any account which leaves us with a mere 'parallelism' of unconnected stances or levels of discourse is unsatisfactory.

Second, the problem of human agency is not really a plausible candidate for a complete 'dissolution'. It is, I think, implausible to assume that the problem arises *only* from an illicit combination of elements from distinct stances or levels of discourse. This would be plausible if the conflicts were to arise only when we compared, say, a neurophysiological explanation of what happens in our body when we act, and a reasons-explanation of action, discovering that the content of the one does not reflect the content of the other. But as we have seen, the problem does not only arise when we make such a comparison. Take, for instance, the conflict between Theses 1 and 2, which arises on the basis of the event-causal view of reality. This conflict is displayed in any third-person description of action which presents this action as part of the natural order—such as the result of the agent's fear of squirrels. Agency conceptually includes activity, and the action's place in nature seems to be directly at odds with this, because the event-causal view claims validity for all areas of reality.

For these reasons, I believe that a mere dissolution of the problem of human agency is both impossible and would not be a completely satisfactory result. Instead, a fully satisfying response to the problem must provide a unified account integrating Theses 1, 2, and 3; and insofar as it truly 'dissolves' some of the tensions between those Theses by presenting them as consequences of mixing up elements from distinct levels of discourse, it must tell us how these levels are interrelated.

But can such a unified account be found? As we have already seen, in view of the tensions between Theses 1, 2, and 3, it may seem that the best we can hope for is an account which takes one of the basic commitments expressed by those Theses as central, and tries to reconcile the other elements with it, as far as possible, in a restricted version. This, I have argued, is the strategy chosen by all the mainstream accounts of agency: agent-causalist, naturalist event-causalist, and intentionalist. But even if one does not share their 'pessimistic' view about a full compatibility of the three basic commitments, clearly there is no viable alternative to starting off with one of the commitments and subsequently trying to reconcile the others to it. The only difference between 'pessimists' and 'optimists' is that for the former the commitment with which we start is truly 'privileged' and the others are 'subordinated' to it, while for the latter it is only 'privileged' in the sense of providing the starting-point for one's account.

So, in order to find an answer to the problem of human agency we will have to examine which of the three basic commitments serves best as the starting-point of a unified account of human agency. While the comparative merits of the proposed solutions to the problem depend on the degree to which the offered account of agency is able to integrate the two commitments which it does not take as its starting-point, there is also an absolute requirement whose satisfaction is a necessary prerequisite for *any* acceptable solution to the problem of human agency. This is the requirement that the offered account must still be recognizable as an account of *human agency*. As all three commitments expressed by Theses 1, 2, and 3 are essential for our self-understanding as human agents, this means that none of these commitments must be completely abandoned nor be modified beyond recognition. Their 'core content' must be salvaged, and the account must contain some version of each of Theses 1, 2, and 3 which can still be understood at least as an 'extremely weak' or 'minimal' reading of these Theses as originally understood.

THE AGENDA FOR FINDING A SOLUTION 27

In the following we shall examine whether on any of the three basic approaches in the philosophy of action—agent-causalist, naturalist event-causalist, or intentionalist—a satisfactory unified account of human agency can be developed. I shall begin with the intentionalist approach, because I believe it can be most easily demonstrated to be unable to accommodate all the commitments—in particular the commitment to agential activity. This will leave us with the opposition between the event-causalist and the agent-causalist approach.

2.2. Performances, agential control, and intentionalism

In my view, there is one central issue about agency which both underlies the failure of the intentionalist approach and whose explanation is the key point of contention between agent-causalist and event-causalist approaches: the issue of 'agential control'. Agential control is the miminal form of activity which the event-causal and the intentionalist approaches have to accommodate in order to count at all as satisfactory accounts of human agency. We will learn about this element in more detail in this section and the next. My concern at the moment, however, is that in order to obtain a clearer view of this essential element of agency we must narrow the focus of our investigation. While hitherto we have been talking about actions in general, we will henceforth restrict ourselves to 'performances', which I believe constitute the most important sub-set of actions.

Performances[4] are those actions which essentially have 'results' consisting in genuine changes. The notion of the 'result of an action' goes back to von Wright, who distinguished 'results' from 'consequences' of actions.[5] For von Wright, actions are not themselves changes in the world, but, as he recognized, many—arguably most—actions involve such changes, either directly or as indirect consequences. For example, when I open a door this entails that the door opens—which is a change from the state of being shut to the state of being open—and it may produce a drop in the temperature of the room, which may cause you to catch a cold. The relations between action and change can either be logical or contingent. In the first case, a type of action is defined as the action of bringing about a change of this kind, and consequently, when an action of this type happens this logically entails that a change of this kind occurs.[6] Thus, the fact that I have opened the door entails that the door has opened. If it has not, I could at best have tried to open the door, but it is impossible that I have successfully done so. If there is a logical connection of this kind, the change is called the 'result' of the action[7]—both

---

[4] With this particular sense, the term was coined by Kenny (1963), 177.
[5] Von Wright (1963a), 35 ff.; (1971), 66 ff.
[6] Von Wright (1963a), 39.
[7] Von Wright himself calls the state of affairs brought about during the change—in our example, the door's *being* open—rather than the change itself, the result of the action, but admits that the change itself could, with equal right, be called the action's result, (1971), 67. For better comparability with the current event-causal theories, I prefer the latter version, because, strictly speaking, only the changes are events, not

generically and with regard to particular actions that fall under this type of action. In the second case, no such logical connection obtains. For example, the fact that I have opened the door does not entail that the temperature in the room has dropped. But the result of a particular action can have other changes as its causal effects, in which case the latter are called 'consequences' of the action.

Now, in a 'minimal' sense, all actions involve changes as a matter of logical necessity, if 'change' is understood as requiring only that some proposition which is not true before the action is true afterwards. Trivially, the change in truth-value of the proposition 'The agent has done F' guarantees that this requirement is satisfied. What is additionally required for a performance, however, is that a 'genuine change' takes place—which means that after the action the *present* state of the world must be different from its state before the action.[8] To take our earlier example: after I have opened the window, the window must be open, at least for a very short time. This additional requirement of a 'genuine change' for performances ensures that von Wright's concept of 'result' can be used to characterize performances even when his view that actions are not themselves changes is rejected, because the required 'genuine change' cannot consist merely in the fact that the action has been performed.

Performances form the most important sub-set of actions in general, and for many philosophers they even exhaust the set of actions.[9] In particular, philosophers who consider all actions to consist in bodily movements, such as Davidson,[10] belong to the latter group, because all movements necessarily involve that the things moved do change their position. However, the sweeping claim that *all* actions have results neglects some important differences between different types of action. Even for some externally observable actions, the model of 'results' can be applied only with the modification that the performance of these actions does not entail that *certain* types of change take place, but only that *some* change in the form of a bodily motion occurs. For instance, that I laugh (intentionally) does not entail that my countenance changes in a specific way, though I do not laugh when no change whatsoever occurs in my countenance. Also, if there are such things as mental acts, not all of these acts have results. For example, the act of imagining how to spend a pleasant evening does not

---

the end-states of these changes (even though the current 'loose' way of speaking about events also includes those states).

[8] This criterion is adapted from the one which Kenny uses to distinguish agent from patient in action, (1963), 181.

[9] For example, for those agent-causalists who think that all actions consist in agent-causings, such as White (1968), 2, or Bishop (1983), 72 ff.

[10] Davidson (1971a), 49. Davidson argues that all primitive actions are bodily movements, and together with his claim that all actions are identical to primitive actions, op. cit., 59, this yields the above thesis. (At the same time, however, Davidson states that he wants to use 'bodily movement' in a very wide sense, so as to capture even 'mental acts like deciding and computing', loc.cit. As he does not make it any clearer in what sense he wants decisions and computings to be considered as bodily movements, it remains somewhat mysterious whether or not this 'liberal view' of bodily movements involves a partial renunciation of his original claim about primitive actions.)

logically involve any change which could count as its result, and is therefore not a performance (in the technical sense).

These caveats notwithstanding, we can rightly consider performances as the central case of human agency—mainly because they best display the difference between activity and passivity that is so crucial to the concept of agency. This distinction clearly has its origin in the cases where there is a change about which the question can sensibly be raised whether the agent is active or passive with regard to it; and when we draw this distinction with regard to mental acts such as imaginings or rememberings, the use of the terms 'active' and 'passive' is mainly due to an analogy to the cases of performances.

Therefore, I will restrict my subsequent examination to performances; and, when I speak of 'actions' in the following, I will, presupposing this restriction, normally mean 'performances', making it clear when I do otherwise. The restriction has no relevance for the force of the subsequent negative arguments against intentionalism and naturalist event-causalism, because, obviously, every successful theory of human agency must also satisfactorily account for performances. It is only when we come to our positive proposal about the nature of human agency that the restriction has any importance. For, as a consequence of this restriction, the positive proposal will, in the first place, explain the nature of agency in performances. How it relates to other kinds of action will still be an open question which we will have to consider at the end of developing this account.

Although we will be talking about performances generally, there is one sub-set of performances that will merit our special consideration: actions consisting in direct peripheral bodily movements. The term 'bodily movements' notoriously contains an ambiguity, which we must clarify before we can proceed further. 'Moving' can be used both in a transitive and an intransitive sense. Both that I raise my arm and that my arm rises are (bodily) movements—though in the first instance the movement consists in my moving something (else), and in the second it consists in something moving or being moved. Only the first instance—the use in the transitive sense—describes an action, while the second use can either describe the result of an action—the result of an action of moving my body—or a change which is unconnected to any action of mine.[11] In order to avoid misunderstandings, I will talk of 'movements' when I talk about actions of moving something, and of 'motions' when I speak about movings in the intransitive sense, further distinguishing between 'actional motions' which are the results of actions, and '(non-actional) mere motions' which are not connected to agency.

After these terminological clarifications we can return to the issue at hand. The reason for the prominent role of bodily movements is that they form the most important type of 'basic actions'—and for some philosophers, even the only such type.[12] The distinction between 'basic' and 'non-basic' actions rests on the fact that

---

[11] The distinction between these two senses of 'movement' has been elaborated by Hornsby (1980), 5 ff.
[12] Davidson (1971a), 49. *Vide supra* fn. 10. The term 'basic action' was originally coined by Danto (1965).

we perform some actions *by* doing something else: for example, in Sarajevo in 1914, Gavrilo Princip killed Archduke Ferdinand by shooting him with his revolver. 'Basic actions' are those actions we perform directly—without doing something else—and it is not only obvious that there are such actions—for example, I can raise my arm directly—but is also necessary to assume, at the basis of every non-basic action, a basic action, on pain of generating an infinite regress of non-basic actions all performed by doing something else.

What a person does directly—what particular basic actions he performs—depends, trivially, on what he is able to do directly, and this varies both among persons and for individual persons during the course of their lives. Thus, some people can wiggle their ears directly, while others can wiggle their ears only with their fingers; and when a person regains control over a limb after an operation or a stroke, he regains the ability to move this limb directly, while before he could move it only by the use of another limb.

Not all basic actions are bodily movements—for example, mental acts are not—but bodily movements play the most important role because they alone generally allow us to change things in the world. Lacking the ability of telekinesis, we must move our bodies if we want to move something else or bring about some other result external to our own bodies, e.g. via communication.[13] There are, however, some exceptions to this. For example, when I know that by imagining a terrible monster I can make my hairs stand on end, I can bring about this effect without performing a bodily movement as a basic action. But such cases are exceptional.

Apart from this overall importance of basic actions which consist in bodily movements, these actions are also of special significance for our project at hand: namely, of assessing the comparative merits of intentionalist, event-causal, and agent-causal theories of action. In particular, accounting for agential control in cases of bodily movements gives rise to the chief difficulty for intentionalist theories, to which we must now turn.

Narrowing our focus to performances throws more vividly into relief the difficulties of intentionalist approaches to provide, on their own, a unified picture of human agency, and, in particular, to account for Thesis 1: the element of activity. As we have noted, according to intentionalism, intentional actions are instances of bodily behaviour by which the agent intends something or aims at something, so that the behaviour can be understood intentionalistically in terms of what it is that he intends by it. For von Wright, this understanding is the crucial factor in distinguishing actional bodily motions from mere bodily behaviour: These events are results of basic actions 'when we "vest" these events with intentionality'.[14] This characterization immediately

---

[13] Pace Goldman (1970), 67 f., for whom also the exercise of the ability of an experienced typist to type the letter 's' can constitute a basic action. Goldman's point has, in my view, been satisfactorily answered by Davidson (1971a), 51.

[14] Von Wright (1971), 130.

raises the question whether all items of behaviour can be so 'vested' with intentionality, by the agent himself or by other persons observing him. If we understand 'bodily behaviour' widely enough to include both actional motions and (non-actional) mere motions,[15] the answer to this question is clearly negative. An agent who is seized by a spasm, for instance, *cannot* intend anything by the convulsive motions of his limbs.

This impossibility is independent of both whether this behaviour can, from the outside, be understood as aiming at something, or whether the agent himself wants it to be thus understood. Thus, imagine that the spasm makes the agent's head shake just when he is asked a question he intends to answer in the negative. The interlocutor mistakenly takes the shaking for a negative answer, and to save himself an explanation, the agent tacitly acquiesces in this interpretation—or even, while his head shakes, he already thinks 'that is convenient; my interlocutor will take this to mean "no"'.[16] Despite all this, the agent would not, by the shaking of his head, have given a negative reply, for this shaking was not even a candidate for intentional behaviour.

So, there is a restriction on the scope of applicability of intentionalistic understanding and explanation, and this restriction does not itself follow from the fact that the behaviour is, *de facto*, intentionalistically understood or that the agent wants it to be so understood. The precondition that must be fulfilled by any item of bodily behaviour, for it to be a proper candidate for such understanding, is that the item of behaviour is under the agent's control.[17] This is the condition that is manifestly not satisfied in the case of convulsive spasms. Intentionalist theories, I will argue, are unable to deal with this element of control, and consequently cannot provide a complete account of human agency.

To begin with, what is the required kind of control? We have already mentioned that agential control is the 'minimal' version of activity which every acceptable account of human agency must capture; but the notion of control which is required for an adequate intentionalistic understanding of behaviour is wider. For we can also intend something by *not* doing something—namely by deliberately refraining from doing it.[18] James can intend to express his disrespect for John by refraining from getting up from his chair when John enters the room, as well as he can intend to express it by positively doing something offensive, such as ostentatiously leaving the room. Nevertheless, our focus here will be on control over bodily behaviour *in action*—both because this is our main overall focus of interest, and because agential control in action forms the paradigm case of control of which control in omissions can be understood as a derivative form.

---

[15] Von Wright, in (1969), 31, clearly suggested a wide understanding of 'bodily behaviour' when he spoke generally of 'certain changes in his body' by which the agent was aiming at something.

[16] Stoutland (1989), 320 f.

[17] It is not sufficient that this kind of behaviour, generically, is under the agent's control, but it must be under his control on this particular occasion. Though shaking his head is generally under an agent's control, it is outside his control when it is caused by a convulsive spasm, as in the above example.

[18] I consider omissions to act not to be actions themselves—at least not generally—because I consider Alvarez's argument as persuasive that *not* doing something cannot, *ipso facto*, be *doing* something, (2001), 66.

Control over something typically involves a counterfactual dependence of what is controlled on some other factor, though this counterfactual element does not exhaust control; for instance, the counterfactual dependence must additionally be based on the right grounds. Leaving the latter complication aside for the moment, let us focus on the relata of the counterfactual dependence relation. What must be under the agent's control in a performance is generally the result of the action: that is, for bodily movements, the corresponding motions of the agent's limbs. In all actions, these motions must depend on the person's agency—a dependence which can be expressed by the counterfactual conditional:

Result-action dependence: *ceteris paribus*, the bodily motion would not have occurred on the particular occasion had the agent not performed a movement of this kind.[19]

Result-action dependence is not the only counterfactual dependence required for agential control, but there are further dependences which vary according to whether the action is performed intentionally or unintentionally. For example, for intentional actions, at a minimum, the following two counterfactual conditionals must also be true: (i) *ceteris paribus*, if the behaviour did not conform to the agent's intention and the agent realized this, the behaviour would be different (because the agent would act differently); and (ii) *ceteris paribus*, when the agent, by doing A, intends to achieve B, then if A turned out not to be conducive to B and the agent realized this, he would cease to do it. However, we can ignore these further complications here, because the problem for intentionalism already lies in accounting for result-action dependence.

Any action theory which does not account for control, and in particular for result-action dependence, cannot be an acceptable complete theory of human agency. At best, it can be an account of *intentional* agency, which explains when behaviour is intentional, *on the presupposition* that this behaviour is already under the agent's control. At first glance this seems to be precisely the case with von Wright's account of intentional agency in *Explanation and Understanding*, which does not itself talk about the necessary precondition of control for a correct application of intentionalistic understanding. As long as von Wright's account is understood to have this limited aim, failure to account for the element of agential control does not, *per se*, constitute a decisive shortcoming. But once the account is understood as a complete account of agency on its own, then such a failure must, indeed, be seen as a crucial weakness.

For in neglecting the counterfactual element of control which is expressed by the result-action dependence, this account—if understood as a complete account of agency—gives rise to a mysterious 'parallelism' between intentional actions and the occurrences of the bodily motions which are the results of these actions. If an intentional action is just behaviour that is intentionalistically understood, it seems to be a 'happy coincidence' that usually, in the situations of action, the results only happen when the actions are being performed. On both agent-causal and event-causal theories

---

[19] Cf. Stoutland (1989), 320.

of action this correspondence is easily explained, because on these theories, whenever an action is performed the result is caused, and it is thus intelligible why, barring causal overdetermination, the result would not have occurred without the performance of the action. But on the intentionalist account, the 'congruence' between actions and the bodily motions which are their results is mysterious.[20]

Interestingly, von Wright, in his earlier work, had apparently recognized this difficulty. Each action, he had claimed, contained the counterfactual element that, without the agent's interference, the result would not have occurred.[21] But in *Explanation and Understanding* he partly retracted this requirement, limiting its scope to non-basic actions. If we find out that the apparent results of those actions come about 'by themselves', the actions cannot be considered to consist in bringing about these results, but must be 'confined to' what the agent does in order to bring them about.[22] For instance, take James, who presses a button in order to call a lift, whereupon the lift promptly arrives. It turns out, however, that the lift was already moving towards the floor where James was waiting, for Jones, who was already in the cabin, wanted to go to this floor and had earlier pressed the button inside the lift. So James' pressing the button was irrelevant to bringing about the result, and it is therefore implausible to claim that he fetched the lift. What he has done is only that he has pressed the button in order to fetch the lift. With regard to basic actions, however, no such 'confining' redescription of what the agent does is possible, because nothing else is done in order to perform those actions. For basic actions, von Wright thus drops his earlier objective counterfactual element altogether, supplanting it by the merely epistemic element 'that the agent *confidently thinks* that certain changes will not occur unless he acts.'[23]

This merely epistemic element, however, is insufficient for a satisfactory account of the relation between action and result, for it does not exclude that the agent's confidence rests on a systematic error of which he has not yet become aware. But even when one dismisses the merely epistemic element, and includes, in one's account of agency, the requirement that the connection must actually hold, as von Wright had done earlier, this still will not suffice on its own. We also need an explanation of *why* the counterfactual element is required, and this can only be an explanation of how actions and their results are connected. Without such an explanation it will continue to appear as a brute contingent fact—a lucky coincidence 'that certain changes will happen only when we happen to be acting'.[24] And given our concept of action, this connection *cannot* be a lucky coincidence.

The necessity of such an explanation becomes especially clear when we remind ourselves that counterfactual connections can have different grounds, and that not all of

---

[20] Stoutland (1976a), 317; (1989), 323 ff.
[21] Von Wright (1968), 43.
[22] Von Wright (1971), 127; however, von Wright is cautious about whether such a redescription of the action under a 'mutilated' aspect is necessary, and claims only that this is what the agent 'undoubtedly does'.
[23] Von Wright (1971), 199 fn. 39.
[24] Von Wright (1971), 130.

these grounds will fit the case of agency. Thus, the relation between cause and effect, between causings and effects, logical interdependence, contingent identity, and also the relation between two parallel effects of a common cause, all give rise to counterfactual conditionals relating the occurrences of the two factors. But the last case, for example, is not an adequate model for the relation between an action and the result which is its effect: Though both may have a common cause, it is not plausible to regard their mutual dependence as being constituted just by this—as if actions were related to effects like the destruction of Herculaneum was related to the destruction of Pompeii; that is, as otherwise unrelated events which only have the same cause.[25]

If this is true, there is a substantial lacuna in the intentionalist account, since it fails to deal adequately with the element of agential control. The only way for the intentionalist to avoid this conclusion seems to be to adopt the following strategy developed—though eventually rejected—by Frederick Stoutland and partly taken over by von Wright.[26] This strategy rejects our earlier assumption that all cases of bodily movements are also cases of bodily motions, without which assumption there is no need to explain a correspondence between the two. Thus, the intentionalist could deny that there is a common element in both the case of the spastic convulsive motion of the head and the case of the agent shaking his head intentionally. He could claim that there is no 'neutral' conception of a 'shaking of the head' by which we could single out one neutral item of 'behaviour' which could be either a mere motion or an actional motion. Instead, there are only two mutually exclusive conceptualizations of items of behaviour *either* as mere motions or as movements: 'behaviour-as-intended-by-an-agent' and 'behaviour-as-mere-behaviour', where no neutral sense of 'behaviour' could be extracted from either conceptualization.

If this course is adopted, our earlier criticism of von Wright's contention that intentional action is 'behaviour by which the agent aims at something' would lose its basis. For the latter locution would then be interpreted as '*movements* by which the agent aims at something', which would lead to the collapse of our argument that not by all items of behaviour could the agent aim at something, because our counter-example has rested on a case of a *mere motion*, and these cases do not belong to the class of movements. In fact, our earlier argument could no longer be consistently formulated without appearing to be obviously false.

But is this escape strategy for the intentionalist viable? Are cases of bodily movements not also cases of bodily motions—of motions which could also occur without a

---

[25] *Pace* Stoutland (1976a), 317 ff., who proposes just this solution to alleviate the mysterious 'parallelism' between action and result in von Wright's theory. What makes this solution implausible is that it bases the 'congruence' between action and result on a factor which is extrinsic to both action and result: namely, their common event-cause. This makes the counterfactual dependence appear a 'coincidence' when we just consider action and result by themselves, which is hardly compatible with the fact that we consider the dependence to be an essential part of our understanding of agency.

[26] Stoutland (1989), 326 ff., developed the strategy from what are at best hints in von Wright (1971), 121 or 135, and (1969), 32 f. Von Wright, (1989), 807 ff.

corresponding movement of the agent, but, for example, due to the interference of another person? Is it not the case that when 'I raise my arm', my arm rises, as Wittgenstein claimed in § 621 PI? The main argument for answering this question in the negative would rest on the following linguistic datum: that it sounds inappropriate for me to say 'my arm rises' when I raise my arm, and similarly for other bodily movements. For using this description always seems to imply that I did not raise my arm—or, at least, that I did not raise it directly, but that I did something else to raise it.

But this linguistic awkwardness does not automatically mean that it must be false to say 'my arm rises' when I raise my arm. For, as Paul Grice has shown, there are pragmatic conversational maxims, whose flouting does not lead to the falsity of statements, but can make them inappropriate due to their being (highly) misleading.[27] One of the most important of those principles is what one can call a 'principle of informativity', that one should not conceal relevant information when making a statement on a question at issue;[28] for by doing so one inevitably gives rise to the impression either that one does not know more, or that one positively believes a further statement to be false. These impressions which one standardly gives rise to are 'conversational implicatures' of one's statement.

Using Grice's notion of conversational implicature, we are able to explain the awkwardness of using the description 'my arm rises' when one raises one's arm, even when we assume that this description is true in this case. For if bodily movements involve bodily motions, 'I raise my arm' is a more informative description than 'my arm rises', because it implies the latter. As—at least for intentional actions—one is expected to know what one is doing, one will therefore, by using the description 'my arm rises', generally produce the impression that one did not raise one's arm on this occasion, because otherwise one would be expected to use the more informative statement. It will thus be a conversational implicature of saying 'my arm rises' that one did *not* raise it, but not a condition of the truth of this statement that one did not.

Now, how can we decide which of the two possible interpretations—that the description 'my arm rises' is false in cases where I raise my arm, or that it is only inappropriate because of its conversational implicatures—is the right one? For Grice, the crucial difference is that a conversational implicature is cancellable: that is, when we explicitly remove the normal expectations of the listener, the statement is no longer inappropriate, while false statements cannot be made true in this way. So, let us consider conjunctions of descriptions of an action and of a corresponding bodily motion, and ask whether such conjunctions can ever be linguistically appropriate.

When we take a statement such as 'I raise my arm, and my arm rises', this statement seems to be generally awkward. But this inappropriateness need not stem from a contradiction. It can also stem from the too glaring redundancy of the second part,

---

[27] On this and the following, see Grice (1975) and (1981) *passim*.
[28] Which, for Grice, together with the injunction that one should not be more informative than required, constitutes the category of Quantity within the general Cooperative Principle, (1975), 26 f.

due to which the second part of the statement has the conversational implicature that the rising of the arm must somehow have been independent of the action. In a similar way, the statement 'At Waterloo the French Army was defeated, and the French Guard was defeated' is not false, though problematic because it implies that the French Guard was somehow defeated independently of the Army, for otherwise we would not be expected to mention its defeat separately. However, when we turn to other conjunctions where the description of the motion contains further information not yet contained in the description of the action, the statements become appropriate. For example, 'I lift my foot, and my foot goes up 30 centimetres' can be totally appropriate in a situation where it is unclear how far I can lift my foot because some heavy weights are attached to it.

So, the normal linguistic impropriety of using descriptions of motions when one is talking about one's direct bodily movements stems from misleading conversational implicatures and not from a falsity of this usage. Switching to the third-person perspective reconfirms the result that descriptions of movements and of motions can be true in the same cases. For instance, as long as the observer does not know whether or not the agent is moving his body, he will choose a description of his behaviour as a motion, and he need not retract this description as false, once he discovers that the agent has actively moved his body, after all. So, when one is observing a person who appears to be asleep, and notes that 'his foot moves', one will not, on discovering that the person is awake and has been moving his foot, retract one's earlier statement and admit 'Oh, your foot did not move after all; you moved it'.

So, *pace* von Wright, we can conclude that cases of bodily movements are, after all, cases of bodily motions. Therefore, the escape route for the intentionalist sketched by Stoutland is closed, and the objection against the intentionalist account that it cannot satisfactorily deal with the element of the agent's control which is necessary for actions remains in force. The intentionalist account, being unable to provide a complete account of human agency on its own, will thus stand in need of supplementation by one of the other two accounts—the event-causal or the agent-causal accounts—and this other approach will then provide the more adequate starting-point for a unified account of agency, into which the positive insights of the intentionalist approach will have to be integrated.

2.3. Event-causalism versus agent-causalism

We are thus left with the naturalist event-causalist and the agent-causalist approach as the remaining contenders for providing the basis of a unified account of human agency, integrating all of Theses 1, 2, and 3, or at least maintaining the 'core content' of each of them. (In conformity to common usage, I will, in the following, also be using the term 'causalist' on its own, to refer to the naturalist event-causalist position.)

Accounts of human agency on both of these approaches accept the result-action dependence and the claim that all cases of bodily movement are also cases of bodily motion; and, for both approaches, what distinguishes cases of mere bodily motion from cases of agency is the presence of an extra causal element which guarantees the agent's control. For the event-causalist, this is causation of his bodily motions by mental states of the right kind, and for the agent-causalist it is causation by the agent himself *qua* substance.

The controversy between event-causalist and agent-causalist accounts of human agency will occupy us throughout the next chapters, and I shall therefore begin my discussion of them with short historical overviews of the 'standard model'—the most important event-causalist theory, on which I will focus—and of the agent-causalist approach. These overviews provide the necessary background for our later discussion of more specific problems for these approaches. Afterwards, I will point out what I consider to be the chief challenge for the standard model: namely, whether it succeeds in 'naturalizing' agential control.

2.3.1. *The event-causalist standard model of agency*

As already mentioned in the very brief presentation of the naturalist event-causal approach in Section 1.2, this approach, due to its commitment to the event-causal view of reality, does not take our talk about agential activity literally, but tries to provide a reductive account of this activity in terms of the causal role of the agent's mental states (or changes in those states). This approach came into prominence practically at the same time as the naturalist materialism which underlies it—the first renowned modern exposition of both these approaches being Thomas Hobbes' *Leviathan*. Hobbes (implicitly) reduced the agent's activity to causal determination by the agent's will, and understood the will itself to be constituted by desires: 'a *Voluntary Act* is that, which proceedeth from the *Will*, and no other... *Will...is last Appetite in Deliberating*.'[29] Due to this explanation of the will in terms which did not contain implicit references to an *active* agent, Hobbes' approach promised to offer a completely reductive account of agency in terms which seemed acceptable to the rising naturalism.

Since Hobbes, most philosophers of action have adopted the same basic 'causalist' strategy to explain the nature of agency in terms of special event-causal antecedents of bodily behaviour, and have usually followed the particular twist added by Hume, who wedded the strategy to his purely instrumentalist account of practical reason.[30] But many causalists abandoned the promise of a completely reductive account, because they did not reductively explain the will, as Hobbes had done. Instead, they assumed that there were 'acts of the will'—volitions, which caused bodily motions and were themselves parts of every (voluntary) action.[31] What lay at the heart of agency, on their

---

[29] Hobbes, *Leviathan*, part I, ch. 6, p. 28.
[30] Hume, *A Treatise of Human Nature*, book I.
[31] The classical statement of volitionalism is Locke, *An Essay concerning Human Understanding*, book IV, ch. x, § 19. The most important twentieth-century defender of this view was Prichard (1949), 190. It is important to note, however, that some volitionalist accounts are reductive, because they consider volitions to be non-actional mental states: for example, Mill, *System of Logic*, book I, ch. iii, sect. 5.

view, was the intrinsic and irreducible action-quality of these volitions, from which the status of bodily movements as actions was derived. However, while the Hobbesian reductive approach was always an important rival to volitionalism, it definitely became the main causalist approach after the heavy criticism against volitionalism at the middle of the twentieth century[32] had temporarily led to a crisis of causalism, ending with Davidson's revival of the causalist approach in his *Actions, Reasons, and Causes*. This revival led to what is today the event-causalist standard account of human agency.

For Davidson, an action is, roughly, an item of bodily behaviour which is caused (in the right way) by a belief-and-desire-complex of the agent, which satisfies the following condition: The propositional expressions[33] of the contents of the belief and the desire rationalize the behaviour under one description, by forming the premises of a practical syllogism whose conclusion is the verdict that an action of this kind is to be performed.[34] (Here we can leave aside some complications—in particular, that it is, strictly speaking, not the belief-desire complex itself but the 'onslaught' of the desire which causes the action; for while the complex is a state, the 'onslaught' is an event.[35]) As clearly not all actions are accompanied by 'desires' in the normal sense of the word, 'desire' in Davidson's analysis must be understood in the very wide sense of a 'pro-attitude', which includes not only felt desires but all kinds of motivating attitudes, independently from their phenomenal quality.[36]

Davidson's characterization of actions trades on the ambiguity in the locution 'bodily behaviour', already encountered in Section 2.2, that it can be understood both in the sense of 'bodily movement' and of 'bodily motion'. For a reductive account of agency, 'behaviour' in Davidson's analysis must be understood as bodily motion, on pain of circularity; but when Davidson talks about the 'rationalization of behaviour' the term can be understood only in the sense of 'bodily movement', because only actions, not bodily motions, are candidates for rationalization through the construction of a practical syllogism. If Davidson's account of action is right, this ambiguity will be innocuous, because then actions will be identical to bodily motions having the right causal antecedents. So, for Davidson, one and the same item will be both a bodily motion caused by the desire-belief complex and an action which is a candidate for rationalization. Still, in order to produce a reductive analysis of action whose analysans does not involve any implicit appeal to agency, Davidson's account must be slightly changed to the following more precise, though clumsier, formulation: An action is a bodily motion which is caused by a desire-belief complex satisfying the following condition: when the bodily motion consists in the body's moving in way X, then the

---

[32] Especially by Ryle (1990), ch. 3. sec. 2.
[33] For beliefs, these are factual statements—for desires, value judgements; cf. Davidson (1970b), 31.
[34] Davidson (1963), (1971a), and (1973a). See ch. 1, fn. 31, for Davidson's slightly different view on the contents of the propositions in the practical syllogism in his (1963).
[35] Cf. Davidson (1963), 11 f.
[36] Davidson (1963), 3 f.

contents of the desire and the belief rationalize an action consisting in moving one's body in way X.

The currently dominant account of agency has introduced only one additional element with regard to Davidson's proposal: the requirement that the belief and desire must first cause an intention, which in turn causes the bodily motion.[37] Appeal to intentions was introduced partly in order to narrow the gap between actions and their mental antecedents which allowed room for 'deviant causal chains' (a topic to which we will return in Chapter 5), and partly due to the recognition of the important coordinating role intentions play for agency over time.[38] Among the intentions viewed as causal antecedents of the bodily motions, a further distinction is usually made between intentions already possessed before the action—'prior intentions', which are meant to explain the possibility that one intends to F long before one begins to F—and 'intentions-in-action'[39] or 'proximate intentions',[40] which are meant to explain intentional agency itself. This distinction will become relevant for our later discussion of deviant causal chains.

2.3.2. Agent-causal theories of human agency

The distinctive claim of agent-causal theories of action is that agents, *qua* substances, can be causes of effects. Now, for many cases the claim that the agent caused a certain effect seems to be trivially true and will hardly be contested: namely, when the agent brings about the effect by doing something else. Thus, when Gavrilo Princip killed Archduke Ferdinand in Sarajevo in 1914, he caused his death, and did so by shooting him. Such cases, however, do not in themselves imply that there is any other kind of causality than event-causality;[41] for when I bring about an effect by doing something else, the result of the more basic action that I perform causes the further effect, and the former result is itself an event.

What is characteristic for agent-causal theories is the thesis that there are instances of agent-causation which are not reducible to event-causation—that there are results of basic actions (i) which the agent causes 'directly' without doing anything else to cause them, and (ii) where his causal role is not reducible to the causal influence of states of the agent or events involving him. If this thesis is right, agents are essentially self-movers when they act—or, at least, when they act freely—because the results of basic actions are not changes external to the agent, but changes in the agent's own states: for

---

[37] An early prominent exponent of the view that actions must include intentions was Searle (1983). Even earlier, 'new volitionalists' had reintroduced mental events such as tryings as successors to volitions, which came very close to what Searle calls 'intentions-in-action'; cf. Hornsby (1980), O'Shaughnessy (1973).
[38] This insight has become widespread since Bratman (1987).
[39] These two terms were coined by Searle (1983), 84.
[40] Mele (2000), 290.
[41] They have this implication only when the additional claim is accepted that causing something by doing something else is conceptually prior to event-causation, and can, for this reason, not be completely reduced to it. This is, for example, the view of Rundle, (2004), 61 ff., for whom the paradigm of causation is not event-causation, but one substance causing an effect by acting on another substance.

example, motions of parts of his body. For this reason, agent-causation is also called 'immanent causation' to signify that its immediate effects rest within the substance-cause itself, in contrast to 'transeunt causation' where the effect is spatiotemporally separated from the cause.[42]

The first expression of a (minimal) agent-causal theory is often believed to be contained in Aristotle's proposal, at the beginning of Book III of the *Nicomachean Ethics*, that the origin of a voluntary action must lie within the agent, so that it depends on him whether he performs the action, while the origin of an involuntary action lies outside the agent.[43] Exegetically, however, the reference to Aristotle as a first proponent of agent-causalism is not completely convincing.[44] Although Aristotle does speak of self-movements—for him, living beings are self-movers[45]—he does not countenance the possibility of self-movement in a strict sense, as a kind of movement radically different from movement by outside factors. For him, it is, strictly speaking, impossible that one and the same substance undergoes a change which it produces itself; in many cases, on his view, producing the instantiation of a certain property even presupposes that the substance producing this change already possesses this very property. As a consequence, self-movement is possible only for composite objects, and in the form that one part of the whole object causes a change within another part.[46]

While medieval and early modern Thomists, such as Suarez, also spoke of immanent causation, the first elaborated agent-causalist theory is to be found in Thomas Reid's *Essays on the Active Powers of Man* from the eighteenth century. Reid's theory of (free) action is a combination of agent-causalism and volitionalism. As a volitionalist, he thought that at the basis of each (free) action there is a volition which causes the agent's bodily motions, and it is this volition—the 'determination of the will'—which is caused by the agent.[47] For Reid, agent-causation consists in the exertion of an active power by the agent to bring about the effect in question.[48]

With his characterization of agent-causation—apart from the volitionalist element in his theory—Reid predetermined, to a large degree, the lines along which the discussion about agent-causation in the second half of the twentieth century was to be led. Three features have been especially influential. First, for Reid the source of our concepts of causation and power is our experience of ourselves as active agents; second, he claimed that exertion of an active power to bring about an effect presupposes the power to refrain from bringing about the effect, which connects agent-causation to *free*

---

[42] Cf. Chisholm (1966), 17; *Handbuch der philosophischen Grundbegriffe*, vol. 3, 780.
[43] Aristotle, *Nicomachean Ethics*, 1110a1 ff., 16 ff.
[44] Cf. Thorp (1980), 96 ff.
[45] Aristotle, *Physics*, 252 b 15 ff.
[46] Op. cit., 257b, 1 ff.
[47] Reid (1983), 602.
[48] Reid (1983), 515. It is doubtful, though, whether Reid had any elaborated theory of powers, apart from Locke's account of powers. Yaffe (2004), 154 ff., claims that Reid lacked any developed conception of exertion, and that his views about exertions were based only on the observed grammatical properties of 'trying'.

agency; and third, as a consequence of this he believed that only human beings with understanding and will can possess active powers.[49]

The last two claims place Reid as the forerunner of a long succession of agent-causalists in the second half of the twentieth century—including C. A. Campbell, Roderick Chisholm, John Thorp, William Rowe, Timothy O'Connor, Randolph Clarke, and Jonathan Lowe[50]—who have appealed to agent-causation in order to solve the problem of free will. When, after a long time of marginalization, agent-causalism was revived at the middle of the twentieth century, this was mainly due to a widespread view that only by appealing to agent-causation could one account for free will and moral responsibility. This view was based on the following kind of argument that had been developed by Chisholm:[51]

> Premiss 1 An agent cannot be responsible for his action if it is deterministically caused by other events (incompatibilism).
> Premiss 2 An agent cannot be responsible for his action if it is not caused at all, for then it happens 'at random' (the 'luck objection').
> Conclusion If the agent is responsible for his action, what causes the action are not other events, but must be the agent himself.

While at Chisholm's time only deterministic event-causation was discussed, later theories of free will, which have accepted premiss 1 and regarded moral responsibility and determinism as incompatible, have tried to explain the possibility of free action by appeal to indeterministic event-causation.[52] So, for the sake of completeness the following premiss must, for current forms of the argument, be inserted:[53]

> Premiss 3 An agent is not responsible for his action simply because this action is only indeterministically caused by prior mental states.

Here I can discuss neither the particular premisses nor the overall stringency of this argument in detail. Only the following point must be noted. For incompatibilists, who believe that universal determinism would exclude free will and moral responsibility, agent-causalism is indeed a very appealing strategy, because it promises a way between the two horns of a putative dilemma.

The normal reason for being an incompatibilist is that one believes that (a) moral responsibility requires that the agent could have acted otherwise, and that (b) this

---

[49] Reid (1983), 523.
[50] Cf. Campbell (1951); Chisholm (1966); Thorp (1980); Rowe (1995); O'Connor (1995) and (2000); Clarke (1993) and (1996); Lowe (2001) and (2002). Both Chisholm and Clarke, however, later gave up their agent-causal views; cf. Chisholm (1995) and Clarke (2000). Taylor (1958) also originally connected agent-causings only to free actions.
[51] The argument was first presented in Chisholm (1958), though it was only in Chisholm (1966) that he drew the conclusion from it that free actions must involve agent-causings.
[52] Most notably Kane (1996) and Mele with his 'deliberative indeterminism', (1995).
[53] Cf. O'Connor (2000), ch. 1 and 2; Lowe (2002), 201 f.

requirement cannot be fulfilled under universal determinism.[54] If one shares these views, moral responsibility will only seem possible if one introduces an element of indeterminism in actions, which gives rise to genuine alternative possibilities. For example, when one adheres to the event-causalist standard model, one will think it necessary that there is a non-deterministic connection between the causal antecedents of the action and the action itself. However, this very move seems to introduce an element of luck or randomness into the action, which diminishes the agent's control over what he is doing. As control is at least as crucial to moral responsibility as the availability of alternative possibilities, it seems that by the very move by which we account for one element of responsibility, we begin to undermine the other.[55] And even if one is more optimistic and believes that indeterminism does not positively undercut control, one must still admit that it cannot, by itself, give the agent control over which of the different possible alternatives in the indeterministic scenario is realized, and that the appeal to indeterminism will not, on its own, solve the problem of free will.[56]

With agent-causalist theories of free will, however, the dilemma does not arise, nor does the element of the agent's control over which alternative is realized remain unexplained. For when an agent causes something, this causing can be regarded as a paradigmatic instance of control over what is happening, whose status as an instance of control does not depend on the event-causal antecedents of the causing (if there are any).[57] For the agent-causing is, on this view, *intrinsically* an exercise of control, and not only extrinsically, in virtue of its relations to other occurrences. Therefore, it will be an exercise of control even if it is not caused by anything at all, or only indeterministically caused.[58]

We can therefore conclude that for an incompatibilist, agent-causalism presents *prima facie* a very attractive solution to the problem of free will which promises an escape from the dilemma between lack of alternative possibilities and control-undermining chanciness.[59] However, besides the strategy *à la Chisholm* to appeal to agent-causation as a solution to the problem of free will, there has also been a second main motivation for agent-causalist accounts, which is more directly related to our overall investigation: namely, the desire to account for the element of agential activity

---

[54] Both parts of this claim are hotly disputed. For (a) see, especially, Frankfurt (1969); for (b) see, for example, the discussion about Van Inwagen's (1983) consequence argument for incompatibilism.

[55] This difficulty for incompatibilists is presented in Mele (2005), 114 f. (Mele, however, does not think that agent-causal accounts can answer the worry about luck either; cf. (2006b), ch. 3.)

[56] Cf. O'Connor's discussion of Kane, (2000), 38 ff.

[57] O'Connor (2000), 58 f.

[58] This important point was overlooked by some agent-causalists and their critics alike: Chisholm, for example, believed that the agent-causing would be 'random' and could not be ascribed to the agent, if it were itself uncaused (1976), 71. Among the critics see Van Inwagen (2002), 173 ff., who argues that appeal to agent-causation does not obviate the 'chanciness' of actions not deterministically caused by prior events.

[59] This does not mean that agent-causalism would offer the only putative solution to this dilemma; deliberative indeterminism, cf. Mele (1995), ch. 12, and volitionalist theories, for instance, are alternative candidates.

expressed by Thesis 1. Philosophers such as Richard Taylor, John Bishop, Maria Alvarez, and John Hyman have all offered more or less elaborate agent-causal theories according to which agent-causation underlies human agency in general.[60] And several other philosophers have expressed the view that the concept of action already includes an appeal to agent-causation, because the basic form of an action description is in terms of the agent bringing about an effect.[61]

As our overall concern here is with the problem of human agency and not with the problem of free will, the latter approach to agent-causation is more relevant for us, and we will therefore ignore any special difficulties that arise in connection to *free* agency rather than to agency in general.

2.3.3. The challenge to the standard model: can agential activity be naturalized?

Which of the two kinds of theory—the event-causalist standard model or an agent-causal account—offers more chance of a successful answer to the problem of human agency? For most philosophers, the answer is clear. Only the standard model stands any chance of success—because it is the only approach of the two which is compatible with naturalist commitments to 'the emerging scientific picture of the world', and because agent-causation is conceptually deeply mysterious. Taking this majority view as our guideline, we will begin by examining the allegedly more promising standard model, and attempt to determine whether it can offer a unified account of human agency.

The project of searching for such an account on the basis of the standard model can best be described as a project of 'naturalizing human agency'—of fitting it within the event-causal view (and possibly, the bottom-up picture) of reality that is the central tenet of 'naturalism'. So, whether the standard model can offer an answer to the problem of human agency depends on whether human agency can be naturalized, or whether the attempt to naturalize it leads to its elimination.

The chief obstacle to a naturalization of agency is, as we have seen, Thesis 1 and the element of agential activity. As we have argued, the event-causal view of nature seems to have no place for genuine activity, but only for a flux of mere happenings. Besides, there are further grounds for scepticism, which rest on the difficulty of how to precisely pin-point actions within the world conceived purely naturalistically, without already presupposing agential concepts. As this difficulty provides a special obstacle to the view that actions could be 'realized' in non-actional event-causal processes, we need to examine it in more detail.

If actions were indeed identical to bodily motions, or to event-causal processes running from intentions to bodily motions, and if actions could be reductively

---

[60] Taylor (1966)—though he later renounced agent-causalism, (1982); Bishop (1983)—he also later rejected agent-causalism in his (1989); Alvarez and Hyman (1998). Also White (1968), Greenwood (1989), and Vossenkuhl (2006), 204 ff. subscribe to agent-causalism.

[61] For example, Kenny (1963), 177 f.; Bennett (1965), 85. Von Wright, in *Norm and Action: A Logical Enquiry* (1963a), 35 ff., also arguably advanced an agent-causalist thesis, though he later explicitly rejected agent-causalism, making clear that for him, causal relations can only hold between natural events, (1974), 49.

analysed, as the event-causalist account proposes, then we would expect that the events which constituted the actions could be described in purely 'naturalistic' terms; that is, without implicitly using agential concepts. But it is extremely difficult to see how this could, even in principle, be done. For instance, which neurophysiological events constitute a bodily movement? How can we even begin to draw a line at the 'beginning' and the 'end' of both the bodily motion and the bodily movement to determine which neurophysiological events 'belong' to the action and which do not? Though we might be confident that some neurophysiological events must be included (if any are included) and others excluded, for many events it does not make sense to claim either. 'Is this muscle-flexion part of the action?' or 'is this neuron-firing part of it?' In many cases these questions seem to be simply absurd.[62] Nor will it help to include the level of internal conscious experiences. Whether or not a certain experience is part of the action, or simultaneous to it, is often both an unanswerable and a misplaced question. Thus it is implausible to expect either a one-to-one fit between action-tokens and any process-tokens picked out by purely neurophysiological descriptions, or between actions and any combinations of processes of neurophysiological and conscious events picked out without using, at least implicitly, agential concepts.

The naturalist might object that this does not undermine his case, because he still has one description available which does not presuppose agential concepts: the descriptions of the bodily motion as 'the rising of the arm', or 'the lowering of my foot', or 'the turning of my hand'. As is apparent from my criticism of the intentionalist approach, I think that in one sense these descriptions are indeed independent from agency. We can describe bodily behaviour in this way without presupposing that it is actually a manifestation of agency. But on the level of conceptual connections it is not the case that these descriptions are independent from agential concepts. For these descriptions are conceptually connected to descriptions of actions, such as 'raising one's arm', 'lowering one's foot', and 'turning one's hand', because the contained verbs are just the transitive and intransitive forms of one and the same verb or verb-stem; and we would not have these motion-descriptions without also having the corresponding action-descriptions. This means that regularly, when we describe bodily behaviour by those terms, (i) we use a description which we can only use because we already have the corresponding act-description, and (ii) we already describe it 'carved up' in a way to be a potential result of an action.[63] Consequently, a thoroughly reductivist approach should not use these descriptions of bodily motions.

If this is right, it is very improbable that actions could ever be picked out, and then analysed, in terminology whose possession does not already presuppose an understanding of agency. At the same time, our considerations make it highly implausible that

---

[62] Cf. Hornsby (1993), 296.

[63] A point related to (ii) is made by Stoutland (1985), 55 f. He argues that actions have both physical and psychological descriptions, but that the psychological descriptions are primary in selecting an action as the—numerically one—particular to which physical descriptions apply.

there can be a one-to-one fit between tokens of neurophysiological processes, or processes consisting of neurophysiological events and conscious experiences, picked out by purely 'naturalistic' descriptions, and action-tokens picked out by using commonplace agential concepts. This provides a strong *prima facie* case against the possibility of naturalizing agency. The case, however, is not yet conclusive, because, for example, even when a one-to-one fit between actions and events picked out by non-actional descriptions in the ways described is impossible, this is theoretically compatible with both being part of the same structure of purely event-causal processes. It might just be that terminology relying directly or indirectly on agential concepts and neurophysiological terminology 'carve up' reality in completely different ways.

But the strong *prima facie* case is sufficient to give rise to a strong initial presumption against the possibility of naturalizing agency. And this presumption is important, because it shifts the 'burden of proof' clearly onto the shoulders of the defender of the event-causalist standard model.

In order to rebut this presumption, adherents of the standard model must show how, within a purely event-causal order, agential activity can be maintained in a recognizable form. Now, as I have already indicated, the minimum 'core' element of agential activity, which *any* account of human agency must salvage, is agential control: It must present a picture of human action on which the agent is recognizably 'in control' of what is happening. 'Control' is, in an important respect, a weaker notion than 'activity', for while the latter is directly at odds with a purely event-causal image of reality, the former is not. Thus, an account of control cannot be criticized merely by pointing out that it is an account in purely event-causal terms. For this reason, it is not *a priori* excluded that adherents of the standard model can provide a satisfactory account of control.

The account that they provide is, as we have seen, in terms of causation of the bodily behaviour by special mental states—especially desires and intentions. For the sake of convenience we can split this account into two claims: (i) about the required '*bearer*' of control—desires or intentions—and (ii) about the required '*mode*' of control—by event-causal influence on the agent's behaviour.

In a parallel way, we can split the requirement that must plausibly be fulfilled for an account of agential control to be satisfactory into two parts: (a) that it must be the *agent himself* who is 'in charge', and not some other entity, and (b) that he must be '*in control*', in the sense that it depends on him what is happening, and is not, from his viewpoint, fortuitous. If we apply these two requirements to claims (i) and (ii) we obtain the following condition that must be fulfilled for (i) and (ii) to jointly form a satisfactory account of agential control: (a★) the 'bearer' of control must somehow represent the agent's 'own standpoint', and (b★) the 'mode' of control must guarantee that this standpoint is realized in the action.

But do (i) and (ii) satisfy this condition? There are two main grounds for scepticism. With regard to (i) and (a★) this is Harry Frankfurt's 'problem of identification', and with regard to (ii) and (b★) it is the 'problem of deviant causal chains'. It is therefore to the discussion of these two problems that we must now turn.

3
Alien desires and Frankfurt's problem of identification

As we saw in the previous chapter, the standard model aims to explain the first necessary element of agential control: namely, that it is the *agent himself* who is in charge, in terms of the causal impact of the agent's mental states, primarily of his intentions and desires to act. This explanation can be successful only if the causal impact of these states can intelligibly be seen to go proxy for the agent's own determination of his behaviour, and this requires that these states can be understood as constituting the agent's 'own standpoint'—or, alternatively, the agent's 'self'. For otherwise it would not be intelligible how their causal impact could constitute an activity *of the agent*, rather than a causal contribution by some other entity. The same point can be made in terms of agential self-determination. If this phenomenon is to be explained in terms of the causal impact of the agent's mental states, it must be intelligible how the causal role of those states could constitute a determination by the agent himself.

The traditional Hobbesian conception of agential control and self-determination answered these requirements by claiming that those desires of the agent which are causally effective in moving him to action constitute his *will*. If this claim were correct, then our query for mental states that express the agent's own standpoint would have found an answer, because if there is to be a standpoint of the agent at all, the content of his will seems to be the best candidate for it.

However, as Frankfurt has shown by a number of examples, the simple Hobbesian account of the nature of the will does not work, because there are desires of the agent which, while moving him to action, clearly do not express his standpoint, but, on the contrary, are obstacles to what he really wants. These are cases of desires with which the agent does not identify, but which he considers as alien or external to himself. We will start with an exposition of these cases, and try to show how they call into question not only the Hobbesian conception in particular, but the whole basic idea of the standard model that the agent's control could be reduced to the causal impact of his desires (Section 3.1).

The most influential attempt to solve this difficulty within the general framework of the standard model is the hierarchical model of the will proposed by Frankfurt, which is, however, beset by a number of objections (Section 3.2). We will discuss a number of attempts—by Frankfurt himself in later writings, by Gary Watson, and by

David Velleman—to provide an event-causal model of self-determination which escapes these objections, and we will see that none of them is completely satisfactory (Section 3.3).

In Chapter 4 we will turn to the most promising approach to dealing with the problem of identification: namely, Michael Bratman's analysis of 'identifying with a desire' as 'treating this desire as reason-giving'. As we shall see, however, the adherent of the standard model cannot draw comfort from this solution, because when understood rightly it goes beyond the resources available to the reductionist project of the standard model.

3.1. The challenge from Frankfurt's cases of alienation

As a starting-point for Frankfurt's cases we do well to remind ourselves of two fundamental features of the standard model. First, this model relies on the idea that what a person wants most is the object of his strongest desire, where the strength of a desire is a matter of its causal efficacy in moving the agent to act, winning out against other desires that would move him to a different course of action. This idea is already expressed in Hobbes' definition of the will; and it is closely connected to the 'hydraulic picture'[1] of human motivation usually ascribed to Hume, according to which desires are like forces moving the agent from rest to motion. Second, as we have already mentioned, when the model claims that the action is caused by a desire, it conceives of desire very widely, in the sense of pro-attitudes. The notion of pro-attitude is meant to cover all kinds of motivating attitudes, including not only attitudes connected to valuational views, but also simple wantings, urges, or yens.

The combination of these two features brings the standard model into difficulties when it is faced with cases in which what the agent is motivated to do—the object of the agent's strongest desire, if strength is understood in terms of 'efficacy in moving to action'—is, in a certain sense, not what he wants most, because it is not what he really wants to do. A by now classical case where what the agent really wants to do and what he is motivated to do come apart is Frankfurt's case of the unwilling drug addict. This addict is regularly moved by his addictive urge to take the drug, even though he hates his addiction and struggles desperately, but unsuccessfully, both to withstand the periodic onslaughts of the addictive urges and to rid himself of them. So, each time, he finally succumbs to the urge, when it becomes insupportable, and takes the drug.[2] Even though the agent acts on his strongest desire—in the sense explained above—in this situation, this is clearly not a case of self-determination or active self-control, because the agent really wants to do something else—refrain from taking the drug— but is prevented from doing so by his own addictive urge.

---

[1] This term is from McDowell (1981), 47, where he describes this picture of motivation as a 'quasi-hydraulic conception'.
[2] Frankfurt (1971), 87.

Frankfurt's case of the unwilling drug addict is not an isolated one; but generally, all cases of Obsessive Compulsive Disorder share the same characteristics: the feeling of an urge which is at odds with what the agent really wants, which can normally be suppressed for some time, but which ultimately becomes irresistible until it is allowed to 'pour out' by performing the relevant action.[3] Apart from these clinical cases, less drastic instances of the same basic phenomenon occur in everyday life when someone is overcome by sudden and extreme passions, of which he disapproves, but which he cannot control: for example, a tennis player who feels a sudden urge to hit his opponent with his racket after losing a point,[4] or other cases of 'seeing red'. If the agent cannot resist those passions, they lead him to behave in ways which he himself experiences as 'discontinuous with his understanding of his situation and his conception of himself'.[5] In these situations we can understand what the agent says when he distances himself from his action by saying something like 'I am sorry, I wasn't myself when I did this, but my resentment overcame me', and we sometimes accept such statements as honest descriptions of the agent's situation rather than disallowing them as insincere attempts to escape full responsibility for the action.

We will call these cases—both clinical and non-clinical—cases of *alienation* from a desire; when an agent is not 'alienated' from a desire of his, we will say that he *identifies* with this desire. The feature shared by all cases of 'alienation' that interests us most is that the motivational efficacy of the agent's strongest desire does not lead to self-control or self-determination, but instead prevents them. Instead of deciding 'himself' what to do, the agent is, in Frankfurt's vivid terminology, 'helplessly violated by his own desires', a 'passive bystander' to his desires, which act on him as 'external' forces and which he experiences as 'alien intruders'.[6]

I believe that these cases teach us a very important lesson, and that there is some justification for Frankfurt's colourful terminology. But in order to better understand the impact of these cases, it is imperative first to distinguish cases of 'alienation' more sharply from some other kinds of cases with which they have sometimes been mixed up.

First, we must distinguish cases of 'alienation' from a desire from other cases of 'alienation' where the agent does not act at all or lacks a sense of agency.[7] Cases of the latter kind are, for example, those of the Anarchic Hand Syndrome. Here the agent temporarily loses control over his hand, which performs, 'on its own', complex movements that the agent cannot stop at will except by using his unaffected hand to hold down the 'anarchic' hand.[8] In the case of 'alien' desires, with which we are concerned here, there is no doubt that the agent has performed an action and has been

---

[3] Cf. Marcel (2003), 79 f.
[4] After Watson (1975), 101.
[5] Frankfurt (1977), 62.
[6] The phrases are, in this sequence, from Frankfurt (1971), 87; (1975), 54; (1977), 61 and 65.
[7] For an overview over these different forms of alienation, see Pacherie et al. (2006).
[8] Cf. Marcel (2003), 77 f. *Vide infra* ch. 5.

aware of doing so. It is only the desire which drives him to action which he experiences as external and uncontrollable. When I refer to alienation in the rest of this chapter and the next, I will always be meaning alienation *from a desire*.

Second, it is crucial to distinguish the phenomenon of alienation from the phenomenon of akrasia. When an agent acts akratically, he does not act in accordance with his judgement about what is best, but willingly does something else, which, on his own assessment, has less value. Clearly, cases of akratic action and cases of being alienated from one's motivationally effective desire have something important in common, for in both cases the agent disapproves of what he is doing and is not acting in accordance with what he believes to be best. It is therefore tempting to regard cases of alienation just as limiting cases of akratic action, where the gulf between the action and the agent's judgement about what is best is particularly large, and which are additionally distinguished from standard akratic actions by the element of compulsion. (Also in the latter respect, there will be no clear-cut distinction between cases of alienation and of akrasia, because extreme pathological cases of akrasia can, with regard to compulsion, be very similar to cases of alienation.)

But regarding alienation as simply a limiting case of akrasia in this way is misleading, because it neglects a crucial difference in the key characteristics of both phenomena. In the standard case of akrasia, the agent believes that he has *some* reason to act as he does, though he does not believe this reason to be a sufficiently justifying one, because it is outweighed by other relevant countervailing considerations. This means that if the countervailing reasons were absent, the agent would view himself as justified in acting as he does. So, the key characteristic of akrasia is (only) that the action fails to reflect the *balance* of the agent's reasons as he perceives them.

In the case of alienation, however, matters are different, because the agent is *completely* unwilling to be moved by the desire in question;[9] that is, he would disapprove of the action even if there were no particular counteracting considerations in the present situation. Thus, imagine a person with an obsessive compulsion to wash his hands all the time,[10] who is alienated from this urge. Now, on one occasion where he feels the urge, a friendly powerful demon offers him the opportunity to wash his hands without any costs or negative consequences. If the person is truly alienated from his obsessive compulsion he will still not choose to wash his hands—at least not until the urge becomes irresistible. He will not do so, even though the demon's intervention excludes negative consequences in the particular situation, for he sees no point at all in washing his hands when they are not dirty. So, the distinguishing characteristic of alienation is not a failure of the action to reflect the *balance* of reasons in an especially glaring way, for such a failure also occurs when the agent acts for a reason which he believes to be much weaker than all perceived reasons to the contrary.

---

[9] Frankfurt (2002), 186.
[10] The example is due to Gerhard Ernst.

The key characteristic is, instead, failure to see *any* point in performing the action which is the object of the desire.

Failure to distinguish the phenomena of alienation and akrasia is not only an exegetical mistake with regard to Frankfurt's own intentions of how his cases of alienation are to be understood—though many philosophers, such as Michael Scanlon, have misunderstood Frankfurt in precisely this way.[11] It also threatens to disguise an important difference of fact, because the phenomenon of alienation presents a particular problem for the standard model that does not arise from the phenomenon of akrasia *per se*. For alienation involves a *complete* breakdown of self-determination and of a characteristic kind of self-understanding, while akrasia involves no such *complete* breakdown. In cases of akrasia it is normally unproblematic to say that it is the agent himself who determines what he is doing. On this occasion the agent normally does what he 'really wants to do',[12] for this is not excluded by a feeling of compunction or of doing something wrong. Because we consider the agent to have decided for himself, akrasia normally does not limit responsibility; but it is different for alienation, because it is a responsibility-limiting factor that what the agent did was not something he really wanted to do.

Furthermore, in cases of akrasia the desire on which the agent acts is not *itself* at odds with his self-understanding and his understanding of the situation. The person on a diet who akratically gives in to his desire to eat a chocolate knows about the pleasures connected with eating chocolate and can therefore well understand why he should desire to have a chocolate. He may even put positive value on having this desire. If his diet only lasts one month, it may be important to him to keep his appetite for chocolates—to enjoy them even more after his diet is over. What is at odds with his self-understanding is only that he acts on this desire—that he prefers the satisfaction of this desire to doing something else which he recognizes to be more valuable. This means that the agent can still understand his own action in terms of a reason for action which he has and for which he acts. He can still view his action as performed for some good, even if only for a lesser good. In cases of alienation—such as hitting one's tennis partner because one 'sees red' after losing a point—this understanding is impossible, because the urge to hit the tennis partner is *itself* completely at odds with the agent's

---

[11] Scanlon (2002) states that he long considered this as the correct analysis of Frankfurt's cases, before realizing that Frankfurt was interested in a 'more radical understanding of the case', 177. That Frankfurt himself understood cases of 'alienation' as radically different from cases of 'normal' akrasia is clear from his discussion of two kinds of decision in his (1977), 66 f.; from his insistence that in the cases of alienation the effectiveness of passions rests on 'sheer brute force', without *any* connected motivational *authority* or claim the passions make on us, (1993), 137; and from his answer to Scanlon in (2002), 186.

[12] One might object that there is a stronger sense of 'really wanting' in which an akratic agent may not be acting as he 'really wants to'—namely, the sense in which 'really wanting' implies wholeheartedness. (For example, when John grudgingly fires one of his subordinates because he has been ordered to do so, he may say: 'I do not really want to lay you off, but I have to.') This stronger sense of 'really wanting' is, however, not directly relevant to our question, which is a question about the agent's *will*. Missing wholeheartedness does not exclude that the agent acts as he wills, or acts self-determinedly, as shown by the case of forcing oneself to act out of duty, though one would like to act otherwise.

self-understanding. The agent does not see *any* point in wanting to hit his tennis partner, and so his urge is not intelligible to him[13] (as a consequence of which he considers the urge to be 'evil'). Consequently, his action is not performed for any perceived good at all.[14]

Besides distinguishing alienation from akrasia, we must also keep it apart from another phenomenon which is the focus of Frankfurt's later work: namely, missing 'wholeheartedness'.[15] An agent acts wholeheartedly when he pursues a course of action to which he is wholly committed, or when he cares about the object of his action. But performing an action only half-heartedly, or not caring about the object of one's action, is clearly not the same as being driven by a desire which one regards as an 'alien intruder'. Consider, for example, actions that are completely inconsequential to us, so that their performance has no importance in our own eyes, such as following an idle impulse to whistle a melody. These actions can clearly be instances of self-determination, where the agent is doing what he really wants, though they are not actions which he cares about or to which he is wholeheartedly committed.[16] So the contrast between identification and alienation is not the same as the one between acting wholeheartedly and acting less than wholeheartedly, and it is only the first contrast that will concern us here.

These distinctions help us to get into better focus the phenomena of alienation and identification. To summarize our characterization of alienation up to now: an agent is alienated from a desire when he altogether disapproves of this desire and of actions issuing from it, when he is completely unwilling to be moved by this desire, and when the desire is still experienced as an urge which often becomes irresistible if remaining unsatisfied. This does not mean that the alien desire *must* be irresistible in the particular case. The agent may have learned to resist the desire, either by self-control—as is hopefully the case with adults who feel the urge to hit their tennis partners—or by using some external means to control the force of the urge—such as in the case of the unwilling addict, by taking a sedative which allays the pressure of his addictive desire.

After having acquired a better understanding of the phenomenon of alienation that we are seeking, we can turn to the question of what specific challenge arises from this phenomenon to the analysis of agency offered by the standard model. At first

---

[13] It is not intelligible insofar as it does not make sense to him. What may be intelligible to him, however, is why, as a matter of fact, he feels this urge. For example, when a tennis player regularly has the described experience and his psychiatrist has explained to him why this happens, the player may understand why he feels the urge. But still, the urge itself continues to be at odds with his conception of the action-situation and of himself.

[14] In urging the distinction between the phenomena of 'alienation' and akrasia, I do not want to deny that it is sometimes difficult or even practically impossible to distinguish a case of 'alienation' from a case of akrasia. In fact, extreme pathological cases of akrasia can be very close to cases of 'alienation'. But the existence of such 'borderline' cases does not refute the general point that the two phenomena are different.

[15] Cf. Frankfurt (1987) and (1988b) onward.

[16] Cf. Frankfurt (2006), 18.

glance, the answer seems to be 'none'—because when an agent acts while driven on by an alien desire, he still possesses agential control, and his action is not a mere uncontrolled reflex. The unwilling addict, who desperately pushes the needle, knows what he is doing, and his control over what he is doing is demonstrated by the fact that he is still able to react to obstacles on the way to realizing his aim—for example, to re-set the needle if it were to slip out.[17] The phenomenon of alienation, it may seem, concerns only the aspect of self-determination that is relevant for free will, but plays no role for the problem of human agency itself.

But this view would be mistaken. For remember, one core idea of the standard model is that the control of the agent can be analysed as consisting in the causal impact of the agent's mental states, and one chief candidate kind for the relevant mental state are desires. This approach can be successful only if the desires, as proposed 'bearers' of control, express the agent's own standpoint—and this is called into question by the lesson that Frankfurt's cases of alienation teach us: namely, that the agent's desires can be obstacles to what the agent really wants.

If this is possible, then why should we think of desires as legitimate candidates for being the bearers of agential control at all? What guarantees that *any* desire we pick out constitutes the agent's will, and not something that instead prevents the realization of his will? Motivational efficacy of the desire does not guarantee this, as the case of the unwilling drug addict has shown—which demonstrates that the simple Hobbesian answer to the question of which mental states constitute the agent's standpoint must be rejected.

As a consequence, the standard model as a whole will have to be abandoned if we cannot find, within its framework, a further criterion which distinguishes cases of alienation from cases of identification with a desire. Fulfilment of this criterion must guarantee that the desire in question cannot be in conflict with what the agent really wants, which will make the desire a legitimate candidate for constituting the agent's own standpoint. This is the key challenge arising for causalists from Frankfurt's problem of identification—from the problem that agents need not identify themselves with the desires which move them to action, and that therefore there must be more to acting as one really wants to act than being moved by one's motivationally strongest desire.

3.2. Frankfurt's hierarchical model

Most of the discussion about Frankfurt's cases of alienation has been dedicated to finding such further criteria which are compatible with the basic tenets of the standard model. The most influential proposal was Frankfurt's own hierarchical account of the agent's motivational structure, which he offered in *Freedom of the Will and the Concept of*

---

[17] On this point Schroeter (2004) bases his criticism of an over-evaluation of Frankfurt's cases.

a Person. In this account, the original Hobbesian view of the agent's will is enriched by a hierarchy of higher-order desires.

This hierarchy is based on the distinction between first-order and higher-order desires—a distinction that is drawn in terms of the desires' contents. First-order desires are directed at certain courses of action—they have the content 'that I perform an action of type F'. Higher-order desires concern either the presence or the motivational efficacy of lower-order desires—they have the content 'that I have a desire to F' or 'that my desire to F moves me to action'; the second kind of higher-order desires Frankfurt calls higher-order volitions.[18] In Frankfurt's view, the motivational hierarchy of ascending levels of higher-order desires manifests the capacity for reflective self-evaluation—the capacity to not merely desire something, but also to detach oneself from one's first-order desires and to form responses of approval or disapproval with regard to them.[19] This capacity and the connected hierarchy are the distinguishing mark of persons, as contrasted to 'wantons', who have desires but do not care about which desires move them to act, and so lack, in Frankfurt's terminology, the capacity to form higher-order volitions.[20]

The distinction between first-order desires and higher-order volitions allows Frankfurt to separate 'what the agent really wants' from the content of his motivationally effective desires in the following way. Whether a first-order desire expresses what the agent really wants depends on whether the agent has a corresponding second-order volition that this desire be motivationally efficacious, by which volition he 'endorses' the desire. In the case of conflicts between first-order desires, the agent, by way of his second-order volitions, can identify with one of the conflicting desires, thereby distancing himself from or rejecting the other contenders, which are now considered as alien intruders. But the desire which the agent endorses may not be the one that eventually moves him to action, because other first-order desires from which the agent distances himself may turn out to be stronger—as is the case with the unwilling drug addict. So the agent may not end up doing what he really wants to do, and the desire that is motivationally strongest may be responsible for this failure, because it prevents the agent from acting on another first-order desire with which he identifies.

Frankfurt's hierarchical model is attractive for an adherent of the standard model because it provides a distinction between different senses of 'wanting most', which allows for an understanding of how our desires can be obstacles to what we really want. So, technically, Frankfurt's account offers a solution to the problem which has turned out to be a decisive stumbling-block for the simple, Hobbesian, form of the standard model. Nevertheless, the account, in its original form presented here, fails to

---

[18] Frankfurt (1971), 86.
[19] Frankfurt (1971), 83, and (2006), 3 f. In other places, Frankfurt speaks, rather, of a 'neutral attitude of acceptance', in order to make it clear that this attitude need not involve a positive evaluation of the desire; (2002), 160.
[20] Frankfurt (1971), 86.

provide a convincing analysis of the phenomenon of alienation, because it is faced by three fundamental difficulties which have—at least *in nuce*—all been developed in Watson's *Free Agency*.[21] These three problems can be called the problems of 'agential authority',[22] of 'potential regress', and of 'the content of practical deliberation'. We must examine these problems in more detail, because they are important for understanding and assessing not only Frankfurt's own proposal, but also the other attempted analyses of the phenomenon of alienation.

a) The problem of agential authority is an expression of the general worry about the possibility of reducing the agent's control to determination by the agent's desires which Frankfurt's own cases of alienation have raised. The central difficulty is to understand how higher-order volitions, in contrast to first-order desires, could have the 'authority to speak for the agent, to constitute where the agent stands'[23]—or, expressed differently, to understand why higher-order volitions should necessarily constitute what the agent really wants, in contrast to first-order desires. This difficulty arises because Frankfurt has introduced higher-order volitions only as desires with a certain content: namely, 'that my desire to F be motivationally effective'; and, given that desires in themselves do not possess any special authority to express what the agent really wants, it is mysterious how some desires should have this authority merely by having a special content. Watson expressed this point succinctly when he stated that 'higher-order volitions are just, after all, desires, and nothing about their level gives them any special authority with regard to externality'.[24]

This problem becomes especially pressing when we imagine that an agent regularly has a desire to F, while he has a second-order volition not to be motivated by this desire. Despite this volition and although the desire to F is not irresistible, the agent always acts on the desire to F, and even appeals to this desire in justifying his behaviour. Would we not then say that the agent's first-order desire expresses what the agent really wants, while the higher-order volition is just an otiose 'hanger-on'?

One might think that higher-order volitions, as they manifest a person's reflective ability to care about what one desires—and not merely to desire it—acquire their special authority from their source: the process of practical reflection. According to this line of thought, higher-order volitions are the results of reflective scrutiny of one's lower-order desires, and contain a reflective endorsement which is the result of such scrutiny. That they necessarily express what the agent really wants would then be due

---

[21] These three difficulties pertain especially to the question of whether Frankfurt's proposal succeeds in identifying the agent's standpoint. As Frankfurt intends to offer a solution to the problem of free will, too, there are further objections against his account to the effect that doing what one 'really wants' may not suffice for moral responsibility, because the source of one's desires may be flawed (cf. Wolf (1990), 35 ff.). However, as we are concerned only with the problem of human agency, we can leave aside these latter objections.

[22] The phrase 'agential authority' for this particular problem was coined by Bratman (2001), 309.

[23] Bratman (2005), 37.

[24] Watson (1987), 149.

to their being formed as responses to the self-reflective question: 'Should I act on this desire?'—which is always a question about whether a lower-level desire can be endorsed by the agent.

I think that such an account of the special authority of higher-order volitions would be highly promising (though I would still be sceptical whether these volitions play the role in our mental lives that Frankfurt ascribes to them). But, on exegetical grounds, this account cannot be ascribed to Frankfurt himself. For the proposed way of anchoring the authority of higher-order volitions in the process of practical reasoning must take into account the key characteristic of practical reasoning that when we are engaged in such reasoning, we ask not (merely) whether we have a desire to act in a certain way, but (also) whether we have *reasons* to act accordingly and whether these reasons are sufficient.[25] Frankfurt, by contrast, has repeatedly stressed that on his view, identification with a desire to F is, in principle, independent from seeing any reason to F—that we can identify ourselves with the forces that move us without thinking that we have any reason to do so.[26] So, the special authority of higher-order volitions in Frankfurt's original hierarchical model will have to be established on grounds other than their supposed status as results of practical reasoning (and it is on other grounds that Frankfurt himself has tried to establish it in his subsequent papers).

If these considerations are correct, Frankfurt's hierarchy of higher-order desires is left open to the problem of agential authority, and does not, by itself, provide us with a criterion for identifying those desires which represent what the agent really wants. Frankfurt himself, at first, failed to see the force of this objection; on his (earlier) view, a person could not be a 'passive bystander' to his second-order volitions, because they *constituted* his activity.[27] It was only in his discussion with Watson that he was eventually forced to recognize that the introduction of a hierarchy cannot, on its own, provide an explanation of identification and alienation.[28]

b) The second problem—of a potential regress of an array of continually higher-order desires—arises directly from the failure of the hierarchical model to explain the purported special 'authority' of higher-order volitions. (This second problem might even be considered just as a particular expression of the general problem of authority. Nevertheless, I will treat both problems separately—mainly because the focus of the discussion about identification has usually been concerned only with the regress problem. This separation will also help us to keep in mind the crucial point that the

---

[25] This would provide the basis for an attractive way to argue for the special 'authority' of self-reflective deliberating processes: for example, Korsgaard (1996), 93.
[26] This point is made most clearly in Frankfurt (2004), 124 ff; but it was already contained in his insistence that identification can be independent of the person's evaluative judgements because 'a person can become resigned to being someone of whom he does not altogether approve'; (1977), 64. However, Frankfurt's position has undergone some changes: At points, he even considered the notion of reflective self-evaluation as more fundamental than the notion of hierarchy itself; (1987), 165 fn. 7.
[27] Frankfurt (1975), 54.
[28] Frankfurt (1987), 167 f.

problem of authority goes deeper than the regress problem. Even if the regress problem is solved, this does not guarantee that the mental state at which the regress stops has the 'authority' to determine where the agent stands.)

The threat of a potential regress emerges because, if second-order volitions do not necessarily constitute the agent's standpoint, the problem of alienation can arise with regard to those desires as well as with regard to first-order desires. That is, the agent can have conflicting second-order desires[29] about how he wants to be motivated, and the desire that finally wins out may not express what he really wants. In order to account for this kind of case, a third-order volition will be needed to constitute the agent's standpoint with regard to his conflicting second-order desires. This process can be repeated at the level of the third-order desires as well, and so on, in principle, *ad infinitum*. But such a regress of continually higher-order desires would be clearly unacceptable—if only because an infinite array of desires is at odds with the finite psychological complexity of human beings.[30]

How can the potential regress be stopped? Two possible answers offer themselves to the defender of the hierarchical model. He might claim that as a matter of empirical fact, the regress cannot be infinite but must stop somewhere, simply because we are finite beings. At one point, the self-reflective process envisaged by Frankfurt—of detaching oneself from one's desires and adopting yet a further attitude towards them—will simply come to an end, if only because 'common sense, and, perhaps, a saving fatigue' prevent the agent from going on.[31] But the possibility that the regress can be averted in this way does not really answer the problem of the regress as it arises for Frankfurt's account; namely, in connection with the problem of agential authority. For, on Frankfurt's view, when the regress is ended the highest-order volition in the series of reflective attitudes is constitutive for the agent's identification with one of his first-order desires. As long as the question about whether the agent identifies himself with the highest-order volition can still be intelligibly raised, it remains hard to see how the volition can be so constitutive. So, the possibility of continuing the

---

[29] Or even, we might say, conflicting second-order volitions—although in Frankfurt's terminology this description is not possible. Although Frankfurt introduces the notion of higher-order volitions simply by specifying their special content, he also implies that there can be only *one* such volition: 'if there is an unresolved conflict among someone's second-order desires, then he is in danger of having no second-order volition'; (1971), 91. This suggests that Frankfurt tries to ensure the 'uniqueness' of second-order volitions by means of terminological *fiat*. But, if we look only at the special kind of content by which higher-order volitions have been characterized, there is nothing to rule out that agents could have conflicting higher-order volitions.

[30] According to an alternative understanding of higher-order attitudes, the reflective content of higher-order attitudes is just a logical expression of the allegedly self-referential content of intentions. On this view, the regress is only a harmless logical and semantical phenomenon, which does not require assuming an infinity of different mental states (cf. Harman (1993), 141 ff.). If one adopts this view, however, it becomes completely mysterious why higher-order desires should be crucial for self-determination, because the logical feature of self-referentiality may be shared by intentions and desires from which the agent is alienated; cf. Quante (2000), 120.

[31] Frankfurt (1971), 91.

series of reflective attitudes seems sufficient to generate the threat of an infinite regress, even if, as a matter of empirical fact, this regress will stop somewhere.

As an alternative to this first answer to the question of how the regress may be stopped, the defender of the hierarchical model can claim that the series of continually higher-order desires can, at some point, be stopped in a non-arbitrary way. As the first answer has turned out to be unsatisfactory, he must hope that this second answer can be substantiated—and, as we will see, Frankfurt, in his later writings, has tried to show how this can be achieved.

c) The third difficulty concerns the question of whether Frankfurt's account allows for an adequate reconstruction of the content of the agent's practical deliberation. At first glance it may appear unfair to allege a difficulty of this kind—if it should exist—as a shortcoming of Frankfurt's account, because Frankfurt, as we have seen, is not particularly concerned about the connection between identifying with a desire and practical reasoning. But it is mainly in practical reasoning about what to do that we come to formulate what we really want;[32] and consequently, if Frankfurt's view of what constitutes the agent's standpoint is at odds with the content of practical reasoning, this will necessarily be a pertinent criticism of his position.

What constitutes the agent's standpoint, on Frankfurt's early view, are higher-order volitions. For him, endorsing a desire consists in wanting to be moved by it. We would therefore expect the question about what we 'really want' to be formulated in terms of which first-order desires we want to be motivated by. But when we turn to our practical reasoning by means of which we try to determine what we really want to do, we rarely find ourselves engaged in reflective reasoning about what desires we want to be motivationally effective. Instead, we are normally concerned with the question which course of action would be most fun, morally right, or simply the best to pursue. So, in Frankfurt's terminology, the 'initial practical question' is in terms of the contents of first-order desires, not of second-order desires.[33] And there is no reason to assume that when the agent has determined what he really wants to do, the answer to this question will not also be directly about courses of action. This strongly suggests that second-order desires are not really pertinent to the question of what the agent really wants, because they need to show up in practical deliberation, and our commitments that are expressed in these deliberations are normally to courses of actions or valuable aims, but not to desires.

Do second-order volitions, then, not appear at all in the agent's practical deliberation and in his motivational economy? This would be going too far. First, in special cases it may indeed be important to us by which desire we are motivated. For a Kantian, for example, it may be crucial, in morally relevant contexts, whether he acts from the motive of duty or from an egoistic desire. But such cases are exceptional, as we are

---

[32] Cf. Korsgaard (1996), 93 f. [33] Watson (1975), 109.

usually concerned only with the question of what to do. Second, as Watson has pointed out, second-order volitions can be 'by-products' of the results of practical reasoning: When we have decided that doing F would be the most worthwhile thing to do, we also have a reason to want to be motivated by the desire to F, because the on-balance reasons in favour of doing F also speak in favour of being motivated to do F.[34] However, the second-order volitions which are generated in this way by deciding what it is best to do clearly cannot play the role that Frankfurt assigns to second-order volitions. They cannot provide the basis for the agent's identification with his desire, because they are generated by decisions of the agent which already possess the authority to express what the agent really wants.

So, second-order volitions do not play the role in practical reasoning that we would expect them to play if Frankfurt's account of identification were correct, for then we would have to expect the reasoning to be conducted in terms of the content of second-order desires. In view of the intimate connection between what the agent really wants and practical deliberation, this result presents a major problem for Frankfurt's account.

The three problems for the hierarchical model as it was originally presented by Frankfurt not only show that this model, as it stands, will not suffice. They also provide challenges which must be addressed by any reductive analysis of the phenomenon of alienation within the framework of the standard model.

3.3. Responses to the three problems: the later Frankfurt, Watson, and Velleman

Several subsequent analyses of the phenomenon of alienation have tried to meet these difficulties while maintaining the basic tenets of the standard model, though they have met with only limited success. In the following, we will discuss the four most influential proposals of this kind. The first two have been developed by Frankfurt himself in his later writings, and the other two by Watson and Velleman, respectively.

3.3.1. The later Frankfurt: decisions and satisfaction

In his paper *Identification and Externality*, Frankfurt had already begun to abandon the attempt to explain identification merely in terms of a hierarchy of desires or other attitudes, for he had realized the threat of an infinite regress which stems from the fact that 'attitudes toward passions are as susceptible to externality as are passions themselves'.[35] This danger, he thought, could be avoided by explaining identification with a

---

[34] Watson, loc. cit. For Kusser (2000), 95, the second-order volition is even identical with the conclusive first-order desire, because both have the same conditions of satisfaction. This, however, is not generally true. As Nida-Rümelin (2005), 89 f., rightly suggests, second-order volitions can have a genuine role to play on their own for the actions of weak-willed persons, because weak-willed persons may be able to change their first-order desires only by a detour via second-order desires, while for strong-willed persons the assessment of reasons is directly effective for action.

[35] Frankfurt (1977), 65.

desire in terms of a decision or a 'decisive commitment' of the agent, because with regard to decisions the problem of alienation apparently does not arise.

The decision that is required is not an ordinary decision about how to act, but a decision about the agent's motivational set-up—it is essentially reflective—and a response to a particular kind of conflict between desires. On Frankfurt's view we must distinguish between two fundamentally different kinds of conflict between desires.[36] The first kind of conflict arises when there are two things both of which we really want, but, due to unfavourable circumstances, we can only obtain either the one or the other. For example, John, who is planning his holiday, both wants to go to the seaside and to make a trip on the Trans-Siberian Railway to Vladivostok; but as the Siberian journey would occupy the entire period of his holiday, he cannot have both. A resolution of this kind of conflict requires that the agent should decide on a preference-ordering among these desires which cannot all be satisfied on the occasion: One desire must be assigned priority. This decision does not, however, imply that the desires which are assigned a lower ranking are no longer legitimate candidates for satisfaction. On the contrary, if the realization of higher-ranked desires happens to be impossible for practical reasons, the agent will normally return to his second choice. So, if John has decided to assign preference to the Siberian trip rather than the seaside holiday, he will probably go to the seaside after discovering that the train to Vladivostok is fully booked for the time of his holiday.

By contrast, the second kind of conflict requires the rejection of one of the desires as an 'outcast'. Imagine that John's acquaintance, James, has just won a literature award for one of his books. John feels that he should buy James a present to congratulate him on his achievement and is inclined to do so, but due to his jealousy he also experiences a nagging desire to annoy James by writing him a letter telling him how much he dislikes his books. Now, clearly this conflict between John's two desires cannot be resolved simply by introducing a preference ordering among these desires, for this would imply that the desire which ranks lower is still considered as a legitimate candidate for satisfaction. Assume, for example, that John decides to buy a present: Then this kind of solution to the conflict would imply that John would set out to write James the offending letter after all, if he fails to find an adequate present for James. This result would be patently absurd. Deciding to buy James a present—at least if the decision is wholehearted—involves a wholesale rejection of the other desire, which is no longer a course of action that John is considering. Instead, this latter desire is now seen as an alien intruder, and John would feel violated by it if it moved him to action despite himself.

It is the second kind of decision—by which the agent decides in favour of one of the conflicting desires, thereby making it fully his own, while withdrawing himself from the counteracting desires—that Frankfurt proposes as the basis for the phenomenon of

---

[36] Frankfurt (1977), 66 f., and (1987), 170 f.

identification. By such a decision, the agent settles the question of what he really wants, and creates 'a self out of the raw materials of his inner life',[37] so that remaining conflicts with counteracting desires are no longer conflicts within the person herself, but are now conflicts between the person and an alien desire.

How does this proposal to analyse identification fare with regard to the three difficulties for Frankfurt's original account elaborated in the last section? At first glance, it patently fails only with regard to the third problem, and basically for the same reason as the original proposal, because the decisions on which the account relies are meant to be reflective—about the agent's desires—and thus have the wrong content for a reconstruction of everyday practical reasoning. Things look much better, however, with regard to the regress problem. For while Frankfurt wants to maintain the hierarchical model, the decision to which he alludes is intended to effectively end the ascent to yet higher orders of desires. That John decides in favour of his desire to buy James a present, implies that it is now no longer an open question for him whether he approves of this desire and of his positive attitudes towards this desire. In this way there is no reason for the ascent to continue, and the regress is averted.

Even with regard to the problem of agential authority, appeal to decisions is *prima facie* promising. Decisions seem to be appropriate vehicles for identification because they seem to be manifestations of an activity of the agent with regard to which the question of externality or alienation does not arise.[38] However, this appearance stems, to a large degree, from the normal sense of the term 'decision', which suggests precisely an active role of the agent in reaching this decision—a suggestion which is exploited by Frankfurt when he uses his colourful terminology of 'activity' and 'passivity', or of 'helpless bystanders'. But it is not a suggestion which Frankfurt can take at face value if he wants to provide an explanation of the phenomenon of identification within the framework of the standard model. Within this framework, talk of agential activity cannot be taken literally—on pain of implicit reliance on agent-causal models—but all such talk must be analysed in terms of the causal influence of the agent's mental states. Talk of 'decision' can therefore be understood only in purely functional terms—as, for example, the forming of an intention to act (where intention, as well, must be understood in functional terms) which is caused by preceding desires and beliefs.

When we understand 'decisions' as functionally defined mental states or events, though, it is no longer apparent why the problem of alienation should not arise for them as well as for desires. In fact, cases of conscious or unwitting decisions show us that a decision can be as subject to alienation as other mental states.[39] Imagine that John has, some time earlier, quarrelled with James and has ever since had the conflicting desires to re-establish their relationship or to definitely sever the friendship. When, on

---

[37] Frankfurt (1987), 175.
[38] Cf. Frankfurt's cautious statement in (1977), 68, fn. 3.
[39] The following example is based on Velleman (1992), 464, though his example is only about an unwitting choice, in Frankfurt's terminology, not an unwitting decision.

an occasion, they meet in the street and begin to talk, John suddenly finds himself raising his voice and shouting abuse at James without any provocation—a behaviour which is completely unintelligible to himself. Later reflection on the event shows John that he had already unconsciously decided in favour of the desire to sever the friendship. Though such a decision was present, John did not identify with this decision, but felt 'violated' by it when it manifested itself in his insulting behaviour—in the same way as he feels 'violated' when overcome by a spasm of emotion. In both cases his behaviour is at first unintelligible to him.

This shows us that the notion of 'decision' that Frankfurt can avail himself of does not exclude that decisions can be as alien for the agent as other mental attitudes, while the notion of 'decision' which would exclude this is not one which Frankfurt has at his disposal, as long as he subscribes to the reductionist project of the standard model.

An alternative analysis which Frankfurt began to develop in *The Faintest Passion* was again based on the hierarchical model, but included the further requirement that the agent must be 'satisfied' with the endorsing higher-order volitions. 'Satisfaction' with a desire does not presuppose the existence of another, yet higher-order, desire, for if it did, the threat of regress would not be averted. Instead, it involves 'an absence of restlessness or resistance. A satisfied person...has no active interest in bringing about a change'.[40] This absence or non-occurrence, however, must itself be essentially reflective, for it must arise from the agent's reflective evaluation of his own psychic condition.

A possible model to understand this kind of 'reflective non-occurrence' is the case of a person who has been calculating and checking his calculation by repeating it several times. This person can reflectively and non-arbitrarily stop checking at a certain point, because his doubts that he might have made an undetected mistake have been allayed. Of course, if the calculation is complicated, at no point will the repeating of the calculation guarantee that the agent has not overlooked a mistake he has been making all the time. Nevertheless, breaking off the process of checking can be non-arbitrary if the agent has no relevant doubts about the correctness of the calculation and the absence of such doubts is due to his understanding of the situation—that is, that after repeating the calculation a sufficient number of times, there is no reason to suppose that such a mistake will appear if he repeats the calculation yet another time. If the absence of doubt is grounded in such an understanding, it is reflective, and in the same sense the absence of an interest for change is intended to be reflective in cases of satisfaction.[41]

Frankfurt's notion of 'satisfaction' involves a stronger requirement on identification than his earlier accounts have done, because the absence of active interest in bringing about a change in one's motivational set-up implies not only that the desire on which one acts is not external to oneself, but also that one acts wholeheartedly.[42] As I have

---

[40] Frankfurt (1992), 103.
[41] This example is modelled on Frankfurt (1987), 167 ff.
[42] Frankfurt (1992), 103.

been arguing earlier, the phenomena of 'half-heartedness' and 'alienation' are not identical, and, on Frankfurt's new account, the notion of identification will have a much more restricted application than on his original account.

However, as our concern here is only the phenomenon of alienation, I want to consider whether by weakening the notion of satisfaction in order to exclude only cases of externality, Frankfurt's new proposal might not still be used to explain the earlier phenomenon. In order to weaken the proposal we will relax the condition of an absence of restlessness, and reduce it to the condition that the agent must have no overwhelming interest in bringing about changes in his psychic condition—or, if he has such interests, that they do not appear at the level of his highest-order volition. In this way, actions performed only grudgingly or resignedly will also be counted as fulfilling Frankfurt's new criterion.[43] I think that even if we weaken the notion of satisfaction accordingly, Frankfurt's notion of satisfaction still fails to adequately address the problem of 'agential authority', and thus does not provide a satisfactory solution for the original problem of alienation.

For Frankfurt has still not provided sufficient reason to think that the agent's higher-order volitions, contrary to his lower-order desires, constitute what he really wants—why we should identify the agent's standpoint with his desires that he be moved by certain other desires to act instead of, say, the desires on which he in fact acts. That a higher-order volition is insufficient for excluding alienation, even if the agent is satisfied with this volition, becomes clear when we look at certain cases of self-manipulation where an agent wants to be motivated by a desire with which he does not identify. For example, a scientist who regularly experiences an urge to drink a can of paint, but who, from repugnance for such an activity, rejects this urge, may for scientific reasons be interested in knowing how it would be to follow such an urge. However, as he rejects and abhors the activity itself, he knows that he cannot do so in a condition of self-control. Therefore, by consuming a huge amount of alcohol he decides to put himself into a state of massively reduced self-control, in which he will be overcome by his urge, and he forms a corresponding higher-order volition. All goes according to plan, and while drinking the can he feels 'helplessly violated by his overwhelming desire' in the same way that the unwilling drug addict does, even though the scientist's existing highest-order volition is that he may be moved to act by this urge.

It seems very plausible that in such cases of self-manipulation, the urge—even though its efficacy is in accordance with my existing highest-order volition—is 'still one I am essentially passive with respect to. It is inflicted on me, even if I am the one inflicting it.'[44] The scientist therefore does not identify with his urge, despite the fact that his existing highest-order volition endorses it. This result is, of course, directly at

---

[43] A case for this restriction can already be made out of Frankfurt's own notion of 'satisfaction', for satisfaction presupposes only the absence of further attitudes towards the highest-order volition—and these would necessarily have to be yet higher-order.

[44] Moran (2002), 199.

odds with Frankfurt's account, on which the fact that the scientist's higher-order volition, endorsing his urge's being efficacious, is higher-order than his desire to not take the drug, by itself would settle the issue of whether he identifies with the urge. For Frankfurt, *how* the scientist's desire moves him to act would not play any role in answering this question.

Even the condition of satisfaction does not enable Frankfurt to deal with this kind of case. For *ex hypothesi*, the scientist's desire not to take the drug—and any corresponding second-order desire—are of a lower level than his highest-order volition to take the drug. So he has not, in the relevant sense, an interest in making changes to his psychic condition, but is, on the level of his highest-order volition, 'content' with it as it is. On Frankfurt's picture, the lower-level status of desires against taking the drug makes them irrelevant to determining what the agent really wants—in a similar way as the lower-level status of the unwilling drug addict's desire to take the drug was supposed to make it irrelevant to determining his standpoint.

Therefore, Frankfurt's hierarchical model, even if enriched by the additional condition of 'satisfaction' with one's highest-order desire, does not satisfactorily explain the distinction between cases of being 'helplessly violated by an overwhelming desire' and cases of full-blooded intentional action.

3.3.2. Watson and the valuational system

The first philosopher who clearly diagnosed the main reason for this failure was Gary Watson, who recognized that Frankfurt's model was bound to fail because it attempted to analyse the phenomena exclusively in terms of higher-order desires, which belong to the same category of mental entities—desires—as those entities with regard to which, as Frankfurt's own examples have shown, alienation is possible. Any successful analysis of identification with a mental state, so Watson claimed, would have to rely on states of a different category. He argued that in order to account for the distinction between what an agent really wants and the content of his motivationally effective desires, we must distinguish the agent's motivational system, consisting of his motivationally relevant states, from his valuational system, which incorporates the agent's conception of the good and generates his evaluative judgements of how it would be best to act.[45] On the most plausible understanding of Watson, the latter system, for him, constitutes the agent's standpoint or what he really wants because with regard to it the question of alienation can no longer arise. The agent cannot distance himself from his valuational system in its entirety, but only from individual values; for a value can only be rejected from the standpoint of some other valuational standpoint, which is retained, and from whose perspective the rejected value is judged to be really worthless.[46]

On this view, the possibility of alienation from a desire stems from the possibility of a split between what one values and what one is motivated to get. We are alienated

---

[45] Watson (1975), 102.   [46] Watson (1975), 106.

from a desire which moves us to action if it is not in accord with what our valuational system judges the best thing to do in the situation, and we therefore see the desire as 'unworthy or in some other way bad'.[47] By contrast, we identify with a desire to F, if F-ing is the course of action favoured by the verdict of our valuational system.

This proposal neatly answers the problems which Watson has raised with regard to Frankfurt's hierarchical account. On the one hand, the special authority of our evaluative judgements in relation to our desires is explained by their special source: the process of deliberating about what it would be best to do. This process of practical deliberation possesses an obvious 'authority', because it is within this process that the agent's standpoint is determined, and only within this process that the question whether a desire expresses what the agent really wants can be raised. Therefore, it is impossible for us to distance ourselves from this process as such, which explains why the answers we find within this process to the question of what we really want are the best candidates for in fact expressing what we really want. As a consequence, the threat of regress is automatically averted, because the phenomenon of identification is not explained in terms of the alleged authority of some other mental state, but ultimately in terms of the authority of practical reasoning. On the other hand, the account allows the adequate reconstruction of the content of our practical reasoning, for our evaluative judgements are normally directly about courses of actions rather than about desires to pursue such courses.

Despite its ability to deal with these difficulties facing the hierarchical account, however, Watson's account falls prey to the different objection of being overly rationalistic and thereby treating the problem of alienation on one level with the problem of akrasia. For as Watson himself later realized, we can knowingly, and even wholeheartedly, act against our judgement of how we should best act.[48] Watson himself considered an extreme form of this phenonemon which he called 'perverse cases', where the agent is supposed to have no desire whatsoever—not even a weak one—to act as he thinks best. But there are much more common examples, such as the normal cases of 'coldly' akratic action, where an agent self-determinedly and deliberately acts in a way he knows to be bad, despite having weaker desires to act in accordance with the good—for example, when a heavily overweight person decides to take another piece of cake, even though he is on a diet. In these cases, the agent's motivating desire does not conform with his judgement about what action would be for the best, but it is not one from which he feels alienated.[49]

These examples tell decisively against Watson's attempt to analyse identification with a desire as conformity of the desire with the verdicts of the agent's evaluational

---

[47] Watson (1987), 149.
[48] Watson (1977), 327 fn. 13; (1987), 150.
[49] Watson himself distinguished 'perverse' cases from cases of akrasia; cf. (1987), 150. In (2003), 131 f.; however, he explicitly mentions the problem arising from cases of akrasia for 'internalist' conceptions of the will, which insist on a necessary link between intentions and what the agent considers as the good. However, he does not, in response, offer a new conception of the will.

system about what it is best to do. Nevertheless, I think that Watson's central idea to take value judgements as expressive of the agent's standpoint is absolutely correct. We will later take up this idea, though in a modified form.

3.3.3. Velleman and the 'desire to act in accordance with reasons'[50]

David Velleman has tried an approach different from Watson's, though he has also recognized the central role of practical deliberation for the question of identification, which is due to the fact that an agent cannot dissociate himself from this process as such. Alienation is possible only with regard to those states that can come under critical review within this process. The conclusion that Velleman has drawn from this insight is that there is a desire which directs the critical scrutiny, and that this desire must be at the basis of identification because it is a desire which cannot itself become an object of critical scrutiny, and thus cannot turn out to be 'alien'.[51] This desire is a formal 'desire to act in accordance with reasons'; and even if Velleman does not want to commit himself to a precise content of this desire, I will, for simplicity's sake, characterize it as the *de dicto* desire to do what is advocated by the balance of reasons.[52]

This *de dicto* desire, as Velleman sees it, plays the role of the agent because its contribution to the agent's mental processes is precisely the contribution we pre-theoretically ascribe to the agent himself, insofar as he is rational: guiding the process of practical deliberation and throwing his weight behind the desire which is seen to be connected with the best reason for action. For the *de dicto* desire not only directs the process of scrutiny, but can intervene in the conflict between other desires by adding its motivational force to the force of the desire supported by the best reasons, and thus helping it to win out against the other contenders.[53] Consequently, Velleman can deny that the (motivationally) strongest desire always moves the agent to action while retaining the 'hydraulic model' of motivation, because the addition of the motivational force of the *de dicto* desire can change the motivational balance, and can help the supported desire to win out against competing desires, even when, on its own, it would be motivationally weaker than they are. Due to these contributions of the *de dicto* desire, Velleman considers its possession as constitutive for being a rational agent.

But can the *de dicto* desire that Velleman introduces really play the agent's role in the way that Velleman envisages? This quickly becomes doubtful once we look more closely at how such a desire would be supposed to work. First doubts arise when we ask how this desire should connect with the agent's practical reasoning. Ever since it became wedded to Hume's view of the purely instrumental nature of practical reason, the standard model contains a certain view of how desires appear in the content of one's practical reasoning. The reasoning can contain practical inferences of the following kind, which are based on the desire and a means–end belief:

---

[50] Velleman (1992), 478. [51] Velleman (1992), 477.
[52] Cf. Velleman (1992), 478, for the possible formulations of the desire's content.
[53] Velleman (1992), 479 f.

(1) I want to do X.
(2) In order to do X, I have to Y.
(C) Thus, I should/will do Y.[54]

For Velleman's *de dicto* desire, this inference would appear like this:

(1★) I want to do what I have most reason to do.
(2★) I have most reason to do X.
(C★) Thus, I should/will do X.

But it is quite clear that an inference of this kind normally does not show up in our practical reasoning. Our deliberations are concluded by the verdict that I should do or have most reason to do X—by something that corresponds to premiss (2★)—and the inference just sketched is not 'tacked on' in addition. A defender of Velleman might respond to this by claiming that the *de dicto* desire need not directly show up in practical reasoning, by yielding premiss (1★), but can instead operate in the background. In this case it will, instead of premiss (1★), provide a premiss of the kind 'I should do/it is best to do what I have most reason to do', or directly license an inference from (2★) on its own to (C★).[55] However, claiming that either the alternative premiss or an inference from (2★) to (C★) normally show up in our practical reasoning is hardly any more plausible than the earlier claim that premiss (1★) itself does. As explained previously, normally our deliberation is concluded by a verdict like the one expressed by (2★), and no further step to infer (C★) is added. It may sometimes happen—when we know what course of action would be best, but are sorely tempted to act otherwise—that we indeed remind ourselves that 'the best reasons speak for doing X, and one should do what the best reasons advocate'; but in such reminders, the second part has only a rhetorical function, and does not add any further argumentative step.

Velleman's alleged *de dicto* desire not only fails to appear in our practical reasoning, directly or indirectly, but it is also altogether implausible to assume that rational agents have such a desire; for this desire is neither required for processes of practical deliberation, nor could it really form the basis of rational deliberation. Let us begin with the first point. Practical deliberation is, roughly, an activity[56] which is aimed at determining what to do and which possesses constitutive internal[57] (or formal) standards of correctness which are partly 'codified' in admissible types of inferences, such as the practical syllogism. The existence of standards of correctness to which an instance of practical

---

[54] Audi calls this the 'simplest basic schema for practical reasoning'; (1989), 99.
[55] Cf. Pettit/Smith (1990), 567 ff.
[56] It is not an essentially 'mental' activity, however, when 'mental' activity is understood in contrast to 'physical', outwardly manifested activity. Practical reasoning can also take the form of joint practical deliberation.
[57] Whether practical deliberation also has an 'external' standard of correctness or constitutive aim—such as 'the Good', as it is claimed by the traditional Aristotelian view, cf. *Nicomachean Ethics*, 1094a 1—is both an ancient and vexed question, which, however, need not concern us here.

reasoning is answerable excludes mere sequences of associations: As Elizabeth Anscombe has expressed it, they lack the feature of being a 'calculation'.[58]

Why should an activity of this kind require the mentioned *de dicto* desire to get started? Perhaps one thinks that consciously performed activity *always* requires a desire for whose fulfilment it is performed, because one generally applies the standard model's picture of intentional agency. But even if it were true that consciously initiated processes of practical deliberation require a desire to 'get started', it would by no means follow that the agent needed to have a *de dicto* desire to do what is in accordance with reasons. *Any* desire which is aimed at something to which practical reasoning would be conducive would be perfectly sufficient. For example, the desire to obtain X would suffice to explain why the agent starts to deliberate how best to obtain X, if he thinks he needs to find out how best to obtain X before starting to act. Alternatively, more specific desires—such as to determine how to obtain X—will do the trick equally well. Besides, consciously deciding to deliberate is not the normal case, as we often begin to worry about what to do, and start deliberating without any conscious decision to do so. For these cases there is not even a *prima facie* argument for the alleged need for a desire that drives the deliberation. We can therefore conclude that no *de dicto* desire to act in accordance with the best reasons is needed in order to explain why the agent engages in practical reasoning.

Nor could this desire, even if the agent were to have it, explain why he engages in practical reasoning. For clearly, the agent could engage in practical reasoning in order to fulfil his desire to act in accordance with reason, only if he is *already* minimally rational and is responsive to reasons. The inference (1★) to (C★), sketched earlier, would be completely lost on an agent who was inaccessible to rational considerations, and so for him possession of the *de dicto* desire would be useless and he would not thereby become a rational agent. But once the agent *is* already minimally rational and responsive to reasons, he is automatically able to engage in some form of practical reasoning, and it is thus unclear what additional work would be left for the *de dicto* desire.

Neither is it clear how the *de dicto* desire could, in this case, add to the motivational force of the desire that is supported by the best reasons. For if the agent is already responsive to reasons, he will thereby have a tendency to act as reason requires. On Velleman's picture, the tendency to act rationally that is connected with the *de dicto* desire will just be the very same tendency—because for Velleman, possessing the *de dicto* desire is constitutive for being a rational agent. Consequently, as the agent must already be responsive to reasons in order for the *de dicto* desire to get a grip, it seems that adding the desire cannot change anything about the agent's tendency to act in a certain way, and thus does not influence the balance of motivational forces.

I think this points towards a basic mistake in Velleman's conception of the rational agent. Clearly, rational agents must have tendencies to act in accordance with what

---

[58] Anscombe (1957), 65.

they think best, and also tendencies to acquire, *ceteris paribus*, more coherent systems of beliefs and desires as results of deliberation. These tendencies, however, do not presuppose an underlying desire; on the contrary, the presence of these tendencies is a presupposition for *any* desire to motivate a rational agent. We would end up in a vicious circle if their presence, in turn, required the possession of a certain desire.

Now, one might object to this criticism of Velleman, that the *de dicto* desire can have a function after all, even if not precisely the function intended by him (which was to guarantee minimal rationality). Instead, the *de dicto* desire concerns a more demanding version of rationality, and possession of the desire makes it more probable that the agent live up to this standard. Rationality, in this sense, can be understood roughly in terms of leading a well-ordered, efficient life. It is true that on such an understanding the *de dicto* desire can have a genuine function, because having this form of rationality is not yet entailed by possession of the minimal rationality that is prerequisite for the *de dicto* desire to get any grip on the agent. At the same time, however, the desire ceases to be a candidate for playing the agent's role. For agents need not really want to lead an efficient, well-ordered life, because they may prefer a certain amount of chaos or uncertainty, or may prefer to live out their emotions without prior planning. Therefore, they may feel alienated from the desire to live rationally in the more demanding sense, considering this desire to be, for example, a remainder of their puritanical upbringing which they want to shed. Also, cases of weakness of the will—which are not cases of alienation, even though the agent acts contrary to what he perceives to be best—show that the agent can act on a desire with which he identifies, even though doing so is not in accord with the *de dicto* desire.

Thus, we can conclude that Velleman's appeal to a desire to act in accordance with the best reasons fails to provide us with a mental state whose causal contributions could explain the 'agent's role' in action, because the proposal is faced with a dilemma. Either we understand the desire too weakly, as only safeguarding minimal rationality, and it does not have any function at all; or we understand it too strongly, thereby giving it a function, but transforming it into a desire from which the agent can be alienated.

4
Identification, desires, and practical reasoning

The most promising approach to dealing with the problem of identification is Michael Bratman's analysis of 'identifying with a desire' as 'treating this desire as reason-giving' (Section 4.1). The chief merit of this account is that it recognizes the main source of Frankfurt's cases of alienation: namely, that the supposed causal impact of the agent's desires can completely bypass the process of practical reasoning. This possibility had traditionally been neglected by adherents of the standard model, who had, as a consequence, failed to provide an adequate account of the relation between the desires' purported causal impact, the process of practical reasoning, and the rationalizing function of reasons-explanations.

However, as I will argue, contrary to what Bratman thinks himself, the analysis cannot be successfully completed within the framework of the standard model. For the standard model intends to reduce the phenomenon of agency, and related notions such as identification, to the causal impact of the agent's mental states, while the proposed analysis already presupposes a notion of practical reasoning which is not thus reducible. One main reason for the latter irreducibility is that practical reasoning is concerned with reasons for action, and that desires themselves are not reasons. In order to show this we need to look in some detail at the nature of 'motivating reasons'—a motivating reason for an action being the reason for which the agent performed the action (Section 4.2). The ensuing account of identification will be a normativist account, on which identification with a desire means that one accepts a corresponding value-judgement about the desire's object and is prepared to treat this judgement as a justifying premiss in one's practical reasoning. This account will be defended against three objections—the first arising from the possibility that the agent's judgements can be wrong, the second from the possibility that an agent might consider it a 'lesser evil' to satisfy an alien desire, and the third from the worry that the proposed account may make identification an altogether too rationalistic phenomenon (Section 4.3).

As a result, the right way to complete Bratman's basic approach will no longer fit into the reductionist project of the standard model. The presupposed notion of practical reasoning is already the notion of an activity, and appeal to it within an intended reductionist account of agency will lead to circularity. Consequently, the attempted explanation of agential control within the standard model must be considered as a failure, because the proposed bearers or vehicles of agential control are not guaranteed to express the agent's own standpoint.

4.1. Identification as 'treating a desire as reason-giving'

As we have seen, none of the five proposals we have been considering has been able to capture adequately the phenomena of self-determination and alienation. Before we go on to look for an alternative analysis of these phenomena, it is instructive to take a step back and take one further look at the failure of Frankfurt's account, asking ourselves whether this failure might not be due to some basic assumptions of the standard model in its traditional form which Frankfurt has not given up.

As we have already seen, the standard model—at least in its Davidsonian form—accords desires two distinct roles in intentional human action. On the one hand they are considered to be effective causes of human behaviour, while on the other[1] they play a rationalizing role by yielding, together with appropriate beliefs, the premisses of a practical syllogism with the conclusion that an action of this kind should or will be performed. It is claimed that if this dual role of desires is fulfilled, they function as rational causes, and can be seen as the vehicle of the agent's rational control over his behaviour.[2]

However, how the two purported functions of desires are related is a continuing puzzle for adherents of the standard model. One famous source of puzzlement is the problem of deviant causal chains—which we will consider in the next chapter—and another is the phenomenon of alienation that we are considering here. Even though the agent has a desire which causes his behaviour and which could rationalize his action, he somehow rejects the rationalizing function; for he does not accept that the object of his desire provides an aim to be pursued, and as a result of this rejection, the desire's causal role undercuts, rather than constitutes, the agent's control. The desire's causal impact—assuming, with the standard model, that it has such an impact—thus bypasses the process of the agent's practical reasoning,[3] in much the same way as it bypasses his agential control in cases of wayward causal chains.

---

[1] Of course, in Davidson's own account—at least from (1970b) onward—what is, strictly speaking, rationalizing the action is the value-judgement that 'F-ing would be desirable in respect K', which he considers to be the 'natural propositional expression' of the desire, (1970b), 31, and which serves as the major premiss in the practical syllogism whose conclusion is that an action of this kind should be performed.

[2] Cf. Lanz's (1993) description of the Davidsonian model.

[3] 'Bypassing' the process of practical reasoning is, in one sense, quite harmless. When we have internalized patterns of behaviour which include responses to perceived reasons, there will be no explicit practical deliberation about what to do in these cases, but we will respond in the right way 'automatically'. We will act only 'as if' we had deliberated, but without actual deliberation (cf. Stoecker (2001), 25 ff.). What is peculiar to cases of alienation is that the desire's impact not only 'bypasses' an actual process of reasoning, but also would 'bypass' a hypothetical process that would obtain if the agent began to deliberate about what to do.

This shows that what we can call an 'objective' rationalizing function of desires will not suffice for self-determination. A desire plays such an objective rationalizing function if it is possible, from the agent's desire and one of his beliefs, to construct a practical syllogism with the conclusion that an action of the relevant kind should or will be performed. In addition to this objective function, it is also necessary that the agent himself should accept the rationalizing function in his practical reasoning. This acceptance cannot be a purely theoretical matter; that is, it cannot just be an acceptance of the abstract fact that this desire *could* rationalize actions of this kind. Instead, the agent must actually be prepared to make use of this function in his practical reasoning, adopting it as the basis of reaching conclusions about what to do, and to justify actions which he has performed. If such an acceptance is present, we can say that the desire has a 'subjective' rationalizing function. The mistaken assumption of the Humean standard model, as defended by Davidson, was that the desire's (supposed) causal impact in motivation and the 'objective' rationalizing function, on the one hand, and the 'subjective' rationalizing function, on the other hand, always go together; but, as the cases of alienation show, this is not the case.[4]

Frankfurt's original approach has also signally neglected the required subjective rationalizing function by focusing exclusively on the effectiveness of the first-order desires in moving the agent to action. Thus, the second-order volitions were only concerned with this effectiveness, and not at all with the *way* in which the first-order desires move the agent to action.[5] But merely wanting to be moved by a desire will not guarantee that one identifies with the desire, in cases where one wants to be moved by the desire in a way incompatible with self-determination—for example, to be 'helplessly violated by it'. As Frankfurt did not change his view about the content of higher-order volitions in his later proposals, the original oversight also lay at the bottom of the difficulties for his latter accounts. This is evident in the case of the scientist's self-inflicted urge to take the drug (discussed in Section 3.3.1), and we can now see the reason behind Frankfurt's failure to deal with a case of this kind. For when the agent wants to be moved in a way that bypasses the process of practical reasoning in the action situation, it is not guaranteed that the subjective rationalizing function of desires, required for self-determination, is fulfilled.[6]

Before continuing to discuss this problem I must insert a remark about terminology. As will become clear later, I do not share the assumption of the standard model that desires have both a causal and a rationalizing function in intentional action. For I neither believe that they necessarily play a causal role in intentional action nor that

---

[4] Cf. Bratman (2002), 67 f., who makes this point slightly differently, in terms of his distinction between 'being an effective motive' and 'being treated as reason-giving'.

[5] This has changed in Frankfurt's more recent writings; cf. (2006), 10 f.

[6] I do not claim that this function *cannot* be fulfilled when we want to be overcome by a desire on a certain situation. If we regard the desire's object as valuable in this situation, being overcome by the desire is no obstacle to identifying with it. The crucial point, however, is that the basis for identification in this case is our assessment that the desire's object is valuable; it is *not* that we want to be overcome by the desire!

they themselves have a rationalizing function. In the following, I will therefore speak, neutrally, of motivational effectiveness instead of causal efficacy; but for simplicity's sake, I will continue to speak of the 'rationalizing' role of desires.

To correct Frankfurt's oversight we must provide an account of the subjective rationalizing function of desires that is needed in addition to motivational effectiveness and the objective rationalizing function, if cases of alienation are to be excluded. What is the necessary impact of the desire on the agent's practical reasoning, which is required when the agent considers the desire as internal to him, rather than as an alien intruder? Obviously, it is not sufficient that the desire sets in motion a process of practical deliberation. For a felt desire can trigger practical deliberation simply via a process of mental association—for example, that I briefly experience an appetite for vanilla ice cream may, by an associative process, make me think of another kind of food, such as chocolate, and I may, as a consequence, begin to deliberate about how I can procure some chocolate. Clearly, this fact does not tell us anything about whether I identify with, or am alienated from, my desire for vanilla ice cream, because the deliberation is not at all about this desire.

Instead, if a process of practical reasoning is set in motion, the content of the reasoning must reflect that I have this desire. There are two fundamentally different ways in which a desire might be taken into account in one's practical reasoning: either as a legitimate candidate for satisfaction, or as a candidate for elimination and suppression.

The first alternative is the way that adherents of the standard model normally conceive of the impact of desires on practical deliberation, which has been defended, in particular, by Davidson since his *How is Weakness of the Will Possible?* On this alternative the impact of the desire consists in providing a premise in a practical syllogism by which the agent can deduce that a certain course of action, which will lead to the fulfilment of the desire, should be pursued.

But an agent can also deliberate on how to eradicate a desire, or how to prevent his acting on this desire. Consider the unwilling drug addict, who regards the regularly occurring onslaughts of his addictive urges as destroying his personality and completely rejects these urges. This addict will deliberate on how to suppress his desire—either completely, for example, by starting a therapy, or at least in particular situations, e.g. by taking a tranquillizer—and about how best to keep the desire under control so as not to be overpowered by it. Clearly, in his case the impact of the desire on the practical deliberation is fundamentally different from the impact normally envisaged by Humeans. For this agent the desire does not provide an aim, but presents a problem to be removed.

It is easily seen that the difference between the two possible impacts of the desire on the agent's practical reasoning is intimately connected to the distinction between alienation and identification that we are seeking to explain. Only in cases of identification does the agent consider the desire to be a legitimate candidate for satisfaction, which provides him with a *reason* to act accordingly. This particular kind of impact of the desire on the agent's practical reasoning has been described by Bratman as the agent's 'treating the desire as reason-giving'; and I will adopt both this description and, provisionally, Bratman's (partial) characterization of 'treating as reason-giving' as treating it as 'end-setting'—that is, 'as potentially justifying, at least to some extent, my performance of the relevant means and/or relevant preliminary steps'.[7] As obviously not all intentional actions are preceded by actually conducted practical deliberation, treating a desire as 'end-setting' cannot require that a corresponding premiss is actually used in practical reasoning; but it must suffice that the agent would have used it if he had engaged in practical deliberation.

That the agent treats a desire as reason-giving in this sense ensures that the desire fulfils the subjective rationalizing function, which is necessary for identification. We can therefore tentatively assume that treating as reason-giving is indeed the distinguishing mark between the cases of identification and alienation. When the agent treats the desire thus, he identifies with it, otherwise he is alienated from it. If this criterion is the right one, the possibility that desires may prevent the agent from doing what he really wants arises simply from the fact that a desire can be motivationally effective, even though it is not one the agent treats as reason-giving.

To obtain a better understanding of what it means to treat a desire as reason-giving, it is useful to think of more common cases in which we decide to completely 'ignore' certain desires only *in a particular context*, though we allow ourselves to act on them outside this context. The notion of 'treating a desire as reason-giving' might then be understood as an extension of such cases, in which the restriction to a certain context is dropped.

For an example of the limited case, take a football referee who decides, for the context of a certain game, to decide strictly and only by the rules. By this decision he determines which considerations will be relevant for the later, specific decisions that he has to take during the course of the match—excluding, *inter alia*, as a relevant consideration that a player in one of the teams is a good friend of his, of whom he is very fond. This means that when during the course of the game the referee has to decide about whether to award this team a penalty, because one of the players seems to have been the victim of a foul inside the penalty area, he will not view his own fondness of his friend as providing him with any reason to award the penalty. For, by his own lights, helping his friend is not an aim that could justify awarding the penalty. The only considerations that he accepts as relevant concern the question of whether a foul has been committed, and whether, according to the rules, this foul should be penalized in this way. If the referee adheres to his earlier decision to decide strictly by the rules, his fondness, in his own eyes, will not even provide him with a weak reason to award the penalty, against which the reasons against awarding the penalty are to be

---

[7] Bratman (1996), 9.

balanced. Instead, the 'fondness' consideration will not appear in his deliberation about how to decide the question at all.[8]

We are well acquainted with cases such as these—especially when people are entrusted with certain official functions or institutional roles which require impartiality, neutrality, or other forms of 'objectivity', and where we consequently expect those people to count certain considerations which may arise from their own desires 'for nought' (though we accord them the right to act on these considerations in their private lives). One might object that in these cases we do not require them to count these considerations strictly 'for nought', but only to subordinate them to the considerations by which they must, *qua magistrates*, be guided. But I do not think that this objection is generally convincing. At least for certain kinds of roles, we do require that, ideally, the magistrate should be *strictly* impersonal in the fulfilment of his role, and we feel that if he could take into account his personal desires even as strictly subordinate or auxiliary considerations, this would still endanger the rule of law or an equal application of the law for all.[9] Whatever the justification of such ideals, it seems clear that quite often such ideals are adopted.[10] This shows that we are generally able to make sense of the idea that desires are treated as reason-giving, or not so treated, in particular contexts.

By dropping the limitations to a particular context, we obtain the notion of 'treating a desire as reason-giving' simpliciter. Imagine that our referee has discovered that his friend is a particularly nasty and brutal criminal, and has consequently rejected his friendship as thoroughly bad and destructive of his own integrity. As a result, the referee begins to despise his lingering fondness for his former friend and to regard it as a regrettable weakness which should be suppressed. In this case, the referee will not consider his occasional fits of fondness for his former friend as providing him with any reason to, for example, meet him for dinner. Instead, he will do his best to avoid such fits—for example, by avoiding any meeting with his former friend—or to efficiently suppress them when they occur—such as by constantly reminding himself of the friend's misdeeds. In this case, the referee does not 'treat his fondness as reason-giving' at all.

After having acquired a better grip on the notion of 'treating a desire as resason-giving' by comparison with more commonplace cases, we can turn to the question of whether this notion really completely captures (as we have tentatively assumed) the difference between identification and alienation that Frankfurt was describing.[11] To answer this question we must examine how this notion is able to explain the different

---

[8] Another case of this kind is provided by Scanlon (1998), 51 f.

[9] So, even if we accept that their personal desires generally provide the magistrates with reasons for action, there is what Raz has called an 'exclusionary reason' ((1975), 132) not to act on these desires in the particular context, and this latter reason can require that the desire is not treated as reason-giving in these contexts.

[10] Traditionally, this ideal is connected either with ancient Romans or with Prussian magistrates.

[11] Frankfurt (2006), 10 f., also admits that treating a desire as reason-giving is an important part of identification, but he does not think that it exhausts this phenomenon.

characteristics of the phenomenon of alienation. I will try to do this with respect to the following three paradigmatic features of the phenomenon.

(i) Self-understanding. As Frankfurt has recognized, in cases of alienation the agent views his desire and the action resulting from it as 'discontinuous with his understanding of his situation and his conception of himself'.[12] The specific understanding of one's own emotional responses and actions that is lacking here is the one which arises from understanding one's actions and emotions as responses to perceived reasons, which is characteristic for intentional agency.[13] With regard to actions, this understanding is lacking precisely if one does not consider the desire on which one acts to be reason-giving, which produces the kind of discontinuity that Frankfurt has described as characteristic for the phenomenon of alienation.

(ii) The basis for the ascription of alienation. Normally, we assume that agents act as they really want to act and are not 'violated by alien forces' when they act in a way appropriate to satisfying a desire which they possess. Thus, an outside observer who views the addict inserting the needle would initially assume that the addict really wants to take the drug. It is only on the basis of certain behavioural phenomena which undermine this initial assumption that we conclude that an agent is alienated from his motivationally effective desire. The required behaviour includes, positively, what we can call 'elimination' and 'avoidance' behaviour, and negatively, that the agent does not justify his actions by appeal to the value of the desire's object (a point to which we will return later). 'Elimination' and 'avoidance' behaviour is behaviour that is aimed at eradicating the desire—either generally or on this particular occasion—or at keeping it under control so that it does not become so strong as to move the agent to action. Thus, an observer will normally only conclude that the addict is alienated from his addictive urge, if the addict has unsuccessfully undergone therapies, or has tried to control his desire by taking tranquillizers, and so on. These behavioural phenomena, as well as being the basis for concluding that the agent is alienated from his desire, are also the basis for concluding that he does not treat the desire as reason-giving, by showing that he does not ascribe any value at all to the desire's object, and no value at all to having the desire.

(iii) Frankfurt's distinction between two kinds of decision. Lastly, let us look again at Frankfurt's distinction of two different kinds of decision in *Identification and Externality*, discussed in Section 3.3.1. Even though this distinction does not completely coincide with the distinction between alienation and identification, because the decision itself could be something from which the agent is alienated, there is an intimate relation. We can even say that provided the decision is one with which the agent identifies, the two

---

[12] Frankfurt (1977), 62.
[13] This connection between an 'activity' of the agent and the self-understanding based on knowing one's reasons has been elaborated by Raz (1999), 20.

distinctions are the same. Now, it is easy to see that under the same condition the distinctions between the two kinds of decision and between treating a desire as reason-giving and not so treating it, also coincide. For as long as the desire is accorded *some* place in the agent's preference-ordering of desires to be fulfilled, it is considered as providing some, if only weak, reason for action. This reason will normally, perhaps, be outweighed by countervailing considerations, but if such considerations are absent it will be seen to successfully justify a certain course of action. However, when a desire is no longer regarded as a legitimate candidate for satisfaction—which is the result of the second kind of decision—it is regarded as not providing any reason at all.

These considerations show that the notion of 'treating a desire as reason-giving' can account for the central features of the distinction between alienation and identification, and therefore provide us with good grounds for concluding that treating a desire as reason-giving is both necessary and sufficient for identifying with this desire. This result can be further strengthened by the following two considerations. First, the analysis is successful in distinguishing the phenomenon of alienation from the phenomena of akrasia and half-heartedness—what Watson's and Velleman's proposals have failed to do. In cases of akrasia, when acting against our judgement of what is best, we still act on a desire we take to provide us with a reason, though with a weak reason that has been outweighed by countervailing reasons; while if the proposed analysis is right, in cases of alienation we do not take the desire which motivates us to provide us with any reason whatsoever. The phenomenon of half-heartedness also involves motivation by desires that we treat as reason-providing, though we have difficulties in settling on which desire to act.

Second, the proposal also succeeds in meeting the three basic problems facing Frankfurt's original account. (a) The problem of agential authority is solved because the proposal explains identification not in terms of possession of a mental state, but in terms of treating the desire as providing a justifying premiss in one's practical reasoning—i.e. in terms of a propensity to conduct one's practical deliberation in a certain way, by using certain premises. And the process of practical reasoning has the authority to determine the agent's standpoint; for it is only within this process that the question of whether a desire accords with what one really wants can arise, and so with regard to the process itself, the question of alienation cannot arise. (b) As a result of (a), the threat of a potential regress is automatically excluded, because with regard to the vehicle of agential authority—the activity of practical deliberation—no alienation is possible. (c) Finally, the difficulty about the content of practical reasoning is evaded, because the proposal does not introduce any new desires or new levels of reflection that would be required to appear within the agent's practical reasoning. What we have required with regard to the content of this practical reasoning is only that desires can be reflected within it in different ways—as legitimate candidates for satisfaction, or as candidates for elimination or suppression. And it should be obvious that desires can be reflected in deliberation in these two different ways.

These points demonstrate that an agent's identification with a desire can, in fact, be successfully analysed as the agent's treating the desire as reason-giving. However, Bratman himself, when developing this approach, thought that a further self-reflective stance is required for identification,[14] and for this reason he combined his 'treating as reason-giving' approach with Frankfurt's hierarchical model. When first developing his approach, Bratman considered a *decision* to treat a desire as reason-giving and satisfaction (in Frankfurt's sense) with this decision as necessary for identification.[15] Later, he abandoned this requirement in favour of the view that the agent must have a 'self-governing policy in favour of the agent's treatment of that desire as providing a justifying reason in motivationally efficacious practical reasoning'.[16]

Why should a self-reflective attitude or decision about treating the desire as reason-giving be required for identification, in addition to the fact that the agent actually treats the desire as reason-giving? In support of his original requirement of a decision to treat as reason-giving, Bratman argued that the phenomenon of identification is always a response to a certain kind of problem: the agent reflects about the desire and about 'what to do with it'—about whether to treat it as reason-giving or to disown it. On this view, identification always requires reflective consideration of the desire; without the latter, the agent is, with regard to the desire, like Frankfurt's 'wanton' who does not care by which desire he is moved and does not form any second-order volitions.[17] When the required reflective consideration has reached a conclusion, this conclusion will, for Bratman, consist in the decision to treat this desire as reason-giving or not to treat it thus.

In one sense, Bratman is simply concerned with a more restricted sense of identification than the one with which I am concerned here. For me, identification is simply absence of alienation, and it therefore does not presuppose any specific genesis: an agent can identify with a desire even if he has never reflected on it. But also on my wider understanding of identification, it presupposes the *possibility* of reflection, while alienation (for reasons that we will discuss later) presupposes an actual process of reflection.

But even where there has been an actual process of reflection and this process has been concluded, the agent need not have formed a self-reflective decision whether or not to treat the desire as reason-giving. Bratman's mistake lies in assuming that the necessary reflection must be about one's mental states and 'what to do with them'. As it is, there are alternatives to this. In particular, the reflection can instead be about the truth of value-judgements. Thus, assume that Davidson is right in claiming that the 'natural propositional expression'[18] of the content of a desire which can appear in one's practical reasoning is a judgement ascribing some value to the desire's object.

---

[14] However, in (1996), 13, Bratman allows for a wider sense of 'identification' which does not require an actual decision but is still more restrictive than the account offered here.
[15] Bratman (1996), 11.   [16] Bratman (2000), 54.
[17] Bratman (1996), 12.   [18] Davidson (1970b), 31.

Then it is sufficient for reflection that the agent can reflect on the truth of such judgements—that is, he can reflect on whether a value-judgement which appears to be true is in fact true. The conclusion of such a reflection is simply the verdict that 'the evaluative statement p is indeed true/false', and so is not a decision of the kind that Bratman envisages, because it is neither a decision nor about mental states. We can therefore reject Bratman's argument for the necessity of a self-reflective decision for identification, because the process of reflection, whose possibility is indeed a prerequisite for identification, need not have such a decision as its conclusion.

In his later writings Bratman switched to other lines of approach, two of which we must briefly consider here. One main line of approach tries to show that dealing with the Milgram experiments[19] requires higher-order self-reflective attitudes. According to Bratman, in these experiments the subjects treat their desire to cooperate with the authority of the supposed scientists as reason-giving, because 'thoughts like "I guess I should cooperate with such an authority" function as end-setting premises in a kind of attenuated practical reasoning.' However, the subjects do not really accept that the norms of cooperating with authority outweigh basic moral norms, and would not appeal to any such precedence in explicit practical reasoning. They are merely 'in the grip of the norm' to cooperate with authority, because 'the norms of cooperativeness, taking directions, doing one's job control the agent in the heat of social encounter'.[20] As Bratman does not consider instances of being 'in the grip of a norm' as cases of identification, he concludes that identification requires more than only the agent's actually treating the desire as end-setting. In addition, there must also be a higher-order attitude in favour of the desire's functioning as end-setting.[21]

Bratman's argument hinges on his claim that in the Milgram experiments, subjects do not identify with their motivationally effective desire to cooperate with the authority of the supposed scientists. But this interpretation is not compelling—at least not if one presupposes a wide understanding of identification and a correspondingly narrow understanding of alienation, as I have done here. For, as we have seen, alienation in this sense is not the same phenomenon as akrasia, and the Milgram experiments are more plausibly seen as cases of 'merely' akratic action. Unfortunately, cooperating with the scientist's orders is what the test persons really want to do, even though they know that they must not do so when this involves substantial bodily harm

---

[19] In the Milgram experiments, test persons were instructed by pretended 'scientists', claiming to perform an experiment, to give electrical shocks to another person when he failed to correctly answer questions which were put to him. Unknown to the test person, the electrical shocks were only simulated by the other person, who was not visible to the test person. A large number of test persons followed the instructions of the 'scientists' and administered shocks of increasing and even putatively deadly intensity, despite hearing the simulated cries of pain of the other person. These cases seem to show that persons can be motivated by norms of comparatively minor importance—such as collaborating in a scientific experiment—despite knowing that moral norms whose greater importance they are aware of make their actions—morally—completely unacceptable. Cf. Gibbard (1990), 58.

[20] Bratman (2002), 74.

[21] Bratman (2002), 75 f.

to other persons. Understanding the Milgram experiments as cases of normal akrasia rather than of alienation also accords much better with our moral assessment of these cases. When we morally condemn the test persons' actions, we do so because we consider them to be fully responsible for what they have done, while alienation would have extremely reduced or even excluded moral responsibility. So, Bratman's attempt to argue for the need of a self-reflective state from the Milgram cases fails, because these states are not plausibly seen as cases of alienation at all.[22]

Another argument provided by Bratman for the need of higher-order attitudes for identification is based on the special solution to the problem of agential authority developed in his *Reflection, Planning and Temporally Extended Agency*. Here he claims that identification requires a 'self-governing policy' to treat the desire as reason-giving, and attempts to show how these policies have the authority to express the agent's standpoint. For Bratman, their authority derives from the role that they play in the cross-temporal existence of the person. He subscribes to a Lockean conception of personal identity over time, according to which this identity is constituted by psychological connections between the agent's successive psychological states—'Lockean ties'. For Bratman, self-governing policies are among those 'Lockean ties', because they guarantee a certain continuity in the agent's motivational structure which is necessary for the continuing existence of the person. Because the policies are thus constitutive for the continuing existence of the person, they seem to be natural candidates for determining the agent's own standpoint—for they are the attitudes without which the agent 'would no longer exist'.[23]

Obviously, if the Lockean approach to personal identity were convincing, and if we were in need of an explanation of agential authority, this proposal would be attractive. But the analysis of identification in terms of treating as reason-giving has already offered an account of agential authority, which rests not on self-governing policies, but on the inescapable authority of practical reasoning. This account is both more economical than Bratman's, because it appeals only to elements which he must also accept, and has the huge advantage of avoiding the controversy about the viability of a Lockean account of personal identity, which makes it clearly preferable.[24]

---

[22] In (2003), 172, Bratman offers another argument for the need of self-reflexive attitudes, on the basis of the Milgram experiments. As he claims, these cases show that the process of reasoning must not simply evolve, but must be 'governed' by the agent. The specific psychological function which underlies this governing must be known to the agent, and this functioning will be included in the content of his self-governing policy to ensure agential governance of the reasoning. But this argument is unconvincing. First, it is wrong to assume that the agential 'governance' must be something external to the structural features of the process of reasoning itself; and second, there is no need to assume that the psychological functioning must be known to the agent. Governing X does not imply knowing what psychological or physiological functioning underlies this governance—consider the ability of an average person to 'govern' the motions of his fingers.

[23] Bratman (2000), 45 f.

[24] Yet a further line of argument is offered by Bratman in (2005), 47 ff. The basic idea is that human agents are faced with a 'pervasive practical problem of self-management' (50), which necessitates a conative hierarchy. Commitments to certain aims, according to Bratman, plausibly include a commitment to management of first-order desires, and have this management as part of their content, which makes them

So, Bratman is wrong in thinking that solving the problem of identification requires appeal to a higher-order self-reflective attitude in favour of treating the desire as reason-giving. Furthermore, ascribing to agents policies of the kind described by Bratman is, for most cases, empirically implausible, because there are normally no grounds for attributing to agents such a high degree of psychological complexity. Such policies are consciously held only by a few people who have attained an unusually high level of self-reflection. Normally, when agents act, policies of this kind play no role. Agents perform actions simply because they believe that they have reasons to do so, and if our considerations until now have been correct, this belief will partly be due to their treating certain desires as reason-giving. But they do not act because, in addition, they have a desire or policy to treat the desires as reason-giving. Therefore, in order to avoid psychological implausibility we should not assume that such attitudes ordinarily underlie self-determined agency.[25]

We can thus conclude that appeal to higher-order self-reflexive attitudes is neither needed to capture the phenomenon of identification, nor plausible. Instead, what is sufficient for identification with a desire is simply that the agent actually treats it as reason-giving.

4.2. The authority of practical reasoning and the nature of motivating reasons

Let us briefly recapitulate the results we have reached so far, and how they relate to our overall topic of investigation—namely, the question of whether, within the general framework of the standard model, adequate vehicles of agential control can be found. The original proposal—that desires by themselves are those vehicles—was refuted by the possibility of alienation, where the desire of an agent presents an obstacle to his acting as he really wants to act. Subsequently, we examined some unsuccessful proposals to identify other mental states, such as decisions, as appropriate vehicles of control. It turned out that what has the authority to determine the agent's standpoint is only the activity of practical deliberation as such, because any question of whether to identify with a mental state can be raised only in deliberation. Identification with a desire, we have argued, requires that the agent treats the desire as providing him with a reason for action; that is, that he uses—or is prepared to use—a corresponding justifying premiss in his practical reasoning. (That he must use a *justifying* premiss is required in order to exclude cases such as mere use of the premiss in a *reductio ad absurdum* argument.)

---

higher-order. However (as Bratman himself admits) this does not constitute a decisive argument for the conative hierarchy, for the commitment to self-management can also express itself in the adoption of value-judgements.

[25] Cf. Hornsby (2004), 14 f.

The failure to find a mental state as the adequate bearer of agential control is a heavy setback for the standard model and its overall attempt to analyse agential control in terms of the causal impact of specific mental states of the agent. This setback is most clearly manifested by the fact that the proposed analysis of agential control involves, on the next level, an appeal to another kind of activity—practical deliberation—and thus seems to have introduced an indirect, but vicious, form of circularity. (The circularity is not direct, because the initial explananda are performances, and practical deliberation, though an activity, is not a performance in the technical sense.) This failure, however, need not be fatal if the adherents of the standard model were to succeed in presenting, in a second step, a reductive analysis of the kind of activity constituting practical deliberation. We must therefore turn to the question of whether such an analysis can be given. In view of our overall enquiry, in this and the preceding chapter, into whether the standard model can identify some mental states as the right 'bearers' of agential control, there will be one aspect of this question which will interest us in particular: namely, whether the authority of practical reasoning to determine the agent's standpoint might not after all be reducible to the authority of certain mental states.

The most straightforward way to provide such a reduction would be to find a mental state which underlies the process of practical reasoning. Extending the way in which the standard model analyses activity for actions consisting in bodily movements, one could then attempt to analyse the activity of practical reasoning as a series of thoughts which is caused—or each of whose steps is caused—by this underlying mental state. In fact, one such state has been proposed by Velleman: the *de dicto* desire to act as one has the best reason to do. Also, the state formed by the agent's higher-order policies postulated by Bratman might be considered as a possible candidate. But as we have already seen, it is implausible to believe that any of these states underlies the phenomenon of identification and the process of practical deliberation. And the difficulties we have discussed with respect to Velleman's proposal render it improbable that any other mental conative state, or belief-state, from which the agent cannot be alienated could be found as a plausible alternative candidate.

If there is a causal analysis of practical deliberation, it is more likely to be one in which deliberation is analysed as a series of mental events, where one step in the deliberation is caused by an earlier step and there are relations of logical inferences between the contents of the mental states involved. This approach would abandon the attempt to explain agential authority in terms of the authority of particular mental states, but instead derive this authority from structural features of the process of deliberation; for example, from its conforming, by and large, to logically valid types of inference. It is questionable, though, whether such a causal analysis could work. First, most of the relevant features are normative ones—not ones that must actually be displayed by the process, but which provide standards according to which the correctness or success of the deliberation is to be measured. It would have to be shown how these normative features could be captured in non-normative terms. And second, this analysis will be faced with the problem that one step in the deliberation might cause a latter step 'in the wrong way', even though the required logical connections between the two obtain. For the causation might proceed in a way that completely fails to reflect the content of those steps, for example by a mere process of free association. This possibility gives rise to a problem of 'deviant causal chains' for causal analyses of deliberation,[26] which is parallel to the problem of causal deviance for the standard model's account of physical actions (discussed in the next chapter). Anticipating the results of our discussion of this latter problem, we can assume that the problem for deliberation is as intractable as the problem of causal deviance for physical actions, and, therefore, that the outlook for a causal analysis of deliberation is bleak.

However, even if a reductive analysis of practical reasoning in terms of purely event-causalist terms turns out to be impossible, one may think that there is a 'short-cut' to demonstrating that the authority of practical reasoning ultimately rests on the impact of certain mental states. For practical deliberation is about *reasons* for action: We try to find out what we should do—which course of action is advocated by the best reasons to act. This makes it plausible to argue that the authority of practical deliberation rests on the claims that these reasons make upon us. Now, according to one influential view, reasons are just desires and beliefs of the agent, and so it may be claimed, ultimately, that the authority of practical deliberation must in essence be the control of the process of deliberation by these mental states. If this were true, desires might yet be vindicated as bearers of control—if only by a detour via the process of practical deliberation and the (alleged) governance of this process by desires.

Whether such a vindication is possible depends on how we should best conceive of the nature of the reasons for which agents act; and it is to this question, which has been at the centre of much controversy since the 1980s, that we must now turn. There is a further reason why we must address this question in connection with the notion of 'treating a desire as reason-giving', for there is still a gap in our account of this notion which must be filled. While we have said that treating a desire as reason-giving involves the use of a corresponding premiss in one's practical reasoning, we have not yet specified what this premiss will be; that is, what content it will have. When we complete Bratman's account of treating as reason-giving by filling this gap, it will turn out—somewhat surprisingly—that such a completion is only possible in a way adequate for distinguishing identification from alienation, if we accept one particular account of motivating reasons. So, Bratman's basic approach to the problem of identification will end up by forcing us to conceive of the nature of reasons in a particular way, which, contrary to what Bratman himself supposes, excludes that the authority of practical deliberation rests on the control of the deliberative process by conative attitudes of the agent.

---

[26] Cf. Wedgwood (2006), who tries to solve this problem by appealing to a causal efficacy of normative facts.

We must begin our examination of the nature of reasons by a preliminary distinction which is crucial for our following investigation. In this context it is common to distinguish two kinds or roles of reason: 'normative' or 'justifying' reasons on the one hand; and, on the other hand, 'motivating' reasons or 'the agent's reason' (the reasons for which or 'in the light of which' the agent acted).[27] Normative reasons objectively—independently from the agent's limited point of view—speak in favour of performing a certain action, and we typically cite them as responses to requests for the justification of an action. Motivating reasons, on the other hand, are what is cited in reasons-explanations of action. They make intelligible why the agent acted by containing something that—from the agent's point of view—spoke in favour of his acting as he did. However, using this terminological distinction does not imply that there must be two distinct kinds of reason. Whether the same reasons are both normative and motivating is a hotly contested issue. It is also important to notice that the term 'normative reason' does not imply that an action for which there is a normative reason is thereby justified overall. Normative reasons only provide objective *pro tanto* justifications for acting in a certain way, and they can be overridden if there are stronger normative reasons to act otherwise.

What concerns us here is only the nature of motivating reasons, because these are the reasons for which an agent acts and decides. So, if any mental states plausibly 'govern' the practical reasoning, they will have to be connected to, or identical with, motivating reasons. What could be the nature of such reasons? Three main types of answer can be distinguished:

(i) 'Psychologist'[28] theories claim that motivating reasons are constituted by mental states. For them, motivating reasons are just motivating psychological states. The most influential version of 'psychologism' is the Humean theory of motivating reasons—according to which, a reason to F consists in a desire to do G and a belief that if one did F one would thereby G.[29] This claim is based on the characteristic Humean view that no motivation is possible without a desire. But there are also 'psychologists' who deny this need for a desire and argue that motivating reasons can consist of beliefs only—so-called 'cognitivists' about motivation.[30]

(ii) Within the 'antipsychologist' camp, a first approach, which has lately come to prominence, is 'realism'.[31] The first truly 'realist' conception of (some) motivating

---

[27] This distinction—sometimes drawn in terms of 'justifying' versus 'explanatory' reasons—can be found, for example, in Raz (1978), 2 ff., Smith (1987), 37, and Dancy (2000), 1 ff. There is also another sense of 'explanatory reason', by which a reason is (simply) a factor which explains some occurrence or fact; cf. Alvarez (2009), 185 ff., who argues against assimilating the explanatory and motivating 'roles' of reasons.
[28] This term was coined by Dancy (2000).
[29] This classical formulation is from Smith (1987), 36. A different version is in Davidson (1963), 5, where the belief is a particular *de re* belief that this action is a G-ing.
[30] One prominent cognitivist is Wallace (1990), 374, and (2003).
[31] This term is from Iorio (1998).

reasons can be found in von Wright's distinction between 'internal' and 'external' reasons. For von Wright, while internal reasons are psychological states of the agent, external reasons consist in 'external challenges', to which one particular kind of action *fits* as the appropriate response. This 'fitting' relation presupposes a normative framework of 'institutionalized practices'[32] which determines certain kinds of response as adequate responses to specific challenges. For example, for an experienced car-driver the traffic lights which have turned red provide a reason to stop his car, because they present a challenge to do so, which derives its particular meaning from the established rules of traffic control.

Taking up von Wright's basic conception of external reasons, but extending it beyond his limited application of it, Marco Iorio and Rüdiger Bittner have recently proposed considering all reasons as challenges to which we respond with our actions and omissions.[33] Typically, these challenges are events or states of affairs which are external to the agent. Iorio combines this claim with a strictly 'naturalist' view of events and state of affairs, insisting that they must be clearly distinguished from the contents of beliefs and lack propositional structure. Neither do motivating reasons, according to Iorio, provide any justification of action (not even a *pro tanto* justification). Bittner, on the other hand, accepts that reasons can be expressed by that-clauses, and thus also accepts that motivating reasons have a propositional structure.[34] In order to better contrast the realist position with its normativist opponent (which we will discuss presently), I will mainly refer in the following discussion to Iorio's strictly naturalist form of realism.

(iii) The alternative position to realism in the antipsychologist camp is normativism, which has gained prominence especially through Jonathan Dancy's *Practical Reality*.[35] According to normativism, motivating reasons are the contents of factual and evaluative beliefs that the agent has, that is, a reason is 'what is believed' rather than the belief itself. Depending on one's view of 'what is believed', motivating reasons will thus come out either as propositions, facts, or states of affairs,[36] which are essentially propositional in form and can be expressed by that-clauses.[37] Normativists can in principle accept the realists' conception of reasons as challenges to which we respond, but, contrary to 'realism'—at least as espoused by Iorio—they insist on the propositional structure of reasons.

---

[32] Von Wright (1980), 39.
[33] Iorio (1998), ch. 6; Bittner (2001), ch. iv, v.
[34] Iorio (1998), 208 f.; Bittner (2001), 109.
[35] Other adherents of this position include Collins (1997), Raz (1999), Stoutland (2001) (although he is ambigous about the propositional structure), Schueler (2003), and Ammereller (2005).
[36] Dancy (2000), 117, claims that reasons cannot be propositions, but only states of affairs. For Hyman (1999), 443, reasons are facts (if the agent knows that these facts obtain).
[37] Darwall (1983), 33 ff.

Which of these three accounts of the nature of motivating reasons we should adopt will depend on the aim of reasons-explanations—which is, as we have seen, the place where motivating reasons naturally show up. As already remarked, reasons-explanations are rationalizations which show the point of the action and make it intelligible as something that was, to some degree, the rational thing to do. This is achieved by pointing out 'what it was about the action that appealed to the agent', showing us 'something the agent saw, or thought he saw, in his action, some feature, consequence or aspect of the action the agent wanted'.[38] Once this aspect—the feature '*in the light of which* the agent acted'[39]—is pointed out to us, we are able to achieve a specific kind of understanding of the action: as something that, had we pursued the same aims as the agent did and seen things as he did, we too would have considered as 'the thing to do'. So, the specific kind of understanding springs from the fact that to an extent we adopt the agent's point of view at the moment of action, when he asked himself what he should do.[40]

If this characterization of the aim of reasons-explanations is correct, then such explanations will fulfil their rationalizing role by reconstructing (partly or completely) the agent's point of view in his practical deliberation at the time of his decision (or else, in the deliberation he would have gone through at the time of the action had it been the result of explicit deliberation), showing us the points which, for him, spoke in favour of acting as he did. They must retrace the course of the agent's reasoning[41]— though this retracing will be quite minimal, omitting considerations speaking against the action, and those in favour on which the agent did not act. The reconstructing or retracing task of reasons-explanations clearly suggests that the motivating reasons that these explanations cite to explain the action should be identical to the considerations that the agent could have produced himself at the time of his decision or action,[42] i.e. to the (justifying) premises he did use, or would have used, in his practical reasoning to arrive at the conclusion that he should act as he did.

Two important requirements concerning the nature of motivating reasons follow from this. First, motivating reasons must be connected to justifying reasons. When an agent uses a consideration in his deliberation, he believes that this consideration does, in

---

[38] Davidson (1963), 3.
[39] Dancy (2000), 129.
[40] This view of reasons-explanations is rejected by Wallace. While, on the view which I am defending here, there is an intrinsic connection between the perspective of explanation and the perspective of justification (or rationalization), Wallace claims that explanation is typically from a third-person perspective and about already performed actions, while the normative question about what to do is typically asked from a first-person perspective and about future actions. Consequently, he argues, motivating and justifying reasons, which show up in those different explanations, can systematically diverge; (2003), 431 f. However, as Dancy has pointed out, the distinctions between first-person/third-person perspective, future/past actions, and normative/motivating reasons, do not combine as Wallace thinks. I can also ask how I should have acted earlier, or whether the action of another person was justified; Dancy (2003), 471. So, there is, *pace* Wallace, in principle no obstacle to applying a normative kind of understanding to past actions of other agents.
[41] Davidson (1987), 40.
[42] Dancy (2000), 110.

fact, justify his acting in a certain way—at least in cases of non-akratic actions—for only then will the consideration help him answer the question that concerns him in practical deliberation, which course of action is, in fact, the best one. And sometimes we believe that agents 'get things right'; that is, they act on considerations that do, in fact, make their actions fully rational. But this is possible only if motivating reasons are capable of being justifying reasons.[43]

Second, our considerations directly entail the following requirement for anything to be a candidate for constituting a motivating reason: that it be an item that could form a premiss in the agent's practical reasoning. Premisses essentially have a propositional structure, for they stand in logical relations, such as entailment, to other statements. Thus, only items which share this structure and are specifiable by that-clauses[44] can be motivating reasons. This immediately rules out not only Iorio's states of affairs, but also the mental states proposed by the psychologist theory as possible candidates. Even though the content of, for example, a belief has a propositional structure, the belief itself as a mental attitude does not, and thus cannot, literally, be a motivating reason.

However, this does not completely settle the issue against the psychologists. For they might accept that mental states *qua mental states* lack propositional structure, while insisting that *the fact* that the agent has a mental state possesses the required propositional structure and is therefore a potential motivating reason. By this move from mental states themselves to facts about the possession of mental states, the psychologist conception of reasons will be upheld in spirit, if not in letter.[45] In particular, with regard to our general question whether the authority of practical reasoning is derived from the impact of desires on the process of deliberation, this move, if successful, will still allow for the answer to be in the affirmative—desires, we would say, would still have a 'mediated' governance of the activity of practical reasoning.

Normativists have tried to answer this challenge by showing that the fact that I am in a mental state may only in exceptional cases be the reason for which I act, and have argued from the exceptional character of these cases that normally a fact of this kind is not the agent's motivating reason.[46] Their main focus has been the fact 'that I believe that p', and they have tried to show that only in abnormal cases an agent takes his possession of a belief to be a reason for action—for example, to go to a psychiatrist to eradicate it. While I think that their arguments in this respect have been successful, our

---

[43] Cf. Dancy's 'normative constraint' on reasons; (2000), 103.

[44] This does not mean that the items could *only* be specified by 'that'-clauses, because facts and propositions can also be specified by singular terms. For example, 'the fact of his playing the violin' or 'his playing the violin' can specify an agent's reason as well as 'that he was playing the violin', but only because the latter specification of them is possible; cf. Ammereller (2005), 70, esp. fn. 20.

[45] This is what Dancy (2000), 121 ff, calls the 'new theory'. It is implied by Steward (1997), 253 f., who argues, on the basis of a causal interpretation of reasons-explanations, against the view that 'he did A because he believed that p' commits us to any causally efficacious entity 'belief' that shares the causal role of the fact that he believed that p.

[46] This strategy has been followed, for example, by Raz (1999), 51 ff., Hyman (1999), 444 ff., Dancy (2000), 124 ff., Stoutland (2001), and Ammereller (2005).

own focus, understandably, must be on the other kind of fact—on 'that I have the desire to p'—because we are concerned here with the question of whether desires can provide the basis for agential authority. Assume that I have a desire to F with which I identify, and a belief that I can do F by G-ing. Does the fact that I have the desire to F then (normally) constitute the reason for which I do G, when I do it, or does the normative fact that it is, for example, my moral duty to F constitute this reason (assuming, for simplicity's sake, that this is indeed a normative fact)?

In order to answer this question we must look back to the gap in the account of treating a desire as reason-giving which is, as we have mentioned, still left to be filled up. We have yet to spell out what the premiss is that we use in our practical reasoning when we treat the desire as reason-giving. On the basis of the view which I have been urging here—that motivating reasons *are* themselves premisses used in the agent's practical reasoning—this question becomes equivalent to the following question: What is the motivating reason for which the agent acts, when his action is motivated by a desire with which he identifies?

Assume, with the modified psychologist position, that the motivating reason is the fact that the agent desires to F. If this is true, then our attempt to draw a distinction between identification and alienation, in terms of treating the desire as reason-giving, will collapse. For, even desires from which the agent is alienated can provide a reason *of this kind*. As Watson has already pointed out, 'any desire may provide the basis for a reason in so far as non-satisfaction of the desire causes suffering and hinders the pursuit of ends of the agent.'[47]

Take the case of our unwilling addict. Under the strain of the onslaught of his addictive urge to take the drug, he might well reason in the following way:

(1) I should not be taking this drug, because it will badly damage my health.
(2) When I have the desire to take the drug, I should take a surrogate medicine in order not to take the drug.
(3) I have the desire to take the drug.
(C) Thus, I should take the surrogate medicine.

In this piece of practical reasoning, premiss (3) clearly functions as a 'justifying consideration' which provides the basis for inferences about what to do. It is also (part of) the reason, for which the agent takes the surrogate medicine, when he takes it as a result of this deliberation. But, *ex hypothesi*, his addictive desire to take the drug is a desire from which the agent is alienated.

So, if the modified psychologist view is right, our overall approach of explaining identification with a desire, in terms of treating the desire as reason-giving, will fail. For Watson's point shows that in one way, all desires can provide us with reasons for action. However, the way in which alien desires are reflected in one's practical reasoning will

---

[47] Watson (1975), 101.

still be essentially different from the way other desires are reflected. As Watson goes on to add after the remark we have quoted: 'it is important that the reason generated in [the latter] way is a reason for *getting rid of the desire*',[48] or, more precisely, for doing something to get rid of the desire. Desires with which we identify, however, will be reflected in deliberation by considerations *in favour* of performing the action which is desired. So, we can hope to salvage our basic approach to the phenomenon of identification by sharpening the notion of 'treating as reason-giving' sufficiently to reflect the different kinds of impact that desires can have on the agent's practical reasoning.

One attempt to do so—which would maintain the modified psychologist view of the nature of motivating reasons—would be simply an elaboration of the point just made. An agent identifies with a desire to F if he treats it as providing him with a reason *to F*, otherwise he is alienated from it. This new analysis would distinguish between identification and alienation not merely in terms of whether the desire is treated as reason-giving, but also in terms of what it is treated as providing a reason *for*. The difficulty for this analysis, however, is the following. In cases of alienation, the presence of a desire can also—albeit indirectly—provide a reason for satisfying this desire, if the urge becomes unbearable and there is no other way to get rid of the desire.[49] Imagine a person with the obsessive–compulsive desire to bite his nails; after reflection, he has rejected this desire and has undergone a therapy to eliminate it—but alas, he is still afflicted by it. Now, in a particular situation he feels the urge to bite his nails, which continually becomes stronger and prevents him from concentrating on other important matters at hand, until finally he decides to allow the urge to 'pour out' by starting to bite his nails, so that he relieves his anxiety and can concentrate on the other matters. Here, even though the agent is alienated from his desire, it provides him with a reason to satisfy it.

It is therefore hard to see how, on the modified psychologist theory of the nature of motivating reasons, we could adequately distinguish between the different kinds of impact made on one's practical reasoning by desires with which one identifies and by alien desires. It is different, however, for the normativist position, which claims that the agent's motivating reason consists in the fact that F-ing is valuable in some respect[50] (assuming the agent has got things right), rather than in the fact that the agent has a desire to F. If we follow the same kind of strategy as the one standardly used by normativists for the case of belief, we will attempt to vindicate this view by showing that only in abnormal cases will it be the agent's motivating reason that he has a desire, while normally it will be the fact that acting in this way has some value.

---

[48] Loc. cit.
[49] Loc. cit.
[50] It is important to note that the reason will not have the content 'that this course of action is, in some respect, valuable, or good.' Instead, in the reason's content, the aspect under which it is valuable will be spelled out, 'that this course of action is what duty requires, will be fun, will be interesting etc.'

And, in fact, once we examine the instances of identification and alienation, we quickly see that this is precisely what is the case. In the normal cases—those of identification with a desire—the motivating reason is 'that F-ing is morally obligatory, is fun, is a fascinating experiment', while only in the abnormal cases—those of alienation—the motivating reason is 'that I have the desire to F'.[51] For the agent who is alienated from his desire cannot use the evaluative premiss of the first sort. The unwilling addict, for instance, cannot use the premiss that it will be fun to take the drug, because he does not believe that it will be fun to take it; while the agent who identifies with a desire always sees some value connected with the object that he is pursuing.[52]

Does this mean that an agent, when he takes a desire as reason-giving, can *never* take the fact that he has this desire as a reason? This would be going too far. Any fact can be a reason to do something, and can be considered as one. In particular, the fact that I have a desire can be a reason for me to do something else; but only in unusual circumstances can it be the reason for which I perform the action which is the desire's object. The only cases of the latter kind are those in which I ascribe a particular value to the fact that I engage in a certain activity only when I feel like it. For example, a gourmet might think that he should only start to eat his favourite dishes when he has a proper appetite, and so having the appetite may be (part of) the reason why he starts eating. But it is important to note that in these cases the fact that the agent has the desire is, strictly speaking, only the agent's reason to perform the action *at this time*, not the reason to perform the action at all. The gourmet also ascribes, to the activity of eating, some value independent of his presently having an appetite; and his reason for engaging in it at all is the fact that in his view the activity has this further value. (We will discuss putative counter-examples to this claim in Section 4.3.3.)[53]

We can thus conclude that if our analysis of identification with a desire in terms of treating the desire as reason-giving is to be successful, we are forced to accept the normativist account of the nature of motivating reasons. For if the motivating reason of the agent, when he identifies with a desire, consisted in the fact that he has this desire, there would be no difference between cases of alienation and identification, because in

---

[51] This does not mean that, in the normal cases, an agent could not also explain his action by appealing to the fact that he had a desire. It means only that the evaluative facts are the real motivating reasons, and that the primary form of the reasons-explanation is conducted in terms of them. An explanation in terms of facts about mental states is only parasitic on this more basic form of explanation.

[52] Raz (1999), 53 ff., appeals to the same criterion to draw the distinction between 'desires' and 'obsessional urges' and to explain what it is for the agent to be in control. However, his version of the distinction is, as I see it, overly rationalistic, *vide infra*.

[53] One class of putative counter-examples springs from a failure to distinguish the fact that I have decided to X from the fact that I want to X. Though often expressed by the same phrases, the first fact can be a motivating reason for action, contrary to the second: that I have decided to X, by itself gives me a reason to X, which can only be overridden if there are strong considerations to the contrary. This possibility is due to the structural function of intentions, that they allow an agent to settle on a certain course of action in advance—a function which desires lack. (The point about decisions has been elaborated by Raz (1975), 136 ff.)

this way also alien desires provide bases for reasons. Only if the motivating reason, when an agent identifies with a desire to F, consists in the evaluative fact that it would be his duty, or fun, and so on, to F, will there be a difference between the two phenomena.

This result, to say the least, provides a very strong argument in favour of the normativist view of motivating reasons, because the analysis of identification in terms of treating it as reason-giving has otherwise been shown to be highly promising. And this entails that the short-cut to showing that the authority of practical deliberation rests on the claim which certain mental states make on the agent, by constituting his reasons for action, is not viable. Together with the reasons for scepticism about the possibility of a purely event-causal analysis of practical deliberation, noted earlier, this provides sufficient grounds for assuming that it will be impossible to reductively analyse the authority of practical deliberation to determine the agent's standpoint by deriving it from the authority of certain mental states which govern this activity.

The normativist view has another attractive consequence. It allows us to see, more clearly than before, how the reflection, of which the agent must be capable for both the phenomena of identification and alienation, can be about the truth of evaluative judgements rather than about the agent's desires. If motivating reasons are the contents of evaluative judgements, then this reflection will plausibly be conducted in terms of the truth and comparative weight of value-judgements. Introducing these judgements as premises into one's practical reasoning automatically makes them subject to potential re-evaluation and revision. When a consideration in our reasoning comes into open conflict with a sufficient number of other considerations upon which we rely, we are forced to re-examine it, and it is, in principle, possible that the first judgement is revised. Even when the consideration is not rejected, it will still be subject to 'comparative weighting' with other considerations, in the course of which it can in principle be accorded lower comparative importance than others in determining what action should be performed. On both alternatives—revision and outweighing—the judgement, simply in virtue of being used as a consideration in the process of practical deliberation, automatically becomes susceptible to potential criticism on the basis of other considerations.[54] This feature of practical reasoning guarantees, on its own, the degree of self-reflection required for identification, without introducing a form of *explicit* self-reflectiveness which Bratman mistakenly held to be necessary.

---

[54] If an agent treats a desire as reason-giving, this desire will be susceptible to motivational counter-influences as far as these are themselves reflected in the content of his deliberation. This shows that there is something to the idea that for cases of self-determination, acting for a reason must involve 'weak reasons-responsiveness' (as Fischer (1994), 164 ff., has proposed for free actions) or 'reversibility' (Audi, for voluntary agency, (1986), 94 f.).

4.3. Three objections

We have so far developed and defended an account of the phenomenon of identification, according to which an agent identifies with a desire to F if he treats it as reason-giving, where this means that he is prepared to use a positive evaluative judgement about F as a justifying premiss in his practical reasoning. So, that an agent acts 'as he really wants' always presupposes that he sees some value in what he is doing. According to this account, the authority to express the agent's standpoint rests with the activity of practical reasoning as such, and not with any specific mental states. As we have seen, this result presents a severe problem for the project of adherents of the standard model to analyse agential control in terms of the causal impact of mental states purportedly expressing the agent's standpoint.

This result, however, may still appear doubtful, because our proposed account of identification is threatened by three fundamental objections which we must address before we can conclude our discussion of the phenomenon of identification. The first objection is one standardly levelled against normativist accounts about the nature of motivating states. It purports to show that the cases where the agent 'gets it wrong' exclude the possibility of evaluative facts constituting motivating reasons (Section 4.3.1). The second objection is based on apparent counter-examples to our proposed criterion for identification, where the agent, though he is alienated from his desire to F, apparently ascribes some worth to 'doing F' (Section 4.3.2). The last objection claims that the account of self-determination which we have offered is overly rationalistic (Section 4.3.3). None of these three objections, I will argue, will force us to abandon the account of identification as treating as reason-giving, although dealing with them will require some further clarifications.

4.3.1. When the agent 'gets it wrong'

Until now we have, for the sake of simplicity, focused only on cases where the agent 'gets things right'. But when we want to present a general account of motivating reasons, we are faced with the by now common objection to normativist theories of motivating reasons that they have difficulties in dealing with those cases in which the agent's judgements are mistaken. As I have argued that our theory of identification as treating as reason-giving must espouse normativism, the objection also pertains to this theory.

The objection can be taken to proceed in the following two steps. First, it is argued that in a certain kind of case—namely, when the agent's judgements are false—the normativist view about motivating reasons *cannot* be true. Assume that Agamemnon believes that it is his moral duty to sacrifice Iphigenia, while we—let us assume rightly—reject this view as mistaken. The crucial premiss in Agamemnon's reasoning will be 'that it is his moral duty to sacrifice Iphigenia'—and, following the argument from the 'retracing' function of reasons-explanations advanced earlier, we should have to conclude that this very consideration is Agamemnon's motivating reason. But this cannot be correct: We cannot say that Agamemnon sacrificed Iphigenia because it was his duty to do so. Saying this would commit us to the view that it was, in fact, his moral duty to do so, and this is precisely what we deny.

This leads us to the second step of the objection. If the normativist account fails with regard to cases where the agent's judgements are wrong, it seems that it must fail in all cases, for it is plausible to assume, with Bernard Williams, that the 'difference between false and true beliefs on the agent's part cannot alter the form of the explanation'.[55] Williams' thesis is supported by our earlier argument that motivating reasons are those considerations 'in the light of which' the agent has acted—and these considerations can be identical in cases where the agent's beliefs are true and where they are wrong. Therefore, it seems that we must accept the result that, generally, the agent's motivating reasons must be understood according to the psychologist account[56]—either as consisting in mental states of the agent or in the fact that the agent has such mental states.

This argument is applicable with regard to the contents of both non-evaluative and evaluative beliefs. Evaluative beliefs appear to present a special difficulty, however, for claiming that they can be true at all commits us to normative facts (in some sense). And while accepting the existence of non-normative facts seems unproblematic, non-cognitivists about the normative reject normative facts and claim that what appear to be normative beliefs are not beliefs about purported facts at all. Such a view would lead directly to a psychologist construal of reasons-explanations.[57] While I consider such general non-cognitivism about the normative to be mistaken, I cannot deal with this position here. So, I will sidestep the special difficulty for evaluative beliefs by simply assuming that there are such things as normative facts—such as that it is the agent's duty to X, or that it would be very interesting for her to X, without, however, espousing any specific account of normativity and normative facts.

My only concern here is the question—assuming that there are such things as normative truths—of whether normativists can answer the fundamental objection to their account which arises from the possibility of mistaken evaluative and non-evaluative beliefs. A first strategy would be to accept the first step of the objection and admit that in cases of mistaken beliefs it cannot be the content of the belief that constitutes the agent's motivating reason, but must be the fact that he so believes. However, the first strategy would go on to argue, this does not imply that all motivating reasons are of this sort, because we should reject Williams' thesis that the truth or falsity of the agent's beliefs has no influence on the form of the explanation.

---

[55] Williams (1979), 102.
[56] This kind of argument against the normativist acount is offered, for example, by Wallace (2003), *passim*. For the reconstruction of this objection, cf. Ammereller (2005), 66 ff.
[57] This line of argument against normativism is sketched—though not endorsed—by Wallace (2003), 433 f.

When the agent truly believes that p—or, as Hyman claims, when he knows that p—the motivating reason therefore still consists in the fact that p.[58]

My main difficulty with such a disjunctive analysis of motivating reasons is that I find Williams' thesis—which this analysis rejects—highly plausible, for it fits so well with the earlier defended view that motivating reasons are the considerations in the light of which the agent acts. Those considerations do not change when what the agent believes ceases to be true—and so the agent's motivating reasons should not change either.

An alternative strategy, which has been proposed by Dancy, consists in rejecting the first step of the argument—that the normativist view about motivating reasons must fail in cases where the agent 'gets things wrong'. Consider, for instance, the agent's belief, or judgement, that it is his moral duty to do X, and assume that he acts on it. Unfortunately, however, he is mistaken, and his duty would lie with refraining from doing X. Dancy has argued that even in this case it could be the agent's motivating reason 'that it is his moral duty to X', because reasons-explanations, he claims, are non-factive.[59] In factive explanations we can infer from the truth of 'the reason why p is/was that q' the truth of both p and q, while in non-factive explanations we cannot do so—and especially, we cannot infer the truth of q. Therefore, Dancy claims, 'that p' can be cited as a motivating reason in a reasons-explanations, even when p is false.

I think that there is an important kernel of truth contained in Dancy's view that reasons-explanations are non-factive, but that the view as he states it is implausible. For taking, as Dancy proposes, 'that p' as the motivating reason even when p is false, means that we would have to accept sentences such as the following as true, though they seem absurd or even contradictory: 'Columbus's reason for sailing westward was that Asia was the first continent to be reached in this direction'; or 'Columbus's reason for sailing westward was that Asia was the first continent to be reached in this direction, though, in fact, it was not.'[60] Considering sentences such as these makes it very plausible to argue that Dancy goes wrong in claiming that by the clause 'that p' in a reasons-explanation we could actually cite something that was false. And even if the impression of absurdity connected with these sentences may on its own not be sufficient to decisively refute Dancy's solution, I take it that any solution which is not committed to these highly counterintuitive results will have a clear advantage over his.

But this does not invalidate what I take to be the important kernel of truth contained in Dancy's claim: that the motivating reason itself need not be something that is true. This follows directly from two claims I subscribed to earlier: the claim that motivating reasons are identical with the considerations in the light of which the agent has acted, and Williams' thesis that it is irrelevant for the reasons-explanation whether or not the agent's beliefs are true. For if these two claims are true, then the explanatory work of

---

[58] Cf. Stoutland (1998), 60 f.; Hyman (1999), 445.
[59] Dancy (2000), 131 ff.
[60] Dancy (2000), 132, is, however, prepared to accept such statements as consistent.

reasons-explanations—at least insofar as the rationalizing aspect is concerned—can be done only by something that is independent of the truth or falsity of the considerations on which the agent acts. And, I believe, this is precisely what is the case. That the reasons-explanation makes an action appear rational to some degree depends on the logical connections between the contents of the agent's beliefs, decisions, and intentions (together with the background assumption that these logical connections are reflected within the agent's practical deliberation). One typical logical connection of this kind would be the practical syllogism: 'it is your duty to do F' and 'in order to F you must do G' logically entail 'you should G'. Such logical connections hold independently of whether the premisses of this argument are actually true. It is a relation between *propositions* which holds regardless of what truth-values these propositions take.

So, the explanatory work in reasons-explanations is done by logical connections between propositions, which are independent of whether these propositions are, in fact, true. But we can even go one step further. The motivating reasons are themselves the considerations connected to verdicts about what the agent should do by such logical connections as the practical syllogism; so, they are themselves propositions—which can be, but need not be, true. If we take a Fregean view of states-of-affairs as true propositions (or thoughts), we can, in case the agent's beliefs are true, consider motivating reasons to be states-of-affairs; but in case the beliefs are wrong, the reasons can, as propositions, still do their explanatory work.

If reasons are propositions, then both their nature will not change whether or not the agent's beliefs are true—they will still be propositions—and they can play their explanatory role in the same way in both cases. The only remaining problem is finding a formulation by which we can express the motivating reason both from the first-person and from the third-person perspective; for we assume that the motivating reason, from both perspectives, is one and the same item. The particular difficulty of this task arises from the two *prima facie* diverging requirements that a candidate formulation must fulfil. On the one hand, on the agent's own view the considerations he uses in his practical deliberation are true; so, from the agent's perspective, the formulation must commit him to the truth of the consideration in question. On the other hand, from the third-person perspective such a commitment is precisely what must be avoided, and instead we must make it clear that the explaining factor is only a proposition, which can be either true or false.

There is one expression of the reason which fulfils both these tasks: 'that, as the agent believes/believed, p'.[61] The enormous advantage of this form of expression is that the commitments as to the truth of p expressed by it change in just the right ways, when used in the first-person and in the third-person perspective. In the first-person perspective it becomes 'that, as I believe, p'—which for the agent himself is tantamount

---

[61] Dancy's 'appositional' account, (2000), 128 f., which goes back to Collins (1997).

to stating just 'that p'. By uttering the former, the agent also commits himself to the latter, and vice versa. But not so from the third-person perspective. When I say 'that, as James believed, p', I avoid all commitment concerning the question of whether p is true. Instead, this part of my statement will be true whenever the agent believes that p, while the truth of p itself is quite irrelevant. Now, the agent's belief that p is, anyway, a background condition[62] which must be fulfilled if the agent acts for the reason that p, both in cases where p is true and where it is false. The formulation therefore succeeds in abstracting from the truth-value of p without introducing any new contested element in its place, and thereby comes as close to talking only about the proposition that p as can be required.

There is one further signal advantage of taking this expression for describing motivating reasons. In both the first-person and third-person perspective, it refers to the same subject-matter—objective circumstances, as they are seen by the agent.[63] From the agent's point of view, the phrase 'that, as I believe, p' is not about his own mental states, but about p; the phrase 'as I believe' does not add anything to the statement, but could equally well be omitted. From the third-person point of view, however, 'that, as he believes, p' cannot be about p, simply because the person who utters this sentence need not himself believe that p. But the expression still talks about the same thing as does the expression in the first-person form: namely, about the objective circumstances, as the agent perceived them. In particular, it is *not* about the agent's mental states, because the use of the phrase 'as he believes' is not descriptive, but parenthetical.[64] That the third-person's formulation has the same subject-matter as the first-person version ensures that the phrase 'that, as he believes, p' satisfies the 'reconstruction' requirement that we have imposed on reasons-explanations, that 'our third-person explanation of the action should be, as far as possible, the agent's explanation'.[65]

Thus, we can conclude that normativists are able to answer the main objection against them without having to reject Williams' thesis that the form of the reasons-explanations is independent of whether the agent's beliefs are true or false. Their answer lies in identifying motivating reasons with propositions. Once we do this we can maintain that even when the agent's beliefs are wrong, still the phrase 'that, as he believes, p' describes his reason for action, which consists in the proposition that p. And both the existence of this proposition and the logical connections to other propositions will be independent of the truth of the proposition.

---

[62] Or, as Dancy called it, an 'enabling condition', which is a 'consideration that is required for the explanation to go through, but which is not itself part of the explanation'; (2000), 127.
[63] The need for the 'same subject-matter' for both reasons-explanation and the agent's deliberation was vividly stressed by Collins (1997), 122 ff.
[64] The first one to notice this point was, to my knowledge, Edgley (1965), 25.
[65] Dancy (2000), 110.

4.3.2. The potential value in satisfying 'alien' desires

The second difficulty arises directly from the possibility which we have mentioned earlier, when rejecting the proposal that the difference between identification and alienation might depend on what the desires are treated as providing reasons *for*. As we have argued, it is not true that only in cases of identification with a desire to do X the agent believes to have a reason to do X which is based on this desire. For in cases of alienation too, the agent, under the stress of the desire's onslaught, might find no other way to get rid of the desire than to satisfy it, and might therefore take the fact that he possesses the desire as a reason to do X. For example, the person with the obsessive desire to bite his nails might, when the urge prevents him from concentrating on other matters, take the presence of the desire as a reason to bite his nails, if this is the only possibility he has to eliminate it. In this case, one may ask, does not the agent necessarily see some value in satisfying his desire, even though he is alienated from it, and does he not thereby treat it as reason-giving on the account proposed here? And if this question should have to be answered in the affirmative, one might want to go on to argue that it is generally the case for all desires that they must be 'reason-giving' in the sense explained here—at least because their satisfaction avoids the frustration arising from their non-fulfilment.

Let us begin with the latter, stronger claim, because it is easier to refute. The refutation has nothing to do with the phenomenon of alienation in particular. Instead, it is clearest when we examine cases which are of no importance whatsoever to the agent, and where he consequently does not care about whether or not the desire is fulfilled. Just think of passing whims—such as the suddenly arising whim to pick a flower—where we know precisely that if we do not pick it we will presently have forgotten all about it and think about something else. Here, there is no feeling of frustration to be expected from a failure to satisfy the desire,[66] and so the general claim that all desires provide reasons because the frustration from their non-satisfaction is better avoided must be wrong.

A greater difficulty is presented by the first type of case. Is it not true that the agent, though he is alienated from the desire to do X, sees some value in X-ing? Indeed, I think that at the end of his practical deliberation about how to get rid of the desire, the agent will see some value in X-ing, after he has had to recognize that this is the only method of doing so. This acceptance of an evaluative judgement is also indicative of a desire to do X with which the agent identifies—for, in fact, during the course of his practical reasoning, the agent has acquired such an instrumental desire.

But the addictive urge to do X, and the desire to do X in order to relieve the pressure of the urge, are, though both desires to do X, not identical. The first desire began as an instance of the more general pattern of urges of the agent, and is not responsive to the presence or absence of reasons. The second desire was adopted only during the course of the practical reasoning, and is what Richard Moran has called a

---

[66] Cf. Raz (1999), 58.

'judgement-sensitive desire';[67] that is, it depends both for its genesis and for its survival on the agent's judgement that it is good to dispense with his urge to do X. Also, the second desire—to do X in order to get rid of the urge—is essentially instrumental, while the first one is not.

All these features speak clearly against an identity between the addictive urge and the desire to do X in order to relieve the nervous pressure. So, we can maintain our general proposal about identification, because only if the agent has a desire with which he identifies, he accepts a corresponding value-judgement. But we should add the following clarification to the proposal: When this value-judgement is only inferred from the judgement that the agent should get rid of this desire, then the agent does not, in virtue of this value-judgement, identify with the non-instrumental desire which he thinks he should get rid of, but only with the instrumental desire to perform the action in question in order to get rid of the other desire.

4.3.3. Is the account of identification too rationalistic?

The third worry that I want to address concerns the question of whether the account of self-determination and identification which I have been defending here is not overly rationalistic.[68] The basis of this worry is that on this account, self-determination requires that the agent sees some value in what he is doing, and this requirement, one might feel, assigns to reasoning about what is valuable an altogether too central place in a self-determined life. There are two forms that this basic worry might take, and each of them will be addressed in turn.

The first is a variant of the worry about Watson's account: that it treats cases of alienation on the same level as cases of akrasia. Has not the failure of Watson's own account already shown that such a strategy must fail because we can identify with desires which do not conform to what we believe to be best? However, this objection would rest on a mistake. What is required for identification on the 'treating as reason-giving' model is not that the desire or the action issuing from it conforms to what the agent believes to be best overall, but only that there is *some* evaluative consideration which, on the agent's view, speaks in its favour. And this requirement does not conflate the phenomena of alienation and akrasia.

The second kind of worry about an overly rationalistic nature of the proposed account cannot be so easily dismissed. As a starting-point, consider Joseph Raz's account of the agent's control over his emotional states, which is in many respects similar to the account of identification that has been defended here. According to Raz, we can only desire to do what, as we believe, we have some reason to desire (as Raz uses the term 'desire', urges from which the agent is alienated are excluded): 'What we want to do...we want for a reason...We cannot want what we see no reason to want

---

[67] Moran (2002), 197.
[68] This general worry has been raised by Frankfurt (2004) against Raz.

any more than we can believe what we think is untrue or contrary to the evidence.'[69] The most plausible way to understand this passage is as requiring that for something to be a desire rather than an urge, there must be an antecedent, and in the agent's view, *independently justified* evaluative belief that backs up this desire. Paradigmatic instances of desires for which this requirement is fulfilled are what Thomas Nagel has called 'motivated desires',[70] which are formed as a result of deliberation. In these cases, the desire has been adopted only because the agent had *already* reached the conclusion that its object had some value. But clearly not all desires (now using 'desires' not in Raz's narrow sense, but in the wider sense in which we have used it earlier) have an independent evaluative belief which backs them up; and for those that lack such a belief, the verdict of Raz's account would have to be that they are only like urges (at least insofar as the agent's control over them is concerned).[71]

If our own account of identification were understood along the same lines as Raz's account of control, this would mean that all desires for which such an independent evaluative belief would be missing would have to be ruled as 'alien'. This result would clearly be unacceptable, for it would equate cases in which we act on whims—'just like that'—with cases of alienation. Consider a person who is walking over a field and suddenly 'feels like picking a flower'. She has no further aim in doing so, and without her 'feeling like picking a flower' she would not believe that she had any reason to do so. Clearly such an action can be an instance of self-determination, and picking the flower can be what the person 'really wants', despite having no independent reason for doing so. So, it would be unrealistic to require for identification that the agent has an independent positive value-judgement about the desire's object.

Do these cases of doing something just because 'one feels like it' refute the account of identification which we have offered? Some philosophers have indeed thought that these cases either refute the claim that an agent must see some good in what he is doing, when he is acting intentionally, or, at least, constitute exceptions to this claim. What the agent takes to be a reason in those cases, it has been argued, *cannot* be a purported value-fact, but can only be the fact that he 'feels like acting in this way'—and this is a fact about his desires.[72] But I will attempt to show that this conclusion is not compelling, and that even in these cases the agent can be understood to act on evaluative facts as he perceives them.

The starting-point is to notice that the account defended here does not include the strong requirement that there must be an *independent* evaluative belief on the agent's part. Instead, we have only required that, for identification, the agent must have some

---

[69] Raz (1999), 52 f.
[70] Nagel (1970), 29.
[71] Of course, this does not mean that Raz must assume that they are, in all respects, like urges, as there can still be differences with regard to irresistibility, and so on.
[72] This possibility—cautiously entertained by Scanlon (1998), 48—is defended, for 'affective desires' in general, by Chang (2004), 84 ff. Both accept, however, that normally the agent sees some value in what he is doing.

positive evaluative belief about the object of the desire whose content he is prepared to use as a premiss in his practical reasoning. In principle, nothing excludes the possibility that the agent has this evaluative belief only because he possesses the desire, while lacking any independent subjective justification for this belief. However, that this possibility is not directly excluded does not really help us to deal with the cases of doing something 'because one feels like it', as long as we cannot positively make sense of the idea of how having an evaluative belief can depend on the possession of a desire. For, *prima facie*, this idea is quite puzzling. Beliefs are about 'what is the case', and therefore can be 'faulted' for not conforming to what is, in fact, the case. Desires, however, cannot be faulted for the same reason,[73] because their possession does not express what the agent considers to be true. As cases of alienation show, they can be possessed even if the agent accords no value whatsoever to their objects. So, how can the possession of a belief depend on the possession of a desire?

The key to solving this mystery lies in recognizing that having a desire can 'colour'[74] one's judgements about what is good because it can involve that the desire's object *appears* to be good to us. This appearance is reflected in a tendency, on our part, to form the *prima facie* evaluative judgement that the object is indeed good, when we have the desire. This tendency to judge need not actually be expressed in an evaluative belief of the agent, because there may be stronger, counteracting tendencies to judge the desire's object to be bad; but the tendency *can* result in an evaluative belief. As a consequence, the connection of desires with 'appearances of value' in their objects will enable us to explain how there can be evaluative beliefs which someone has only because he has the desire, without thereby committing us to the stronger claim refuted by the cases of alienation that having a desire entails acceptance of a corresponding value-judgement.[75] This is the rough sketch of the solution, which must now be filled out.

How can desires 'colour' one's evaluative judgement ? Watson—who originally mentioned this possibility—was arguably only thinking of rather exceptional cases where the agent is under the strongly experienced 'onslaught' of a desire. For example, when an agent strongly feels a 'thirst for revenge', he is disposed to view acts of revenge as 'manly' or worthy of admiration, while otherwise he regards them as morally repugnant. However, the 'colouring' influence is not, on my view, restricted to such cases, but *all* desires involve a tendency to positively judge the desires' objects. This influence on one's judgements works in either of the two following ways.

---

[73] The same point can be made in terms of the distinction between different 'directions of fit' for beliefs and desires; cf. Smith (1987), 51 f.

[74] Watson (1975), 104.

[75] A significantly stronger version of the thesis that desires involve 'appearances of value' is defended by Tenenbaum (2007). He defends the view that desires should be identified with positive evaluations, which would rule out that one strongly desires something to which one attributes only a small value; cf. (2007), 23. My claim here is much weaker. Neither need desires be identified with evaluations, nor need the motivational strength of a desire exactly correspond to the greatness of the attributed value.

The first alternative involves what Thomas Scanlon has called a 'desire in the directed-attention sense'. When a person has such a desire to P, 'the thought of P keeps occurring to him…in a favorable light', and his attention is constantly being drawn towards considerations 'that present themselves as counting in favor of P.'[76] Thus, imagine that I have the desire to buy a new car, and that this desire is a desire in the 'directed-attention sense'. Then, I will constantly be finding ideas in favour of doing so—for example, that my present car is very old and already rusty in many places, that the new car will not be particularly expensive and I can well afford it, and so on—occuring to my mind and occupying my attention. As a result of these considerations, which keep 'popping up', it will appear to me that it is really a good idea to buy a new car, and I will consequently have a tendency to judge that this is what I should do.

Now, desires in the 'directed-attention sense' are indeed important instances of the phenomenon of 'appearance of the good' that has been mentioned. As a result of having such a desire, the agent might arrive at a value-judgement that he would not have accepted independently. But I do not think that these desires provide the correct solution to the cases of acting because 'one feels like it'. For the considerations which keep appearing when we have such desires are *really* considerations that speak in favour of doing P.[77] Thus, it is really a consideration in favour of buying a new car that my old car is rusty, and a consideration which I accept independently from having the desire itself. The desire's influence consists only in distorting my overall perspective on the course of action in question, by occupying my mind with the positive considerations while shutting out the negative ones, thus diminishing the latter's influence on my overall assessment of what course of action is best. But, to repeat, this distortion functions only on the basis of positive assessments of particular features of the action, which are or would also be accepted independently of the possession of the desire. Only the perceived balance of these assessments is affected.

In cases where the agent acts only 'because he feels like it', however, this distortion of balance will not suffice for creating an 'appearance of value', because here the agent cannot, independently from having the desire, tell us of any positive consideration in favour of acting as he does. There is not even a *pro tanto* value-judgement about a positive feature of, say, picking a flower, which the agent could adduce, and which could, by the distorting influence of the desire, appear to be speaking decisively in favour of picking the flower.

Instead, the second alternative of a 'colouring' influence of desires becomes relevant here, where the object *simply*—that is, not due to emphasis of particular features of it—appears to us to be 'a good thing to do', and this impression is connected with a tendency to judge accordingly. This kind of 'colouring' influence is best understood in parallel to the impact of sensual impressions or experiences on our empirical judge-

---

[76] Scanlon (1998), 39.
[77] Scanlon somewhat misleadingly writes that these considerations (only) 'present themselves as counting in favor of p', (1998), 39.

ments. Consider the Müller-Lyer illusion, where two lines, which are really equally long, appear to be of different lengths because one has arrow-heads pointing outward at each end, and the other has arrow-heads pointing inward. Looking at a drawing of these lines, we have the impression that one of the lines is longer, and have a connected tendency to judge that it is. But (contrary to cases of desires in the 'directed-attention' sense) there is no particular feature of the picture to which our attention is drawn and which we regard as a reason to believe that one line is longer. In particular, the differently pointed arrow-heads are no such features, because we do not take them as *evidence* that one line is longer, they only create this impression on us.[78]

Desires, on my view, typically have this second kind of influence—often in addition to the first—and therefore have the same impact on our evaluative judgements as sense-impressions have on our judgements based on experience.[79] They involve an appearance that their object is of value, without thereby presenting us with independently holding reasons to believe that it is, or giving us grounds to believe that there are such reasons.

Nevertheless, the mere appearance can sometimes be the basis on which we judge that the object is indeed of value[80]—namely, if we trust appearances. Such a judgement need not be irrational. Appearances of value entitle us to corresponding judgements if (i) nothing relevant hinges on our action, if (ii) it would be too troublesome to think through whether the apparent value is a real value, and if (iii) there is no conflict with other things that we value. Using value-judgements which are formed merely on the basis of how things appear in one's practical reasoning will be possible so long as there is no conflict with other evaluative judgements. If there is, we will, of course, need to reflect on the justification of the different judgements, and then the judgement that X is valuable, which was adopted only because X appeared to be valuable, will be rejected because it is not supported by independent reasons (assuming we do not find further support for it within the system of beliefs that we already possess). But crucially, as long as no conflict arises, it can perfectly well be that we maintain the judgement for a considerable time, and act on it.

This point vindicates our earlier contention that alienation from a desire always presupposes an actual process of practical deliberation. For alienation from a desire always requires rejection of the corresponding value-judgement as false; and as desires involve that their objects appear as valuable to us, we must reject these appearances as unfounded, which always requires deliberation about their credentials. Without

---

[78] For this reason, Chang's comparison of cases of optical illusion such as the Müller-Lyer case, to desires in the directed-attention sense, (2004), 65, is unconvincing. Chang argues that in such cases 'our attention is drawn to features...that present themselves as reasons to judge' in this way, and that these cases 'necessarily involve a tendency to judge that one has reasons.' Neither of these claims is plausible. There are no such particular features in the case of optical illusions which present themselves as reasons, and we need not have a tendency to judge that we have such reasons. Instead, the two lines simply appear to be of different lengths, and we have a tendency to judge that they are.

[79] *Pace* Chang (2004), 66, who denies this for desires other than desires in the directed-attention sense.

[80] The value accorded to the object in such cases will typically, but not always, be a hedonic value.

deliberation we would continue to trust appearances and adhere to the value-judgements which we adopt on their basis.

These considerations provide, I take it, the correct analysis of the cases of doing something because 'one feels like it', which shows that these cases do not refute our claim that when an agent acts as he really wants, he sees some value in acting as he does. In these cases, the agent, as a result of having a desire to, say, pick a flower, has the impression that this action would be of some value. As this action is completely inconsequential, there is no conflict with other things which he values, and so he may judge that picking a flower would indeed be a 'good thing to do', merely on the basis of the impression. (Of course, he need not judge so. If he is a highly self-reflective person, he may ask himself whether there really is value in picking a flower, and, finding none, he may reject his impression as illusionary.)

This result answers the second worry about an alleged overly rationalistic character of our account of identification. As we have seen, identification with a desire can require acceptance of a value-judgement by the agent without thereby becoming a too rationalistic phenomenon, because the value-judgement need not be derived from other independent and antecedently held value-judgements, but can be based merely on 'appearances of value' that are connected with desires.

4.4. Conclusion

The answers to the three objections addressed in the preceding section complete our discussion of Frankfurt's problem of identification and its consequences for the event-causalist standard model of human agency. Our main results have been the following. First, that the most plausible analysis of the phenomenon of identification is in terms of the agent's treating the desire as reason-giving, where the latter notion must be spelled out as the agent's accepting a positive value-judgement about the desire's object which he is prepared to use as a justifying premiss in his practical reasoning. An agent, it follows, can only act self-determinedly when he sees some value in what he is doing. And second, that this analysis is at odds with the overall reductive project connected with the standard model—both generally, and specifically, with regard to the standard model's particular strategy to analyse agential control.

Generally, our analysis is at odds with the reductive project, because it appeals, within the analysans, to an activity of the agent: namely, practical deliberation. And as we have seen, the outlook for a reductive analysis of this activity is bleak. As a consequence, the analysis—if taken as a reduction of the notion of agential activity—threatens to be circular. More specifically, the analysis shows that the attempt of the standard model to reductively analyse agential control in terms of the impact of certain mental states which are the bearers or vehicles of agential control fails. For there are no mental states which would be plausible vehicles by necessarily expressing what the agent really wanted and thereby constituting the agent's own standpoint.

We must therefore conclude that the standard model cannot even fulfil the first part of the overall task of naturalizing agency, presented at the end of Chapter 2. This overall task chiefly consisted in presenting a reductive account of agential control by finding both adequate mental states as bearers and an adequate mode of control. But, as argued in Chapter 2, a successful naturalization of agency is a prerequisite for a unified account of human agency on the basis of the standard model. Thus, the failure to provide the first half of the intended analysis already shows that no satisfactory response to the problem of human agency can be given on the basis of this model.

5
Deviant causal chains

Let us turn to the other half of the causalist project, i.e. to spelling out the right 'mode' of agential control. According to the causalist standard model, the adequate mode of control consists in an event-causal link between the mental states and the bodily motions which are the results of the action and which must fit the content of the mental states which cause them. When examining this proposal we will temporarily leave aside the result of the preceding chapter, that the mental states specified by the standard model are no adequate bearers of agential control. Instead, we will focus only on the question of whether—assuming those mental states could express the agent's own standpoint—an event-causal link between them and the agent's bodily motions would ensure that these motions are under the agent's control and the results of actions that he performs.

The main obstacle to a success of the event-causal analysis of the mode of agential control is the problem of deviant (or wayward) causal chains. It arises from the possibility that even when mental states of the kinds envisaged by the standard model—combinations of desires and beliefs, or intentions—cause a bodily motion which fits the content of those states, the bodily motion which is produced may not be the result of an (intentional) action because it may be caused in the wrong way.

5.1. The problem of antecedential waywardness

The problem of deviant causal chains does not arise solely for the causalist analysis of action, but, taking on different forms, it poses a general threat to causal analyses of phenomena concerning human agency.[1] In particular, it also threatens the causalist analyses of intentional action and of acting for a reason. Causalists usually explain intentional action in terms of causation of the action by an intention, and acting for a reason R in terms of causation of the action by a desire-belief complex which embodies R.[2] The following four cases demonstrate how the problem of deviance arises for these two analyses, as well as for the causalist analysis of action itself.

---

[1] And also for causal analyses of perception, representation, or knowledge; cf. Enc (2003), 99.
[2] Cf. Davidson (1963), 11 f.

Case 1: Nephew I has decided to shoot his uncle, who is taking his afternoon nap. Just as the nephew is standing in front of his uncle's bed and intends to pull the trigger of his gun, his intention so unnerves him that he begins to tremble uncontrollably. The trembling makes his finger press the trigger, and the gun fires, killing the unfortunate relative.[3] In this case, the motion of the finger which touched the trigger was caused by an intention and fitted this intention, because it was, after all, an intention to press the trigger. Thus, the conditions for agency specified by the standard model are met. Nevertheless, the nephew did not perform an action when his finger pressed the trigger, because he had no control over this motion.

Case 2: Nephew II intends to kill his uncle by running him over with his car while the uncle is taking his daily evening stroll. While driving to his uncle's home, his intention makes the nephew so nervous that he cannot concentrate on his driving. As a consequence, he drives too fast and, by mistake, steers the car off the road, running over a pedestrian who, unknown to him, is his uncle.[4] Even though the nephew's movements leading to his uncle's death were caused by his intention, and he did what he intended to do, he did not intentionally kill his uncle.

Case 3: Nephew III intends to kill his uncle by shooting him. The shot he fires misses the uncle, but stampedes a herd of wild pigs which trample the uncle to death.[5] Here, while the agent did something intentionally—he fired a gun at his intended victim—and what he did caused the latter's death, he did not kill his victim intentionally. For the way in which he caused his uncle's death was completely different from the way that he had envisaged.

Case 4: Nephew IV intends to kill his uncle in order to inherit his fortune. The intention agitates him so much that it gives him a terrible stomach-ache, which turns him into an angry maniac. Forgetting about his earlier intention to kill his uncle, he goes out into the street and, out of sheer anger, kills the first man he meets, whom he recognizes to be—by chance—his uncle.[6] In this case, the nephew killed his uncle intentionally, and his action was caused indirectly by his desire to inherit his uncle's fortune. Nonetheless, he did not kill his uncle in order to inherit the latter's fortune.

These examples show that none of the proposed causal analyses will go through without modification. As Case 1 makes clear, the causation of bodily behaviour corresponding to an intention's content by this very intention is not, on its own, sufficient for the performance of an action. Cases 2 and 3 show that when an action is caused by an intention, the action need not be intentional. Lastly, Case 4 demonstrates that even when an intentional action is caused by a desire, this does not ensure that the agent acts on this desire.

---

[3] After Morton (1975), 13.
[4] After Chisholm (1966), 29f.
[5] The example is due to Bennett; Davidson (1973a), 78.
[6] Modified after Searle (1983), 136.

Following a distinction introduced by Myles Brand, the problem of causal deviance is normally divided into two sub-problems: the problem of antecedential deviance, which concerns the connection between the mental antecedents and the bodily motions which are the results of the agent's *basic* actions (as in Case 1); and the problem of consequential deviance, which concerns the connection between more basic activities of the agent and their further consequences (as in Case 3).[7] While the latter problem concerns the analysis of *intentional non-basic* action—because it calls into question whether the agent has intentionally brought about further consequences of his more basic actions—the problem of antecedential waywardness directly pertains to the event-causalist analysis of human agency as such.

As our overall concern here is the analysis of agential control in general, and not of special forms of control required for intentional agency in particular, it is only the problem of antecedential deviance which we need to investigate. For only this problem calls into question the key causalist contention that the right mode of control required for agency in general is the event-causal link between mental antecedents and bodily behaviour.

However, in discussing this problem we will not be able to make a clear-cut distinction between agential control in actions, in general, and in intentional actions. For as we have seen, for most contemporary defenders of the standard model, the necessary antecedents of actions in general include intentions, and thus, for them, an analysis of agential control in basic actions also provides, automatically, an analysis of agential control in intentional basic actions. I think this approach is misguided, because not all actions involve intentions (think of the cases of purely unintentional actions mentioned in Section 1.2). But this latter point has nothing to do with the problem of deviance in particular, and so it would not fully address the issue to dismiss the causalist analyses of the latter problem simply by rejecting their assumption that actions always involve intentions. Therefore, I will follow adherents of the standard model in focusing the discussion of antecedential waywardness on cases of intentional actions, or actions allegedly involving intentions.

Adherents of the standard model have tried to answer the challenge arising from cases such as Case 1 by modifying the standard model and specifying additional requirements in order to exclude the possibility of causal deviance.[8] The additional requirement that most readily suggests itself is that the mental antecedents must cause

---

[7] Brand (1984), 18. Mele has introduced a third category, 'tertiary waywardness', (1987), 58, in order to cover cases where the agent has made a mistake prior to the action and it is only by accident that he successfully does what he intends to do (for examples, see Ginet (1990), 78, and Mele and Moser (1994), 247 f.). It is questionable whether such an additional category is truly needed; but we can leave this question aside, because we only have to discuss the problem of antecedential waywardness.

[8] Ironically, the most prominent proponent of the causal analysis—Davidson—came to believe that an elimination of 'wrong' causal chains is impossible without thereby abandoning the standard model. This was a consequence of his thesis of the anomalousness of the mental, due to which a strictly reductive account of agency in physical terms—which would presuppose strict psychophysical laws—could not be presented, anyway. Cf. Davidson (1973a), 80.

the bodily motion *in the right way*. But how can we spell out the difference between the right way and wrong ways in which the result might be caused ? Obviously, the right way cannot simply be specified as the way required for an (intentional) action, if the standard model is to offer, as intended, a *reductive* account of human agency. But is it possible to provide an adequate, non-circular account of what counts as the right causal route from mental antecedents to bodily behaviour?

It might be objected here that this is not a task which can fairly be put to philosophers. In the course of time, the 'right' causal route will be discovered by neurophysiologists when they enquire more closely into the functioning of the nervous system when actions are performed, but this result cannot be expected from philosophical analysis. Along these lines, Alvin Goldman has argued that solving the problem of waywardness is not a genuinely philosophical task, but should be delegated to neurophysiologists, because only the latter, by empirical research, can discover the 'detailed delineation of the causal process that is characteristic of intentional action'.[9]

But is this a plausible answer to the problem of waywardness? The overwhelming majority of causalists have not thought that it is—and, I think, rightly so. For in the discussion between naturalists and non-reductivists, it is precisely at issue whether the 'right way' in which the behaviour must be caused can be spelled out in purely naturalistic terms, in which a neurophysiological account would be couched. Goldman's proposal already assumes that this is, in principle, possible, which makes it, in the context of this discussion, simply question-begging. What Goldman would need is an additional argument that the task he sets to neurophysiology is a coherent one in the first place, and without such an argument his claim that one day neurophysiology will be able to provide the details is nothing more than a mere expression of faith.[10]

Furthermore, even if we assume that the task Goldman sets to neurophysiology is coherent, it is not plausible to think that it is really a task for neurophysiologists rather than for philosophers. What neurophysiologists could do, on their own, is to delineate, in detail, the particular neurophysiological processes involved in human actions, or to discover statistical prevalences of some such processes in cases when people act (intentionally). But this does not yet amount to distinguishing between deviant and non-deviant causal chains—and it is completely mysterious how this further step is something which natural scientists could do on their own. Deviant causal chains are not necessarily very unusual. Agency is neither guaranteed by statistical prevalence of the causal chain involved nor excluded *per se* if this chain is very unusual. Nor do deviant causal chains flout any natural laws. What they do not conform to are only the conditions arising from our concept of human agency and agential control. This kind of deviance is not one that could be read off from neurophysiological processes themselves; from the point of view of natural science, one causal chain is as good as

---

[9] Goldman (1970), 62.
[10] Cf. Bishop (1989), 144; Wilson (1989), 250.

any other.[11] What will be needed, instead, for qualifying a causal chain as being of the right kind, will be an argument that this chain realizes the agent's control over his behaviour—and I, for one, cannot see how this further argument could be anything but a philosophical one.[12]

Causalists, in general, have therefore been correct in attempting to describe for themselves the right causal route from mental antecedents to bodily behaviour required for realizing agential control, rather than delegating this task to neurophysiologists. Among the different proposals that causalists have put forward, we can distinguish four main strategies[13] which are both most widely defended in the philosophical literature today and appear most promising with regard to answering the challenge of antecedential waywardness:[14]

(a) *Causal immediacy*: According to this strategy, a simple structural requirement on the event-causal chain can exclude deviance. There is an older version which claims that temporal immediacy—simultaneousness of cause (intention) and effect (behaviour)—excludes the possibility of deviance.[15] A more recent version focuses on causal immediacy, arguing that in intentional action the intention must be the immediate (or proximate), initiating cause of the physiological chain that leads to the overt behaviour.[16]

(b) *Sensitivity*: The key idea of this strategy is that in intentional action the agent's behaviour must be sensitive to the content of the agent's intention in a way that it is not when it is caused by intervening nervousness which prevents the agent's control.[17] One way to spell out the required sensitivity is Christopher Peacocke's requirement of differential explicability of the behaviour by the intention.[18] Alternatively, the sensi-

---

[11] Cf. Kenny (1975), 121 fn. 6.
[12] Cf. Brand (1984), 19; Keil (2000), 85.
[13] Another strategy, which enjoyed some popularity in the 1980s, relied on self-referential intentions or decisions. When one has an intention, it was claimed, the intention's content is not merely that one will do A, but that 'because of that very intention, it is guaranteed that one will do A'—Harman (1976), 158—or that one's intention or choice will explain one's action; cf. Donagan (1987), 91. In cases of waywardness, it was argued, such an explanation is impossible and the intention is not fulfilled. This strategy faces two main difficulties. On the one hand, there are doubts whether the underlying view about the self-referential content of intentions is plausible or even coherent in the first place; cf. Moya (1990), 128; Mele (1992), 204. On the other hand, even in cases of waywardness the resulting behaviour *can* be explained by appeal to the agent's intention, and so it seems that even an intention with a self-referential content would be satisfied here. Therefore, the self-referential explanation strategy seems no better off in dealing with the causal deviance problem than the original causalist analysis, and will not have any advantage over the latter so long as no workable account of self-referential explanation is developed which shows how this notion is more restricted than the notion of causal explanation.
[14] Not all of these strategies are mutually exclusive; for example, Bishop (1989), 171, combines (b) and (c).
[15] Mitchell (1982), 353, Alston (1986), 278.
[16] Brand (1984), 19 ff., (1989), 423 ff.; adopted by Mele (1992), 201.
[17] This core idea of the sensitivity strategy was first spelt out by Morton (1975), 14.
[18] Peacocke (1979a), 128 ff., (1979b) 66 ff. An even stricter version of this requirement, connecting it with the causal powers account of Harré and Madden, forms the centre of Shope's analysis, (1991), 265 ff.

tivity can be understood in terms of patterns of counterfactual dependence of the behaviour on the content of the agent's intention.[19]

(c) *Sustaining causation*: While the approaches (a) and (b) can, in principle, restrict the causal role of intentions to the initiation or triggering of the causal chain leading to the behaviour, this strategy insists that the intention must continue to causally interact with the behaviour for the duration of the action, sustaining or guiding its course. The notion of sustaining causation is normally explained by appeal to feedback systems as they appear in cybernetic theories of purposive behaviour.[20]

(d) *The new 'manifestation' approaches*: Contrary to the earlier approaches, this strategy altogether discards the idea that deviance might by excluded solely by structural requirements on the event-causal chain from mental antecedents to bodily behaviour. Instead, the strategy takes into account the underlying system which produces the behaviour and its characteristic functioning, its Aristotelian nature or causal powers. Only in cases of (intentional action), the agent's behaviour is a manifestation of the well-functioning of the system, or a realization of the system's potentialities or causal powers.[21]

In the following sections we will examine these four causalist proposals in turn. However, before we can do this we must complete an important preliminary task. In order to provide the basis for assessing the merits of the particular proposals, we must first determine which standard of adequacy has to be met by a successful proposal that can claim to convincingly naturalize the phenomenon of agency.

5.2. The standard of adequacy for a causalist analysis

To determine which standard of adequacy a causalist analysis has to meet, we must, first and foremost, answer the question to what extent a causalist analysis has to accord with our pre-theoretical views and linguistic intuitions about the extension of the concept of action and the grounds for its application. In other words, we must determine to what extent a naturalist analysis has to respect, and to what extent it can ignore, both the intensional and the extensional aspects of this concept. Doing this is crucially important for assessing the outlook of the project of 'naturalizing human agency', and the widespread neglect of this question by causalists is not merely a matter of lacking self-reflection. It also becomes acutely relevant when we deal with the analysis of deviance, where the dialectical impact of counter-examples and the importance of certain aspects of the meaning of 'action' can be decisive for the result of the discussion.

---

[19] Bishop (1989), 150, sketches this possibility—without, however, endorsing it over Peacocke's version.
[20] Frankfurt (1978), 74 f.; Bach (1978); Thalberg (1984), 257; Alston (1986), 284 ff.; Bishop (1989), 167 ff.; Adams/Mele (1989), 511 ff.; Mele (2000) und (2003) 54 ff.
[21] Enc (2003), 106; Stout (1996), 51, 89; (2005), 95. Stoecker (2003), 310.

To answer this question we must become clear about what the causalist analysis really wants to achieve. At first glance, the aim is simply to provide a reductive analysis of action that does not rely on any of the concepts entailing agential activity which we normally use and which does not contain any agent-causal residues. This general reductive aim obviously rules out certain 'simple' ways of answering the problem of antecedential waywardness—such as saying that the causal chain must realize the agent's control.

So far, the matter seems quite straightforward. But when we characterize the causalist enterprise as the project of giving an event-causal *analysis* of action, this characterization is ambiguous. It can be understood to mean that causalists want to provide a *conceptual analysis* of our existing concept of action—that they want to explain what we *mean* when we assert that an action has been performed. But, alternatively, causalists might not care about synonymy or conceptual connections between our everyday assertions and the proposed explanation of the term,[22] and only be concerned with spelling out necessary and sufficient conditions for an action to take place. The crucial difference is, of course, that the connection between these conditions and the occurrence of the action need not be conceptual in the latter case, but can be conceptually contingent, e.g. based only on laws of nature.

One might even think that the causalists' aim is a still weaker sense of 'analysis': namely, only that of spelling out the conditions that are contingently satisfied whenever an action is performed, without even the requirement of necessity and sufficiency by natural laws—only of explaining what happens whenever someone acts (and vice versa).[23] But as this possible interpretation of the causalist project does not, in the present context, raise any other difficulties than the second one, I will not discuss it separately here.

Causalists have rarely been explicit on which of the two senses of 'analysis' they want to rely.[24] So, in order to decide which sense is relevant for the causalist enterprise, we can do no better than turn to the general naturalistic project of which their analysis of action is a particular instance. This general project can plausibly be understood as the enterprise to fit various phenomena into a naturalist framework, which, so it is claimed, accords with the 'scientific picture of the world', as we have seen in Chapter 1. What causalists want to show with regard to the phenomenon of 'action' is how it 'has a place' or 'can be realized' in such a framework. Given the naturalist assumption that this framework *is* the framework of reality, this would amount to clarifying what actions really are. The notion of natural realization that is relevant to this project does not amount to a notion of synonymy, and therefore causalists do not have to provide a

---

[22] Like an 'analysis' or 'explication' in Quine's sense; cf. Quine (1960), 258 f.
[23] I presuppose here that the third sense is really different from the second—that the notions of sufficiency and necessity cannot be analysed in terms of mere coextensionality of concepts.
[24] A notable exception is Bishop. The following formulation of the causalist project is, for this reason, based to a large extent on his considerations in (1989), ch.1 and 3.

conceptual analysis of action in the strict sense—that is, one where the analysans is synonymous with the analysandum.

That synonymy is not required for this project becomes clear when we compare the project of naturalizing action with another particular naturalist project: that of showing how mental states fit into the presumed framework—for example, by a functionalist analysis. Here too, the analysis is not intended to capture the whole meaning of the mental-state concept, though it is claimed that the functionally defined state *constitutes* the mental state. For example, a philosopher who presents a purely functional analysis of 'love' need not claim that 'love' is synonymous with 'a mental state that causes…and is caused by…', but may accept that there are certain aspects of the meaning of 'love' which his analysis fails to capture. It may happen that these further aspects of our everyday concept cannot be captured within what naturalists consider as the 'framework of reality', and naturalist philosophers could (and would) deny either that they are part of the descriptive content of such concepts or that they are anything more than misconceived elements of our existing concepts.

So, if we look back at our original dichotomy concerning 'analysis', it seems that the causalist analysis must only provide necessary and sufficient conditions for an action to take place. But will the specification of *any* such conditions suffice, even if it is conceptually contingent that they occur whenever an action occurs? Or must the analysis fulfil a further constraint?

Assume that neurophysiological research would somehow succeed in establishing that certain neurophysiological processes must obtain whenever an action is performed (given the extension of our everyday concept of action), and that these processes can obtain only in cases where an action is performed. This result would provide necessary and sufficient conditions for actions, where the relevant sense of necessity is necessity based on natural laws and regularities. But this result would *not* suffice for a successful naturalist 'analysis' of action, and it would not (yet) provide all that is required for realizing the general naturalist project. For there is a crucial difference between 'what must happen whenever A obtains and can happen only when A obtains' and 'what constitutes A'—that is, a difference between the relation of necessary concomitance in nature and the relation of constitution. Without further argument we cannot infer from the fact that the first relation holds that the second one also holds. Thus, consider the case of a person whose neurophysiological set-up is such that when and only when he raises his arm, his lip must twitch nervously in a certain way. In the case of this person, the particular twitching of his lip is a necessary and sufficient condition of his raising his arm—but obviously we cannot infer from this that the twitching of the lip is a constitutive part of his arm-raising.

Similarly, with regard to underlying neurophysiological processes, many such processes have to occur when I raise my arm, because without them I would not be able to raise my arm; and probably some of these processes can, as a matter of fact, happen only when I raise my arm. But this does not yet show that these processes *constitute* my raising my arm, for they might only be necessary and sufficient conditions for the execution of my ability to raise my arm, and the imagined neurophysiological findings have not shown that this latter factor could be cancelled out from the action.

In order to make the step from necessary and sufficient conditions for actions to a claim about what actions consist in, we need a further argument that shows us that the regularly concomitant structures really do constitute actions. Without such an argument, it would be mere dogmatism on the causalists' part to insist that since the regularly concomitant structures are all that can be found in the event-causal framework, they *must* constitute the action—for this would amount to just dogmatically presupposing the framework, instead of being prepared to adapt it in the light of recalcitrant phenomena. This point is conceded by Bishop, who agrees that if the causalist could only provide necessary and sufficient conditions for action, he would leave 'open the possibility of continued puzzlement about how *the actions themselves* can be naturally realized'.[25]

We can go even further than Bishop, though, when we remember the dialectical situation between naturalist causalists and their opponents concerning the naturalization of agency, discussed in Section 2.3.3. As we saw there, the initial presumption is against the possibility of naturalizing agency, and so the burden of proof in the discussion clearly lies with the causalist. This means that failure to provide an argument that the putatively concomitant neurophysiological structures really constitute the actions amounts not only to leaving room for a 'possibility of continued puzzlement', as Bishop claims, but to a wholesale failure of the project of the naturalizing project, because the burden of proof will not have been discharged.

What further argument is required of a causalist analysis to establish the constitution claim, if we do not want to go so far as to claim that synonymy is needed? Bishop himself suggests that the correlation must 'emerge[s] from a conceptual investigation of agency'; that is, it must be inconceivable—at least for worlds similar to ours—that the natural conditions identified by the analysis obtain without the occurrence of an action, and vice versa.[26] If an analysis satisfies this requirement, it would be reasonable to suppose, so Bishop argues, that, 'at least across all possible worlds with the same natural ontology and causal order as the metaphysics of naturalism holds the actual world to have', the necessary and sufficient conditions identified by the analysis ontologically *constitute* actions.[27] For, he argues, the requirement of a further non-naturalist element of action which has not yet been captured would then only amount to a dogmatic rejection of naturalism.

A comparison with other instances of the general naturalist project suggests that this is the standard generally followed by such analyses. Functionalist analyses of mental states—although they do not claim synonymy of analysans and analysandum—argue

---

[25] Bishop (1989), 97.
[26] Loc. cit.
[27] Loc. cit.; cf. also Bishop (1989), 179.

that there is a conceptual link between the claims 'A has a belief' and 'A is in a mental state that together with desires can cause actions and…', which we discover when we investigate how our concept of this mental state is connected to the concepts of other states. In consequence, they will claim that competent speakers can acknowledge that in a sense, belief is 'nothing but' a functionally characterized mental state.

Given our considerations about the dialectical situation, Bishop's requirement should be seen as the minimum that a naturalist has to satisfy in order to give plausibility to his claim that actions are constituted by events or event-causal chains. For as we have seen, there is the *prima facie* suspicion that the event-causalist 'scientific picture of the world', which naturalists take to be the adequate picture of reality, fails to capture the phenomenon of agency, with which the natural sciences are not concerned. In order to dispel this suspicion, the naturalist has to show that within this framework we find something that we can reasonably identify with actions, because it follows from our concept of action that 'nothing more is required' for an action to take place.

Contrary to Bishop's own view, however, I think that even if the causalist succeeds in satisfying Bishop's requirement, we are not forced to accept that actions are ontologically constituted by the event-causal processes which the causalist describes. For in addition to the problem of identification discussed in Chapters 3 and 4, we may in any case have good reasons for rejecting a purely event-causal framework (as I will argue in the next chapters). But in discussing the problem of antecedential waywardness we can primarily focus on Bishop's requirement. For if the causalist can provide an analysis satisfying this requirement, this will at least show that accounting for the right mode of agential control will not force us to reject the naturalist event-causal framework.

We should thus adopt Bishop's adequacy condition. The main difference to the stronger requirement of synonymy lies in the appeal which an analysis can make to newly developed models of scientific explanation—to cybernetic models, for example. It would be a tall order to claim synonymy with the term 'action' for an analysis based on such models. But if we only require that it should emerge from a conceptual investigation that the occurrence of a process described in terms of such a model is necessary and sufficient for an action to take place, it is much more plausible that this requirement might be satisfied. For this only presupposes that when presented with such models and understanding them, competent speakers would accept the analysis based on them as a reasonable account of 'what actions really are', and accept that actions are 'really *nothing but* this'.

Though primarily concerning the intensional adequacy of an analysis—such as the question of whether a conceptual connection of analysans and analysandum is required—the adoption of Bishop's requirement also has consequences for the degree of extensional adequacy required for a satisfactory analysis. This is the question as to what extent, for the phenomenon F to be analysed, the extension of our pre-existing everyday concept of F and the extension of F on the offered analysis must coincide. While what we may call a revisionary approach will react to divergences by telling us to 'doctor our linguistic intuitions' about the cases in question, so as to fit the proposed analysis, a descriptive approach will take cases of divergence as decisive arguments against the proposed analysis.[28] Of course, a revisionary approach must also require considerable overlap between what the analysis rules as actions and what our pre-existing concept does, in order to plausibly claim that agency, instead of another related phenomenon, has been shown to be realized in nature. But, on the edges, so to speak, this approach will allow for trade-offs.

Causalists themselves are rarely very clear about the degree to which they think themselves at liberty to follow a revisionary course.[29] But if a causalist analysis is to satisfy Bishop's requirement, clearly it must accord with our key intuitions about the application of the concept of action. This means that at least insofar as counter-examples rely on central intuitions about agency, a causalist cannot neglect these counter-examples by appealing to the general explanatory value of his theory. When such cases occur, the causalist analysis must be modified or abandoned if the idea of a conceptual connection is to have any force.

We can thus conclude that a causalist analysis of action will be successful only if it offers necessary and sufficient event-causal conditions for the occurrence of an action, and we cannot, given worlds similar to ours, conceive that these conditions are fulfilled without an action taking place (and vice versa). This also means that a satisfactory analysis must be generally descriptive; that is, whenever central intuitions about the concept of action are concerned, recalcitrant counter-examples cannot be dismissed, no matter how successful the analysis is in dealing with other cases.

5.3. The 'immediate causation' strategy

After preparing the ground by examining the standard of adequacy which a successful causalist answer to the problem has to meet, we can now turn to the task of assessing the four causalist analyses of action sketched in Section 5.1.

Let us begin with the causal immediacy strategy, which tries to solve the problem of waywardness by a structural requirement on the causal chain running from mental antecedent to overt behaviour. The simple idea behind this strategy is that wayward causal chains can occur only because there is a temporal or causal gap between the antecedents and the behaviour for such chains to fill up. By eliminating this gap we would also exclude the possibility of waywardness. This idea is suggested by looking at older causalist analyses, such as Davidson's in *Actions, Reasons, and Causes*, which

---

[28] To borrow two terms of Strawson (1959), introduction, i—although the 'descriptive'/'revisionary' distinction used here does not exactly coincide with Strawson's distinction of 'descriptive' versus 'revisionary' metaphysics.

[29] Bishop, when considering a case of what he calls heteromesial waywardness, ponders whether, given the explanatory benefits of his proposed analysis, we should not tutor our intuitions about these recalcitrant cases to fit the analysis; (1989), 163. Brand proposes a totally 'revisionary' analysis when suggesting the 'naturalization of action theory'; (1984), introduction, x.

focus exclusively on the action's prior causal history, thus courting the possibility of intervening factors shortly before or during the time of the action itself.

Earlier versions of the immediacy strategy have focused only on the temporal aspect, and have tried to eliminate the time-span between the mental antecedents and the behaviour by requiring the mental state to be temporally concurrent with the behaviour. For example, Searle's appeal to intentions-in-action, which are simultaneous with the behaviour which they cause, can be seen as part of such a strategy.[30] But although it is true that older causalist theories, such as Davidson's, were particularly vulnerable to cases of waywardness[31] by neglecting what was happening at the time of the action itself, it is mistaken to think that the introduction of a causal factor simultaneous with the behaviour could, by itself, solve this problem.

First, the idea that simultaneousness of cause and effect excludes the possibility of intervening causal waywardness is only as plausible as the idea that simultaneousness between cause and effect excludes any intermediary *causal* links; for once we allow any such links, nothing guarantees that these links do not constitute a deviant causal chain. But the idea that simultaneous causation excludes intermediary causal links is implausible on its own once we accept the possibility of simultaneous causation at all. For instance, take Kant's classical example of simultaneous causation—of a weight sinking into a cushion, thus causing a depression in the cushion's surface.[32] In this case we could equally well imagine that the weight causes the depression only indirectly, such as by causing the depression of a cushion placed on top of the other one, while cause and effect are still simultaneous. So, simultaneousness between cause and effect cannot guarantee causal immediacy. Second, excluding intermediary causal links between the mental antecedents and the ensuing behaviour would raise great difficulties for the causalist analysis of action itself, because the mental antecedents certainly do not cause the bodily behaviour directly, but only via intervening neurophysiological processes.

The latter problem also faces the more recent version of the 'immediacy' strategy. This version, recognizing that simultaneous causation does not exclude indirect causation, postulates *causal* immediacy between mental antecedents and behaviour *tout court*. For example, Brand's 'immediacy strategy' is based on a notion of proximate causation which includes the absence of any intermediate events that are caused themselves by the proximate cause, and in turn cause the result. As Brand is aware that there will be intervening neurophysiological mechanisms between intention and behaviour, he does not claim that intentions proximately cause the outward behaviour, but only that they proximately initiate the neurophysiological event-causal chain leading to the bodily motions. But what about the possibility of waywardness during the neurophysiological processes? Surprisingly, Brand considers the route from the initial neurophysiological events to the bodily motion as irrelevant for the question of

---

[30] Searle (1983), 84 ff.
[31] Cf. Frankfurt (1978), 43.
[32] Kant, *Critique of Pure Reason*, B 248.

whether an action has been performed—with the sole exception that this causal route must not contain the intervention of another person.[33] However, this gives up the whole point of the intended analysis; for obviously, some courses which the event-causal neurophysiological chain can take will exclude agential control, even if we leave out cases of intervention by another person. For example, if nervousness is neurophysiologically realized, then all the classical cases of antecedential waywardness, where the intention causes the behaviour only via control-preempting nervousness, can be replicated against Brand's account.[34]

Basically, the same objection can be raised against the arguments proposed by Alfred Mele, who adopts Brand's immediacy strategy for his analysis of intentional action. Mele tries to exclude the possibility of waywardness on the causal pathway from intention to bodily motion by claiming that the intention proximally causes the action. For this, he must assume that the action includes the whole neurophysiological chain leading to the bodily motions, beginning with the neurophysiological events purportedly immediately caused by the intention.[35] However, as a result of this move Mele's thesis that intentional actions are those immediately caused by intentions can no longer be used to deal with the possibility of waywardness arising within the neurophysiological chain now included in the action. (Mele has, by his 'sustaining causation' account, a different answer to this question, but this answer has nothing to do with causal immediacy.)

This objection is, on my view, already decisive against the appeal to immediate causation to solve the problem of antecedential waywardness. But even if this problem for the immediacy strategy could somehow be solved, there remains the even more fundamental worry that the notion of immediate causation of one event by another is conceptually suspect.[36] Brand claims that it follows, from the assumptions that chains of causally related events are not dense and that events have temporal duration, that all events which have causes have proximate causes—and he thinks that these assumptions are borne out by 'the common-sense vantage point'.[37] But this is highly implausible. It is true that we often say that event A caused event B without thereby claiming or implying that there was another event, C, via which A caused B. But this is very different from positively assuming that the event-causal chain is not dense; that is, from assuming that at one point we could not, for any given events A and B, ask via which event A caused B. There is no reason to think that we make any such positive assumption. In fact, if common sense takes any stand on the question at all, it is more

---

[33] Brand (1984), 20 ff.
[34] Brand's own arguments for neglecting the causal route of the neurophysiological processes fail to address this issue, because he only discusses cases where there is an unusual intervening mechanism, which does *not* (obviously) exclude the agent's control; cf. op. cit., 21.
[35] Mele (1992), 202.
[36] Doubts of this kind are tentatively voiced by Bishop (1989), 139, who asks whether we have reason to think this notion any more coherent 'than a corresponding notion of "proximate" points on a line'.
[37] Brand (1989), 430.

likely to be the contrary assumption that for any event-causal link, however close cause and effect might be, science could dig even deeper and uncover the stages of a causal chain connecting the two. But without the assumption that event-causal chains in nature are not dense, the whole notion of proximate causation becomes unintelligible.

Thus, we must conclude that appealing to simultaneous or immediate causation will not help us to solve the problem of wayward causal chains.

5.4. Sensitivity strategies

While the causal immediacy strategy tries to exclude the possibility of antecedential waywardness simply by a requirement on the structure of the actual causal chain from intention to bodily behaviour, sensitivity strategies recognize this focus as too limited. What is needed for agency, on their account, is sensitivity of the behaviour to the content of the agent's intention. That *some* such requirement must hold is clear; for, normally, in cases of intentional actions, it must be true that the agent would act differently if he intended to do so—at least for a sufficient range of possible alternatives. Adherents of the sensitivity strategy explain the notion of sensitivity either in terms of counterfactual dependence, or in terms of a requirement on the explanatory connection between the intention and the resultant behaviour. As the differences between these two accounts are not decisive for the following discussion, I will mainly concentrate on one form of the latter version which has been developed by Christopher Peacocke.

On Peacocke's view, cases of deviance are distinguished from cases of intentional actions by failure of a certain kind of differential explanation of the bodily behaviour by the intention-state. Differential explanation of A by B requires, roughly, on Peacocke's account, (i) that B is a non-redundant part of the explanation of A, and (ii) that the laws backing this explanation contain functions correlating the relevant features of A with the relevant features of B.[38] A condition of mere differential explanation, however, will not suffice to exclude cases of deviance, for even constant functions, which clearly fail to capture the idea of sensitivity of outcome to input, would satisfy this condition.[39] Instead, what is needed is what Peacocke calls a condition of 'strongly differential explanation', which presupposes one-to-one functions between the relevant features of A and B, thus allowing recoverability of the cause-state from the effect-state.[40] On this account, what is characteristic for cases of deviant causal chains is that there are no such one-to-one functions correlating the relevant features of the behaviour and of the intention.

While Peacocke's account has been subjected to a number of criticisms, I will focus only on what I consider to be the two main objections.

---

[38] Peacocke (1979b), 66.
[39] Cf. Sehon (1997), 207.
[40] Peacocke (1979b), 79 f.

a) A major controversy has developed over Peacocke's treatment of cases of 'alien interveners'. Imagine a scenario where a very clever neurophysiologist reads off the intentions you have and brings about exactly the bodily behaviour you intend to perform.[41] In this case, the condition of strongly differential explanation is satisfied with regard to your intentions and your bodily motions, for the neurophysiologist would cause another bodily motion if you intended to act differently. However, his intervention preempts your own control over your behaviour, and thus excludes the latter from being a result of *your* agency.

Peacocke himself has reacted to this difficulty by stipulating that in non-deviant cases, the causal 'chain from intention to movement must not run through the intentions of another person'.[42] But from the standpoint of the sensitivity approach as a whole, this move is very much ad hoc, and the need for an independent additional condition makes it doubtful that sensitivity really provides the key to understanding causal deviance.[43]

Even worse, Peacocke's amended analysis will not work, because his general exclusion of causal chains running through another person's intentions is too strict, as the following case shows. Due to an accident, A has suffered severe nerve and muscle damage to his left arm, with the consequence that he is now no longer able to clench his left fist, except if he holds the biceps of the arm tightly to prevent it from trembling.[44] It is crucial that tightly holding the biceps does not make A's fist clench automatically, but that it is still A's decision whether or not he clenches his fist. Normally, A is able to hold the biceps with his right hand, but unfortunately, in another accident, he breaks his right hand. Being unable to use it to hold the biceps of his left arm, he asks B to hold the biceps for him, and now A is able to clench his fist, which he finally does. In this case there is no reason to assume that A did not clench his fist himself; after all, we are often able to perform actions only because others make it possible for us to do so. Nonetheless, the causal chain from intention to behaviour runs through B's intention and behaviour, and so the case would be ruled—falsely—as deviant on Peacocke's account.[45]

Thus, with regard to the intervention of other persons, Peacocke fails to provide a rationale for distinguishing deviant from non-deviant cases—which is a decisive failure of his account. An adherent of the sensitivity approach cannot successfully argue that

---

[41] Op. cit., 87.
[42] Op. cit., 88. Peacocke here takes up a suggestion of Pears (1975), 66.
[43] Peacocke was attacked on this ground by Bishop (1981), (1985), and (1986), 240f.; while Montmarquet defended Peacocke's account in (1982) and (1986), arguing that it could exclude cases of alien intervention without circularity by relying on a 'recursive' definition of action. Bishop (1989), 158, has accepted this defence of the sensitivity strategy, while McCann (1998), 122, still raises the arbitrariness objection.
[44] A person suffering from Parkinson's disease can at least lower the intensity of the fits of trembling to which he is subject by exerting pressure on his chin, I have been told.
[45] Bishop (1989), 159, has a more fanciful example of broken electric wires of a prosthetic device being held together by another person.

failure to deal with alien interveners is irrelevant because these cases are too fanciful or absurd to play a role in determining what actions really are, for the standard of adequacy for causalist analyses developed in Section 5.2 excludes that scenarios which we can well conceive and where we are, pre-theoretically, certain that the agent has (not) acted, may be assessed differently by a successful causalist analysis. The scenarios of alien interventions are of this kind, and therefore cannot be ignored by the causalist.

b) The second main difficulty for Peacocke's account arises from cases of 'coarse-grained' abilities to act, which show that actions do not really *require* strongly differential explanations. To develop this objection we must first clarify which features of the intention-state the sensitivity approach takes to be correlated with features of the behaviour by one-to-one functions. Peacocke himself thinks that the relevant features of the behaviour depend on the *neurophysiological* features of the intention-state;[46] alternatively, the features of the behaviour could depend on the *content* of the intention.

Peacocke's own version of the differential requirement is faced with the difficulty that it is not at all clear how a requirement of this kind is supposed to exclude causal deviance. For there is not even a *prima facie* reason to assume that there cannot be one-to-one functions relating neurophysiological features of the intention-state to features of the behaviour, when the latter is caused via a control-preempting intermediate state like nervousness.[47] On the contrary, it is even plausible to positively assume that such one-to-one functions can be found, for in some respects the nervousness state and the behaviour are always bound to be different, from one occasion to another. As Peacocke thus lacks any positive grounds for claiming that strongly differential explanation between the features he envisages will exclude antecedential deviance, we do well to discard his version and turn to the alternative version which correlates features of the behaviour to features of the content of the intention.

This latter version has some intuitive appeal, for as we have already noted, dependence of the behaviour on the content of the agent's intention is an essential part of intentional agency. Nevertheless, a strongly differential explanation of the behaviour by the intention's content is not necessary for agency.

This becomes clear when we consider cases where the agent has a very precise intention, but his abilities to act are too coarse to allow for a one-to-one fit between the content of his intention and his behaviour. Consider the following example by Scott Sehon:[48] A baseball pitcher tries to move his arm at a speed of 70 mph, and

---

[46] This is, at least, the most plausible reading of Peacocke's claim that the behaviour is differentially explained by the neurophysiological state that realizes the intention, (1979b), 70.

[47] As Sehon (1997), 211, has rightly pointed out, the reason for this lack of even a *prima facie* case is that, on the level of neurophysiological features, there are simply no intuitions parallel to the one about a rough correlation between the content of the intention and the behaviour in intentional action, which has originally motivated the sensitivity approach.

[48] Sehon (1997), 209.

succeeds. Though the fast movement of his arm is an intentional action, we need not assume that the movement would have had a correspondingly greater or smaller velocity had the agent's intention been to move his arm at 69 or 71 mph. Instead, we may well believe that even if the pitcher had intended to move his arm at 69 or 71 mph, his actual speed would have remained the same. So we need not assume that there is a one-to-one function correlating the behaviour with the content of the intention in order to classify the pitcher's behaviour as an (intentional) action.[49]

A defender of the sensitivity strategy might react to such cases by claiming that no precise one-to-one fit between the intention's content and the ensuing behaviour is required for agency, but only a 'sufficiently tight' correlation—a correlation of certain ranges of the intention's content to ranges of behaviour. However, such a move seems to give up the central idea of strongly differential explanation as the key to agency, because this kind of explanation requires one-to-one-correlations. Besides, the move will not help the causalist to escape the problem of antecedential deviance, as limiting cases of 'coarse-grained' abilities to act—'on–off' abilities—make clear.

To see this, compare the case of agent A, who is able to wiggle his ears at will and does so, with the case of another agent B, who mistakenly thinks he is able to wiggle his ears and forms an intention to do so, which deviantly causes a wiggling of his ears. Let us assume that A is not a perfectionist ear-wiggler: The wiggling is an 'on–off' affair with him; that is, he can only 'simply wiggle', but cannot wiggle in specific ways. Now, with regard to sensitivity of the ensuing bodily motion to the content of the intention, both cases are identical. Both agents' ears would not have wiggled had they failed to have the intention, and no relevant further dependences between bodily motions and intentions hold in either case. So, an adherent of the sensitivity approach must either rule both as cases where the differential explanation criterion is satisfied, and therefore both as cases of actions, or neither. But both solutions are wrong. While A has performed an action, B has not, because, *ex hypothesi*, he could not wiggle his ears at will.

The same difficulty arises for all cases of 'on–off' abilities, where the agent can move a limb in only one way without further control over how it is moved—for example, when an agent's finger is almost totally paralyzed by gout and he can only move it in one direction, without any control over the distance or force with which he moves it.[50]

---

[49] This does not refute the principle discussed in Section 2.2, that for intentional action, when the action does not conform to what the agent intends to do and the agent realizes this, he would act differently—for this principle does not require the existence of one-to-one correlations between bodily behaviour and intentions, but is already satisfied by much looser correlations.

[50] Using cases of 'on–off' abilities, we can even construct—rather fancifully—examples which show that sensitivity is not always *sufficient* for action. Assume that an agent is able to move his finger in all directions but one (because, for example, the nerves for the control of motions in this direction are damaged). Unaware of this, the agent forms the intention to move his finger in exactly this direction, and his intention deviantly causes the right motion. In this case, the required counterfactuals hold. Had the agent intended to move his finger differently, the finger would have moved in the right way. Nonetheless, the agent did not move his

These considerations show that sensitivity strategies, despite their advantages over immediacy accounts, still fail to cope with the problem of causal deviance.[51] This does not mean that the underlying claim—that in intentional action, the behaviour must be somehow sensitive to what the agent intends to do—must be rejected. It only shows that the sensitivity approach is mistaken in trying to turn this correlation into the basis of a purely event-causal interpretation of agential control.

5.5. Sustaining causation

The strategy to deal with antecedential waywardness which enjoys the widest following among causalists rests on the insight that when we want to explain agential control by the causal role of some of the agent's mental states, we cannot exclusively focus on the *initiation* of the behaviour by these mental states. No 'one-dimensional' causal chain from the mental antecedents to the bodily behaviour, whatever structure it might have, can plausibly be considered as a realization of the agent's control over his behaviour, for this control also includes possible correction of the behaviour and adaptation to changing intentions and circumstances. Strategies like the immediate causation and the sensitivity strategy, which in principle focus only on the triggering causal function of intentions, cannot account for these aspects, and thus neglect an essential element of the agent's control.

In order to account for this element, many philosophers have thought that the intentions must not only initiate the overt behaviour, but continue to causally 'sustain' or 'guide' it throughout the performance of the action. What underlies this locution is the suggestive simile of the guidance of processes by persons—for instance, in Frankfurt's famous example, in which the driver of an automobile controls its course and speed by intervening with adjusting actions whenever he is not satisfied with the course it takes.[52]

However, Frankfurt's simile presupposes an agent who acts intentionally in order to reach an aim and who monitors the movement of the car in order to see whether it is

---

finger on this occasion. Thus, strongly differential explanation of the motion by the content of the intention is neither sufficient nor necessary for the motion to be the result of an action.

[51] Enc (2003), 105, has pointed out a further difficulty for the sensitivity approach which arises from the possible exploitation of non-sensitive mechanisms. For example, an actor may know from experience that whenever he intends to shake his hand as if nervous, and imagines how to do it, he really becomes nervous and his hand (deviantly) begins to tremble. As he has understood this mechanism, he is now able to consciously exploit it to produce shaking motions, and when he exploits it the resulting trembling motion is the result of an action which he has performed. As the causal chains are identical when he exploits the mechanism and when he does not, and therefore satisfy the sensitivity requirement to exactly the same degree, this seems to show that sensitivity is not required for non-deviance. However, exploitation cases are not counter-examples to a sensitivity account for *antecedential* deviance, for in exploitation cases the result is brought about by doing something else—in our case, imagining how to shake one's hand as if nervous—and is not the result of a basic action. So, for our question of antecedential waywardness, exploitation cases are inconclusive.

[52] Frankfurt (1978), 47 f.

necessary for him to intervene correctively. Thus it cannot be directly transferred to the case of sustaining causation by a mental state, because the latter, trivially, cannot literally perform these functions.[53] Can causalists explicate the notion of 'causal guidance' by mental states also without recourse to anthropomorphic similes?

5.5.1. How sustaining causation works: negative feedback models of action

What seems to provide an explication of causal guidance is the notion of servosystems which incorporate negative feedback mechanisms. This notion, developed in cybernetics, has proved a very powerful tool for understanding many biological systems. Negative feedback mechanisms in general are systems which keep certain features—of the system's output, its internal state, or external conditions—relatively stable despite tendencies to the contrary, because they counteract deviations from a certain pre-set range of values by means of feedback loops.[54]

A very simple instance of a negative feedback mechanism is a thermostat which keeps the temperature in a room at an approximately constant level. The thermostat incorporates an electric circuit connecting a power supply to a heating mechanism, and this circuit contains a connecting/disconnecting device that is differentially responsive to changes in temperature. A simple device of this kind is a bi-metallic strip that changes its form as a result of sufficient changes in temperature, due to the different expansion and contraction behaviour of the two metals. By changing its form, the strip disconnects the circuit when the temperature has risen sufficiently, thereby disconnecting the heating mechanism from its power source, and reconnecting it when the temperature has fallen sufficiently. In consequence, as soon as the temperature in the room rises above a certain level, the thermostat switches off the heating mechanism, while switching it on again when the temperature falls beyond a certain level. In this way, the thermostat keeps the room temperature roughly between these two levels.

This simple case already displays all the essential ingredients of a negative feedback mechanism which keeps a certain feature F relatively stable: (i) the system must be capable of emitting at least two different kinds of behaviour, A and B; (ii) A and B must influence the environmental or internal circumstances C1 and C2; (iii) A is adequate for either keeping the values F takes on stable, or bringing them back into the relevant range under circumstances C1, and B under circumstances C2; (iv) the system is able to react to a change from C1 to C2 by switching from A to B and vice versa. What is essential for the system's keeping F stable by negative feedback is that it is *neither* simply a matter of F's remaining constant in the presence of the system, *nor* simply a matter of the behaviour that the system emits; for F may remain constant for other reasons which have nothing to do with the thermostat, and the system may just by chance sometimes

---

[53] A transference of the simile would amount to what Bennett and Hacker (2003), 68 ff, have called the 'mereological fallacy'.

[54] See Woodfield (1976), ch. 11, for a useful general discussion of servosystems and Nagel (1953) for a general discussion of negative feedback.

exhibit the right behaviour to keep F constant, without reacting to changes in the values of F. Instead—crucially—negative feedback is always a *process* rather than a persistent state or a single occurrence, which must involve a system possessing the minimally complex structure described.[55]

Some servosystems, other than thermostats, are much more complex. They can react differentially to many more kinds of circumstances, and they can not only keep certain features stable, but also keep them changing in a specific way. Nevertheless, they all follow the basic model described above.

This explains why servosystems exercise such an enormous appeal for causalists. Not only do we naturally describe their behaviour as 'goal-directed' or use mentalistic vocabulary to describe them, but they also seem to provide us with an explanation of 'control' which cannot be suspected of relying on any hidden agent-causal notions, because the control mechanism is straightforwardly event-causal.

When causalists apply the model of negative feedback processes to actions, they assume that actions too contain negative feedback loops, by means of which the agent's bodily motions are controlled. A natural candidate for determining the pre-set aim—conformity with which is monitored by means of these feedback loops—is the content of the agent's intention. On this picture, the intention itself would sustainingly cause the bodily motion, and its continuing 'control' over this motion would ensure that the agent's body moves in the way that he intends.

The resulting picture of agential control is, roughly, the following. The (acquisition of an) intention starts a process producing a bodily motion which it controls by means of feedback loops. First, a sub-initiating event is caused, which we can understand as the occurrence of a kinaesthetic representation of the first part of the motion to be performed: the motor command (or efferent image). This sub-initiating event causes the first part of the bodily motion, which in turn causes a feedback event: for example, the occurrence of sensory feedback containing a kinaesthetic representation of the motion that has taken place (afferent image).[56] The information transported by the afferent image is then informationally processed; that is, it is checked for match or mismatch with the original representation of the motion to be performed, and a new motor command for the next sub-stage of the bodily motion is emitted. If the checking yields the result that the hitherto produced motion matches the original representation, the motor command for the next part of the bodily motion is emitted; but if the result is one of mismatch, a motor command for a corrective motion is emitted. (In addition, at this stage new information about changes in the agent's environment relevant to the intended bodily motion can be processed and can influence what motor command is emitted next.) This cycle is repeated until either the bodily motion is completed or the performance of the action is finally given up.

---

[55] Woodfield (1976), 186.
[56] Cf. Bach (1978), fn. 12; Adams/Mele (1989), 524 f. For James' ideo-motor theory, which originally introduced these notions, see James (1890), vol. II, 486 ff.

While, naturally, there are many aspects of this model which would merit further discussion, I can, in the following, focus on only two aspects which are of particular importance.

First, the checking event. Talk of 'checking for match and mismatch' is particularly open to anthropomorphic interpretations, which causalists must take care to avoid when describing processes at the sub-personal level. The only acceptable way to understand these descriptions is in terms of systematic causal connections of the different states and events involved. The system must have the disposition to react differentially to sensory feedback; that is, different motor commands must be produced at the next step according to whether or not the afferent image matches the original efferent image.[57] The checking event is, on this model, just the causal interaction between the feedback, the state underlying the whole process, and possibly of other influx of relevant information, which determines what new motor command is emitted. But again it is crucial to remember that also talk of 'content' or 'match of images', when applied at the sub-personal level, is metaphorical, and any literal content of these locutions must be spelled out in terms of the causal role that these 'pictures' play in the feedback process. Only at the personal level of intentions, beliefs, perceptions, and so on, can we non-metaphorically speak of 'representations' or 'content'. Therefore, the ultimate 'cash-value' of such metaphors as 'comparisons of efferent copies with afferent representations' is only (roughly) that a state causes motor commands leading to the completion or the correction of the motion, according to whether or not the motion already matches the content of the intention.

Second, the role of intentions. So far, we have worked on the natural assumption that intentions causally sustain the feedback process, and that their content determines the pre-set aim conformity with which is monitored by the feedback process. But this assumption is too simplistic, and two important modifications are required.

On the one hand, not any intention will do, for we must exclude the possibility of last-minute akrasia or change of intention on the agent's part. Therefore, the acquisition of the intention must be close enough to the beginning of the action—requiring the intention either to be a proximate intention 'to act straight away' or an intention-in-action 'that one is now acting'.[58]

On the other hand, a closer look at the supposed feedback process reveals that we need more fine-grained standards for monitoring the bodily motion during the feedback process than can be provided by the content of an intention. For the content of an intention is 'I am going to F' or 'I am F-ing', where F is an action-type. Thus even the most specific intentions will never be more fine-grained than choosing basic

---

[57] An influential account of the supposed mechanism of 'comparison' in neurophysiology suggests that the central monitor system of the agent uses 'efference-copy' signals of the motor command to 'predict' the sensory outcome. These 'predictions' can then be compared with the actual sensory feedback—which comparison is also crucial for determining whether or not the occurring bodily motions are self-produced. Cf. Frith, Blakemore, and Wolpert (2000), and Blakemore and Decety (2001), 563 f.

[58] Terms from Mele (2000), 290, and Searle (1983), 84. Cf. Section 2.3.1.

actions to be performed. But this standard would only allow for checking *after* the performance of a basic action, not *during* its performance—and it is the latter that is required to account for the agent's control over his bodily motion, if the sustaining causation model is correct.

Causalists therefore have to assume that there is an intermediate and more detailed representation of the bodily motion to be produced, which functions at the sub-personal level and breaks down the bodily motions into smaller parts, thus providing a standard for monitoring during the feedback process. Such representations are normally called 'action-schemata',[59] which are supposed to function as intermediate sustaining causes between intentions and bodily motions. This provides us with a two-level picture of intentional action:[60] the bodily motion is the product of a feedback process which is sustained by an action-schema, which in turn is activated and causally sustained by the proximate intention. That the action-schemata are themselves monitored by intentions is necessary to ensure reaction to changes in our intentions about what basic actions are to be performed, and how.

This two-level picture of intentional action has the signal advantage over a single-level picture—which only includes monitoring by intentions—of promising an analysis of action which shows how both intentional and unintentional actions have the same basis. On the two-level picture, what is crucial *for action* is the level of action-schemata sustaining bodily motion, and it is the feedback process at this level which distinguishes actions from mere bodily motions.[61] In the case of intentional action, only the involvement of the higher level of intentions and its interaction with the lower level is added.

But it is crucial to realize that even in non-intentional actions, mere sustaining causation of a bodily motion by an action-schema cannot be sufficient for agency, but that in addition, some connection to intentions is always needed. This requirement is demonstrated by cases of the Anarchic Hand syndrome, mentioned in Chapter 3.

In Anarchic Hand cases, patients find one of their hands performing movements that they can neither control nor suppress at will, except by using their 'good' hand (or some other part of their body over which they have control). What is striking is that the movements which anarchic hands perform are often highly complex and of an apparently goal-directed structure. In many cases, the affected hand tries to compete with and undo what the person is doing with his good hand—for example, unbuttoning the shirt which the agent is trying to button up.[62] The complexity of the activities

---

[59] Cf. for the 'schema' approach Jeannerod (1997), sec. 2.4.
[60] Cf. Perner's (2003) dual-control model of action, which distinguishes between two such distinct levels of information-processing in action. This basic strategy is widespread among adherents of the control model of action in neurophysiology, though there is an ongoing debate about whether there is an independent 'lower' level of information-processing, separate from the level of intention, which in cases of completely unintentional and automatic actions can produce the behaviour on its own. (Roessler/Eilan (2003), 6 ff., provide a useful overview of this discussion.)
[61] Cf. Perner (2003), 227.
[62] Marcel (2003), 77 f.

of anarchic hands, and their occasionally analogous structure to motions that are part of intentional actions, strongly suggest that their motions can be sustainingly caused by action-schemata (assuming that actional motions are so caused). Thus, if the two-level picture of action only required sustaining causation by action-schemata for agency, the anarchic hand's movement would satisfy this criterion.

But the anarchic hand's motions are not results of actions which the agent performs. The motions, though controlled by inner states at the sub-personal level, are alien to the agent—not only at the phenomenological level, but also, as the complete lack of direct control at the personal level shows, as a matter of fact. In this respect they differ crucially from cases of completely unintentional actions, such as cases of double capture errors. For in the latter cases, the agent could change his behaviour were he to become aware of what he was doing. Due to the lack of agential control we cannot ascribe agency with regard to the anarchic hand's motions to the agent himself, and as we cannot plausibly ascribe agency to the hand itself, we have to conclude that no action is performed at all.[63] This shows that sustaining causation by an action-schema is not sufficient for action.

To deal with cases of anarchic hand, causalists must enrich their analysis of non-intentional action by an element of hypothetical control by the agent's intentions. Even though there is no actual monitoring of the action-schema level by the intention level in unintentional actions, there would be if the agent were both aware of his motions and intended not to perform such motions. This modification yields the following proposal for analysing intentional and non-intentional action on the sustaining causation model:

(1) *Analysis of intentional action.* The agent acquires an intention to move his body in a way F, and by this event an action-schema, which initiates and causally sustains the ensuing behaviour by way of feedback loops in the way described, is activated; the intention continues to causally sustain the functioning of the intervening mechanism involving the action-schema; and the feedback process continues until the basic action specified in the intention has been completed.[64]

(2) *Analysis of unintentional action.* An action-schema initiates and sustainingly causes a bodily motion that fits the content of the action-schema; if the agent were aware of the motion and had the intention to stop it, the intention would deactivate the action-schema.

---

[63] Pace Marcel (2003), who continuously calls them 'actions'.

[64] That intentions normally cause bodily motions only indirectly, via action-schemata, does not mean that they always do so. While the fine-grained monitoring must involve action-schemata, intentions can be directly involved in monitoring and correcting when the agent consciously registers and corrects more significant deviations from what he intends. An illuminating model of the interaction between action-schemata and intentions in monitoring behaviour is suggested by Jeannerod's experiments; cf. Jeannerod (2003), 134 f. These experiments suggests that the conscious level of checking is involved only in greater deviations which make significant perceptible differences to the outcome, while minor corrections are performed at the subconscious level of action-schemata.

5.5.2. *Assessment of the sustaining causation strategy*

The strategy of analysing actions in terms of negative feedback processes has important advantages over the causalist strategies discussed previously. Not only does it provide the causalist with a model of the agent's continuing control over his actions—which has been completely missing from the earlier accounts—but the success of negative feedback models in explaining many biological processes also makes it attractive for an understanding of human action in terms of the same basic notion, in order to assign human action a place not merely in the 'natural order', but also 'in the order of living beings', making it continuous with other phenomena from the realm of biological enquiry. Furthermore, the strategy seems to fit well with many results in neurophysiology, for it appears that many of the neurophysiological functions involved in the performances of actions can be explained as negative feedback processes.[65]

However, all of this does not imply that we can explain action in general as the occurrence of such a process. Even if there are feedback processes that take place whenever we act and only when we act, this at best shows a regular concomitance between actions and such processes. It does not yet show that these processes *constitute* the actions. For, as argued at length in Section 5.2, the constitution claim presupposes, over and above regular concomitance, satisfaction of Bishop's requirement that—at least for worlds similar to ours—it is not conceivable that the specified processes obtain without the occurrence of an action, and vice versa.

This further requirement is not satisfied by the sustaining causation strategy. This becomes clear when we consider two kinds of cases which show that the obtaining of such feedback processes is neither sufficient nor necessary for agency. That the feedback processes are not sufficient is shown by cases of alien intervention; that they are not necessary, by cases of actions not involving feedback.

a) *Alien interveners.* The problem of how to account for cases of interventions by another person in the course of an action is one that we have already encountered when discussing Peacocke's differential explanation strategy. As we have seen, Peacocke tried to deal with these cases by excluding wholesale any such intervention within the causal chain running from the agent's intention to his bodily motion. However, this condition turned out to be too strong, because it excluded cases where the other agent's intervention made possible the agent's own exercise of his ability to act, rather than preempting his control. Is the sustaining causality strategy in a better position to distinguish between the cases of preempting and merely enabling intervention—between the neurophysiologist who reads off your intentions and realizes them for you, and the friendly assistant who tightly clasps the injured man's biceps in order to enable him to clench his fist?

---

[65] For example, those involving 'optimization' principles; cf. Jeannerod (2003), 128f.

Bishop thinks it is, because the feedback loops which occur in the case of the intervening neuroscientist are going back from the bodily motions to the neurophysiologist's apparatus, not to the agent's own brain. Thus, adding a condition on the specific structure of those feedback loops seems to do the trick to distinguish cases of preemptive intervention from merely enabling intervention: namely, the condition that the feedback must go back to the agent's own central mental processes,[66] whose involvement is seen as constitutive for the agent's control.

However, this proposal neglects the possibility that even when the feedback loops must go back to the agent's central mental processes, there is still the danger of deviance within such feedback loops.[67] For we can easily imagine a clever neurophysiologist—as in the counter-example to Peacocke's original account—who now interferes in the stage between the motor command and the motion, causing the latter in accordance with what he 'reads off' from the former, and then allows the feedback loop to go back to the agent's central nervous system where the information continues to be processed. (As the action is itself a continuous process, or the result of one, rather than a one-track causal chain, the neurophysiologist's interventions would also be continuous rather than a one-time affair and adaptive to informational 'updating'.)[68]

With regard to dealing with these cases, Bishop is in no better position than Peacocke. To cope with them, he would have to exclude wholesale the possibility that the relevant feedback processes contain any kind of intervention. But, as in Peacocke's case, this condition would be too strict, because there can be enabling interventions in these feedback processes. We only have to think of cases where another person's continuous contributions are necessary for sustaining the feedback process.

So, in a very similar way to Peacocke, sustaining causation analyses are confronted with the problem of how to distinguish cases of agency-preempting interventions from cases of non-preempting 'helpful' interventions. And, as in Peacocke's case, there seems to be no principled way in which they could do this. Thus we must conclude that sustaining causation accounts fail to satisfactorily deal with deviance in the case of other agents' interventions.

b) *Actions without feedback.* Furthermore, the sustaining causation strategy places too high requirements on the performance of an action. Bishop, in defending his account, admits that there are actions not involving feedback to the agent's central processing system because they are performed too fast to allow for feedback—such as 'the finger movements of an accomplished violinist, or in catching an egg after it slips from one's

---

[66] Bishop (1989), 170.
[67] Bach (1978), 375, admits that the feedback sequence cannot, *per se*, exclude the possibility of deviance.
[68] A similar case is envisaged by McCann (1998), 123—for whom, however, feedback is important not for the completion of an adopted intention, but for the altering of an intention by 'filling in the final details of my action plan', and whose example is consequently somewhat different.

hand'.[69] Actions may also fail to involve feedback for other reasons. An old person may have lost the feeling in his gouty finger, or this same effect may take place due to an accident in which many nerves are severed, thereby destroying the feedback mechanism, even though the person might still be able to move his arm.[70] Similarly, a doctor may tell a patient, whose arm has been anaesthesized for an operation and is completely numb, to raise his arm, in order to determine whether the patient is already able to do so. If the patient succeeds in raising his arm, he has performed an arm-raising action, even though there was no functioning feedback mechanism involved. In such cases of actions with or without any properly functioning feedback, coordination of behaviour is difficult and—apart from cases of actions 'too fast for feedback' which form part of behavioural patterns which the agent has learned—the necessary monitoring will not happen automatically, but will require conscious effort by, for example, visual control.

How are such cases, where feedback control is not necessary for agency, but initiation control is sufficient, to be treated on the sustaining causation strategy? One solution would be that even if there need not be feedback loops from all the stages of the process leading to the bodily motion, there has to be agential control based on feedback at least for the first part of the process. Thus, Mele claims that 'direct ballistic continuations'—in which feedback governs only the first part of the process and ceases at one point, after which the agent can no longer control his movement—are sufficient for actions. A case of this kind would be snapping one's fingers.[71] Probably some of the cases of feedback failure previously mentioned fall under this category of direct ballistic continuations. For example, when the agent with the anaesthesized arm tries to move his arm, there will arguably be (unconscious) feedback control of the nervous processes up to, though not including, the nervous mechanisms in the anaesthesized arm.

But even for the cases of direct ballistic continuations, the original account of sustaining causation will have to be extended in some way or other. For once we reach the stage of the causal process not governed by feedback control, we still need to distinguish between an outcome of this process that is the result of a basic action of the agent and an outcome which is a mere bodily motion which has been caused deviantly. *Ex hypothesi*, we cannot apply the feedback criterion to answer this question, which makes the need for an alternative criterion pressing. The same need arises, even more clearly, for actions not involving feedback at any stage at all.

To some extent, adherents of the sustaining causation approach have tried to answer this difficulty by applying one of the other causalist strategies to the cases of feedback failure; thus, Bishop proposes to apply the differential explanation approach to these cases.[72] But, as we have seen, this approach does not work *inter alia* because there are

---

[69] P. S. Churchland (1986), 430. Cf. Bishop (1989), 171, who endorses this possibility.
[70] Using James' terminology, such patients are called 'deafferented'. Without visual contact with their limbs they may fail to identify what they are doing; cf. Proust (2003), 306.
[71] Cf. Mele (2000), 291 f., (2003), 57.
[72] Bishop (1989), 169.

cases of 'on–off' abilities to act, where we can expect a differential explanation either for both cases of deviance and non-deviance, or for neither; and the difficulties we have discussed in connection with the other causalist strategies make appeal to them for cases of feedback failure equally unpromising.

Alternatively, one might argue that even if the production of the motion itself does not involve feedback in these cases, at least the movement is embedded in a larger feedback process, which often constitutes a more comprehensive behavioural pattern. So, even if the violinist's movements, considered in isolation, are too fast to involve feedback, there is the more comprehensive activity of playing a piece of music of which the movement forms a part and in which there can be some corrective measures for errors.[73] But this way of accounting for feedback control is not open to the causalist; for the behavioural pattern involving correction and feedback consists of particular *actions*, not of mere bodily motions, and thus cannot be appealed to in an explanation of feedback control without already presupposing an analysis of action.

Cases of feedback failure therefore continue to present counter-examples to the sustaining causation strategy, for which its defenders have not yet provided a satisfactory answer. We must therefore conclude that the sustaining causation strategy, despite its signal advantages over many other causalist strategies, fails to meet Bishop's requirement and cannot be considered as successfully discharging the task of 'naturalizing agency'.

5.6. The new 'manifestation' or 'well-functioning' analyses of action

Let us now turn to three more recently developed strategies that I have categorized with the label 'new manifestation theories'. What unites these strategies is a rejection of the idea that causal deviance can be excluded by requirements on the present and actual properties of the event-causal chain going from mental antecedents to bodily motion. They all agree that the occurrence of an event-causal chain whose steps are connected by certain lawful regularities (such as laws strict enough to guarantee sensitivity) can never guarantee that an action takes place—and in this respect they crucially differ from all the strategies which we have discussed hitherto.

The degrees to which these new theories reject the picture underlying the earlier accounts differ, though. Berent Enc thinks that the idea of a causal chain must only be supplemented by an historical account, based on a theory of natural selection which explains what it means for the system to produce a result in the way that *it is supposed to do*.[74] Rowland Stout, on the other hand, altogether rejects the idea of a causal process as a chain of events, and wants to supplant it with an Aristotelian notion of process—

---

[73] For major errors, that is, such as slipping to the wrong line of the piece, while not for each single false note.

[74] Cf. Enc (2004), 157.

where 'process' is understood as the realization of an underlying potentiality.[75] Ralph Stoecker agrees with the second line of approach in regarding actions as *actualizations* of powers, but understands such powers on the model of reductively construed dispositions.[76]

I will argue that the strategy underlying the last two approaches—understanding actions as realizations of causal powers—indeed points in the right direction, both specifically with regard to solving the problem of waywardness, and more generally with regard to providing an adequate account of human agency. However, the strategy will be successful, in both respects, only if we choose the right kind of causal power— and this power, I will try to show, cannot be specified in other than agential or agent-causal terms—as a power to act or to produce results. As long as the power is described differently, the strategy will fail—and once we describe it correctly, the resulting account will no longer be an event-causal reductive analysis of agency.

5.6.1. Enc's 'well-functioning' analysis

Enc relies on the general intuition that causal deviance constitutes a *malfunctioning*. The system that is involved—though it achieves the result that it is supposed to achieve— does not function as it is supposed to. The answer to the problem of causal deviance must therefore lie in spelling out the conditions for the well-functioning of the system, according to which one can assess whether the actual causal chain leading to the result is a 'normal' one. For Enc, we cannot provide a general account of these conditions merely by structural or statistical requirements on the causal chain; for a causal chain of exactly the same structure may, for one system, be the way it is supposed to work, while for another system it is an instance of malfunctioning. Thus, for *any* structural requirement R we are bound to find some system where a causal chain flouting R constitutes an instance of well-functioning.[77]

What alternative way is there to spell out the conditions for well-functioning? For artefacts the answer is easy, because we can refer to the purpose of the producer. For organisms, according to Enc, the criterion must be provided by the evolutionary processes that have shaped these organisms. Certain features of an organism are retained in a population over the generations because they are well fitted to certain tasks necessary for survival or propagation, while others die out during the course of natural selection because they are not equally well fitted, and thus organisms having them tend to die out more quickly. For example, many flowers have retained striking colours and smells because these have attracted insects which carry the pollen necessary for fertilization, thereby giving flowers possessing these features an evolutionary advantage. Such historical accounts of the development and retaining of features in a population during the process of natural selection reveal the biological functions of these features.

---

[75] Stout (2005), 88 ff.
[76] Stoecker (2003), 308 ff.
[77] Cf. Enc (2003), 105 f.

What is characteristic for explanations in terms of functions is that we can explain the possession of the feature by a member of the population by the fact that the feature serves this function—that its possession contributes to attaining a certain result.[78] For example, that a rose has a striking colour can be explained by the fact that the colour attracts insects, because a rose would not have this feature if it did not serve this purpose.

Enc exploits this notion of the 'function' of biological features to explain the well-functioning of systems which produce results by causal processes. Cause C, so Enc argues, causes a sequence leading to a result S, in the way that it is supposed to, if for any intermediate step X in the causal chain from A to R, 'the fact that C causes X is explained by the fact that X results in S.'[79] Consider, for example, the process of the capturing and devouring of a fly by a carnivorous plant, which is triggered by the fly's touch on the inside of the calyx. Each single step of the causal chain initiated by this touch—from the closing of the calyx to the absorption of material from the dead fly—is caused by the triggering event, because it contributes causally to the end-stage of the whole process: the digestion of nourishing material. If a step in the process were to fail to do this—if, for example, closing of the calyx proved unnecessary to capture the fly because the fly could be totally immobilized immediately—it would (normally) be eliminated from the process by natural selection over the next generations of this kind of plant. Actions, for Enc, are also causal processes which are to be understood on the same model—their special characteristic being that an intention to A must cause the behavioural output of the organism in the way that it is supposed to do.[80]

Enc's proposal is attractive because it makes the specific structure of the causal chain leading from intention to behaviour irrelevant to the question of agency, thus evading the impossible task of spelling out a kind of structure that is necessary and/or sufficient. However, the proposal is successful only if the (biological) function of intentions, and of the steps in the causal chains issuing from intentions, is limited to producing items of behaviour which are, at the same time, the results of actions. In other words, the proposal hinges on the assumption that the class of (in Enc's sense) 'well-functioning' causal chain-structures issuing from intentions coincides with the class of action.

And this assumption is false. The biological function of intention-states is clearly not limited to producing things over which we have agential control. In particular, for intentions to perform biologically crucial actions such as eating or having sex, the fulfilment of these intentions typically presupposes physiological changes over which we have no direct agential control—production of saliva, stiffening of the penis—and these changes are (usually) caused by (the acquisition of) the intention when the biological system is functioning properly. This makes possible deviant causal chains which are not captured by Enc's analysis. We can imagine an ignorant person who does

---

[78] Enc (2003), 108 ff.
[79] Enc (2003), 111.
[80] Enc (2003), 112.

not know that he cannot effectuate these changes at will, and therefore regularly intends not only to eat but also to form saliva at the same time. When such an agent 'succeeds' with his double project, all the conditions of Enc's analysis of action are satisfied with regard to the non-actional behaviour of forming saliva. The agent had an intention to form the saliva, saliva was formed, and it was produced in the way that the intention was 'supposed to produce it', because it was produced by the same well-functioning but non-actional mechanism connecting food intake and saliva production that human beings have acquired as a result of evolutionary processes. However, forming saliva (or stiffening his penis) is not something the agent can do at will, and therefore is not something that could constitute a (basic) action.

So, Enc's proposed analysis of action is defeated by the fact that the biological role of intention-states in the production of physiological changes is not restricted to the production of actional behaviour.

5.6.2. Stout's and Stoecker's 'realization' accounts

For Stout, the failure of the traditional causalist analyses of action is due to their subscribing to what he calls a 'Russellian' understanding of causal processes as mere series of causally connected events. Once this conception of causal processes is abandoned in favour of an Aristotelian conception, on which 'a process is the realization of a potentiality for a certain structure of stages to occur',[81] the problem of causal deviance will disappear. By his rejection of the Russellian conception of causal processes, which is the strictly Humean event-causalist conception, Stout's solution already goes beyond the limits of naturalist event-causalism, and shares several characteristics with the agent-causal accounts discussed in the next chapters.

On Stout's Aristotelian conception, the occurrence of a causal process requires both a series of events and the continuing presence of an underlying nature or potentiality, which is realized in this series throughout the whole process. Stout identifies this potentiality with the set of operational conditions whose continuous fulfilment is necessary and sufficient for the process to evolve. Potentialities have two key aspects. First, they are essentially potentialities *for* something, and what they are potentialities *for* is characterized by the structure of stages. Second, they are grounded in the underlying nature of the system in which the process occurs.[82]

Of the two elements of the Aristotelian notion of a process—the series of events and the persisting presence of an underlying state that is realized by this structure—the second is clearly dominant in Stout's account. Identification of processes does not depend on the identification of a structure of stages, but on the identification of the underlying set of conditions for such a structure.[83] This applies both to 'identification' in the sense of the numerical identity of particular processes—for what counts as one

---

[81] Stout (2005), 89.
[82] Stout (2005), 89 f.; (1996), 50 ff.
[83] Stout (1996), 53.

process—and in the sense of characterizations of kinds of process—for what particular processes are instances of the same kind of process.

For Stout, an action consists in a causal process, and the potentiality which is realized in this process must be described in terms of the sensitivity to the agent's aims that is characteristic to intentional agency—i.e. the fact that a different action would be performed if the agent were aiming at something different, or realized that something else was more conducive to his aim. As we do not always succeed in what we intend to do, this sensitivity requires only that the agent does what he should do in order to achieve the intended goal—that he takes the means to the intended goal, even though he may fail to reach this goal. This provides us with the following analysis of intentional action: An intentional action is a process (or the result of a process)[84] that is 'the realization of a potentiality to produce what should be achieved in order for the agent's intended goals to be achieved'.[85]

Stout's strategy to explain actions in terms of Aristotelian causal processes, whose identity depends on underlying potentialities, is much more powerful to exclude deviant causal chains than any of the proposals that we have considered so far. For, arguably, the main source of this problem is the following. When causal processes are understood as event-causal chains, however minutely we describe the structure of such a chain, it is *always* possible to insert between its steps a series of further steps, which can turn the original chain into a deviant chain. When we understand causal processes as realizations of potentialities, such a move is no longer possible. When we take a causal structure realizing a potentiality, we can, of course, still interpolate a deviant chain between two steps—but then the whole structure is no longer the realization of the same potentiality (or, at least, not necessarily), and thus no longer the same kind of causal process. Thus, the possibility of inserting wayward chains will not constitute a counter-example to Stout's analysis.

But Stout's strategy will be successful only if he can provide a characterization of the potentiality supposedly realized in action that is extensionally correct; that is, the characterization must be such that all and only cases of the realization of this potentiality are, in fact, cases of action. As we have seen, Stout himself takes the potentiality to be the potentiality to produce the behaviour that 'should be achieved' in order to reach the agent's intended goals; that is, as a potentiality to produce behaviour that is teleologically explainable.[86] He thus commits himself to the view that teleological explicability of the resulting behaviour is sufficient for agency.

A first problem with this proposal is the obvious need for making the standard for what behaviour 'should be achieved' more subjective. This standard cannot depend on

---

[84] While Stout's (2005), 95, formulation favours the first alternative, in (1996), 157, he considers both.
[85] Stout (2005), 95. The analysis in (1996), 155—that the process must be governed by a method of practical justification—is basically equivalent, because this method must also embody means–end sensitivity.
[86] Stout (1996), 99.

the objective circumstances, but must take into account the agent's possibly mistaken beliefs about what is conducive to his aim. For Stout, this modification is problematic because his overall project of teleological behaviourism is intended to present an account of intentional action that is independent from the concepts of belief or of other mental states.[87] But we will leave this special difficulty for Stout's project aside here, and only consider the more fundamental question of whether the production of behaviour in accordance with a means-end justification is really limited to the case of actions.

At first glance, the answer is clearly negative. It is not only in cases of human actions that a system's behaviour can be explained in terms of the aims that the system pursues, but also in cases of negative feedback systems not directly connected to human agency, such as thermostats. Even when we restrict ourselves to teleological explanations of human behaviour, there are many bodily motions which subserve the agent's intended aims, but are not things that he can do at will and therefore do not qualify as actions. Consider the earlier counter-examples against Enc's account, such as the production of saliva at the beginning of the eating process. This seems to directly refute Stout's proposal.

Stout, however—who is aware of the difficulty that things other than actions appear to be teleologically explainable—thinks that these cases do not present genuine counter-examples to his theory. He thinks that systems such as thermostats and bodily organs lack the right degree of sensitivity to changing circumstances, and that their behaviour is therefore not, after all, 'really' teleologically explainable. Under many conditions, thermostats or bodily organs will continue with one kind of behaviour or functioning, even though this behaviour clearly fails to serve the system's aim in these circumstances and other behaviour would be better suited. This characteristic is called 'sphexishness'. 'Real' teleological explanation is incompatible with 'sphexishness', and requires, so Stout claims, that whenever a certain kind of means to a pursued end is apparent and falls within the system's repertoire, this kind of means-behaviour will be emitted by the system.[88]

Does this move make the realm of teleologically explainable behaviour coextensive with the realm of (intentional) actions? There are two worries here. First, why should teleological explanation exclude, as Stout claims, *any* measure of sphexishness? Though, when something is done in order to achieve an end, there must be *some* sensitivity to facts about the necessary means to this end, why should this exclude that there are *any* situations in which the system would not do what it was required to do, even though it could do it? Could not sensitivity restricted to a range of standard situations suffice for teleological explanation? Stout's answer is that this strategy will not work for non-agential systems, because we cannot spell out in a non-circular way the

---

[87] Stout (1996), 3.
[88] Stout (1996), 113, 118. His answer for evolutionary explanations is different, however; cf. (1996), 99 ff.

restrictions to the sensitivity of such systems by explicitly excluding problematic situations. For there are, he argues, too many problematic situations for which, for example, the thermostat was not designed and with which it is unable to cope.[89]

But if Stout is right about this, we are immediately faced with the second worry. Is not the situation the same with regard to human intentional action? We often act irrationally and fail to take the means to our ends. Should this not also exclude our actions from the realm of 'real' teleological explanation? Stout thinks not, because intentional agents will do what they need to do in order to achieve an end, if the necessity is made apparent to them and they are able to do it.[90] But this latter claim is ambiguous, depending on different ways of understanding what it means 'to be apparent', and while on some readings this claim is clearly false, on others, though true, it is trivially true of all feedback systems, and thus also of things such as thermostats, which do not act.

One way to understand that a means to an end is apparent is that it is somehow objectively apparent; that is, it is clearly perceptible for anyone who looks at the matter or thinks about it. When we take this notion of apparency, Stout's claim is false, because no matter how obvious something is, an agent may still fail to recognize it and therefore fail to act accordingly. Alternatively, we can switch to the subjective perception of the agent. A means is apparent only if it is apparent to the agent—if he recognizes that this is the means to his end. But on this understanding, the possibility of akrasia falsifies Stout's claim. No matter how clear it is to me what I need to do, I may still fail to do it. The only reading on which Stout's claim *is* true about human agents is one on which 'being apparent' is understood as 'persuasive for the agent'; that is, already implying a motivational impact on what he is doing. In this case—barring preemption of the action or other more important aims—the agent will indeed do what he should do. But this reading reduces the claim to a trivial truth, and a parallel claim also holds good for the thermostat case, when we understand 'being apparent' as already implying a tendency to show an appropriate reaction.

The result which we can draw from these considerations is that Stout's strict view of teleological explanation, that is incompatible with any degree of sphexishness, either fails to apply to human actions because these too can exhibit a degree of sphexishness, or also applies to feedback processes which do not constitute actions, if we presuppose a strong enough notion of 'being apparent'. In both cases, teleological explanation will not provide a differentiating criterion between actions and non-actions. But Stout needs a criterion to adequately characterize the potentiality which is purportedly realized in actions, and not in other causal processes. As his proposed criterion fails, and the potentiality he characterizes can be realized in non-actional processes as well, Stout's account must be rejected.

---

[89] Stout (1996), 116 f.   [90] Stout (1996), 118.

Stoecker's account of actions as realizations of intentional atttitudes radically differs from Stout's proposal in not sharing the latter's Aristotelian approach to causal processes. For Stoecker, actions are actualizations of causal powers, but the latter have nothing to do with underlying potentialities. Instead, he understands causal powers on the model of dispositions—such as 'being water-soluble'—and for him, disposition-ascriptions are to be explained reductively. Having a disposition means only that it is probable that in certain circumstances the object 'behaves' in a certain way—for example, it dissolves when it is put in water—and when this happens we can explain the resulting behaviour by the object's possessing that disposition.

In addition to dispositions, which are restricted to what happens to the object itself, there is a further kind of tendency: causal powers, which concern the object's effects on other things. Consider the property of being scary. When we say that a film is scary, we do not thereby imply anything about what will happen to the film itself, but about what effects it has on persons watching it—for example, that it will make a child who watches it cry.[91] Such tendencies play the same kind of explanatory role as dispositions. We can explain the child's crying by appeal to the film's being scary in the same way as we can explain the dissolution of the cube of salt in water by its water-solubility.

Now, Davidson, on whose remarks Stoecker extensively draws, repeatedly described pro-attitudes, that were, for him, the 'primary causes' of actions, as special dispositions, which he also called 'causal powers' of agents.[92] A desire for X was characterized as (*inter alia*) a disposition 'to be caused to cause' X (its own fulfilment), given the right circumstances (beliefs, opportunity, and so on).[93] As Davidson famously believed that all actions are identical with bodily motions,[94] he therefore regarded 'causal powers' of the agent as, roughly, complex dispositions for displaying certain bodily behaviour.

Stoecker's own theory is more complex, because his focus is on explaining *results* rather than actions, and it is the former that must, on his view, be explained by intentional attitudes. This is due to his general suspicion of actions as entities on their own, and his consequent desire to eliminate them from the explanation of human agency.[95] For this reason, while adopting Davidson's characterization of an agent's intentional attitudes as his 'causal powers', Stoecker does not regard them as dispositions, but as belonging to the second kind of tendency mentioned earlier, which concern the object's effects on other things.[96] But this special feature of Stoecker's account does not add any substantially new aspect with regard to the discussion of causal waywardness. For our purposes, it suffices to note that on both Davidson's and

---

[91] Stoecker (2003), 309 f.
[92] For example, Davidson (1987), 41; (1973a), 64.
[93] Davidson (1990), 22.
[94] Cf. Davidson (1971a).
[95] Cf. Stoecker (1993).
[96] Stoecker (2003), 310 ff.

Stoecker's accounts, intentional actions consist (roughly) in the realizations of causal powers of the agent.

Both these accounts can draw on the same powerful resources to avoid the problem of wayward causal chains as Stout's account. If intentional attitudes are causal powers and actions their actualizations, this problem is circumvented, because an actualization of a power is not the same thing as the occurrence of a causal chain involving the power and leading to the right kind of result. Consider again the causal power of scariness. When a child watches a film and starts crying because he is frightened, his crying is a manifestation of the film's scariness. But the crying of a child can also be caused 'deviantly' by the scariness of a film without being such a manifestation. A child may cry because his parents, who have already watched the film, will not allow him to watch it because they think it is too scary.[97] The crucial distinction between a (mere) causal role and a realization of a causal power thus provides the key to answering the challenge of causal deviance on the basis of Davidson's and Stoecker's manifestation analysis of action.

And, indeed, I believe that this analysis would succeed in dealing with the problem of deviant causal chains and provide a satisfactory account of agency, if two additional conditions were satisfied: (i) If they did not rest on a reductive account of causal powers or dispositions which reduces them to event-causal relations, and (ii) if they picked out the right kind of causal powers—that is, those powers the sets of whose realizations are, combined, coextensive with the set of human actions. Condition (i) is important because, as we shall see in the next chapters, a reductive account of causal powers is itself faced with problems of waywardness. Here, though, we can postpone discussion of this point and focus on condition (ii) instead.

With regard to this condition, Stoecker's and Davidson's accounts, which pick out intentional attitudes as the relevant causal powers, face the following problem. Actions are not the only kind of actualization of intentional attitudes, but there are many other results in which these attitudes manifest themselves. For example, the desire to do something particularly shameful may cause a person to blush, the desire to see the football World Cup final may cause one's eyes to sparkle in anticipation when one settles down to watch it, or my fear of a wild animal will make me tremble when I encounter it. All these are characteristic manifestations of the complex dispositions that make up intentional attitudes. Fear, for instance, would not be fear as we know it if it did not involve a tendency to tremble. Therefore, with regard to our earlier distinction between a (mere) causal role and an actualization of a causal power, these cases clearly fall on the side of actualizations. Nevertheless, they are not cases of actions, and therefore seem to falsify the proposed accounts.

---

[97] Stoecker, loc. cit.

For Davidson's account, this verdict is adequate, because for him the relevant causal powers are just dispositions for bodily motions, and in the case of trembling from fear such a disposition is actualized, even though the trembling is not an action. With regard to Stoecker's proposal, however, the situation is more complex, because he characterizes the causal power actualized in intentional actions more specifically as a 'rational capacity' that we have specifically as rational *agents*. At times, he even speaks of an additional causal capacity of the agent beyond his intentional attitudes: 'the agent's rational causal power', whose realization he considers to be crucial for agency. This extra power is based on 'the agent's learned control over his limbs that allows for a basic causal power to move his limbs as he wants them to', and if the result of a basic action is not due to this control, it will not be intentionally explainable.[98] The appeal to such an extra basic causal power could indeed save Stoecker's account from the objection we have raised. For if actions involve the actualization of a basic causal power to move one's limbs as one wants them to move, then the actualizations of desires which are not also realizations of this power will be excluded, and his analysis will capture precisely those cases that are actions.

As will be seen in the development of the agent-causal account, I think this kind of analysis of action is, in general, along the right lines (leaving aside, for the moment, problems about Stoecker's view of dispositions). But what concerns me here is only the following point. By relying on a basic causal power to move one's limbs, the account can no longer be seen as a reductive event-causal account of action at all. For this causal power, whose actualization is necessary for intentional agency, cannot be explained in purely event-causal and non-actional terms, if the problem of causal waywardness is not to be brought in again 'by the back door'. If the account is to solve this problem, the causal power to move one's limbs as one wants to cannot be understood as a disposition for *mere* behaviour, but, at best, as a disposition for a certain *activity*—for example, a disposition to move one's limbs if one has a desire to do so. In this case, the account will include unreduced agential terms in the analysans, and therefore will not be reductive.

Stoecker himself seems to accept this result when he introduces the unanalysed 'causal power to move one's limbs as one wants to'. And, indeed, for his own account, the failure to eliminate such agential or agent-causal residues completely need not necessarily lead to a vicious circularity, because his explanatory focus is on *intentional* agency rather than on agency simpliciter, and on the explicability of *results* rather than of actions. However, for a reductive event-causal analysis of action this failure does entail a vicious circularity.

The conclusion which can be drawn from the discussion of the manifestation analyses is therefore the following. With regard to solving the problem of waywardness, these analyses point into the right direction; but when we try to characterize the

---

[98] Stoecker (2003), 316. For non-basic action types, this basic power must be enriched by our ability to manipulate further outcomes by skilful use of our bodily movements.

power or potentiality that is realized in actions extensionally correctly—so that all and only the realizations of this power are actions—we cannot do so without using agential or agent-causal notions. Therefore, such analyses cannot provide the basis for successful reductive accounts of action.

5.7. Conclusion

What lessons can be drawn from our discussion of antecedential waywardness? We have discussed four causalist strategies to cope with this phenomenon. While the first three of them—the proposals based on causal immediacy, sensitivity, and sustaining causation—have failed in the task, the manifestation strategy has offered, at least in one form, a solution to the problem, but only at the price of abandoning the reductive project. So, the outlook for this project is bleak.

Though we have discussed the specific reasons for the failure of each reductive account in detail, it is still instructive to ask whether there is some common, more fundamental reason for the failure of these accounts which is manifested in the more specific difficulties. The answer to this question has already been indirectly suggested in our discussion of the manifestation approaches. Actions are essentially manifestations of *abilities to act at will*. In cases of deviance, the exercise of this ability of the agent is 'bypassed' in the production of the bodily motions,[99] either because the agent has no opportunity to act at all, or because, even though an opportunity has presented itself, the exercise of the ability is pre-empted, as in the case of alien interveners. Though this description of both actions and cases of deviance is fairly trivial, we can deduce from it an important requirement for a possible causalist analysis. Such an analysis has to explain, in purely event-causal terms, what abilities to act and their manifestations consist in.

In fact, we can understand some of the proposals that we have discussed as including implicit, though unsuccessful, attempts to provide such analyses. For instance, the standard model in its original form—equating actions with bodily motions caused by desires or intentions—implicitly relied on the idea that abilities to act are dispositions to display a certain behaviour when one has specific desires and beliefs, and that these dispositions could be reduced to the presence of an event-causal structure. But abilities to act are not dispositions of the envisaged kind, if only because they are two-way powers, which we can exercise or refrain from exercising. Furthermore, as we shall see in the next chapter, dispositions cannot be reductively analysed in the envisaged way. The sensitivity and the sustaining causation strategies also made implicit proposals about what the manifestation of an ability to act consists in: the counterfactual dependence of bodily motions on the content of the agent's intentions (or the possibility of differential explanation), or the existence of feedback mechanisms to monitor

---

[99] Cf. Gustafson (1987), 176.

bodily behaviour. From our discussion of these proposals, we can draw the conclusion that the manifestation of an ability to act can be equated with neither of the two.

This leaves us with two important results—one positive and one negative. The negative one is that it will not, after all, be possible to provide a reductive, purely event-causal, and naturalist account of the mode of agential control; for whatever mental states of the agents we take to be bearers of agential control, an event-causal connection between those states and the agent's bodily motions, even if enriched by the additional elements proposed by the different theories, will not guarantee that the agent is in control.

Together with the results from Chapters 3 and 4, where we saw that the adherent of the standard model is unable to specify the adequate bearers of agential control, this shows that the project of naturalizing human agency is unsuccessful. Consequently, the standard model of human agency should be rejected, because it does not allow for agential activity and therefore fails to provide an answer to the problem of human agency. This negative result has the important consequence that only the agent-causal approach—which was, besides the standard model, the only remaining candidate for providing a satisfactory unified account of human agency (at the end of Chapter 2)—is now left in the running. If this approach also fails, we will not be able to answer the problem of human agency.

But there is also a positive result of our discussion of causal waywardness: namely, that we have identified, as the fundamental problem at the base of this phenomenon, the failure of the reductive event-causal analyses of actions to do justice to the insight that actions are manifestations of abilities to act. This result strongly suggests that if the agent-causal approach takes this insight seriously, it has a good chance of solving the problem of human agency, evading the difficulties that have beset the standard model. In the following chapters I shall argue that this is just what an agent-causal account, if suitably developed, is able to do.

6

How agent-causation works I: the problem, and a brief theory of powers

Our discussion in the previous two chapters has shown that the standard model cannot, even if modified, provide an adequate account of agential control. As agential control is the minimum core element of agential activity which any satisfactory account of human agency must capture, this failure means that the standard model cannot provide a unified account of human agency.

If we are to find an answer to the problem of human agency, we must therefore turn to the agent-causalist approach which, at the end of Chapter 2, remained as the only rival to the naturalist, event-causalist approach. And an answer to the problem will only be forthcoming if we succeed in developing a viable agent-causal model, vindicating a notion of agent-causation which is both conceptually and ontologically irreducible to event-causation. This is the task which will occupy us in the following three chapters.

Because agent-causalist approaches take seriously the idea that agents, when acting, are genuinely active, there is no real worry that they will fail to account for the first of the three Theses encountered at the beginning of Chapter 1. That the huge majority of contemporary philosophers of action rejects agent-causal accounts is, on the one hand, due to an alleged incompatibility of agent-causation with Theses 2 and 3—that is, with the status of actions as part of the natural order and with the possibility of explaining (intentional) actions by appeal to the agent's reasons. Some sources of these worries have already been sketched in Section 1.1. On the other hand, there is also a deeply rooted suspicion against the coherence and explanatory value of the notion of agent-causation, and this more fundamental objection to agent-causation must clearly be the first object of our concern.

Since Hume's criticism of the traditional theories of causation, the huge majority of philosophers have considered the notion of agent-causation to be, at worst, incoherent, or at best, totally parasitic on the notion of human agency, and thus unilluminating with regard to this latter notion. In one form or another this has become a standard objection to agent-causation in analytical philosophy of action. To invoke just two voices from different parts of the huge chorus of sceptics: Searle claims that it is simply 'bad English' to say that an object causes something *tout court*, because he considers it to be a constraint on our notion of cause that there must be some feature of the object or event involving the object that causes the outcome we only parenthetically ascribe to the object's causal activity.[1] More benignly, von Wright argues that the only sense we can make of the notion of agent-causation (or immanent causation) is by *calling* human agency agent-causation[2]—but if this is true, any attempt to illuminate human agency by appeal to agent-causation will be unavoidably circular. Let us call this objection about the coherence or explanatory value of the notion of agent-causation the 'mysteriousness' objection.

The scepticism about the coherence or explanatory value of the notion of agent-causation is often combined with the view that even if the notion could not be positively shown to be incoherent, agent-causation could nevertheless not be part of the natural order. As Davidson has expressed it, agent-causation would be a 'kind[s] of causation foreign to science'[3] and its instantiation therefore be incompatible with our 'emerging scientific picture of the world'. Often, this worry takes the special form that agent-causation would be committed to substance-dualism because it is understood as causation by an immaterial 'self'.[4]

In this chapter and the following three chapters I will be concerned with answering both the 'mysteriousness' objection and the scepticism about agent-causation as part of the natural order, for I believe that developing a viable account of agent-causation which answers the first objection will also automatically meet the second kind of worry.

The first key step towards answering both questions lies in recognizing that agent-causation is nothing unique in the world, in the sense that only human agents performing actions can cause effects, while all other natural objects are incapable of doing so and figure purely passively in event-causal processes. Though the huge majority of agent-causalists ascribe a genuinely causal role only to sentient and intelligent beings with a will,[5] this restriction has been a mistake of great consequence, because it has contributed greatly to the impression that agent-causation is either completely mysterious or a mere synonym for human agency. For restricting agent-causal activity to human agents (among the objects in the world) tends to make agent-causation appear either as some unnatural extra force with which human beings are endowed, and which can only be compared to divine causation[6]—a comparison which is unlikely to improve our understanding of the notion—or as simply another name for the phenomenon we want to understand: human agency.

---

[1] Searle (2001), 82.
[2] Von Wright (1971), 192; also Hornsby (1980), 101.
[3] Davidson (1978), 83. The same kind of objection (especially against libertarian agent-causal accounts) is developed at length by Pereboom (2001), 69 ff.
[4] For example, Honderich (1993), ch. 3.
[5] For example, Reid (1983), 523; Chisholm (1966), 28; Taylor (1966), 20; Donagan (1987), 167 f.; Clarke (1993), 201 f.; O'Connor (2000). Notable exceptions are Alvarez and Hyman (1998), 243, who follow Harré and Madden (1975), 82 ff., and Lowe (2002), 209 ff.
[6] Cf. Chisholm (1966), 23, for a comparison with 'the prime mover unmoved'.

In addition, the denial of a genuinely causal role of any natural objects other than human agents is also, on its own, *prima facie* implausible. Ordinary parlance suggests that other objects, as well as human beings, can be causes. We not only talk about Attila causing the downfall of the Roman Empire, but about an acid causing a logwood solution to turn red, or HIV being the cause of AIDS. Ordinary talk abounds with such mention of general and particular inanimate substance-causes. Once we proceed, following this hint, on the assumption that if substances can be causes at all, other natural objects as well as human agents can be such causes, the task of meeting both the 'mysteriousness' and the 'natural order' objection becomes much easier.

Of course, neither objection is answered *per se* simply by admitting other substance-causes than human agents. But this admission significantly widens the scope of strategies at our disposal to explain the nature of agent-causation, because its nature now no longer has to rely on a specific characteristic of human beings, but can rely, alternatively, on a general feature common to all active substances. If one successfully explains this nature in the latter way, one can meet von Wright's worry that explaining agency in terms of agent-causation will be circular. For suppose we can explain agent-causation as an instance of a wider genus of substance-causation. Then it will already be sufficient to avert the threat of circularity if the explanation of the wider genus is not a mere anthropomorphic simile, because this will guarantee that we have at least one way of understanding agent-causation that does not presuppose a pre-existing understanding of human agency.

Starting from this first insight, I will try to develop, in this chapter and the following three chapters, an account of agent-causation which both provides a coherent notion of agent-causation and shows how this kind of causation can be part of the natural order. The fundamental idea on which the account rests is as follows.

It only appears that there is no coherent notion of agent-causation, other than one which defines agent-causing as acting, because modern philosophers in the wake of Hume have used a too impoverished notion of causation, and consequently have relied on a too impoverished picture of nature, which has falsely been elevated to the status of 'the emerging scientific image'. This picture is the Humean 'event-causal' picture of reality encountered in Chapter 1. The key points of impoverishment have been the following: the Humean view that nature is constituted by 'atomic' self-contained events, which are tied together only by regularities or laws of nature, the consequent elimination of the notion of 'power' from the concept of cause, and, *pari passu*, a neglect of causal talk involving the notions of powers and dispositions in ordinary and scientific explanatory practices. I will argue that without accepting powers as bona fide properties of objects, we are left without an appropriate understanding of much of these explanatory practices and would have to renounce both these practices and our ordinary view of the world. Substance-causation, I will claim, is no more 'mysterious' or 'unnatural' than are powers themselves, so that it can and should be included together with powers in our 'picture of the world'. The 'respectable' standing of agent-causation will be assured by showing that agent-causation is an instance of this more general notion in the special case of substances that are persons, where abilities to act are the causal powers of persons in whose exercise agent-causings consist. And this result will answer directly the 'natural order' worry, because it shows that the apparent tension between agent-causal accounts and Thesis 2 rests on a false picture of the 'natural order'.

As the overall argument will be quite lengthy, it will be useful to provide a more detailed overview of it at the start. The argument will proceed in the following steps. In this chapter I will begin with some negative 'clearing' work in preparation of the positive account that will be developed (Section 6.1). This 'clearing' work is required because there is an influential argument against the intelligibility of agent-causation which to many philosophers seems to rule out the possibility of agent-causation and substance-causation from the start, and which would, if successful, make our search for an account of agent-causation pointless. I will begin by looking at this argument in its classic form, which has been presented by Davidson (Section 6.1.1). Against this, I will argue that the implicit premiss on which the argument rests, which is the validity of the regularity theory of causation (in one version or another), has not been established, and that it is highly doubtful whether this theory can be true as a general theory of causation (Section 6.1.2). This will show that we need not regard Davidson's argument against agent-causation as compelling, and thus opens up the possibility that there *might* be a viable account of irreducible agent-causation.

In the following section I will begin to develop such an account, which on my view should be based on a theory of powers (Section 6.2). The first step will consist in developing an account of powers as genuine properties of objects. Though since Hume it has been common to regard powers with scepticism, I will argue that in order to provide a satisfactory understanding of our ordinary and scientific explanatory practices, we have to accept powers among the bona fide properties of objects (Section 6.2.2).

In the next chapter I will argue that, furthermore, powers must be seen as both conceptually (Section 7.1) and ontologically (Section 7.2) irreducible to non-power properties. In an appendix I will show that contrary to appearances, the acceptance of irreducible powers does not commit us to problematic doctrines about 'natural necessities' or 'essences of individual objects', which one may justifiably wish to avoid (Section 7.3). These considerations will complete our defence of irreducible powers. As the account of agent-causation to be developed rests on the account of powers, and many of the basic sceptical worries against the first can also be raised against the second, the defence of powers will be the step of my argument that will occupy most space.

In Chapter 8 I will develop a theory of agent-causation from the account of powers elaborated in Chapters 6 and 7. A first step will take us (exemplarily for inanimate substances) from powers in general to substance-causes, by way of 'active powers' (Section 8.1). It will be argued that among the powers of substances we can distinguish a sub-group of 'active powers' (Section 8.1.1), and that when such an 'active power' is exercised, the cause of the resulting event is the substance which possesses the power itself. This instance of substance-causation will be shown not to be analysable in terms of exclusively event-causal processes or in terms of a causal role of the power itself (Section 8.1.2). It will further be argued that the relation between substance and effect fulfils the traditional requirements for a causal relation, so that these requirements present no obstacle to regarding the substance as the cause of the effect (Section 8.1.3).

This leaves me with the task of showing how the general concept of substance-causation can be applied to the specific case of human agency (Section 8.2). I will show that human agency, in a rather trivial way, turns out to be an instance of the more general concept of substance-causation, when the causing substance is a human person (Section 8.2.1). Proceeding one step further, I will address the worry that though the model of substance-causation might apply to non-basic actions, it fails to apply to cases where we produce certain results directly. Against this worry, I will argue that the concepts of substance-causation and causal power in general do not exclude the possibility of direct causation, and that consequently, we have no reason to exclude basic actions from the agent-causal model (Section 8.2.2). I will conclude my defence of agent-causation by checking the list of standard objections against the possibility of agent-causation, showing why they do not apply to the account which I have developed (Section 8.3).

Chapter 9 is dedicated to an examination of the worry that agent-causal powers of human persons might be completely reducible to the physical structure of the agent's body and the constituent powers of its parts, and that consequently there might, after all, be no 'real' agent-causation by human beings.

6.1. The classical argument against the possibility of agent-causation

While there is a number of more specific arguments against the intelligibility of agent-causal talk—to which we will turn only after presenting a positive account of agent-causation—there is a general worry about the conceptual possibility of agent-causation that is best addressed before even beginning to develop this account. This worry relies on a certain widely accepted paradigm of causal explanation connected to the predominant view about causation, and for many philosophers clinches the issue against the possibility of agent-causation from the start. Furthermore, this worry sets the stage for the later discussion by yielding an important requirement on any positive account of agent-causation. Such an account must either rely on the same paradigm of causal explanation, or it must provide an alternative paradigm to which agent-causal explanations are supposed to conform.

6.1.1. The regularity theory of causation and Davidson's intelligibility objection

To this day, the predominant view about the nature of causation is based upon Hume's arguments in the *Treatise* and the *Enquiry*, in which he claims to have established that the obtaining of the causal relation depends upon the cause and the effect falling under two kinds of events which regularly succeed one another. Though Hume's followers have modified his own theory of causation in several respects, two core theses of Hume's have successfully established themselves and have become the basis for what was, well into the second half of the twentieth century, the 'orthodox' view about causation: (i) the anti-singularist claim that the causal relation between two individual events always presupposes a general regularity or natural law, so that there cannot be a case of 'private' causation between individual events, and (ii) the reductionist claim that the obtaining of causal relations and facts can be reduced to non-causal facts. I shall summarily call the theories of causation which follow Hume in both these claims, 'regularity theories of causation'.

Though both claims came under heavy criticism in the second half of the twentieth century—famously voiced by Anscombe when she called the resulting theory one of the 'dogmatic slumbers of the day'[7]—they still enjoy widespread acceptance, and have to a large extent shaped the discussion about causality. They also provide the basis for much of the scepticism about agent-causation—the most important strand of which is expressed by Davidson's intelligibility objection. As Davidson's objection itself relies on the regularity theory, it is profitable for us to briefly recapitulate Hume's argument for these two claims in order to provide the background for Davidson's objection.

Hume's discussion of causation is set within the general framework of the *Treatise* and the *Enquiry*, which is shaped by Hume's basic methodological commitment that we must decide on the meaningfulness of a term by an enquiry into the origin of the supposed idea which is expressed by the term.[8] This commitment derives from the empiricist theory of concepts to which Hume subscribes. According to this theory, all concepts are ultimately derived from sensory impressions, and the *contents* of the concepts are functionally dependent upon the contents of those impressions, because the concepts are the results of the application of a limited range of mental processing operations on these impressions.[9] In the application of his general method to the concept of cause and the connected idea of a necessary connection, two theses about the origin of this concept become the prime targets of Hume's criticism: (a) the view advocated by, for example, Hobbes and Malebranche,[10] that the connection between cause and effect is one of logical necessity that can be established *a priori*;[11] and (b) the claim that in a single instance of causation we can directly perceive the obtaining of a necessary connection with our senses.[12] According to Hume, both (a) and (b) are false,

---

[7] Anscombe (1971), 104.
[8] Cf. Hume, Enquiry, 22.
[9] Hume, Enquiry, 19, 22. Cf. Strawson (1989), 102 ff.
[10] Cf. Hobbes, *Elements of Philosophy: De Corpore*, ch. 9, where he claims that a cause is nothing else than the set of states of the objects involved, so that when one imagines them to obtain one cannot imagine the effect to fail to ensue; and Malebranche, *Recherche*, VI.2.iii., whose 'liaison nécessaire' between cause and effect is also a connection of logical necessity; cf. Nadler (2000), 113.
[11] Cf. Hume, *Enquiries*, 27.
[12] Cf. Hume, *Enquiries*, 63.

and the individual case fails to provide us with any adequate basis for our concept of causation and the connected idea of a necessary connection.

Instead, there is only the impression of a necessary connection that originates from our experience of a regular succession of events of certain kinds, which makes us expect an event of the one kind whenever we witness the happening of an event of the other kind. 'This connexion, therefore, which we *feel* in the mind, this customary transition from the object to its usual attendant, is the sentiment or impression from which we form the idea of power or necessary connection.'[13] Coupled with this claim about origin is a corresponding thesis about the content of the concept of cause, which finds its classic expression in Hume's first definition of cause in the *Enquiry*[14] as 'an object, followed by another...where all the objects similar to the first are followed by objects similar to the second'.[15] The holding of causal relations is thus reduced to the obtaining of regular successions of 'objects' or, more precisely, events, and the idea of causal necessity is claimed to arise only from a projection of our subjective customary transition onto the perceived events themselves.[16]

Reduction of causation to regular successions holding merely *as a matter of fact*, as advocated by Hume, has, however, fallen out of favour among philosophers who have followed him in his reductionist project, and has been superseded by reduction to *law-like* regularities or to laws of nature. The central motivation for this move—which reintroduced an element of 'natural', non-logical necessity repudiated by Hume—was the desire to retain the implication from singular causal statements of the kind 'A caused B' to contrafactual conditionals of the kind 'If A had not happened, neither would have B', which plausibly holds when there is no case of causal overdetermination or hypothetical substitute causes.[17] Regularities which hold only as a matter of fact are not sufficient bases for this implication, because the counterfactual 'If A had not happened, neither would have B' does not necessarily hold if the regular succession between events of kind A and B is merely accidental; only regularities based on laws of nature or connected with analytic necessity yield the required counterfactuals. The result of this development of Hume's regularity theory was the view—predominant in philosophical discussion since Mill—that a cause of A is a condition that is *ceteris paribus* sufficient and/or necessary for A's obtaining, where the sufficiency/necessity is not of a logical kind but is derived from laws of nature ('physical necessity').[18] This view—

---

[13] Hume, *Enquiries*, 75.
[14] The definition in the *Treatise*, 170 f., also includes the contiguity of cause and effect.
[15] Hume, *Enquiries*, 76.
[16] This rough sketch of Hume's arguments perforce neglects many important exegetical questions, especially concerning the question of whether Hume makes a claim about 'causation considered as it is in the objects', or only an epistemological claim about what we can know about causation; cf. Strawson (1989), 10 f. I can, however, neglect these exegetical questions here, for it is in the form presented by the 'standard' view that Hume's theory has become so influential. Cf. classical Humeans such as Ayer (1973), 183.
[17] Hume himself based his second definition of 'cause' in the *Enquiries*, 76, on this counterfactual conditional.
[18] Cf. Mill (1879), b. iii., ch. 5; Hempel (1965), 349; Popper (1972), 91.

which shares both Hume's reductionism and anti-singularism about causation—can be called the nomological version of the regularity theory.

According to the nomological theory, the explanatory power of a causal explanation rests on the subsumption of cause and effect under types of events and reference to a law-like connection holding between these two types. Relying on this law-like connection, it is possible to *explain* why the effect happened by deducing a statement that it took place from statements about the occurrence of the cause, its concomitant circumstances, and laws of nature, and, analogously, to *predict* that a certain effect will happen by the same kind of inference. This deductive account of explanation has found its most influential formulation in Hempel's covering-law model of scientific explanation.[19]

After this short overview over the regularity theory of causation, we can now turn to the question of why adherents of this theory will find talk of agent-causation, when it is not understood metaphorically or reducible to event-causal talk, unintelligible, or, at least, lacking any explanatory value. Their fundamental worry has found its classic formulation in Davidson's *Agency*, in which he sketches a dilemma for agent-causalists about the explanation of basic actions.[20]

Davidson addresses agent-causal theories, such as Taylor's,[21] according to which agents cause their (voluntary) actions (an action is not the causing of an effect by the agent, but the effect of the causing). For such a view, according to Davidson, the following dilemma arises when we consider the causing of a basic action by the agent. Either this causing is itself a separate event from the action, or it is not. In the first case, according to Davidson, we must ask whether or not this distinct causing-event is itself an action. If it is, then according to the agent-causal view Davidson is attacking—that actions are caused by agents—the causing-event too must be caused by the agent; and because the question about the action-character of the causing event arises again at the next step, we are neatly led into an infinite regress of agent-causings and actions.

So, staying on the first horn of the dilemma, let us assume that the causing-event, though an event distinct from the action, is not itself an action. Davidson simply dismisses this possibility by saying that the notion 'of a causing that is not a doing'[22] is too obscure a notion to be of any help in explaining the notion of agency. But even if an agent-causalist is prepared to go along with the idea of 'a causing that is not a doing', he is faced with a further dilemma, depending on whether he is willing to consider that at least *some* causings are actions. If he is not willing to do so, he seems to renounce the basic motivation for appealing to agent-causation: namely, to account for agential control over the results of actions. If, however, he is willing to count some causings as actions, he faces the task of providing a criterion to distinguish those causings that are actions from those that are not—and, as Alvarez and Hyman have rightly pointed out, he is unlikely to succeed. Any plausible additional criteria for actions, such as inten-

---

[19] Cf. Hempel (1965), *passim*. [20] Davidson (1971a), 52 f.
[21] Cf. Taylor (1966), 115. [22] Davidson (1971a), 52.

tionality, are likely to be satisfied by *all* agent-causings of actions, whenever they are satisfied by the actions themselves.[23]

This embedded dilemma, though not decisively refuting the possibility of 'a causing that is not a doing', shows that a solution which relies on this possibility encounters serious difficulties—and this result completes the first horn of Davidson's overall dilemma. We should note, however, that this first horn—which Davidson develops from the assumption that the causing of a basic action is an event distinct from the basic action which is caused—arises quite independently from this assumption. What is responsible for the first horn of the dilemma is instead the view which Davidson ascribes to agent-causalists in general: namely, that agents cause their actions. For on this supposition the causing of the action must either be an action itself, which would start off an infinite regress, or be 'a causing that is not a doing', which would lead to the embedded dilemma just discussed. This shows that the right agent-causalist response to the first horn of Davidson's dilemma is to reject the supposition that agents cause their actions. Instead, actions should be seen as consisting in agent-causings; that is, when an agent performs the basic action of raising his arm, what he causes is not the raising but the *rising* of the arm.[24]

Though this agent-causalist response suffices to escape from Davidson's dilemma as it is explicitly presented in *Agency*, agent-causalists would nevertheless be ill-advised to neglect the second horn of the dilemma, which contains the crucial objection. For the second horn begins with the assumption that the causing of a basic action is not a distinct or discrete event from the basic action—and this is an assumption that the agent-causalist should, *mutatis mutandis* (substituting 'result of basic action' for 'basic action'), accept, because the causing of an event is not plausibly seen as an event distinct from the event caused, but at best as a more comprehensive event including the latter event. This admission is enough for Davidson's objection in the second horn to take hold, for in the absence of two discrete events, Davidson claims, talk about causation completely lacks explanatory power. For him, as an adherent of the nomological theory of causation, this explanatory power totally depends on the possibility of distinguishing two events which can be subsumed under types of event connected by lawful regularities. 'The ordinary notion of cause', he stresses, 'is inseparable from this elementary form of explanation. What distinguishes agent-causation from ordinary causation is that no expansion into a tale of two events is possible, and no law lurks. By the same token, nothing is explained.'[25]

---

[23] Alvarez and Hyman (1998), 222 f. Their generally formulated claim that 'if actions are events caused by agents, then an intentional action is surely one that was intentionally caused' needs some qualification, however. If actions can be caused, then not all causings of intentional actions will be intentional. For example, a pupil can unintentionally make a simple mistake in calculation, thereby causing the teacher to intentionally scold him. Their claim is plausible only in the special context of where the agent's control over his actions is understood to rely on the agent's causing these actions.

[24] Cf. Bishop (1983), 77; O'Connor (1995), 181; and Alvarez/Hyman (1998), 223 f.

[25] Davidson (1971a), 53.

Indeed, agent-causation resists expansion into two events subsumable under a natural law, because the only two events involved are the event caused and (arguably) the causing-event, which is no plausible candidate for the cause because the caused event is one of its components. But what follows from this?

One could understand Davidson's point here to be simply that the regularity theory of causation allows only for event-causation. For the regularity theory, which appeals to regular or law-like *successions*, causes must be datable in the same way as effects; for only then can effects follow in the right way upon causes which precede them. Agents, being substances, cannot precede and be followed by the changes which they are normally said to cause, and thus do not belong to the category of entities—namely, events—which the regularity theory exclusively admits as causes. This way of understanding Davidson's argument reduces it to a mere reassertion of the regularity theory.[26]

Plausibly, however, Davidson's real worry goes deeper and relies on the covering-law model of explanation which he considers as paradigmatic. Agent-causality fails to conform to this paradigm, because (even without the problem of datability) there is no law-like connection between an agent and the effects of his action to which we could appeal in order to explain or predict the effects from the agent-cause. Therefore, as causation is connected to causal explanation, another paradigm of explanation to which agent-causality conforms seems to be needed—and as agent-causalists have been very reticent about such a paradigm, the explanatory power of agent-causal statements appears dubious. Davidson therefore seems to be *prima facie* justified in denying that these statements have explanatory power.

On similar grounds, Irving Thalberg has voiced doubts about the intelligibility of agent-causal talk, when it is not understood elliptically. Thalberg, too, argues that our ordinary notion of causation involves the possibility of explanation and prediction of the effect, which finds no application in the case of irreducible agent-causation; therefore agent-causation must differ from our ordinary understanding of causation.[27] Thalberg is pessimistic about finding any illuminating model for agent-causation outside the area of human agency; for he thinks that all such attempts will end up explaining agent-causation by appeal to what persons (or substances) *do* (or bring about by doing something).[28] If agent-causalists nevertheless want to adhere to the notion of irreducible agent-causation, according to Thalberg, they are left with two equally unsatisfactory alternatives: either to claim that the agent-causal relation is a primitive and totally uncharacterizable relation, or to introduce the notion with a formal axiomatic calculus which remains uninterpreted.[29] Both solutions will obviously fail to allay the doubts of sceptics about agent-causation, because they will leave the nature of this form of causation obscure.

---

[26] This is the essence of Goldman's objection against agent-causation in (1970), 81.
[27] Thalberg (1976), 216 f.
[28] Thalberg (1976), 228 f.
[29] Thalberg (1976), 229. With the first alternative Thalberg probably alludes to Taylor's claim that the notion of agent-causation is unanalysable; while the second alternative is an allusion to Chisholm's method of providing an axiomatization of his agent-causal theory; cf. Chisholm (1969), 209.

If Davidson and Thalberg are correct, there is indeed a fundamental problem about the notion of irreducible agent-causation, both because agent-causation is incompatible with the presently predominant view about causation, and because it is unclear what explanatory content the locution 'agent-causation' could have. Therefore, the first preparatory step towards constructing a positive account of agent-causation which meets the demand for intelligibility must consist in showing where Davidson's and Thalberg's arguments go wrong. For only in this way can the strong *prima facie* impression raised by their arguments—that causation can only be event-causation—be dispelled, and the quest for an alternative or supplementary account of agent-causation be motivated.

We will try to do this in the next part of this section by attacking the regularity theory of causation and, implicitly, its concomitant model of causal explanation, on which both Davidson's and Thalberg's arguments tacitly rely. First, we will try to show that Hume's considerations about the origin of our notion of causality, which may seem to exclude the possibility of a notion of cause not tied to regularities of successions, are unconvincing (Section 6.1.2.1). Second, we will raise some doubts about the capacity of the regularity theory to provide a satisfactory exhaustive account of causation, focusing on a problem that continually confronts adherents of this theory: the problem of accounting for the asymmetry of causality (Section 6.1.2.2). Though these doubts will not amount to a conclusive refutation of the regularity theory, they will show that the validity of this theory is far from established, and remains doubtful. This result will suffice to motivate the search for an alternative account, because the regularity theory can then no longer be regarded as the default theory of causation, and the burden of proof for claims that other forms of causality are impossible will clearly be shifted onto the shoulders of adherents of the regularity theory.

6.1.2. Difficulties with Hume's arguments and the regularity theory of causation

We will begin by looking critically at Hume's argument aimed at establishing that the notion of cause and the concomitant idea of necessary connection must involve regular connections between events. It has already become clear from our very short sketch that Hume's argument relies on two different premisses. The first premiss is provided by his empiricist theory about the dependence of the content of a concept on the 'impressions' from which it is derived. The second premiss is Hume's thesis that the impression from which the idea of cause and necessary connection is derived *must* be the customary transition that we make on the basis of the experience of regular successions of kinds of events, because 'there is not, in any single, particular instance of cause and effect, any thing which can suggest the idea of power or necessary connexion'.[30] Leaving aside the first premiss with its psychological assumptions

---

[30] Hume, *Enquiries*, 63.

about concept formation, I will focus on the second premiss here, trying to show that it is implausible because one of the alternative sources of our concept of causation that Hume dismisses—observation of causation in single cases—is a more promising candidate than Hume is willing to accept.

6.1.2.1. The observability of causation As we have seen, Hume rejects the possibility that our idea of causation might be derived from observation, because he holds causation to be unobservable in the individual case. As Hume argues, what we can observe in the individual case is only the sequence of events succeeding one another—as in his famous example: the succession of (i) a motion of one billiard-ball, followed by (ii) its hitting another ball, and, consequently, (iii) a motion of the second ball. Beyond that, according to Hume, nothing can be observed that would constitute or suggest a necessary connection.[31]

Hume's argument against the observability of causation suffers from two basic defects: his 'atomization' of causal processes into distinct and independent events, and his restrictive view of what counts as a 'sensible quality', which leads him to rule out anything that might count as 'observing causality'. These two factors combine to give the following train of thought some *prima facie* plausibility. Causal processes are successions of distinct events which are, at first, unconnected, because they consist of instantiations of 'sensible' qualities such as 'solidity, extension, motion' that 'never point to any other event that may result from them'.[32] When cause and effect are two such distinct events, this restriction on 'sensible' qualities already precludes that observation of the qualities instantiated in the two events on their own could count as an observation of causality. Instead, we could observe the causal connection in the individual case only if we could observe something *in addition* to those two events that could constitute the causal connection.[33] If we put the question of observability of causation in this way, we are indeed hard pressed to find an additional element that could constitute a causal connection. Therefore, with regard to 'atom', independent events of the kind that Hume envisages, his claim that causal connections between them are unobservable is very probably true.[34]

But this would only imply that causation is unobservable in general, if we could assume that all causal processes can be 'atomized' into successions of distinct events, which are instantiations of properties that 'never point to any other event that may result from them'. This assumption, however, is wrong. Characteristically, we can witness continuous causal processes, involving active substances, without breaking up this continuous experience into successions of separate experience-'atoms'. Standard cases of exertions of powers and forces which constitute observable causal processes are,

---

[31] Hume, *Enquiries*, 63.   [32] Hume, *Enquiries*, 63.
[33] Harré and Madden (1975), 57, point out this mistake on Hume's part.
[34] Cf. Strawson (1985), 120.

as Peter Strawson has argued, mechanical transactions between physical objects, such as pulling, pushing, and so on.[35]

Three points are characteristic for such mechanical transactions, and serve to refute Hume's general claim.[36] (1) In observing such processes we do not observe two distinct changes which we then connect as cause and effect, but instead we directly observe a change-as-brought-about-in-a-certain-way. For example, when I see a person lifting a suitcase I do not have two distinct experiences of the person raising his arm and subsequently of the suitcase going up, but only one experience. Perhaps the most obvious case of one experience comprising both cause and effect is when someone feels physical pressure exerted on his own body, where he often experiences the cause only *as causing* the feeling of pressure. (2) It is appropriate to describe such transactions which we can directly observe, as *causal* processes, because a new state of affairs is brought about and there is a substance or change which we can describe as causally responsible for bringing it about; for example, when the man lifts the suitcase, the state which is brought about is a new position of the suitcase, and the man is responsible for bringing about this state. (3) The observed change already provides us with a completely satisfactory explanation of the outcome, and so there is no reason to assume that what we have observed has somehow not comprised the 'real' causal element which alone would provide such an explanation. These three points show that Hume's claim that, in general, causal connections are unobservable, cannot be upheld; for once we abandon Hume's focus on separate events as causes and effects, we easily find continuous causal processes which are observable and include causal connections.

That such cases are not isolated, but pervade our lives and constitute the huge majority of causal transactions which we encounter, becomes clear once we realize the connection between our general concept of 'cause' and more specific causal concepts that are typically expressed by transitive verbs.[37] As linguists have pointed out, such verbs characteristically contain a causative element. They systematically relate to verbs describing changes, and what we do in applying such verbs is, on the one hand, to describe the correlative change or effect that is brought about, and on the other hand, to identify the subject of which we predicate the verb as the source of this change or effect.[38] Clearly, processes which we describe by such transitive verbs are ubiquitous in our daily lives, and equally clearly there is no reason to assume that such processes are something that we could not perceive directly, or only 'less directly' than some of the other 'sensible' qualities which Hume accepts, such as motion or solidity. Short of Cartesian scepticism,[39] seeing how an avalanche crashes a house or experiencing how the wind blows away one's hat must be accepted as a paradigmatic case of an 'experi-

---

[35] Strawson (1985), 123 f.
[36] Cf. Strawson (1985), 120 ff.; and Harré and Madden (1975), 53.
[37] Anscombe (1971), 92 f.
[38] This systematic connection and the 'causative' element have been explored in detail by Lakoff (1965).
[39] Anscombe (1971), 93, points out the parallel between Hume's procedure and Descartes' sceptical arguments.

ence of the senses', in the same way as witnessing the motion of a billiard-ball is a case of such an experience. Hume's denial of this point is even more surprising when we remember that on a strict atomization of causal processes into distinct events, motion—which Hume himself counts among the 'sensible qualities'—would also have to count as non-observable, because one could only observe the object in different places at successive times, but not observe an additional 'element of motion'.

The pervasive phenomenon of observing changes being brought about by substances or by other simultaneous changes not only refutes Hume's non-observability claim, but also calls into question Hume's negative phylogenetic claim that such observations cannot be the source of our idea of cause. In fact, as Strawson has eloquently argued, our experience of exerting force on physical objects and suffering the exertion of force upon us is the most obvious and plausible candidate for the basic experience that Hume is seeking.[40] In particular, these feelings are experiences of 'force' and 'compulsion', and therefore could serve as the basis of some, albeit anthropomorphic, idea of causal necessity connecting cause and effect. For, from the perspective of the 'suffering' object upon which the cause acts, it is 'unavoidable' that the effect obtains. When I am pushed along a ramp by a cupboard sliding downwards, 'I cannot help' sliding downwards myself, when I unsuccessfully try to resist the pressure. If the idea of causal necessity corresponds to any specific element of experience at all, it will arguably be this particular aspect of unsuccessful resistance to physical impact which is anthropomorphically projected onto other causes and effects. However, what the relevant specific experiences are ultimately remains an empirical question about actual processes of concept formation in childhood, whose resolution is independent from the central philosophical point that causality can be perceived at all, and that this perception *could* form the basis for the acquisition of this concept.

We can thus conclude that Hume's arguments about the sources of our concept of causality, and against the 'direct' observability of causality in particular, should be resisted, for they rely on a mistakenly 'atomized' view of processes in reality as constituted by a series of self-contained and independent events. If one subscribes to this view, one is naturally led to Hume's reductionist and anti-singularist views about causation, because then, regularities and causal laws seem to be the only candidates for what could connect those distinct events. Once we recognize that causation is observable in the individual case, Hume's reason for claiming that particular causal relations always presuppose general relations, and that causal relations could be reduced to non-causal relations, simply vanishes. With regard to questions of concept formation, the

---

[40] Strawson (1985), 122 f. Interestingly, in the *Enquiries* Hume himself discussed the possibility that the 'strong endeavour' in exerting power to overcome physical resistance might be the basis for our idea of causation, and he rejected this possibility because we could know only through experience which effects followed upon this feeling of endeavour (p. 67, fn. 1). However, this argument rests on Hume's problematic atomization of the process by which he separates the feeling of endeavour from the experience of the whole situation, and is therefore unconvincing.

concept of causation needs to be neither anti-singularist nor reducible to non-causal concepts.

Obviously, this point does not yet refute the regularity theory of causation as such. Even if, *pace* Hume, we can observe that causal relations obtain in particular cases, it might well be true that such relations can obtain only if there are corresponding general regularities. But our result removes the presumption in favour of the regularity theory that has been underlying the widespread acceptance of this theory as 'the default theory of causation' in the centuries following Hume. Consequently, it also removes the presumption against agent-causation which one may believe to result from Davidson's argument in *Agency*, because this argument relies on the regularity view and its connected paradigm of causal explanation. In the end, it may still turn out that we are unable to provide a satisfactory account of agent-causation—but Davidson's general consideration should not stop us from trying.

6.1.2.2. The regularity theory and the direction of causation The argument presented in the previous section has only removed an often accepted presumption against the possibility of agent-causation. In order to positively motivate the search for an agent-causal account, I will sketch one problem that continually haunts adherents of the regularity theory, and strongly suggests that this theory omits a crucial element of causality, so that it cannot be a satisfactory and comprehensive account of causation. This notorious problem is that the causal relation is not symmetrical, but 'has a direction': if A and B are particular events or substances,[41] then if A causes B, B need not and normally does not cause A.[42]

When we look back to the reductionist analysis of cause as, *ceteris paribus*, a necessary and/or sufficient condition, it is easy to see that this analysis fails to account for the asymmetry of the causal relation, and therefore fails to distinguish between causes and effects. For if A is, *ceteris paribus*, necessary and sufficient for B, then the same clearly also applies to B with regard to A. If it is, *ceteris paribus*, necessary and sufficient for a completely dried up cistern to be filled with water tomorrow morning that it rains during the night, then conversely, the cistern's being filled with water tomorrow morning is also, *ceteris paribus*, necessary and sufficient for it having rained during the night. This converse dependence of sufficiency and necessity is what enables us to infer what has happened from what is now the case.

Normally, adherents of the regularity theory try to solve this difficulty by distinguishing between cause and effect by their temporal order. Among two mutually

---

[41] It is different when A and B are general types of event or substances; then 'reciprocal' causation is quite common. For example, a rise in workers' wages in an economy can cause, via an increase in demand, an increase in production, and the latter increase can in turn cause a rise in the workers' wages.

[42] One might even think that if A causes B, then B *cannot* cause A. But I do not see why we should not include cases of reciprocal simultaneous causation—for example, of two events mutually sustaining each other, such as Pollock's case of 'two cards leaning on each other', among cases of 'causation proper'; Pollock (1976), 173.

necessary and sufficient conditions, the cause is the one that temporally precedes the other (following Hume's first definition of cause in the *Enquiry*).[43] But, as Taylor has rightly argued, this distinction fails to account for the asymmetry of causation generally, because cause and effect can be simultaneous. If a person moves a pen which she holds in her hand by moving her hand, then the movement of the hand is, *ceteris paribus*, necessary and sufficient for the movement of the pen, and vice versa; also, both movements are completely simultaneous.[44] But obviously, only the movement of the hand is the cause of the movement of the pen, and not vice versa.[45]

Taylor infers from these cases of simultaneous causation that the adherent of the regularity theory is generally unable to distinguish between cause and effect. Instead, he argues, we must reintroduce concepts such as 'activity' and 'bringing about' to capture the direction of causation.[46] Of course, this inference is premature, for there are other attempts by adherents of the regularity theory to explain the asymmetry of causation, so that the possibility of simultaneous causation is insufficient to refute the regularity theory as such. But our aim here is more modest than Taylor's. We are not concerned with a thorough refutation of the regularity theory, but only with showing how its difficulties should motivate the search for an alternative or supplementary account of causation. And the difficulties of the theory with the direction of causation remain, by and large, when we substitute or supplement the temporal criterion by another criterion, as a summary perusal of popular attempts in this direction makes clear.

These attempts can be classified, very roughly, with regard to three different kinds of concern which make it improbable that they can salvage the regularity theory:

(i) First, the account may be unpromising with regard to an explanation of direction or asymmetry, because the feature on which it is based allows for symmetrical relations. This worry applies to attempts to explain the direction of causation by the direction of probability-enhancement[47]—attempts which would claim that the occurrence of the cause raises the probability of the occurrence of the effect, but not vice versa. However, this idea does not seem a promising basis for explaining the difference between cause

---

[43] Hume, *Enquiries*, 76.
[44] Adherents of the regularity theory might try to challenge this example by arguing that the movements *cannot* be completely simultaneous, because there is a transfer of energy from hand to pen, the connection hand–pen can never be completely rigid, and the hand *must* begin to move first. (Mellor (1995), 223, and Molnar (2003), 193, have argued in this way against another example for simultaneous causation from Taylor (1966), 35.) However, the underlying assumption is unwarranted in the case of the hand moving the pen. Of course, I have to exert some (often minimal) pressure with my hand before the pen begins to move, and so a 'transfer of energy' is required to overcome the initial friction and make the pen move; but it is quite possible that my hand too, only begins to move when the pen does, because the energy transfer necessary to overcome the initial friction has been completed previously (though, of course, further energy-transfer is necessary to keep the pen moving, this further transfer continues simultaneously with the movement).
[45] Taylor (1966), 35 ff.
[46] Taylor (1966), 39.
[47] Tooley (1990), 475, argues for a connection between these two directions (without, however, attempting to explain the direction of causation in the 'simple' probability-enhancement form which I am addressing here).

and effect, because probability-enhancing relations of this kind are often symmetrical:[48] If the effect at t2 is more probable given the cause occurring at t1, then typically it is more likely that the cause has occurred at t1, if the effect occurs at t2. The probability may even rise in precisely the same way; remember the pen-pushing example, and compare the probabilities of the hand moving and the pen moving in connection with each other. So, probability-enhancing will not suffice to explain the direction of causation.

(ii) Second, even if the account is successful in providing some explanation of the asymmetry of the causal relation, it may still fail to cover the case of simultaneous causation, because the explanation of 'direction of causation' that is offered is no stronger than the explanation in terms of temporal succession. This is the case with the 'open fork' strategy,[49] which tries to explain the direction of causality by appeal to 'conjunctive open forks' rather than to temporal succession. The underlying idea is that there can be two co-occurring events A and B, such that there is an event C in one temporal direction making the co-occurrence of A and B more probable than it would be without C, while there is no such event in the opposite temporal direction. In this case we have an 'open fork', with C at the bottom and A and B at the two upper ends. Reichenbach and Salmon contend that all open forks which satisfy a set of four conditions about the relations between the probabilities of A, B, C, non-C, and A-and-B— forks called 'conjunctive'[50]—point into one temporal direction; that is, they are always open to the future. This unique direction of 'open forks' then determines the direction of causation (and time).

There are major difficulties confronting this account, especially concerning the question of why all 'open forks' should point in the same temporal direction, and how this account is to be supplemented for deterministic processes which do not allow for 'open forks'.[51] But even if we leave these worries aside, this strategy clearly cannot account for the direction of simultaneous causation, because 'open forks' are always directed from one point of time to a preceding or succeeding one.[52] Thus, the account would

---

[48] When we consider only conditional probabilities, on standard probability theory, this relation will even be symmetrical *tout court* (under some additional conditions): When the probability of the effect, given the cause, is higher than the probability of the effect *tout court*, the same holds vice versa (if the probability *tout court* of neither cause nor effect is zero); cf. van Fraasen (1980), 26 f.

[49] Reichenbach (1956), sect. 19; Salmon (1973), *passim*.

[50] Salmon (1973), 158 f.

[51] Cf. Sosa and Tooley (1993), 23; Swinburne (1997), 85.

[52] The same kind of difficulty confronts Lewis's explanation of the direction of causation; cf. his (1973) and (1979). On the basis of his counterfactual account of causation, he argues that in our world, events typically have many effects, but seldom many causes, and so the F-worlds closest to our own will be those which differ from our world with regard to the future rather than to the past. Even if this were true, it would clearly not help us with regard to the direction of simultaneous causation. What would be needed to transfer Lewis's account to simultaneous causation would be to show that in cases of simultaneous causation, in the absence of the effect the cause would not have been absent, because it is a smaller change of reality to hold the cause fixed than to change the relevant laws. (This is the general line which Lewis takes in (1973), 441, without explicitly addressing the problem of simultaneous causation.) But for many cases of simultaneous causation,

have to deny the possibility of simultaneous causation, and is therefore unable to fill the gap we have found to exist in the regularity account.

(iii) Lastly, the account may seem to be explanatorily adequate, but go too much beyond the resources of the regularity theory to be compatible with its central tenets. For instance, von Wright's manipulation account of causation—which argues that what distinguishes cause from effect is that we can bring about the latter by manipulatively bringing about the former[53]—promises to provide an explanation of the direction of event-causation. But it reduces the asymmetry of causation to the asymmetry of the 'by'-relation between non-basic actions and those actions by which we perform them, and therefore has to presuppose a notion of activity or agency. Without a prior non-causal explanation of activity, this is not something that an adherent of the regularity theory can accept without running the risk of bringing in the repudiated notion of agent-causation by the back door.[54]

I do not want to claim that this classification is exhaustive, or that the three kinds of worry that I have mentioned are necessarily insurmountable. But I think these worries show that there is a strong case for assuming that the regularity theory has a fundamental difficulty with the direction of causality. As the latter is an essential feature of causation, the regularity theory, it seems, cannot tell the whole story about causation, and we are well advised to look for an account that either supplants or, at least, supplements it.

6.2. Powers as genuine properties

When one starts looking for an alternative account of causation that allows space for agent-causation, there are, in my view, two main promising lines of approach: first, an 'interventionist' model of causation; and second, a 'causal powers' model. The core claim of the 'interventionist' model of causation is that causation, as we ordinarily understand it, is 'the intervention of an agent in a system, thereby bringing about changes which would not otherwise have occurred'.[55] Agents, on this view, are external to the systems in whose ongoing processes they interfere.[56] This model allows

---

this claim is simply incredible, because taking away the effect while holding the cause fixed entails splitting up one naturally continuous causal process—as in the pen-pushing case.

[53] Von Wright (1971), ch. 2.
[54] The same point applies to transference theories of causation which explain causal interactions as transmissions of conserved quantities—of charge, energy, or tropes; cf. Ehring (1986). As the bearers of such quantities are objects or systems composed of objects, it is no surprise that the earliest proponents of transference theories—for example, Aronson (1971)—took objects rather than events to be the relata of the causal relation—and this is not compatible with the view connected to the regularity theory that all causes must be events.
[55] Sellars (1966), 142.
[56] Cf. Byerly (1979), 60 f.

for substance-causation, because the agents are seen as causal sources of effects: namely, of the results of their interferences. But it creates difficulties for our general project of finding an agent-causal account that explains the agent's control over the results of his basic actions; for the results of basic physical actions are motions of the body of the agent himself, and are therefore not changes in a system to which the agent is external. Consequently, I will follow the 'causal powers' model and try to show that the latter allows for substance-causes bringing about changes in themselves.

The central idea of the 'causal powers' model of agent-causation that I will defend is that objects are bearers of causal powers, which are 'directed' at certain effects, and that causation consists in the manifestations of a certain sub-group of those powers—'causal' or 'active' powers. Even though causal powers can be accepted by agent-causalists and their opponents alike,[57] the specific agent-causalist claim is that when causal powers are exercised, the cause of the effect is the substance-bearer of these powers, and not (or at least not exclusively) the event which triggers the exercise of the power. Furthermore, while event-causalists can be either agnostic about the reducibility of causal powers to other properties or advocate such a reduction, an agent-causalist theory which is based on causal powers is well advised to argue for the irreducibility of causal powers as a genus. For if powers are reducible to non-power properties, this reduction may imply a reduction of agent-causation, understood as the realization of such powers, to event-causation (where the relevant events will presumably be the events triggering the power's exercise).

The claim that there are irreducible powers is by no means uncontested—at least since powers became the object of Hume's criticism in his overall attack on the traditional notion of 'cause'.[58] The rejection of powers is part and parcel of Hume's 'atomized' view of reality and experience, which we have already discussed, and the ongoing influence of this view in the empiricist tradition underlies the widespread rejection of irreducible powers up to the present day. As D. Mellor very aptly characterized the situation when he undertook the project of rehabilitating powers in the 1970s, they are regarded as 'shameful in many eyes as pregnant spinsters used to be—ideally to be explained away, or entitled by a shotgun wedding to take the name of some decently real categorical property.'[59] Due to the persistence of this 'Victorian prejudice', irreducible powers are viewed by many present-day philosophers with almost as much suspicion as substance-causation itself; and so our contention that there are such powers will require a lengthy defence against both scepticism about the existence of such powers, and even more against scepticism about their irreducibility.

---

[57] Cf. among the opponents of agent-causation, Davidson (1973a), 64, whose 'definition' of causal power makes it reducible to event-causation, or Armstrong (1997), ch. 15 and 16, which contain his explanation of causal powers as based on contingent relations between universals.

[58] Cf. Hume, *Enquiries*, 61 f.

[59] Mellor (1974), 157.

Our vindication of agent-causation on a causal powers model must therefore proceed in two steps: showing that there are powers that are irreducible to other properties, and showing how the exercise of these powers involves agent-causation. In this section I will begin by tackling the first task, by presenting a general overview of the genus 'power' and its sub-kinds (Section 6.2.1), and then by defending a 'realist' view of powers—the view that powers are genuine properties of objects (Section 6.2.2). This will set the stage for our argument, in the next chapter, that powers are not reducible to non-power properties or relations among them, both conceptually and ontologically.

6.2.1. What are powers? – Different types of power

In a general sense, powers are properties of substances, or of other stuff, that are by definition directed at certain changes called (effects of) 'manifestations' of those powers, which are distinct from the powers themselves. Thus, powers are necessarily powers *to* X: to behave in a certain way, to produce a certain effect or to undergo a certain change. Ascriptions of the power to X to an object implies that the object can or will do X, and behaviour of this kind can be expected from it. The identity of a power as a distinct property is determined by the conjunction of three criteria: (a) its manifestations—what it is a power *to*—(b) the conditions for the manifestation or 'exercise' of the power, and (c) how tightly the manifestations are linked to the obtaining of those conditions—whether the power must be manifested under those conditions, probably will be manifested (and how probably), or simply can be manifested.

The best-known subclass of powers is formed by *dispositions*—properties of an object to behave in a specific way under certain circumstances. Dispositions are closely tied to conditional statements of the kind 'if circumstances A obtain, the object will behave in way B'; we will call A 'triggering conditions' or 'stimuli', and B 'manifestation behaviour'. When the triggering conditions obtain, the manifestation behaviour must occur unless there are intervening factors which prevent it; for example, a water-soluble object must dissolve when put into water, except if the water is immediately frozen into a block of ice. Dispositions—which we normally describe by suffixing '-ile' or '-ble' to a verb stem, yielding the myriad of commonplace dispositional verbs such as combustible, flexible, breakable, or by putting the adjective 'disposed to' in front of a predicate—are ubiquitous in our daily lives. In our daily use of dispositional terms, the claim about a necessary connection between triggering conditions and manifestation behaviour is often implicitly restricted to a range of background circumstances considered as 'normal'. Beginning with dispositions, four important distinctions can be drawn among powers—the first three of which correspond to the three identity criteria for powers that we have mentioned.

First, following Gilbert Ryle, we can distinguish between more or less *generic* (or 'determinable') and *determinate* dispositions. While a determinate disposition, such as water-solubility, is closely correlated with *one* specific manifestation, more generic dispositions are connected with a range of *different* manifestations as responses to different stimuli. An instance of a generic disposition is elasticity, which is not tied to just one specific kind of manifestation, but to several, such as expanding when pulled, contracting after having been expanded, and so on. Characteristically, the mark of a highly 'determinate' dispositional word is that the verb stem is the same as of the verb used for describing the manifestation behaviour, while for generic words it is different. For example, while the correspondent manifestation description for 'water-soluble' is 'dissolves in water', there is no such correspondent description for 'elastic'.[60]

Orthogonally to this first distinction, there is a further distinction to be drawn according to how closely triggering conditions and manifestation behaviour are connected. For example, water-solubility can be ascribed only if the object, when placed in water, dissolves, save for extraordinary factors. In contrast, 'dispositions' of human beings, such as irritability, are not only highly generic, but their possession does not necessitate manifestation behaviour on *all* specified occasions—even if the background conditions are right. An irritable man need not be offended *every* time he is provoked, but only sufficiently often.

When the link between triggering conditions and manifestation behaviour is sufficiently loosened so that the behaviour will only regularly or probably occur under those conditions, we no longer talk of dispositions but of *tendencies* or propensities of objects. As Ryle explained: 'A has the tendency to B under circumstances C' licences us to positively expect that A will B, when C obtains, though we cannot rely on its doing so with certainty.[61] Further along the line of loosening the connection are potentials or *capacities*[62] of objects. When an object possesses a capacity to A under circumstances B, the object *can* do A in these circumstances, but need not do so nor is especially likely to do so. For example, a certain medicine can produce, as a side-effect, an inflammation of the liver, if certain specific conditions obtain; but even under those conditions, the inflammation occurs in only 10% of the cases, so that even then it cannot be positively expected. As the obtaining of the specific conditions does not even make the effect probable, we will not call those circumstances 'triggering conditions', but '*occasions*' for the exercise of the capacity.

The third distinction concerns the specificity of the conditions for the manifestation of the power: Does the manifestation require more specific circumstances—as in the case of a disposition to dissolve in water only at a specific temperature, where both the right temperature and contact between the object and water are necessary for the manifestation—or can it be manifested in a wider variety of situations, requiring fewer conditions for its exercise, such as a disposition to dissolve in fluid water irrespective of

---

[60] Ryle (1990), 114.
[61] Ryle (1990), 126.
[62] Capacities in the sense used here must be distinguished from capacities as understood by Kenny (1989), 83, where capacities are 'more removed from action' than dispositions—that is, they function as capacities to acquire an ability or disposition. Also, they must be distinguished from Cartwright's usage, (1997), 74, for whom capacities are simply highly generic dispositions.

its temperature? The limiting case of the latter kind would be that no special circumstances are required at all, so that the manifestation is always possible. Though it is doubtful that we can find instances of this limiting case among natural objects, we can find instances of *unconditional* powers which can be manifested without requiring much more than the absence of intervening factors. For example, unstable explosives can explode practically all the time and in all kinds of situations, as long as those situations are not completely abnormal and no special precautions for masking the explosive force are taken.

Crucially, unconditional powers have no corresponding conditionals linking manifestations to conditions for exercise, such as dispositions or tendencies have. One might challenge this claim by pointing out that also with regard to those powers we describe as 'unconditional' there are corresponding conditionals of the kind, 'if intervening factors are absent, and under ordinary conditions, A can B'. However, this objection is unsuccessful, for in those conditionals, the 'if' clause does not describe triggering conditions, as it does in the conditionals connected to dispositions or tendencies. Instead, it states background conditions which are also relevant for the latter conditionals, *in addition to* the triggering conditions, and which we implicitly assume to be satisfied when asserting the conditional.

The fourth distinction concerns the question of what the manifestation of a power consists in. When it consists in the acquisition of a further power by the object, we can talk of a 'higher-order' power; and when the power is not 'directed' at such an acquisition it is a 'first-order' power. For example, while brittleness is a first-order power because its manifestation—breaking—is not itself a power[63] or the acquisition of a power, the disposition to become brittle when heated is a second-order power, because it is 'directed at' the acquisition of the further power—brittleness.

As our first three distinctions are gradual, they yield three different gradual spectra of power. The fourth distinction, on the other hand, is categorical, and yields a hierarchy of powers of different orders. We can freely combine the spectra generated by the first three distinctions, thereby discovering new types of powers—for example, of highly generic tendencies or capacities, such as the spontaneous 'wittiness' of a person which can, but need not, manifest itself in a wide variety of ways and without presupposing any specific circumstances. Combining two extreme points of the second and third spectra, we can even find powers that are necessarily continuously manifested, as long as they are possessed by their bearers, that is, powers that are always manifested when there is an occasion for manifestation, while lacking preconditions for their manifestation. According to General Relativity Theory, rest mass is such a power.[64] There is, however, something *prima facie* puzzling about such continuously manifested powers, for the impossibility to separate possession of the power from its manifestation seems to remove the characteristic mark of powers. These powers appear to cross the line

---

[63] *Pace* Molnar (2003), 166, who claims that occurrences themselves can be dispositional.
[64] Molnar (2003), 87.

dividing powers and those properties which are normally contrasted to powers: namely, 'categorical' or 'occurrent' properties.

The notion of 'categorical' properties can be seen, at a first approach, as an heir to Hume's notion of 'observable properties', comprising the same cases as paradigms, such as location, geometrical form, size, and so on. Some modern philosophers have even followed Hume so far as to contrast the dispositions of an object with the properties of it which we can observe.[65] To draw the distinction between powers and categorical properties in this way, however, will not work, if the distinction is intended to be both exclusive and exhaustive for all properties described by one-place predicates. For on the one hand, when we understand 'observable' narrowly enough to exclude powers—as, for example, 'what we can see with our eyes, without presupposing specific factual knowledge'—there are also categorical properties which are unobservable in this sense, such as molecular or subatomic structure, which is, at a certain level, simply too small to be so observed (even in principle).[66] On the other hand, when we understand 'observable' more widely, so as to include as many of the categorical properties as possible, we quickly reach a point where some powers will count as observable too; for in a sense, we *can* observe that an object has certain powers—namely, when we witness the object exerting its power by producing a certain effect (cf. Section 6.1.2.1) or undergoing a certain change.

The distinction between powers and categorical properties should therefore be better based on our original characterization of powers. While powers essentially point towards an object 'beyond themselves'—their manifestations—, 'categorical' properties do not. The best way to explain this difference in a non-metaphorical way is in terms of a general difference in the conditions for mastery of power concepts and categorical concepts. Having mastered a power concept requires that one knows which kind of manifestation is connected to this power, and that this manifestation is not identical with the power. By contrast, it is not necessary for mastering the concept of a categorical property to know about any *specific* connection to another property or its instantiation (with one exception: if the other property is a determinable property of which the first property is a determinate). Therefore, someone would not count as knowing what 'fragile' means when he does not know the essential connection of this property to breaking; while for mastery of the concept 'triangular', no such specific additional knowledge is required.[67] (This does not mean that one need

---

[65] For example, Goodman (1955), 40.

[66] Mumford (1998), 4 f. One might object that even at a level where, admittedly, we cannot 'see the structures through the microscope', we can still observe them 'indirectly' in experiments, in the same way as we can 'see' an electron in the cloud-chamber. But this objection does not succeed in saving the proposed criterion for distinguishing categorical properties from powers, because once one accepts cases of 'indirect' perception of this kind, one must also admit powers as observable. For example, in the cloud-chamber experiment we can 'perceive' in this way that the particle flying around is charged, and its charge is among its powers.

[67] This connection is *not* merely a logical connection between power-ascriptions and statements about other occurrences—for both disposition ascriptions and categorical ascriptions *a priori* imply statements about

not know many other things in order to count as having mastered any concept at all; it only means that for categorical property concepts one need not know about any *particular* such connection.)

When we use this difference in the conditions for concept-mastery as the criterion for distinguishing powers from categorical properties, it turns out that we are right to treat 'rest mass' as a power concept, even though the possession of rest mass is always connected with the manifestation of this power. For the manifestations are different from the power itself, consisting in the object's behaviour when accelerated, its specific interactions with other objects, and so on, and at the same time we have to know something about the connection to those manifestations in order to count as having mastered the concept of rest mass.

This rough sketch of powers, their main sub-types, and the rule-of-thumb distinction between power concepts and concepts of categorical properties, will suffice as the basis of our further discussion of powers.

6.2.2. *The reality of powers*

The first question that arises with regard to powers is whether we should accept them as genuine properties of the objects to which they are ascribed (leaving aside, for the moment, the question of whether they are reducible to non-power properties). This question cannot be settled by merely pointing out that powers are ascribed by using predicate-terms—for not all predicates express genuine properties.[68]

Nevertheless, it seems quite obvious that powers must be bona fide properties, like categorical properties. For, plausibly, it is jointly sufficient, for an alleged property to be indeed a genuine property, that (1) there are statements appealing to this property which we regard as clearly true and about whose truth-value we are unwilling to change our mind even if pressed, and that (2) the truth of those statements can be explained only if we assume that there is a genuine property of this kind. With regard to powers, this condition is fulfilled, for there are power-ascriptions, descriptions of processes as manifestations of powers, and corresponding explanations of results in terms of powers, which we believe to be true, and which we could not consider to be false without giving up an enormous part of our quotidian and scientific explanatory practices. An important practice of this kind is constituted by dispositional explanations—such as explaining the dissolution of a lump of sugar in water by pointing out that sugar is water-soluble, which we regard as a perfectly satisfactory and sound explanation of why the sugar dissolved. Furthermore, it seems that for the truth of

---

further occurrences. For example, while an object's being fragile implies that it breaks when it is knocked, *pari passu*, an object's being knocked implies that it breaks when it is fragile. Therefore, we must turn to the knowledge required for concept-mastery in order to draw the distinction between power concepts and concepts of categorical properties—as Hawthorne and Manley (2005) rightly point out for the case of dispositions.

[68] There cannot, for example, be a property of 'being not-self-exemplifying', because postulating such a property would lead to Russell's paradox; cf. Lowe (2006), 122.

these statements, powers must be genuine properties, because we treat them as such properties—that is, as properties that can be acquired, lost, and whose possession makes a difference to the object's behaviour. It is difficult to see what more could be required for qualifying as a genuine property.

In agreement with the result of this argument, powers have traditionally been viewed as genuine properties of objects, on a par with their categorical properties. Acceptance of powers as bona fide items within the ontology is usually dated back to Aristotle's discussion of δύναμις and ἐνέργεια in book θ of *Metaphysics*. This realist view commanded widespread acceptance until the Early Modern age, as Locke's realist theory of powers in his *Essay concerning Human Understanding* especially testifies. But in the eighteenth century, powers began to fall into disrepute, due to Hume's eloquent criticism, and scepticism about powers continued throughout most of the empiricist tradition and logical positivism well into the second half of the twentieth century. Only in the 1970s did the slow rehabilitation of powers, particularly of dispositions, begin—especially through the work of Rom Harré, E. H. Madden, and D. H. Mellor.

The difficulty about viewing powers as genuine properties was mainly thought to be the following. While it is obvious that we have disposition-verbs and other power-verbs in our language, one can think that in predicating such a verb of an object we do not ascribe a real property, but only make a statement about how the object might possibly or probably behave. What would make the statement 'A has a disposition to F' true, it was thought, would not be A's possession of a dispositional property, but only the possibility or probability that A would F. If this view were true, we could explain the truth of such statements without assuming that powers are genuine properties on their own, and therefore our argument for realism about powers would collapse.

The best-known exponent of such scepticism about powers was Hume, who claimed that power was no more than 'the possibility or probability of any action, as discovered by experience',[69] and denied powers any existence as distinct from their manifestations. Insofar as a power was manifested, Hume claimed, it was identical with its manifestation(s), while otherwise it was no real property of the object at all: 'the distinction, which we sometimes make betwixt a power and the exercise of it, is entirely frivolous.'[70] Nelson Goodman expressed similar worries when he wrote that dispositional predicates 'seem to be applied to things in virtue of possible rather than actual occurrences', and therefore, in comparison to observable properties, dispositions and capacities seem 'rather ethereal.'[71] Ryle's famous 'inference-ticket' view denied that disposition ascriptions are describing facts, and so we can conclude that they ascribe any real properties. Instead, Ryle argued, these ascriptions are similar to law statements, for they license us to infer from a statement about the obtaining of the triggering conditions a statement about the occurrence of the manifestation.[72]

---

[69] Hume, *Treatise*, 313.　　[70] Hume, *Treatise*, 311.
[71] Goodman (1955), 40 f.　　[72] Ryle (1990), 120.

The result of these worries need not be a straightforward eliminativism about powers, but can also be a strictly reductive view of powers.[73] At the moment, however, I am concerned only with the eliminativist alternative. As both eliminativists and realists about powers agree that power-ascriptions are sometimes truthfully asserted, the crucial question is whether eliminativists are correct in denying that these ascriptions must be construed as statements about genuine present properties of the object. Must we really accept powers as genuine properties in order to account for everyday and scientific explanatory discourse involving power-predicates, or not? I think we must, and one important part of showing that we do is to demonstrate that power-ascriptions are not reducible to statements containing no power terms. However, this latter task will have to be postponed until the next chapter, where I shall be dealing with the general question of the reducibility of power-statements. Here, I will only present two arguments directed specifically against the eliminativist account—the first applying to Hume in particular, and the second to eliminativism in general.

The first concerns Hume's proposal to identify powers, insofar as they are exercised, with their manifestations. This proposal will not work because, for conceptual reasons, powers are distinct from their manifestations—this distinction, one might say, is precisely the point of power concepts. As a consequence of this distinction, the occurrence of an F-ing does not imply that a power to F is exercised, for there can be occurrences of F-ing that are no exercises of correlated powers. For example, an object which is not brittle may still break when it is shattered by a nuclear explosion. But if we assume, as Hume does, that manifested powers are nothing but their manifestations, an F-ing event on its own would be sufficient for a power-manifestation, because there is *ex hypothesi* no extra element required; so we could not distinguish cases of F-ing which are manifestations of the power to F from cases which are not. This amounts to a *reductio ad absurdum* of Hume's proposal.

Second, and more generally, the possibility that powers, like other properties of an object, can change over time, poses an insurmountable problem for eliminativists. An object can lose its flexibility, cease to be water-soluble, or become brittle. For an eliminativist about powers it is impossible to explain this fact while maintaining the difference between powers and higher-order capacities to acquire these powers. For instance, compare an 'unconditional' capacity, such as the power possessed by an unstable explosive, and the higher-order power to acquire this capacity, such as the power of an explosive that can become unstable, though it has not yet done so. On the realist view of powers, the difference between the two objects is easily explained, because the first explosive possesses a power which the other lacks, though it can acquire this power. On the eliminativist view, however, we would analyse *both* 'A is an unstable explosive' and 'B can become an unstable explosive' in the same way as 'A can explode' (for when analysing the second ascription, we would obtain, as a first step of

---

[73] As, for example, in Goodman's case, (1955), ch. 2.

the analysis 'B can (can explode)', and the two subsequent 'cans' can be 'conflated' into one). But being an unstable explosive and being capable of becoming one are obviously not the same thing. Having the second capacity is much less dangerous than having the first, and this difference can be of the greatest practical importance for us when we can determine whether or not an explosive has already become unstable; for example, if the explosive will turn red on becoming unstable.

The eliminativist might try to save this crucial distinction by saying that the 'can' in both sentences must be understood differently; but it seems that he cannot explain this distinction in the correct way, because the relevant sense of 'can' in which 'A can explode' while 'B cannot explode' is that A can explode without first changing its properties, while B must change its properties first—and the eliminativist, denying that powers are real characteristics of objects, cannot add this qualification.

So, the eliminativists' difficulties with changes in the powers of objects provide sufficient grounds for accepting powers as genuine properties, though it is yet unclear whether these properties are reducible to non-power properties. Further arguments for the reality of powers will be implicitly added when we show that power-ascriptions are not reducible to other statements which do not contain any reference to powers; for if these arguments are successful, power-ascriptions must be more than only talk about the possible, probable, or certain behaviour of objects, as eliminativists such as Hume and Ryle have thought.

7
How agent-causation works II: the irreducibility of powers

Even if powers are genuine properties of objects, this does not exclude the possibility that they are completely dependent on and reducible to non-power properties; in this case, the possession of a power could be construed completely in terms of the possession of categorical properties and relations among them. As we have already stated, reducibility of powers would be an unwelcome result for our general project of developing an account of agent-causation on the basis of a theory of powers. For if powers were reducible to categorical properties, their possession could not confer on their bearers any causal role that extends beyond the role bestowed by the possession of categorical properties; and there is good reason to assume that the possession of the latter does not give rise to substance-causation, but only to event-causation by the triggering event or the instantiation event. Thus, for an agent-causal account we need to show that possession of powers cannot be reduced to possession of categorical properties and the obtaining of relations among those properties and their instantiations.

The most straightforward form of reducibility would be conceptual reducibility. It would hold if statements about powers could be translated without any change in truth-conditions into statements without any explicit or implicit appeal to power-concepts. This kind of reducibility will be treated in Section 7.1, where we will address the question of whether such a translation is possible for power-ascriptions. But even if power-ascriptions should turn out not to be reducible in this way, it might still be argued that powers cannot confer a genuine causal role on their bearers because they are not ontologically distinct from categorical properties and, in this sense, reducible to them. This worry about ontological reducibility will be stated more fully and also answered in Section 7.2. In an appendix to the chapter, I will try to allay worries that accepting powers as irreducible properties might commit us to philosophical doctrines about 'natural necessity' or 'essence', which, with good reasons, many philosophers would want to reject.

7.1. The irreducibility of power-ascriptions

In order to answer the question of whether power-ascriptions are conceptually reducible, we will examine the three most influential reductive proposals of how to 'translate' them. We have already discussed and rejected Hume's proposal that such ascriptions should be analysed as mere statements about possible behaviour. The analysis with which we will start our examination in this section is implicit in Ryle's 'inference-ticket' view of dispositional statements: the 'simple conditional analysis' of power-ascriptions. Understood as a general reductive analysis of the concept of 'power', it goes as follows: 'Object A has the power to R under triggering conditions T iff: if A undergoes (were to undergo) triggering conditions T, then it shows (would show) reaction R.' The alternative material or counterfactual conditional in the analysans is meant to capture both cases of manifested and unmanifested powers.

This 'simple conditional' view of power-ascriptions is often connected with eliminativism about powers—the position that, in the last section, we rejected as a general thesis about powers. Nevertheless, it is useful to begin our overview of the main attempts at reductively analysing power-ascriptions by investigating the main objections against the 'simple conditional analysis'—both because its shortcomings are important to understand the motivation for the following analyses, and because many of those shortcomings have been inherited by the analyses which have succeeded it.

7.1.1. The simple conditional analysis

Why are power-ascriptions not equivalent to the conditional or counterfactual conditional that we have stated?[1] The first and most obvious reason is that not all powers are dispositions, and that the conditional analysis clearly fails for unconditional powers and capacities. However, more interestingly, the analysis even fails for disposition-ascriptions—primarily for the following three reasons.

(1) *Internality of powers*. Firstly, the analysis neglects the fact that manifestations of a disposition are due to the special internal characteristics of the object, rather than to external circumstances or relations to other objects.[2] (Pending a later further specification of the notion 'internal' in Section 7.3, we will, for the moment, be content to qualify as 'internal' what lies within the object's 'spatial envelope'.) When we say that, for example, a sleeping-pill has the power to make people who have taken it sleepy, we imply that it is something *in this pill*—something about its chemical constitution—which is relevant for the production of this effect. This can be seen by comparison with the opposite case of a placebo, which lacks the power to produce the effect. Here the sleepiness typically does not come about by a process in which the specific chemical

---

[1] The following points of criticism also apply to Carnap's 'reduction sentences' for dispositions (where D is the disposition, T the triggering conditions, and R the response behaviour): 'For all objects x, times t (T (x,t) → (D (x,t) ↔ R (x,t)))'. Cf. Carnap (1953), 52 f.

[2] Molnar's 'intrinsicality' condition for powers; (2003), 58, 84.

properties of the pill become efficacious in producing the sleepiness, but only via the person's beliefs about the pill, while the real internal chemical constitution of the pill can be completely irrelevant.[3]

(2) *Finkishness.* Secondly, as Charles Martin has shown, there are 'finkish' powers which falsify the conditional analysis because they are acquired (or lost) under exactly the same conditions as the conditions that would trigger their manifestation. To take one of Martin's examples, consider a live wire which, *qua* live wire, has the disposition to produce electrical current in a conductor that touches it. Nevertheless, it will not be true that it would produce such current if touched by a conductor, if the wire is connected to an electro-fink which registers whenever a conductor is about to touch the wire and reacts by making the wire dead for the time of the contact.[4] Therefore, Martin concludes, the truth of the conditional is not necessary for the truth of the power-ascription. His finkishness examples have not passed by without criticism,[5] but I consider them as convincing because they make basically the same point as the one mentioned against the eliminativist view—that purely conditional analysis fail to account for the possibility of changes in the powers of an object.

A defender of the conditional analysis might try to deal with the finkishness examples by adding restrictive conditions to the biconditional which rule out the set-ups making the disposition finkish. But the question is whether he can do this in a non-circular way—which leads us directly to the next fundamental objection to the conditional analysis.

(3) *Ceteris paribus conditions and circularity.* Lastly, there is the well-known general problem for reductive analyses, which arises through the need of introducing a *ceteris paribus* clause. The simple conditional analysis is clearly wrong if it claims truth under unrestricted generalization; that is if we put unrestricted universal quantifiers 'for all A, R and T' in front of the analysis-biconditional. For then, an object could have a power only if it would always show the adequate response, whenever it was placed under the relevant stimulus conditions. But counter-examples to this are not difficult to find, for our common dispositional terms all allow for the possibility of interventions which prevent the occurrence of the response. For example, a deadly poisonous plant does not necessarily cause the death of a person who has ingested it, if immediately after the ingestion an antidote is taken which prevents its harmful effects.[6] Thus, if a person

---

[3] They *need* not be irrelevant, however; for example, the smell or taste of a placebo may influence the person's beliefs about its effectiveness, and thus indirectly contribute to the effect.

[4] Martin (1994), 2 f.

[5] Cross, for instance, has argued that disposition-attributions typically presuppose background conditions that are violated in the finkishness cases; (2005), 324. But this criticism appears too ad hoc to be convincing. Also, it is difficult to see why the presupposed background conditions should generally exclude finkishness, because finkishness is not a highly extraordinary phenomenon, but is, for example, the basis of many safety mechanisms.

[6] In this case, the antidote 'masks' the power of the plant; cf. Molnar (2003), 92.

proposes to eat the poisonous plant and to ingest the antidote immediately afterwards, and is able to do so, the relevant counterfactual 'if it were ingested by a human being, this human being would die' would not be true of this particular plant in this situation, though it would still be poisonous.

Therefore, the counterfactual and the power-ascription do not always have the same truth-value, and it is necessary to restrict the quantifier to be placed in front of the analysis-biconditional, if one wants to save the conditional analysis. Because there are, in principle, innumerable possible interveners which could prevent the response from occurring under the stimulus conditions, the task of spelling out explicitly all the possible exceptions is impossible to fulfil. As in the case of natural laws whose proper formulation faces the same difficulties, the normal strategy to solve this problem is to introduce *ceteris paribus* clauses, or 'under ideal conditions' clauses.[7]

These clauses, however, are treacherous when inserted into reductive definitions, for in order to exclude circularity we must possess an understanding of these clauses that does not reduce them to the clause 'when possible interveners to the power-realization are absent', for this latter clause would reintroduce an appeal to the analysandum 'powers'. With regard to particular powers, we may be able to have the required understanding of *ceteris paribus,* or at least to have a good grasp of when this condition is satisfied, which we can use in experimental verification of power-ascriptions. This understanding in the case of particular powers, however, rests on a grasp of the context-dependent features which are relevant for both the power and the kind of situation in question. Since these relevant features are context-dependent and a general analysis of 'A has the disposition to F under conditions T' wants to abstract from the particular contexts, we cannot expect to have the required understanding of the *ceteris paribus* clause as it appears in the general analysis. Thus, *ceteris paribus* clauses will serve only to introduce circularity into the general analysis of power-ascriptions, because we cannot understand them in any better way than as 'if possible interveners to the power-realization are absent.'[8] The same difficulty arises, *mutatis mutandis,* for 'ideal conditions' clauses.

This result is decisive against the general analysis of the concept 'power' that the conditional analysis proposes. However, a defender of the conditional analysis might react in the following way. Though giving up on the claim that we can analyse the general statement 'A has a power to R under conditions C', where R and C are variables ranging over possible responses and conditions, he might argue that we can still uphold the weaker claim that for *each particular* power type we can analyse the power-ascriptions as '*ceteris paribus*, if conditions C obtained, A would give response R'. The generalized analysis-biconditional closed under universal or restricted quantification would thus be changed into a substitution scheme for particular power types, and

---

[7] For the analysis of power-ascriptions, this strategy was followed by, for example, Goodman (1955), 39.
[8] Cf. Martin (1994), 5 f.; Molnar (2003), 88 f.

power-ascriptions could still be reducible one by one. In defence of this new scheme the adherent of the conditional analysis might add that since for particular power types we can know the context-dependent features which determine the content of the *ceteris paribus* conditions, our objection about the circularity of the conditional analysis will no longer apply.

But does this shift from a general analysis to a piecemeal reduction of particular power-ascriptions really save the conditional analysis, as a reductive analysis, from the problem of *ceteris paribus* clauses? In order to answer this question it is vital to keep separate the following two reductionist projects, as parts of which the conditional analysis may be offered. First, the general reductionist project to reduce *all* power-ascriptions, one by one, to non-power statements; and second, the more modest project to reduce ascriptions of particular powers to statements containing no reference to those *very same* powers. A conceptual reduction of power-concepts as such will necessarily involve the first kind of reduction, because if statements about powers were reduced only to other statements about powers, nothing whatsoever would follow about the reducibility of the genus 'power' or 'power-concept'. On my view, if the conditional analysis is intended to make possible this kind of reduction, the answer to our question is clearly negative. In order to see why this is so, it is instructive to take a look at how we can experimentally confirm a power-ascription.

I take it that we can distinguish two general methods for doing so, of which only the first one will concern us here. The first is to check whether the conditional '*ceteris paribus*, if triggering conditions T obtain, A shows response R' is true for the specified T and R. The second presupposes that we already know that objects of type X have the power to R, and can separately check whether the particular object A is of type X. Then we need only do so in order to verify our power-ascription. We will leave the second kind of experimental confirmation aside here, because confirmations of this kind obviously presuppose the possibility of confirmations of the first kind, and the first kind is problematic with regard to the *ceteris paribus* condition.

The crucial question now is, how can we ensure that this condition is satisfied, when we want to confirm a power-ascription? Basically, there are two methods for doing this—each with one corresponding kind of experimental procedure. The first is to know all the other possible influencing factors and control them, which would correspond to what Nancy Cartwright has called the 'totally controlled experiment'.[9] The second is to establish that the *ceteris paribus* condition is satisfied without knowing all possible intervening factors—namely, by 'averaging out' possible interveners, which can be done without knowing what those interveners are. The corresponding experimental procedure is the 'randomized experiment'.[10]

Let us illustrate these two procedures with a simple example. We want to determine whether a particular metallic object A has the power to attract another metallic object

---

[9] Cartwright (1989), 66.
[10] Cf. Cartwright (1989), 62 ff.

B, of which we know that it is not magnetic. Let us assume that A is relatively, though not rigidly, fixed inside a wooden box, perhaps suspended on a string hanging from the top of the box—so an obvious procedure for establishing what we want to know is to shoot object B into the box and determine whether it changes its course towards A. But how do we establish that the *ceteris paribus* condition is satisfied, and that there are no other forces that might change B's course when it enters the wooden box—for example, that the box is not placed within a magnetic field independent of A, which could also explain B's changing its course? When we know about such a field we will take measures to shield off the box by, for example, placing coils of wire around it. In the totally controlled experiment we would install such shielding with regard to all the possible intervening factors. More realistically, however, we will not know about all of them, and so we will try to balance their distorting effects by introducing a 'randomizing factor'. For example, we could initiate a series of trials, during which we would rotate the box or shoot B into it from different directions or angles and decide about A's attracting force on the average effect of these series.

Let us now consider whether these two confirmation procedures provide support for the reductivist project. The totally controlled experiment seems to be more promising in this respect. If we can ever completely reduce power-ascriptions to statements about non-powers, this seems to be a case, because here we know about all possible intervening factors and thus can eliminate the *ceteris paribus* clause. However, with regard to general reductivism about powers, even this case is insufficient; for in order to support the envisaged kind of reduction, the possible intervening factors themselves must not include powers—and it is just absurd to think that this requirement could ever be satisfied. Because the intervening factors are characteristically the manifestations of counteracting powers, we simply cannot assume that the *ceteris paribus* conditions could be completely spelt out without an appeal to powers. (Even if this were possible, it is highly doubtful whether the completely controlled experiment would be possible for any powers at all, because in practice we never know about all possible intervening factors.[11]) The randomized experiment even more obviously provides no support for the reductivist project, because the whole idea of the randomizing procedure is to balance out interfering manifestations of *powers*.

What we are left with is merely an equivalence (for the purposes of experimental confirmation) between a particular power-ascription and a statement containing no reference to the very same power—but only to other powers. For example, our statement 'A has the power to attract B' has turned out to be equivalent to 'If B is shot into the box and no other forces that could influence B's course are present or these are balanced out, it changes its direction towards A'. But this equivalence is a trivial consequence of the fact that, assuming a background theory, we can experimentally test whether A has the power to attract B. Our conditional just describes the experimental procedure.

---

[11] Cf. Cartwright (1989), 71, who rightly suggests that in practice all experiments contain some elements of both methods: controlling and randomizing.

Testability, however, does not on its own support reduction—neither of powers in general, nor even of the particular powers whose possessions are tested, because it is possible that, if we were to test the other powers which we shielded off or balanced out when testing A's power to attract B, we would in turn have to shield off or balance out A's own power.

We can therefore safely conclude that even the manoeuvre of defenders of the conditional analysis of power-ascriptions to turn the proposed biconditional into a substitution scheme for particular power-concepts does not save this analysis from the problem of *ceteris paribus* conditions.

7.1.2. The causal conditional analysis

Another proposed analysis of power-ascriptions seems to remedy some of these grave defects of the simple causal analysis: the causal conditional analysis, which is, again, primarily intended for disposition-ascriptions. According to this analysis, 'A has the disposition to R under conditions S' is true iff A has a property that would cause A to give response R if conditions S obtained. The latter property is itself not a power, but a categorical property—the 'categorical basis'[12] for the power.

Historically, the central motivation for thinking that power-ascriptions are not equivalent to simple conditionals, but necessarily include an appeal to a categorical property of the object as well, rested on verificationist scruples about unmanifested powers. How could we ascribe an unmanifested power if there was no property of the object which made it true that the object possessed this power? In the final analysis, this further property would have to be categorical, because if it were itself a power, the same problem would again arise with regard to this further power; and thus, it seemed, all powers needed an ultimately categorical basis. This line of thought directly leads to the result that power-ascriptions must include an appeal to this categorical basis, if one accepts both the verificationist principle that the meaning of a statement must somehow reflect its verification-conditions, and plausibly assumes that power-ascriptions have the same meaning when we talk of manifested and unmanifested powers.[13]

While the simple conditional analysis was often connected to eliminativism about powers, as in Ryle's case, the causal conditional analysis reconciled empiricists with power-concepts and allowed them to be realists about powers—but, at least in the beginning, only at the price of the marginalization of powers. For initially, due to the verificationist scruples mentioned previously, power-terms were still widely regarded with suspicion as long as no categorical basis was found; while after the discovery of the basis, power-terms were considered to have become, as Quine expresses it,

---

[12] Or 'vehicle'; Kenny (1989), 72.
[13] These verificationist scruples were at the heart of Armstrong's theory in (1968), ch. 6, sect. 6. Also, Quine's and Goodman's views that acceptable dispositional predicates must have a suitable non-dispositional basis was motivated by the problem of unmanifested dispositions; cf. Goodman (1955), ch. 2, and Quine (1969), 238 ff.

'respectable, and, in principle, superfluous'.[14] But the causal conditional analysis, as other philosophers have realized, also allows for more substantial realism about powers as genuine properties, in either of the two following ways: either by identifying them with their categorical bases,[15] thus securing their status as bona fide properties by turning them into categorical properties; or by construing them as higher-order functionalist properties—of possessing a causally efficient lower-order property.[16] This latter alternative became attractive after the importance of higher-order properties had been recognized in the debate about functionalism in the philosophy of mind in the 1970s.

Although the causal conditional analysis allows us to regard powers as genuine properties of objects, its truth would still be fatal to our project of constructing a causal-powers account of substance-causation. For on neither of the two forms of realism about powers just mentioned does it seem possible that possession of a power confers on its bearer a genuine causal role that is not reducible to the causal role of the categorical basis. This is clear for the first alternative, where powers are identical to their categorical bases; but also on the second alternative, powers only involve a causal role of categorical properties (or the correlated instantiation-events), because the latter's role is sufficient for an exhaustive causal explanation of the results of power-manifestations, and no causal role of the bearer-substance is required in addition.[17]

Thus, if our general project stands any chance of success, the causal conditional analysis must be false. But is it false? When we go through the list of difficulties mentioned with respect to the simple conditional analysis, we find, first, that the account, as it stands, clearly fails to account for ascriptions of unconditional powers, as do all conditional analyses. But one might reply that the account is primarily intended for dispositions, and can be extended to tendencies and unconditional powers by slightly adapting the analysis. Thus, tendencies could be accommodated by changing the analysans so that it is no longer required that the categorical basis would cause response R, but only that it probably would. And for the analysans for unconditional power-ascriptions we would simply need to remove the clause 'if conditions S obtained' from our analysans, whereby we would obtain 'A has a property that does/can cause R' as the proper analysis of those ascriptions. Thus, the causal conditional analysis can be naturally modified to include ascriptions of powers other than dispositions.

Also, the second objection we have considered against the simple conditional analysis—that powers must be somehow intrinsic to their bearers—can be met by defenders of the causal conditional analysis, if they require that the categorical base-

---

[14] Quine (1969), 241.
[15] This is Armstrong's solution, (1968), ch. 6, sect. 6; and Quine's (1974), 11.
[16] This is the 'role-functionalist' analysis of dispositions advocated by Prior, Pargetter, and Jackson (1982).
[17] Nor of the powers themselves as higher-order properties, as Prior, Pargetter, and Jackson (1982) argue with their impotence thesis.

property be internal (in some relevant sense) to the object A— for example, its chemical composition.

The third difficulty, about Martin's finkish dispositions, however, remains in force. The peculiarity of these dispositions was that the triggering conditions S for this disposition also caused the object to lose the disposition—that is, in terms of the causal conditional analysis, that the conditions S either prevent the causal effect of the categorical basis of the disposition, or cause the object to lose this categorical basis altogether. In either case, the analysans proposed by the causal analysis 'object A possesses a property that would cause response R under conditions S' is false, though *ex hypothesi* the object possesses the finkish power as long as conditions S do not obtain.

Also, the fourth difficulty, about *ceteris paribus* conditions, applies equally to the causal conditional analysis as it applied to the simple causal analysis. For, obviously, the categorical basis need not always cause the response, due to the possible presence of preventing interveners. This possibility makes it necessary to include *ceteris paribus* conditions, with the consequences examined at length in Section 7.1.1.

There is, however, one problem peculiar to the causal conditional analysis: deviant causal chains. This problem, which we have discussed at length with regard to the causalist theory of action, again arises with regard to the connection between the causal basis and the response. Even if the response is caused by the categorical basis of the object under stimulus conditions, it can be caused 'in the wrong way', and thus the occurrence of the response can fail to count as a manifestation of the power.[18] For example, assume that the categorical basis for water-solubility of sugar is property C, and that a specific lump of sugar, A, possesses property C. Imagine now that A is being used by a mad scientist for an experimental set-up, where a sensor is inserted into A, such that whenever A is put into water, A's possessing C, together with its being inserted in water, jointly cause a signal to be sent by the sensor with the effect that A is immediately dissolved by a strong bombardment of X-rays, before it can be dissolved by the water. When this scenario is realized, then A's dissolving is not a manifestation of the disposition of water-solubility, though it has the causal pedigree required by the causal conditional analysis.

This possibility implies that the possession of a categorical property which has the causal role of producing R responses in S conditions is not by itself sufficient for possessing the power to R, and this result refutes the causal conditional analysis. To see this, imagine that in the case just mentioned, C is *not* the categorical basis of water-solubility, but some property which normally plays no causal role for the dissolving process; and assume further that A is not really water-soluble. Nevertheless, when A is used in the mad scientist's experimental set-up, C plays the requisite causal role—and so, on the causal conditional analysis, its possession would have to suffice

---

[18] The first to notice the possibility of causal deviance in the case of powers was Smith (1977), 441.

for being water-soluble, because the counterfactual conditional of this analysis is satisfied. As A is, *ex hypothesi*, not water-soluble, this amounts to a reductio of the analysis.

The strategies of adherents of the analysis to exclude deviant causal chains have paralleled the attempts to save the causal analysis of actions—and have been equally unsuccessful.[19] For instance, A. D. Smith has proposed the additional requirement that the response must be caused in an 'immediate', 'direct', or 'standard' way by the stimulus conditions.[20] These proposals neatly mirror Goldman's proposal that mental states must cause bodily motions in the 'standard way', or Brand's immediate causation strategy. And they suffer from the same basic flaws as those proposals because, on the one hand, without being able to spell out explicitly what the 'standard way' consists in, this clause introduces circularity; and on the other hand, there is no reason to assume that the stimulus conditions could not cause the response via a number of intermediate steps when a disposition is manifested. Therefore, we can safely conclude that attempts to rule out deviant causal chains from the causal conditional analysis will either fail to rule out all and only those chains, or be circular.

This allows us to reject the causal conditional analysis of power-ascriptions, because even though, after due modification, it can deal with unconditional powers and the requirement of intrinsicality of powers, it founders on the problems of finkish dispositions, of the circularity involved in *ceteris paribus* clauses, and of deviant causal chains.[21]

7.1.3. *Lewis's reformed causal conditional analysis*

As an answer to Martin's finkishness objection to the causal conditional analysis, David Lewis has developed a more sophisticated version of this analysis. Lewis's version is based on the notion of an 'x-complete cause', which is the notion of 'a cause complete in so far as havings of properties intrinsic to x are concerned',[22] and proceeds as follows. An object x has the disposition to give response R under stimulus S, at time t, iff there is an intrinsic property B that x possesses at time t, such that for some time t' later than t, if

---

[19] A more radical defence of the causal analysis has been proposed by Lewis, who has argued that dispositions are not generally process-specific with regard to their manifestations. He claims that in the case of lethal viruses it does not matter by which way the virus causes the victim's death, and concludes that insofar as some dispositions are process-specific, this is just a peculiar characteristic of these dispositions; (1997), 153 f. But this view is unconvincing, for even in the case of lethal viruses *some* causal chains will count as deviant—for example, if some other person regularly takes infection by the virus as a reason for killing the infected person; cf. Molnar (2003), 92. In a similar way, all disposition-manifestations will require more than causation of the response by the stimulus and an internal property via an arbitrary causal chain, because some causal chains will always be ruled out as deviant.

[20] Smith (1977), 444 f.

[21] The same criticisms apply to analyses which are relevantly similar to the causal conditional analysis, though they do not speak of the response being caused by a property of the object, but only of the response occurring 'in virtue of' the object's intrinsic nature (cf. Harré and Madden (1975), 86), insofar as these analyses of power-statements are intended to be reductive.

[22] Lewis (1997), 156.

x were to undergo stimulus S at time t and retain B until time t', stimulus S and x's having B would jointly constitute an x-complete cause of x's giving response R.[23]

Lewis's proposal indeed succeeds in dealing with finkishness cases, as far as finkish powers that have categorical grounds are concerned; for the peculiarity of finkish powers—that the stimulus conditions cause the loss of the power—is dealt with by requiring that the power is retained after the stimulus conditions occur. (At least, it is dealt with if we require the power to be retained until the response R begins; though Lewis' formulation is not quite clear as to whether or not he intends t' to be the time of the beginning of response R or not, I will interpret him in this way, because if t' could be a time before the beginning of response R, there would be space for a more complicated kind of finkishness.[24]) Ungrounded powers, however, escape his analysis—and in the next section we will see that we have good reasons for supposing that there are such powers.

Furthermore, Lewis's analysis is faced by two other problems which it inherits from its predecessor, the causal conditional analysis. The first is the difficulty of how to restrict the universal quantifier over x, R, and S to be placed in front of the analysis-biconditional—a difficulty which leads to the by now well-known problem of *ceteris paribus* conditions.

The second is, again, the problem of deviant causal chains, though it appears in a slightly different form than before, and its recognition requires one additional argumentative step, as follows. When Lewis requires that stimulus S and having property B jointly constitute an x-complete cause of response R, this cannot mean that they must be the only events or states involving intrinsic properties of object x that contribute causally to R's occurrence. Other intermediate steps may be necessary on the way from the stimulus to the occurrence of response R—between time t and t'. For example, before finally transmitting energy, a conducting wire may first have to become hot. So, the requirement can only be that stimulus S and having property B together constitute an x-complete cause of R as far as causal factors obtaining *at time t* are concerned.[25] But this leaves space for causal deviance, as the following example shows. (As in our discussion of causal deviance in Section 7.1.2, our argument against Lewis's proposal will proceed in two steps. First, we will show how in a case of causal deviance the relevant power is not manifested; and second, how this refutes the proposed analysis.)

---

[23] Lewis (1997), 157.

[24] Namely the following: Imagine that response R usually follows upon stimulus S after 10 seconds, but that S causes the object to lose the categorical base-property after 5 seconds. In this scenario, even though the object has the disposition to R at time t of the stimulus, and retains the base-property till a later time t', stimulus S and the possessing of the base-property are not an x-complete cause of R, because R is not caused at all. To avoid this possibility, the categorical base has to be retained up to the beginning of the response.

[25] Not at t' (the time of the beginning of the response), because the stimulus can occur earlier than the response.

Take the disposition of an object to submerge in water. On Lewis's analysis its ascription would require only that an object x had a categorical property, which, in conjunction with the object's being placed on the surface of water, would be an x-complete cause of the object's submergence. We will further assume that the object stays, for a very short time, at the surface before submerging. A first difficulty for a Lewis-type analysis would be to find an adequate categorical basis. The relevant factor for the object's submergence is its having a specific density which is higher than the density of water—and, plausibly, density is not itself a categorical property. But for the sake of argument, assume that we can somehow specify the required categorical basis. Even then, the following scenario is still possible. A mad scientist stands next to the bowl of water in which we put the object. He registers immediately when an object possessing the relevant categorical property is placed in water, and reacts by pushing the object under water before it can submerge on its own. In this case, the object's being placed in water and having the relevant categorical property is an x-complete cause of the object's submergence, as far as causal conditions at the time of placing the object on the surface of the water are concerned. For though the later event of the object's being 'thumped down' by the scientist is also part of the cause of the submerging, it is not part of the x-complete cause of this event, because the scientist's reaction is itself an extrinsic factor. At the same time, however, the object's submergence is not a manifestation of its disposition to submerge. Therefore, the fulfilment of Lewis's conditions does not guarantee that the response is the manifestation of a power of the object.

Pari passu, we can show that Lewis's analysis does not provide sufficient conditions for power-ascriptions. The only factor that we need to change in our example is that this time the object is not disposed to submerge in water, but would, on its own, continue to float on the surface. Then the interference of the mad scientist—who would now react to the categorical property responsible for the disposition to float by pushing the object under water—would verify the analysans clause of Lewis's analysis, although *ex hypothesi* the object does not have the disposition to submerge.

Therefore, there are still cases of causal deviance which falsify Lewis's reformed conditional analysis, though these cases are rather more complicated than the standard cases applicable against the causal conditional analysis.

This brings to an end our survey of the three most influential attempts to reduce power-ascriptions to statements not containing any power-terms. All these three attempts—the simple conditional analysis, the causal conditional analysis, and Lewis's reformed conditional analysis—have turned out to be subject to decisive criticisms, especially concerning the possibility of deviant causal chains and the circularity implicit in the unavoidable insertion of *ceteris paribus* clauses in the analysis. Power-ascriptions, we can thus conclude, are irreducible—and this completes our first step towards demonstrating the irreducibility of powers to categorical properties. If there is such reducibility, at least it cannot be conceptual.

7.2. The ontological irreducibility of powers

Can there be ontological reducibility without a conceptual one? Applied to our particular investigation, could powers still be ontologically no more than categorical properties, even though power-concepts are clearly distinct from non-power-concepts? Though intuitively it may seem that conceptual irreducibility of 'A's having p' to 'B's having q' implies that there are two different kinds of properties p and q, or objects A and B, and two different kinds of events, the discussion about functionalism in the philosophy of mind since the 1970s has taught us that there is no general implication of this kind. In particular, the discussion about functionalism has shown this with respect to events or states.

This discussion turned around the following question. Once we accept that mental concepts are irreducible to physical concepts, and therefore the claim 'A has mental property M' is irreducible to any statement of the form 'B has physical property P', do we then have to assume that the event of A's instantiation of M at time t is a mental event distinct from any physical event, or could the event still be identical to a physical event? The answer given by the functionalists who rejected type–type identity of mental and physical properties, was, famously, to affirm the latter alternative; and its consequence was a token–token identity theory of mental and physical events construed, for example, in the following way.

According to the 'functional state identity thesis',[26] state descriptions in terms of mental concepts are nothing more than functional specifications of states—for example, as causes of other states or as instantiations of causally relevant properties. Although these functional specifications are not conceptually reducible to purely physical specifications, mental states are identical to the states that play the specified functional role, and thus *realize* the mental states. If we assume that as a matter of empirical fact, all the realizing states are physical states, then all the states referred to when using mental vocabulary are physical states, so that there need not be, in addition, any separate mental states.

While token–token identity does not imply by itself an ontological reduction of mental events to physical events so long as one refuses to see either the physical or the mental descriptions as more basic than the other,[27] it naturally leads to a reduction once one considers the physical properties to be more basic. The latter view seems very natural to adopt, once one accepts the premises of the functional state identity thesis; for the mental concepts are supposed to be specifications of events by causal roles, and the realization of these causal roles is due only to the physical properties of the events in question. Furthermore, once mental concepts are considered only as specifications in terms of causal roles, it seems that mental properties would themselves have to be causally epiphenomenal, for all the 'causal work' would already be done by the physical

---

[26] Block (1980), 179.
[27] A possibility defended by Davidson (1993b).

'realizer' properties,[28] and this consideration would provide further pressure towards considering the latter as more 'basic'. Mental states, we will then say, do exist, but are nothing more than physical states, and not vice versa. As this kind of reduction does not imply that statements ascribing a mental property can be translated into equivalent statements ascribing only physical properties—that is, as it does not imply what we have called 'conceptual' reduction—it can be called a merely ontological reduction.

The important question for us is whether this kind of functionalist argument from the philosophy of mind can be transferred to the question of the relation between powers and categorical properties. Stephen Mumford has claimed that such a transfer is possible, and that in the same way as all mental events are token–token identical to physical events, all instances of powers are token–token identical to instances of categorical properties, because power-concepts are just specifications of categorical properties by their causal role.[29] As a consequence, Mumford rejects the idea that powers are a type of property different from categorical properties, and argues that the categorical property/power distinction is 'only' a conceptual distinction; that is, that there are only distinct categorical and dispositional *ways* of talking about the instantiations of properties.[30] If this claim is true, then an ontological reduction of power-instances to instances of categorical properties becomes possible in the way just sketched for mental and physical events, once we consider the descriptions in terms of purely categorical property concepts as more basic. (Mumford himself wants to remain neutral about which description is more basic, and thus opts for a 'neutral monism' about properties.[31])

The possibility of an ontological reduction of this kind would be as damaging to our project of a causal-powers account of substance-causation as the possibility of a 'conceptual' reduction. For if all instantiations of powers were really nothing more than instantiations of categorical properties, then, as in the case of conceptual reduction, this instantiation could not confer on the substance that possesses the power a causal role that goes beyond the causal role conferred by the instantiation of the categorical property. And it is very plausible to think that the causal role conferred by possession of a categorical property is completely reducible to the *event*-causal role of the event consisting in the instantiation of this categorical property or of a triggering event.

Thus, we have to demonstrate that ontological reduction is not possible here, and the most straightforward way to do this is to show that Mumford's claim of property

---

[28] The epiphenomenalism problem for higher-order properties arises because they seem to be 'shielded off' from causal influence by the first-order properties, and their causal influence would involve over-determination; cf. Jackson (1998), 91 f., Kim (1998).

[29] Mumford (1998), ch. 9.

[30] Mumford (1998), 145.

[31] Mumford (1998), 192. Neutral monism is also defended by Martin—cf. his contributions in Crane (ed.) (1996), Heil (2003), ch. 11, and (2005), and Cartwright (1997), 74, where she claims that the distinctions between the occurrent properties and powers are only 'distinctions in language', because all properties bring powers with them.

monism is false, and that power instantiations cannot be token–token-identical to instantiations of categorical properties. I will offer two kinds of argument to this effect. The first applies specifically to Mumford's token–token identity thesis about instances, and shows that even when there are two such correlated instances—even when the power has a categorical base—the identity-conditions for instantiations will rule out Mumford's identity-claim. The second argument applies to monist theories about properties in general, and shows that not all powers have corresponding categorical bases with which they could be identified.

a) *Property-instances and their identity-conditions.* When the issue about identity of property-instances arises, the crucial question concerns the individuation criteria for such instances. We can hope to deduce these conditions from a better understanding of the nature of property-instances. For Mumford, property-instances are particular properties of particular objects—for example, the particular weight of this particular book—and for him, these instances are themselves particulars.[32] Unfortunately, however, Mumford does not provide a detailed account of property-instances, and his notion remains somewhat obscure:[33] For to all appearances, it involves a mistaken treatment of the properties that an object possesses—such as its redness—as particular *things*; but properties are no such things, whether or not instantiated in an object.[34] In order to avoid this mistake, and in view of the lack of clarity about Mumford's understanding of property-instances, I will, in the following, try to assess Mumford's identity-claim for instantiations understood as facts—namely that a property is instantiated—though the arguments I will offer should also be applicable to alternative viable notions of 'instance' which Mumford might offer.

If there are such 'things' as property-instances, their character will be exhaustively specified by the instantiated property and the instantiating objects (and possibly the temporal and external circumstances). This implies that instances can be identical only if both the objects and the properties involved are identical. Applied to our case of instances of powers and categorical properties, this immediately raises the question of whether this condition can ever be satisfied with regard to them. As a precondition, powers and categorical properties that are instantiated would have to be identical properties—and it seems clear that they cannot be so, if only because not all powers are coextensional to categorical properties, and coextensionality seems a minimum criterion for identity. That there is no general coextensionality can be seen from the fact that powers can have variable categorical base-properties—a fact which

---

[32] Mumford (1998), 159 ff.
[33] As also noticed by Prior (1985), 76.
[34] Mumford's account is particularly mysterious because he rejects the only account of properties that would allow him to regard the properties of particular things as 'abstract particulars'—trope theory; (1998), 160.

Mumford accepts.[35] For example, the power of inflammability has, supposedly, different categorical bases in paper and in petrol because the features of the constitution of paper and petrol that are relevant for their inflammability are different. Therefore, it seems obvious that the property of inflammability cannot be identical to any of those categorical base-properties.

It is quite mysterious how Mumford expects to deal with this difficulty—and the more so because he seems to accept, as a result of this argument, that 'properties *qua* universals are indeed not identified'.[36] But, as property-instances must be characterized by what property is instantiated, this implies that the instances also must be distinct. Instead of directly answering these worries, Mumford advances an argument for his identity-claim from the 'identity of causal role'. Two property-instantiations, he claims, are identical if they occupy the same causal role,[37] and the instantiations of a power and of its categorical base-property fulfil this condition. However, this proposal about identity-conditions for instantiations is unconvincing. Assume that instantiation A causes instantiation B, and A is the only direct cause of B, and B the only direct effect of A (where 'only direct cause' means that all the other causes of B have only caused B via causing A, and *mutatis mutandis*, for 'only direct effect'). Then A and B have precisely the same causal effects and antecedents—except one another[38]—though they are not identical.[39] Consequently, Mumford's proposal that 'identity of causal role' implies the identity of instantiations should be rejected, and with it, his argument for the identity-claim.

Given its incompatibility with an intuitive understanding of property-instantiations, Mumford's identity-claim is thus hardly tenable. He would probably object to our criticism by claiming that there will be a viable notion of property-instance with concomitant identity-conditions which do not depend on the identity of the instantiated properties. But such an objection would not only lack force so long as no such notion is proposed. There are even positive reasons for thinking that there can be *no* such notion that would both yield the identity-criteria that Mumford needs for his identity-claim and be compatible with our pre-theoretical intuitions about what counts as one instantiation of a property. For there are cases where there is not even a one-to-one correlation between instantiations of powers and of their categorical base-properties on particular occasions, and consequently, identity between the instantiations is clearly excluded.

---

[35] Mumford (1998), 157 ff.
[36] Mumford (1998), 160.
[37] Mumford (1998), 145 ff.
[38] This cannot be counted as a distinct cause or effect on Mumford's proposal, on pain of circularity.
[39] If Mumford thinks that *only* property-instantiations could cause and be caused—which does not become clear—his proposal also faces the circularity objection raised against Davidson's proposal for the identity-conditions of events by Quine (1985).

One such case is the following.[40] As we have seen, powers can have variable categorical bases, and if those bases can be possessed simultaneously by one object it is also possible that the bases are switched while the object continuously possesses the power. For example, assume that power P can have either base-properties B or C, and object E, which possesses P, can possess B and C simultaneously. Then the following three-stage process is possible: (a) the object possesses power A in virtue of possessing property B, while lacking property C; (b) the object acquires property C in addition, so that now its possession of A is 'overdetermined' by the possession of both B and C; and (c) the object loses B but continues to possess property C, and therefore still has power A, though now in virtue of having C. As the object continues to have power A throughout the whole process, it seems unavoidable to conclude that there is only one instantiation of A by the object. At the same time, the instantiation of B at the beginning of the process cannot be identical to the instantiation of C at the end, because B and C are, *ex hypothesi*, different categorical properties. Therefore, the instantiation of A cannot be identical to the instantiation of its causal bases, because otherwise, by the transitivity of identity, these latter instantiations would also have to be identical with one another.

Cases of this kind present fundamental obstacles to developing any convincing theory of property-instantiations that would support Mumford's identity-claim. Therefore, we can safely conclude that Mumford's claim—that all powers are identical to their categorical base-properties—must be false.

b) *Powers without bases.* The second kind of argument is not directed specifically against Mumford's token–token identity-claim, but against all monist views about properties, which claim that all powers must also have categorical aspects. The argument shows that this view cannot be true of all powers, because there are some that have no correlated categorical property with which they could be identical.

A necessary presupposition of the monist claim is that all powers must have correlated categorical properties (at least, on each particular instantiation), which will plausibly be the categorical base-properties; for without a correlated categorical property there is simply no candidate property with which the power could be identical. Consequently, if there are powers without a categorical base—either because the object having those powers possesses no categorical properties at all, or the categorical properties it does possess are clearly not candidates for the categorical base—for these powers the identity-claim must be false.

And we have good reason to think that there are powers of just this kind. According to modern physics, fundamental sub-atomic particles possess powers, such as charge or spin, without possessing correlated categorical properties which could serve as their categorical bases.[41] For these objects are characterized only in terms of their powers and

---

[40] Cf. Rives (2005), 22 ff.
[41] Cf. Molnar (2003), 131 ff.

causal role, and not in terms of any further internal properties to which this role would be due; in particular, they have no internal structure which could explain the possession of the powers. The external categorical properties they do possess, such as location, are not plausible candidates for categorical bases—both because of their externality, and because the powers are retained even when the location is changed. So, at least for fundamental sub-atomic particles, it seems that powers cannot be identical to categorical properties, because there are no suitable corresponding properties.

Defenders of the identity-claim can, of course, object to this argument that it is far from conclusive. The lack of categorical bases for fundamental powers could at best be an empirical matter, and we cannot assume that this is already established; and perhaps, as science progresses, the structural basis of the powers of what we now assume to be fundamental particles will be discovered. And indeed, it is quite true that for any *particular* kind of particle that is proposed as lacking microstructure, it might eventually turn out that it does, after all, possess a microstructure. But the objection must go deeper than this, and show that this must be so for all kinds of particles in general—that is, that no particle can be fundamental in the sense of possessing no microstructure. But it is unclear why this should be so. The powers of sub-atomic—supposedly fundamental—particles in physics demonstrate that we have no conceptual difficulties with powers lacking corresponding categorical bases. Therefore, the burden of proof will clearly rest with those who want to claim that there cannot be any such powers—and I do not see how they could acquit themselves of this burden.

To do so, they would have to provide a general argument for the need of categorical bases—and no such general argument seems to be available.[42] In particular, correlated categorical bases are neither necessary for experimental testing of power-ascriptions, nor are they needed in order to successfully refer to the object possessing the power. First, as the two experimental procedures for establishing that an object possesses a power (presented previously) have shown, establishing that an object possesses a power neither involves nor presupposes demonstrating the possession of a related categorical property. Neither the result of the experiment using the randomization procedure, nor of the controlled experiment, establishes that the object in question possesses a categorical property correlated to the power. Second, we do not need correlated categorical properties for referring to the objects possessing the power—neither in the experimental situation nor elsewhere. For we can refer to objects successfully by

---

[42] *Pace* Prior, Pargetter, and Jackson (1982), 251 ff., who have tried to present such an argument. It rests on the idea that in a deterministic world there must be a causally sufficient antecedent condition that accounts for the occurrence of the response in power-manifestations, and that this condition constitutes the causal base of the power. For non-deterministic but probabilistic dispositions, the argument proceeds, the assigning of different probabilities necessarily depends on different causal bases. Even if this argument were to be successful in establishing the need for causal bases, it would not prove that these have to be categorical properties of the object possessing the power *itself*, because the causal base in the argument comprises both intrinsic and extrinsic conditions. But only properties of the object itself can constitute the categorical basis for a power or be identical with the power, because powers are *intrinsic* properties of their bearers; cf. Molnar (2003), 129 f.

definite descriptions, and (i) these descriptions might appeal only to the possession of powers, and (ii) even if they do appeal to the possession of categorical properties, might only appeal to external properties or to internal properties that are no possible categorical bases of the powers in question. For example, by using the description 'the electron in this cloud-chamber', one can successfully refer to an object, even though the spatial location of the object is not an internal property and 'electron' is only a description of the object's powers. So there seems to be no general need for categorical bases of powers, and consequently, no obstacle to assuming that there can be powers without such bases.

If there are powers without categorical bases, the general identity-claim collapses. The consequences of this collapse are not restricted to the powers of fundamental particles alone, but also pertain to the powers of larger, composite objects, in the following way. It is extremely plausible to assume that the powers of larger objects depend not only on the categorical properties of the object itself or its structure, but also on the powers possessed by the component parts of the structure. An object composed of water-soluble materials is liable to behave differently, when placed in water, than is an object composed of water-resistant materials. And the same dependence holds 'one level down'—that is, when we talk about the powers of the component parts, and so on. This implies that powers of larger objects can have a purely categorical basis only if the powers of the component parts are themselves, in the last analysis, identical to categorical properties. But our argument that the powers of fundamental particles are not identical to categorical properties shows that this is not the case. And as the powers of the component parts of larger objects ultimately depend on these fundamental powers, the powers of the larger objects will not have a purely categorical basis—and therefore no correlated categorical property to which they could plausibly be identical.

Thus we can conclude, from the two arguments which we have considered, that the identity thesis about powers and categorical properties that is defended by monism about properties is false, and that the same applies to the idea that power instantiations are token–token identical to instantiations of categorical properties. This forces[43] us to accept a dualist view of properties: Powers and categorical properties are distinct kinds of properties.[44] This dualism removes the threat of an ontological reduction of powers, and opens up the possibility that possession of powers can confer on the substance which bears them a causal role not conferred by the possession of categorical properties.

---

[43] Dualism is only forced on us if we accept that categorical properties are properties in their own right—i.e. that not all properties are powers. Pan-dispositionalism rejects just this latter thesis. I will neglect the possibility of pan-dispositionalism here—both because the position is of much less influence compared to eliminativism or reductivism about powers or neutral monism, and because I think that it has been convincingly refuted by Armstrong, (1997), 80, and Lowe, (2006), 138, who have shown that it does not allow for the possibility of real change, and leads to a vicious regress when we try to fix the identities of powers.

[44] Place—cf. his contributions in Crane (1996)—and Molnar (2003) are the most important contemporary defenders of this view.

7.3. Powers without 'natural necessity' and essentialism

Even though the arguments advanced so far have shown that we should accept powers as properties in their own right, there will still be a lingering worry about the 'respectability' of powers which must be addressed. Powers may still appear to have a dubious standing because they appear to be closely connected to two notions which are regarded with suspicion by many philosophers: natural necessity and essentialism. I will first try to show why it is natural to think that a connection with these two notions exists, and then try to argue that an account of powers can well do without these notions.

The apparent connection to 'natural necessity' arises as follows. When a power is manifested in a certain stimulus situation, this manifestation seems to be *necessary*, given that the objects involved 'are what they are': acid *must* turn logwood red, water-soluble material *must* dissolve in water. This necessity seems to be independent of the existence of intelligent observers and their ways of thinking about the process. Even if nobody were to think about the present situation, a cube of sugar that is placed in water would *have to* dissolve. Thus, it is *prima facie* plausible to think of the necessity involved as a 'metaphysical' or 'natural' necessity that is different from 'logical' or 'conceptual' necessity, because the latter hold only between *descriptions* of the participants and of results of the situations and are, in this sense, dependent on the conceptualization of the situation.

One might think of two different relations that they hold by 'natural' necessity. First, the effect—for example, the dissolving of a cube of sugar—can be considered as being tied to the possession of the relevant powers by the objects involved and the presence of the stimulus conditions by 'natural' necessity. And second, the powers themselves, together with their manifestation, can be considered to be tied to the 'nature' of the substance—its other properties, internal structure, and properties of its constituents—by this kind of necessity. Harré and Madden advocate the latter view. For example, the dispositions of a chemical substance are said to follow from its chemical structure and the nature of its constituent parts 'by natural necessity',[45] and once we have discovered these features we will see that the substance 'must' behave as it does.[46] Discovering these features is never merely a matter of *a priori* reasoning, but necessarily involves empirical research: The relations of 'natural necessity' are only discovered *a posteriori*.[47]

The combination of these two ideas—(i) that there is a connection of natural necessity between 'what a thing really is' and what powers it has, and (ii) that the relevant features of the objects are discovered only by empirical research—quite naturally leads to the idea that objects, both individually and as types, have 'real essences' which are independent of the concepts with which we describe those objects,

---

[45] Harré and Madden (1975), 14.
[46] Harré and Madden (1975), 47.
[47] Harré and Madden (1975), 18.

but are a matter for scientific investigation into the grounds of the objects' behaviour. And if one adopts this idea one has adopted the essentialist doctrine of 'real natures' of particular objects which we have mentioned as the second dubious doctrine to which theories of 'powers' seem to be intimately connected.

In fact, many of those philosophers who nowadays affirm the reality of powers also embrace essentialism—at least for fundamental particles—claiming that individual substances have essential properties which they must possess as long as they exist.[48] For them, essentialism is a primary ingredient of their anti-Humean metaphysics, because essences of objects and connected natural necessities supplant natural laws and regularities as the basis of scientific explanation. While Humeans assume that the fundamental fact in explaining why an event of type B has happened is the existence of a law connecting A-type and B-type events, the essentialists whom I am considering here (such as Harré and Madden) believe that the essential natures of the objects involved in these occurrences are fundamental to explaining the occurrence of the B-type event, because these objects, in virtue of their essential natures, could not have behaved differently from how they did.[49]

The 'real essence' of an object is normally considered as constituted by those properties that most advanced science regards as responsible for the properties which the object manifests. An important consequence of this view is that properties—both powers and categorical properties—are no longer regarded as freely combinable, even beyond logical and conceptual restrictions; for if science tells us that both electrical charge and a possession of a certain mass are both essential properties of an electron, then we cannot change the combination by switching to the mass of a proton while retaining the negative charge.[50]

One of the chief advantages that essentialism appears to offer with regard to an account of powers is the promise of sharpening the vague notion of 'intrinsicality' or 'internality' which we have used when characterizing powers as 'intrinsic' properties of objects. Intuitively, the distinction between 'internal' and 'external' is drawn in spatial terms; and in the examples we have mentioned so far, this approximate distinction has worked. However, this distinction does not always yield the correct results. For example, ingested food is spatially 'inside' the human digestive system during the process of digestion, but the food's properties are not 'internal' to the system, nor do they contribute to the system's powers; instead, the powers of the digestive system are powers directed at doing something with the ingested food. Essentialism might be able to draw the internal/external distinction in a more appropriate way by relying on those properties that are essential to the object.

Many contemporary philosophers might hope to reap this advantage because, following Kripke's arguments about *a posteriori* necessity and rigid designation in

---

[48] For example, Harré and Madden (1975), 101 ff.; Ellis (2001), 127 f.; and Molnar (2003), 182 ff.
[49] This program is set out in Ellis (2001), ch. 8.
[50] Cf. Molnar (2003), 182.

Naming and Necessity, they will have no qualms about 'natural' necessity understood as a non-logical kind of necessity, or, as neo-Aristotelians, they have no difficulty in accepting essential properties of particulars. Since this is the normal route which theories of powers take, so much the better for those philosophers when they want to accept a realist view of powers. For my part, however, I have grave difficulties in understanding both these notions, and therefore I would prefer an account of powers that would not commit me to any of them. As I cannot discuss these difficulties at length here, I will simply mention the two most fundamental of them.

The first problem is the well-known difficulty concerning essentialism about particular objects, that it seems to lead us into contradictions. This has, in particular, been argued by Quine.[51] The second problem is to understand what role 'natural necessity' could play in scientific explanations and enquiry, if it is conceived as something distinct from the notion of conceptual necessity or epistemic necessity (the necessity to conclude that p, given the premises and our background knowledge, because all the alternatives to p are implausible). Connections of 'natural necessity' are supposed to be determined by empirical research. But for A to be 'necessary', given B, in the context of empirical investigation, it seems, epistemic necessity is all that is required; it is sufficient that given the body of scientific knowledge we possess and our knowledge about the experimental situation, we can only conclude from the occurrence of A that B will occur or obtain. 'Natural necessities' as something distinct could only function as idealized and never-attainable end-points for scientific investigation, without, however, providing any guidelines for this investigation; and, therefore, they seem to be dispensable.

I do not want to claim that these problems provide a conclusive argument against essentialism and 'natural necessity'; but they certainly provide grounds for scepticism about these notions, which makes it attractive to have a theory of powers that accounts both for the appearance of necessity of power-manifestations and for the 'intrinsicality' of powers without relying on these two notions.

The crucial hint for the solution to the first task is provided by Harré and Madden, who stress that there is often a conceptual relation matching the supposed relation of natural necessity. These conceptual relations, as they rightly point out, are the results of changes in the concepts involved under the influence of experimental discoveries. As they demonstrate with regard to the history of copper: when we discover that a type of material formerly characterized as being of a certain colour and fusible with gold also conducts electricity, we may, as a consequence of this empirical discovery, come to change our definition of 'copper' to include conductivity.[52] When such a conceptual relation is established, the appearance of a necessary connection between the nature of the object and the power is easily explained: From the object's being copper, it follows, *ceteris paribus*, that it will conduct electricity. The necessity involved here is conceptual or logical

---

[51] Quine (1961), 139 ff.   [52] Harré and Madden (1975), 22.

necessity, based merely on the nominal or stipulated definition of copper, and we need not assume any natural necessity in addition to explain why the effect *must* follow. Furthermore, the appearance of a necessary connection between power, manifestation, and effect is easily explained by the obvious conceptual connection between our power-concepts and descriptions of stimulus and effect.

But even when the change in meaning of the original concept has not yet taken place and no conceptual connection is, as yet, established, there can already be an epistemic necessity when the empirical findings and the scientific background knowledge make all possibilities but one highly implausible or rule them out directly.[53] (In this context, 'plausibility' can also arise from 'inference to the best explanation', when one hypothesis has the greatest explanatory power.) Epistemic necessity of this kind also explains the impression that the effect 'cannot but' happen under the circumstances.

Perhaps one could accept the idea of natural necessity as innocuous if this necessity were simply understood as a projected counterpiece to conceptual and epistemic necessity which was completely reducible to these notions. Natural necessity, one would then claim, connects two events exactly if there is a connection of conceptual or epistemic necessity holding between the propositions describing these events. But this way of talking would still be highly misleading, because the term 'natural' necessity suggests that the necessity holds between events independently from our conceptual schemes, and from what types of inferences and arguments we accept as rational beings. This suggestion is quite wrong, for connections of both logical and epistemic necessity are not independent in this way, and if natural necessity were just a projection of these two kinds of necessity, it couldn't be independent, either. Therefore, it would be better to altogether avoid the term 'natural necessity'.

To avoid the apparent connection between 'intrinsic' properties and essentialism we can also exploit Harré and Madden's idea of concept development through adaption to new *a posteriori* discoveries and scientific explanations. Assume that we begin with the concept of a type X of chemical material defined by a number of observable categorical properties and contributions to causal processes (a 'nominal essence'). An object is, by definition, of type X if it conducts electricity, is of a reddish colour, and is fusible with gold. Let us call these features the defining features of kind X—the D-features. Now, by experiment it may be determined that objects of type X have a certain internal structure Y (where internal can at first be understood as 'inside the spatial envelope'), and on the basis of this fact and of our background knowledge, we may be able to explain why these objects also possess the D-features. In this case, the fact that an object possesses structure Y is explanatorily more fruitful than the facts about the possession of the D-features. For the latter facts are, at the beginning, without systematic connection

---

[53] Cf. Rundle (2004), 51 f.

among each other, while possession of Y unifies these different facts in a systematic way by allowing us to determine how they have the same basis and, for this reason, regularly appear together.

In this case we may be tempted to say that Y, rather than the D-features, constitutes the 'real nature' of objects of type X. But what would be the basis of this claim? *Only* that an explanatory relation of the kind just described holds, and that the fact that the object possesses structure Y has a 'unifying power' in explaining the object's behaviour, because it makes intelligible the connection between the D-features. If this relation holds, we may be well advised to change our definition of type X by substituting the possession of Y for the possession of the D-features as the defining property of the kind—as it has happened in chemistry with regard to the definition of the elements. However, it would be erroneous to think that this rational pressure for change arises from the existence of a 'real essence of X' which we have now discovered, and to which our concept of X, with its criteria of application, must conform. Concepts themselves cannot be false nor true, and so even if there were such a thing as a 'real essence', pressure for conceptual change would not stem from the need of conformity to such an essence in order to avoid factual mistakes. Instead, the pressure is due only to pragmatic considerations connected to general principles of explanatory practice in science—such as simplicity, parsimony in the concepts used, and so on. For example, when we have sufficient reason to believe that structure Y is responsible for the D-features as well as for the other features of the object, it may be advantageous to take possession of structure Y as the ascription-criterion for X, because this allows us to say more about the object's properties by calling it an object of type X.

Appeal to 'real essences' is therefore unnecessary for explaining why discovery about the structure of an object can rationally give rise to conceptual change. Nor do we have to appeal to them once the conceptual change *has* taken place, because then Y constitutes the 'nominal essence' of X, and, for conceptual reasons, no object can be an X without having this structure. This means that we can avoid all talk of 'essence' or 'nature' outside the realm of 'nominal essences'. If we want to talk about 'essences' at all, they should be seen as nothing more than defining criteria. Consequently, not as such, but only as described in a certain way, do individual objects possess any properties 'in virtue of their nature'.

This rejection of 'real essences' may be misunderstood as implying a rejection of certain other doctrines with which I have no quarrel. In order to avoid this misunderstanding it is important to stress what I do *not* want to deny when I reject 'real essences'. I do not want to deny that there are characterizations of objects that we see as the 'natural' and even 'unavoidable' ways of thinking about those objects. In fact, on my view we think of non-sentient material objects primarily *as* such i.e. as material objects, or of human beings *as* persons. These basic categories are embedded in our way of conceptualizing the world, and they unavoidably pre-form the ways in which we think about particular objects, because they determine the ways in which we learn about those objects and learn how to refer to them.

The main reason for their unavoidable influence is—as Strawson has rightly argued—the connection between reference and the possibility of reidentification: namely, the possession of criteria of numerical identity.[54] Whenever we refer to a particular object we must possess some criteria of numerical identity for this object, because we must be able to decide—in principle, and leaving aside possible vagueness—what counts as the same object as the one to which we refer, and whether an object to which we refer later is (numerically) the same object or a distinct one. The criteria for identity differ for different kinds of object. For example, they are different for inanimate physical objects such as a chunk of salt, and living beings and persons; while the numerical identity of material components is largely irrelevant to the numerical identity of living beings and persons, it is relevant to the identity of the chunk of salt. This difference between identity-criteria, taken together with the necessity of having some grasp of the identity-criteria of the objects to which we refer, implies that we can refer to an object only *qua* object of some kind—however unspecific or vague this kind may be—not 'just so' by ostensive definition.[55]

Normally, the identity-criteria for the objects to which we refer are automatically provided by very fundamental categories of objects—fundamental to *our* thinking, that is—such as the categories of material objects or persons, because we learn about these objects, at least implicitly, *qua* members of these categories. Thus, we learn about a particular A not as some indeterminate being, but we learn *about the person* A, or are shown *a material object* B, not some being B which might be a material or immaterial object, for otherwise we could not know *which* object we are being informed about or which is being pointed out to us. Perhaps some of the fundamental categories—such as the category of material objects—are even necessary to our thinking if we are to refer successfully to any objects at all. But even if no single such category is necessary as such, the fundamental categories still, as a matter of fact, unquestionably govern our thinking about objects and the ways in which we refer to objects.

I do not want to deny any of this. I do not even want to deny that because of the connection between fundamental categories and identity-conditions, we are normally unable to imagine that an object introduced as falling under one category ceases to belong to this category without ceasing to exist—simply because the criteria for saying that the object we are talking about 'is still numerically the same' as before are no longer satisfied. This inability on our part may produce the appearance that belonging to this category is an essential property of the object. But the crucial thing to keep in mind is that this appearance stems only from *our way to conceptualize* and to think about the world, from the necessary conditions which must be fulfilled if we can identify objects and refer to them. The appearance does not reflect essential properties 'in the

---

[54] Cf. Strawson (1959), ch. 1, sect. 1 and 2.
[55] Ostensive definitions themselves are impossible without a framework of fundamental kinds and identity-conditions for the objects pointed at. This point is rightly made by Wittgenstein, *Philosophical Investigations*, part I, § 30.

things themselves' that could be discovered by empirical research; instead, what it reflects—the preconditions for reference—can be found, if at all, by a 'transcendental' enquiry into the preconditions for our thinking about the world. So, even though there are 'natural' and even 'unavoidable' ways to think about particular objects, this does not entail a problematic connection to 'real essences' possessed independently of description and conceptualization.

After having shown that a theory of powers need not appeal to 'natural necessity' or 'real essences', I want to conclude my treatment of this topic by returning to the distinction between 'internal/intrinsic' and 'external/extrinsic' properties, to which essentialism promised a better answer than the rough-and-ready distinction based on inclusion within the object's 'spatial envelope'. Can we draw this distinction in a more satisfactory way, and explain in what sense powers are 'intrinsic' properties, without appeal to 'real essences'?

I think we can, if we recognize that properties are 'intrinsic' or 'extrinsic' primarily with regard to *kinds* of object, and with regard to particular objects only insofar as they belong to these kinds. This insight renders it unnecessary to appeal to 'real essences' of particular objects in order to draw the distinction that we are seeking. Instead, we can develop this distinction via the following two steps.

The first step is to single out one important class of extrinsic properties: 'relational' properties. *The* paradigm 'relational' property is relative spatial location for objects which can change their place. But what are 'relational' properties in general? In the intended sense they can be characterized as follows. If F is a verb by whose predication this property is ascribed to an object, then 'Object A has F' implies, logically, that an object other than A exists, and that A stands in a certain relation to it.[56] The property 'being the ruler of Scotland' is relational in this sense because someone can have this property only if Scotland exists and he rules over Scotland. Singling out relational properties as extrinsic allows us to deal with the counter-examples to the 'spatial envelope' criterion of 'internality'—such as the case of the ingested food inside the digestive system. The food is not a proper part of the system, but a distinct object, and so, if it does not induce a change in the system itself, its properties can only contribute to the system's properties via relational properties of the system.

In a second step, we must pick out those extrinsic properties that are not 'relational' in this sense; in particular, this includes properties which are too 'observer-dependent' to be considered intrinsic. Take properties such as 'being beautiful'. If we do not think that there are objective standards for beauty, the ascription of beauty must rely on the object's impact on potential observers, and this impact will primarily depend on the

---

[56] Cf. Molnar's definition of intrinsic and extrinsic properties; (2003), 39 f. For Molnar, the crucial characteristic of intrinsic properties is that their possession by an object does not depend in any way on what other objects exist. This is too restrictive, because it would, counterintuitively, turn all properties of objects which cannot, *de facto*, exist without the existence of other objects—such as human beings—into extrinsic properties.

observers' tastes—according to the adage that 'beauty lies in the eye of the beholder'. For this reason, beauty cannot be counted as an intrinsic property (if it is to be counted as a genuine property at all). But beauty is not a 'relational' property in the sense just described, because its possession does not imply the existence of some further object or person, who finds the object beautiful. Only the 'manifestation' of beauty—an observer actually finding the object beautiful—would require the existence of a further entity if the object is unable to observe itself. But in this respect, beauty is no different from many bona fide powers—such as the power of a solvent, whose manifestation also requires the presence of another object which is dissolved.

The reason why beauty cannot be an intrinsic property is that it depends on the object's effects on potential observers, and these effects are not connected in the right way to 'what the object is really like', because observers can like 'practically anything'. What the object is 'really like' can be, on our earlier considerations, either (i) its 'nominal essence'—the defining features of objects of this kind, and, if there is no clearly defined 'nominal essence', to the other crucial features of the concept—or (ii) the structure which explains possession of the properties included in the 'nominal essence'. An 'internal property' will be one that is rightly connected to either (i) or (ii), as the case requires.

A connection with (i) is required for objects that do not possess any structure, such as electrons. An electron's internal properties are only those included in the 'nominal essence'—electrical charge and mass—and the properties that can be directly derived from the former, such as the power to attract or repel other particles, which is included in the electrical charge. However, even for some kinds of object which possess an internal physical structure, this structure may not be crucial to our concept of those kinds of object and to our understanding of their characteristic behaviour *qua* objects of this kind—the most important such case being human persons. For though human persons are physical beings, we do not think of them simply as such, and to our understanding of 'what they are' their physical constitution is mostly irrelevant, contrary to their capacities to think, act, have emotions, and so on. With regard to those beings, intrinsic properties are, roughly, these very capacities and (some of) the properties that are acquired as a result of their manifestation. As a consequence, for human beings—who are both material objects and persons—the set of powers which they possess *qua* persons need not be coextensional to the set of powers they possess *qua* material beings, because the criteria for properties to count as intrinsic are different. This is reflected in the different identity-criteria for something to count as the same person and to count as the same material structure. For example, a corpse may consist of the same amount of matter as a living human being, but is not the same person. (We will return to this point in Section 8.2.1.)

A connection with (ii) is normally required when we know the internal physical constitution of the object and when this constitution plays the unifying role in explaining the object's properties described earlier. When we have knowledge of such a constitution, we will normally expect all internal properties to be explanatorily connected to it, and lack of such connection indicates that a property is extrinsic. Thus, if an object possesses a natural colour that is internal in this sense, and the colour is changed by artificially adding another layer of paint, this new colour will be typically external, because it will not be explainable—not even indirectly—by the internal physical structure of the object. However, lack of explanatory connection can sometimes be tolerated in intrinsic properties, when these properties are possessed temporally stably by the object and their ascription is not at odds with the underlying structure. Thus, as we have seen when discussing the case of the randomized experiment, it is possible to discover new powers of an object without knowing how its structure could explain these powers, and even without later finding such an explanatory connection. As long as manifestations of the alleged power occur regularly, and the known structure of the object would not, by itself, rule out that the object can possess this power, we can accept that this power is indeed among the object's intrinsic properties.

When we apply these considerations to our earlier example in Section 7.1.1—placebos and their alleged power to produce sleepiness—we can see why placebos must lack this power. In this case, the only relevant factor in producing sleepiness is the person's false belief that he is taking an effective sleeping-pill. But as the pill can be believed to be effective regardless of its internal structure or nominal essence, neither of the two is explanatorily connected to the effect. Nor is the effect regularly manifested, because not every person believes that the pill is effective. Ascribing the power in question is even positively at odds with the placebo's known chemical structure, because we know that medicines cannot produce effects in human beings directly, as if by magic, but only via chemical or physical interaction with their bodies, and from our knowledge of the pill's chemical constitution we know that the interaction which takes place in the body cannot itself lead to sleepiness. For these reasons, placebos, on the above criteria, cannot have an intrinsic power-property of producing sleepiness, and any powers would have to be intrinsic.

We can therefore conclude that the 'internal/external' distinction for properties can be explained without appeal to the essential properties of particular objects, but instead by singling out 'relational' properties as external and appealing to explanatory connections to 'nominal essences' and physical/chemical constitution of the objects. This result completes our argument that despite appearances, a viable theory of powers can do without the notion of 'natural necessity' and can get along with logical and epistemic necessities only, and that it does not have to appeal to 'real essences' of objects which would include or ground those powers.

7.4. Conclusion

Let us briefly summarize the main results of Chapters 6 and 7. The aim of these chapters was to argue for the existence of powers and their irreducibility to categorical properties. We have defended the need to accept powers as genuine properties by showing that this is required to account for the difference between statements about the possession of powers, and statements about (possible) changes in the possession of powers. We have also argued for the irreducibility of powers—first by refuting the claim that power-ascriptions are conceptually reducible to statements about categorical properties, and second, by showing that a purely ontological reduction of powers to categorical properties is also impossible. Lastly, we have shown that powers do not commit us to the doctrines of natural necessity and essentialism.

Our considerations so far should not only have dispelled doubts about accepting powers as genuine properties. They have also shown that powers are properties whose possession might confer on their bearer a causal role not conferred by the possession of a categorical property. What we have still to explain, however, is how the role which they confer can be the role of a substance-cause. Answering this question will be our concern in the following chapter.

8

How agent-causation works III: from causal powers to agent-causation

After developing an account of irreducible powers in the last chapter, we must now turn to the task of elaborating this account into a theory of agent-causation. As already mentioned in the overview of the overall argument at the beginning of Chapter 6, I will proceed via the following steps. First, taking the case of inanimate substances as an example, I will show how the account of powers allows us to develop a viable notion of substance-causation not reducible to event-causation (Section 8.1). Afterwards, I will apply the general notion of substance-causation to the particular case of human agents, which will yield the account of agent-causation that we have been seeking (Section 8.2). I will conclude this chapter by showing how this account evades the criticisms traditionally levelled against agent-causal theories (Section 8.3).

8.1. Substance-causation among inanimate substances

In order to develop an account of substance-causation for inanimate physical objects on the basis of the theory of powers from the preceding section, I will proceed in three steps. First, I will elaborate the crucial distinction between 'active' and 'passive' powers (Section 8.1.1); second, I will show how exercise of an active power provides a genuine causal role for the bearer of the power which cannot be reduced to purely event-causal processes (Section 8.1.2); and last, I will demonstrate that substance-causes, thus understood, are indeed bona fide causes, and that their relations to the effects produced by the exercise of the power satisfy all plausible requirements for a causal relation (Section 8.1.3).

8.1.1. Active and passive powers

The fundamental distinction between activity and passivity—between what substances do and what happens to them—is reflected, among powers, by the traditional distinction between 'active' ('causal') and 'passive' powers (or between 'powers' and 'liabilities').[1] As Locke explains this distinction, power is 'twofold, viz. as able to make, or able to receive any change'.[2] When active and passive power are defined in this way it is natural to see the two kinds of power as systematically interrelated: to the power to produce a certain change, such as the power to ignite, corresponds the power to suffer this very same change, such as inflammability, and both are normally manifested together.[3]

The distinction between active and passive powers is not an exhaustive distinction for all powers; that is, not all powers are either active or passive. For the manifestations of both active and passive powers consist in productions or sufferings of changes, and thus necessarily include changes which are produced or suffered. These changes cannot be identical to the manifestations themselves; that is, the change cannot consist merely in the fact that the power has been manifested, while it had not been manifested before. Instead, some further change in the properties of the substance itself or some other substance is required (the limiting case being that one substance comes into being or ceases to exist). And not all powers have manifestations that necessarily include such further changes; for instance, the human powers of thought do not. Therefore, not all powers can be active or passive.

The traditionally assumed 'duality' of active and passive powers came under criticism in the late seventeenth century and the eighteenth century. The earlier attacks were mainly based on doubts about whether non-sentient physical substances could possess anything but passive powers, without yet calling into question that intelligent beings with wills could possess active powers.[4] The ensuing 'mechanistic' view of physical matter as purely passive was, in a further step, transferred to voluntary actions, when actions were also begun to be understood on the mechanistic model. As our concern at this point is with the active powers of inanimate physical substances, we can restrict our attention to the first kind of attacks.

8.1.1.1. Scepticism about active powers of inanimate substances Locke himself was among the number of seventeenth-century philosophers who were sceptical or openly dismissive about the possibility of active powers of substances other than intelligent beings capable of voluntary actions. The other two most famous exponents of this group were Descartes and Newton, and with the success of Newtonian mechanics in the eighteenth century the denial of active powers of inanimate objects became quite

---

[1] Cf. Harré and Madden (1975), 88 f. The distinction goes back to Aristotle's distinction between δύναμις τοῦ ποιεῖν and δύναμις τοῦ πάσχειν; cf. *Metaphysics* Θ, 1046a.

[2] Locke, *An Essay concerning Human Understanding*, II, ch. xxi, § 2.

[3] Though not necessarily so—for powers can only be possessed by substances (or amounts of stuff), and there can be causal factors triggering the manifestation of a power that are not substances themselves and therefore have no powers; for example, an inflammable object may be set afire by a lightning strike.

[4] A notable exception is Malebranche, for whom even human beings did not possess any active powers, but only God; cf. *Recherche*, VI.

standard.⁵ Here we will focus only on the arguments of two important critics: Locke and Reid.

As Locke argues, the observation of physical motion 'gives us but a very obscure Idea of an active Power of moving in Body, whilst we observe it only to transfer, but not to produce any motion'—a transfer which he describes as a mere 'Continuation of Passion'.⁶ This verdict presupposes a very demanding notion of active power according to which it is not sufficient for 'activity' that the power exerted is a power to bring about change, but it must even be a power to initiate a change 'all by itself'—without an earlier impulse. Given the principle of energy conservation, it is difficult to see how *any* physical body could satisfy this condition; and probably the only changes among inanimate objects that Locke would be willing to consider as involving a genuinely active power are completely spontaneous activities, such as radioactive disintegration, which, although conforming to the laws of energy conservation, appear to be self-initiated 'from zero' because of their spontaneity.⁷

Thomas Reid's requirement on something to count as an 'active power' is even more strict. Reid—who thinks that for terminological reasons only 'active powers' can adequately be characterized as powers at all[8]—draws a sharp distinction between powers and dispositions of objects to behave in a certain way under specific circumstances. The difference between the two can best be expressed in terms of a difference between the manifestation of a disposition and what Reid calls the *exertion* of a power. While a disposition is 'simply' manifested on the relevant occasions, a power to produce an effect must be exerted by its bearer when the effect is produced, and this exertion presupposes, for Reid, that the bearer is also capable of refraining from exerting the power. Thus, Reid claims, the 'power to produce any effect, implies power not to produce it',⁹ and we cannot infer lack of a power from failure to exert the power even though there is an occasion for its exertion. As a consequence, for Reid, possession of powers is restricted to intelligent beings having a will, for only with regard to them the idea of a 'power not to produce the effect' makes sense, because it involves the idea of a choice between exerting a power and refraining from doing so.[10]

Clearly, once we accept Locke's or Reid's strict criteria for active powers, non-sentient physical beings—as well as plants and non-human animals—would almost exclusively count as devoid of active powers and activity. This result would undercut our general project of making the causal powers of human persons intelligible as an instance of the more general genus of active powers of substances, because it would practically reduce this genus to just the class of properties that we want to explain.

---

⁵ Descartes, *Principia Philosophiae*, II, § 4, §§ 36 ff.; for Newton, see Thayer (1953). For an overview over the general historical development, see Ellis (2001), 107 ff., 263 ff.
⁶ Locke, *An Essay concerning Human Understanding*, II, ch. xxi, § 4.
⁷ Cf. Harré and Madden (1975), 115.
⁸ Reid (1983), 514.
⁹ Reid (1983), 523.
¹⁰ Reid (1983), 523 ff.

Fortunately, however, there are good reasons to reject both Locke's and Reid's overly demanding criteria for what should be deemed an active power.

The answer to Locke's doubts about the activity of non-sentient beings rests on distinguishing more clearly than he does *with regard to what* an object is said to be active or passive. Consider the following scenario. A billiard ball is set in motion by a player who hits it with his cue. Moving over the table, it strikes a second ball, thereby also setting this ball in motion. With regard to its role in the overall process it would not make sense to refer to the first ball as 'active' *tout court*, because it does not self-initiate its own movement. So far, Locke is correct. But from this it does not follow that we can rightly call the ball 'passive' *tout court* either, because it is possible that the ball is active with regard to some aspects or stages of the scenario, and passive with regard to others. And this is indeed one natural way of viewing the scenario. The ball is passive when set in motion by the impulse of the cue, but active when setting the second ball in motion.

This can be true even though the ball was passive in acquiring the active power manifested at the second stage, because the acquisition of an active power need not be an activity itself. The post-Lockean concept of energy in classical physics captured this idea quite clearly.[11] Energy is the power to produce effects, which can, metaphorically, be 'stored' and 'transferred' in quantified packages. Activity involves the 'transfer' of such 'packages' onto other objects to produce changes in them, and passivity is the 'reception' of such packages. As the transfer from an 'active' object presupposes that the object has built up a sufficient store of energy in advance, and this in turn requires that sufficient energy has been transferred to the object, activity presupposes an earlier process of power-acquisition with regard to which the object itself has been 'at the receiving end' and is therefore passive.

So, *pace* Locke, we need not assume that all production of change through motion that is not self-initiated is only a 'continuation of passion'. Even without the concept of energy expounded in modern physics, Locke could have arrived at the same result had he not focused exclusively on cases involving only one kind of change and one kind of behaviour. In the cases which Locke considered, the change induced in the first object was of exactly the same kind as the change later produced in the second, and there was no further change in the behaviour of the first object between the two impacts. For example, in the case of the billiard balls, the first ball is set in motion by external impulse, moves, and, on hitting the second ball, induces the same kind of change in it as previously induced in itself—that is, it sets it in motion. In cases such as these, Locke's contention that when motion is imparted on the second ball by the first it is merely a continuation of the original change in the first ball,[12] may, *prima facie*, appear quite plausible. But clearly not all cases are like this. The first object can change its behaviour before it acts on the second, or the second may be caused to display behaviour of a

---

[11] Cf. Harré and Madden (1975), 115.
[12] Locke, *An Enquiry concerning Human Understanding*, II, ch. xxi, § 4.

different kind from the first. For example, the first object may be heated, whereupon it starts to emit radiation which causes the second object to change its colour. When we are faced with such cases, the impression that the impact of objects consists only in 'transmitting' changes externally induced in them soon vanishes.

When we turn to Reid's argument that only intelligent beings with a will can possess active powers, we quickly realize that his underlying requirement on the possession of an active power—that the substance which has the power must also have the power not to bring about this effect—is implausible; for it rests on conflating the notion of active powers with that of freely exerted powers, with the result that for Reid all active powers must be freely exerted, because their bearers must be able to refrain from exerting them. But on the traditional view of active powers as powers to produce change, it is by no means necessary that they are freely exerted. An object can also produce an effect when the circumstances make it unavoidable that it does produce this effect; indeed, far from being precluded from producing the effect, it is then necessitated to do so.

Insofar as it is intended as an explication of the traditional concept of active powers, Reid's thesis is therefore simply mistaken. Its apparent plausibility as such an explication stems from a failure to keep apart separate two kinds of case: (i) that circumstances make it unavoidable that effect E is produced independently of A, and (ii) that circumstances make it unavoidable that A produces effect E. In case (i) it is indeed plausible to deny that A—apart from cases of over-determination—has any role to play in the production of E. It may appear that the same applies to case (ii), and that what 'really' produces E here must be the necessitating circumstances and not the bearer of the power, A. But this impression is misleading, for in case (ii) the mentioned circumstances may not even be jointly sufficient for E, but the existence of an object possessing the power to produce E may be required in addition to those circumstances, even though these circumstances are jointly sufficient for such an object, if present, to exert this active power and thereby bring about E. Therefore, there is no need to assume that active powers, as powers to produce changes, are incompatible with the existence of necessitating conditions for their exercise.

8.1.1.2. The distinction between activity and passivity So, *pace* Locke and Reid, there can be active powers of inanimate physical objects. But how are we to distinguish an object's active powers from its passive powers? Given a particular power whose manifestation necessarily involves a 'real' change, under which conditions is it a power to produce this change, and under which conditions is it a power to suffer this change?

This question is far from trivial, though at first glance there seems to be the following obvious answer. As we have already seen, many transitive verbs contain causative elements, which characterize them as verbs ascribing the production of a certain change to the objects of which they are predicated. So, it seems, we can use the following grammatical criterion: A power is active if the verb by which we describe the manifestation of this power is a transitive verb of this kind, used in the active voice, such as 'turning logwood solution red'; while if the verb is a transitive verb in the passive voice or is not a transitive verb with a causative element at all, the ascribed power is passive.

But this proposal, as well as other proposals of purely grammatical criteria for the distinction, is faced with an apparent paradox which seems to prevent *any* successful answer to our question. The manifestation of practically all powers that are active on this criterion, as well as on our intuitive assessment, involves changes not only in other objects, but also in the object which possesses the power itself. This is obvious in the case of allegedly active powers to produce a change in oneself, but the same point also applies to powers to interact with other objects. For instance, take the power of water to dissolve water-soluble objects, which, on the proposed criterion, qualifies as an active power. When water contained in a bowl dissolves a lump of sugar which has been thrown into the bowl and the power is thus manifested, not only the lump of sugar changes—it dissolves—but also the water itself, which becomes sugar-water. As a consequence, it seems, almost all supposedly active powers are not only powers to produce, but also powers to suffer change—and so, it seems, practically all active powers are, at the same time, passive powers. *Pari passu*, we can make this argument 'from the opposite direction' and reach the conclusion that the manifestation of practically all passive powers involves producing changes in other objects, so that almost all passive powers must also be active powers. As a consequence, the distinction that we are seeking seems to collapse, because almost all powers are both active and passive.

If we take this apparent paradox seriously, we will say that the alleged difference between active and passive powers cannot be a real distinction between two different kinds of property, but merely a matter of different perspectives in describing one and the same power.[13] Thus, when we say that the water in the bowl has the power to dissolve the sugar, we would adopt an 'active' perspective, while we adopt a 'passive' perspective when we claim that the water has the disposition to turn into sugar-water when sugar is put into it. But in both cases we would be talking about the same power of the water.

However, it is wrong to think that the distinction between active and passive powers reduces to a difference between perspectives only. The apparent dilemma can be dissolved when we notice the following two points. First, from cases of self-produced changes of objects, we must recognize that the crucial point for distinguishing between activity and passivity is not *where* the change occurs, but whether the object passively undergoes it or actively produces it. But this first point does not yet dissolve the paradox for cases like the dissolution of sugar by water, because in these cases there is a chemical interaction between the objects involved, so that in the overall process of

---

[13] At one point, Harré and Madden (1975), 83, also suggest that the distinction between activity and passivity is merely one of perspective, though they explain later that there is a 'real' distinction, (1975), 89.

dissolution both objects suffer some changes which are produced by the other. In order to deal with these cases we must get rid of the idea which is primarily responsible for the apparent paradox—namely the idea that the distinction between a passive and an active power is a sharp categorical distinction, so that in the manifestation of an active power its possessor must be 'purely active', not undergoing any change itself, and, respectively, for passive powers. Instead, the distinction between active and passive powers is one of degree, with all powers situated on a more or less continuous spectrum of more or less active and passive powers.[14]

Once we accept that the 'active/passive' distinction is one of degree, this rules out a purely grammatical criterion for this distinction of the kind we have mentioned, for this criterion would yield a clear-cut distinction instead of one of degrees. This immediately raises the question of by what other criterion the activity or passivity of objects and their powers—or rather, the degree of activity and passivity—is determined.

Harré and Madden have suggested that what is crucial is 'the degree to which we assign responsibility for particular behavioural manifestations between intrinsic conditions and extrinsic circumstances'.[15] If we place the emphasis on 'powers' rather than 'intrinsic conditions', I think this proposal is basically right and explains the fundamental distinction between activity and passivity. The degree of activity depends on the relative weight of the contributions of the object's powers (and, only secondarily, its other intrinsic properties) and of external factors, such as the obtaining of triggering conditions, to the producing of the effect. (Of course, on pain of vicious circularity, 'powers' in this sentence must be understood neutrally; that is, the powers could be either active or passive.)

The reason for drawing the distinction in this way is the following. That an object is active with regard to a change—that it produces this change—means that the object is the crucial factor for the occurrence of this change. Not only would the change not have occurred if the object had been absent, but the object must also have played the 'chief role' in comparison to other factors whose presence has also been necessary. An object plays this role when it is the crucial factor in the *explanation* of the occurrence of the effect, and this condition is satisfied if the intrinsic properties of the object—especially its powers—are the crucial features in the explanation of the occurrence, while the external conditions that obtain are completely or largely irrelevant. What determines an object's active role is therefore the relative weight of the explanatory contribution of its powers (and other intrinsic properties) in explaining why the effect has occurred. When its powers are crucial to the explanation and the external circumstances are not, the object is active; and the more important external circumstances become for the explanation, the less active and more passive the object is with regard to the effect.

---

[14] Harré and Madden (1975), 89.   [15] Harré and Madden (1975), 89.

Connecting activity to explanatory contribution may raise doubts about whether we have succeeded in explaining a notion of activity that is truly non-perspectival, as the explanatory relevance of factors in particular cases is notoriously dependent on pragmatic and highly context-dependent considerations concerning what can be presupposed and what factor is extraordinary. Therefore, it seems that we can—depending on perspective and explanatory interest—pick out *any* factor as 'crucial' in the explanation, and so the distinction between activity and passivity would turn out to be merely a matter of perspective after all. But this conclusion would be unwarranted. It is true that explanatory relevance depends, to some degree, on what factors we consider as extraordinary, and which background conditions we consider as 'normal'. But the question of activity does not thereby become a mere matter of perspective, for there are some general principles for the relative explanatory relevance of factors, which sometimes force us to regard one factor as more important than another, and consequently, one object as active, regardless of our particular perspective.

In order to show this, we have to spell out our rough characterization of activity in more detail. What does it mean that the powers of an object are crucial in explaining the occurrence of E, while the external circumstances are irrelevant to the explanation? It means that while we *must* mention the power which was manifested in explaining the effect, mention of the specific external circumstances is unnecessary,[16] because (i) the effect could also have occurred under other circumstances, and (ii) this effect need not have occurred under the actual external circumstances, because either no change at all or a different effect might have occurred. (In the extreme case the effect could have occurred under any external circumstances, but need not have occurred under any of those circumstances.) If both conditions (i) and (ii) are met, the manifestation of the power and the effect in which it issues are independent from external circumstances, and we can therefore assign responsibility for the effect only to the object and not to those circumstances. In these cases it would indeed be a mistake to do otherwise, regardless of the perspective on the situation which one adopts.

From conditions (i) and (ii) we can easily construct a general measure for the degree of activity or passivity, which spells out the notion of different weight of explanatory contribution more precisely. The activity and passivity of an object simply depends on the degree to which (i) and (ii) are satisfied. As the satisfaction of both conditions can come apart, the question arises which one is more crucial. Clearly, condition (i) must take precedence over (ii), because whenever the object's power could have been manifested under a sufficiently large range of occasions, knowledge of the specific external circumstances will be less important or even unnecessary for understanding why the effect has occurred, because it would also have occurred had the circumstances been very different. This is true whether the power *can* or *must* be manifested under

---

[16] This is *not* a case of leaving out one factor in the explanation, because the factor is already known to the interlocutor. Even if the interlocutor does not know about the specific circumstances, we need not tell him about them, because even without knowledge of them he can understand why E occurred.

those circumstances. Therefore, the power of a magnet to attract iron objects by its magnetic force, and the power of material objects to attract one another by gravitational force, are active according to this criterion—for as the concepts of magnetic and gravitational fields show, we believe that these powers are continuously exercised in one way or another.[17] (However, as both these powers necessarily involve interactions between different objects, there will be a modification of the activity/passivity distinction to which we will turn presently.)

The proposed way of drawing the distinction between the activity and passivity of objects introduces a distinction between active and passive *powers*. For whether conditions (i) and (ii) are met, and to what degree, depends on what kind of power is being exercised. If the power to E is both 'unconditional' and a capacity—i.e. if it can be manifested under an extremely wide range of circumstances, but need not be manifested under any of those circumstances—(i) and (ii) are satisfied and the object will count as active. Unstable explosives are paradigmatic cases of this kind. If, however, the power is a highly specific disposition whose manifestation presupposes highly specific external stimuli, but *must* occur when those circumstances obtain, then clearly the obtaining of the external circumstances is at least as important to the explanation of the effect as the disposition of the object itself, and in this case the object is highly passive. It is crucial to note that in this case the qualification as passive does not depend on the fact that the disposition is highly specific *per se*, but on the fact that the *external* triggering conditions are so specific, while the specificity of the *internal* conditions is irrelevant. In order to better distinguish between the two we will call the external conditions for the exercise of a power *opportunities*,[18] which are contrasted with the occasions and the triggering conditions, which include both external and internal conditions.

Active and highly passive powers are located near the idealized 'poles' of a continuous spectrum in which powers are distributed according to their active or passive character. The idealized end-points are formed by 'purely active' powers which could, but need not, be exercised on any occasion whatsoever, and 'purely passive' powers which could be exercised in only one situation in the entire history of the universe, because their triggering conditions are too specific. No such 'purely active' or 'passive' powers, however, exist in nature.

Whether we consider a power to lie 'sufficiently' near the idealized pole of an 'active power' depends on what we regard as a 'sufficiently large' range of opportunities for the manifestation of a power. The range must be regarded as 'sufficiently large' at least if it covers all those external circumstances which we regard as 'normal'—for the

---

[17] Harré (2001), 97, although also considering continuous exercise as a chief characteristic of a causal power, places emphasis on the fact that causal powers are not 'in need of stimulation'—that the bearers of powers do not have to be activated in order to act. However, in order to avoid circularity in our account of the activity/passivity distinction, we must spell out this (perfectly sound) intuition merely in terms of the range of circumstances for exercise, without already presupposing that these circumstances involve activation.

[18] The term is taken from Kenny (1989), 68 (who, however, restricts it to human abilities).

'normal' circumstances need not be mentioned in an explanation of the change, because they are already tacitly assumed as the background of the explanation. The range of active powers therefore includes at least those things which an object can be expected to 'do by itself'.

This characterization of powers—with activity determined by the degree of satisfaction of conditions (i) and (ii), and correspondingly for passive powers—forms the 'basic distinction' between activity and passivity.

This 'basic distinction' must, however, be modified in two ways. The first is specific to cases of interactions between different objects. When there is a change in the properties of one of two interacting objects, and we want to know which of the objects 'actively produced' the change, we usually already presuppose that one of the objects was 'active' and that the change was not produced by conditions external to both of them. To answer the question of whether one object actively produced the change, it therefore suffices to decide whether one object is clearly 'more active' than the other; that is, we have only to decide about the explanatory weight of the powers of the objects *compared with each other*, and we need not, as in the 'basic distinction', compare the relative weight of the powers of each object with *all* the circumstances external to this object (which would include the powers of the other object). Typical scenarios where we are interested in the first, more restricted question, when determining the 'activity' or 'passivity' of the involved objects, are mechanical interactions in classical dynamics—for example, when one billiard ball hits another, setting it in motion, or attractions of objects by magnets.

Do we have to regard this modification as a distorting 'falsification' of the distinction between activity and passivity, or can we accept that an object is active with regard to changes under the modified conditions, even though it would not count as active according to the 'basic distinction'? I think we can accept the latter result, because the modification reflects a very natural two-step procedure in assigning responsibility for a certain change, successively narrowing our focus of search for the explanatorily crucial factor. First, finding out the crucial process, before looking for the crucial factor within this process. Thus, the restriction to the relative contributions of the two objects involved in the interaction reflects our prior belief that what is crucial to the occurrence of the change is this interaction, not other factors lying beyond it; and as far as this belief is true, we are justified in applying the two-step procedure just mentioned. Whether this belief is true depends on a criterion parallel to that used in the 'basic distinction' between activity and passivity: it is true if the interaction was necessary for the change, (i') the change could also have occurred had factors external to the interaction been different, (ii') it need not have occurred given those external factors.[19] As with the 'basic distinction', it suffices that (i') and (ii') are satisfied to a sufficiently large degree.

---

[19] Factors which are not themselves constitutive parts of the interaction, but have been part of the objects' acquiring those properties that are relevant in the interaction, such as prior acceleration of one object by

We can therefore accept that among interacting objects, the object whose powers and properties are more important for the explanation of the change is active, and the other is passive. This consideration modifies our 'basic distinction' between activity and passivity—for example, in cases of reciprocal attraction of material objects by gravitational force or by magnetic force—for we often consider the contribution of one object to the change comparatively greater than the contribution of the other, and therefore consider this object as (relatively) active, and the other as (relatively) passive.

This first modification of the 'basic distinction' is often combined with a second modification which arises from the fact that many powers are introduced in an explanatory framework *as* powers to produce change, and are therefore, conceptually, active powers. An important case is the concept of energy in classical mechanics which was, in essence, introduced as part of a framework to explain changes in the motions of objects. Within this framework, energy is explained as the power to do 'work'—that is, as the power to exert a force on an object which moves it for a certain distance. This means that energy is conceived of as a power to produce a certain quantified amount of motion—and therefore, energy is conceived, by definition, as an active power to bring about a change. The original conception that the energy of an object must be 'stored' in the object's own motion—now known as kinetic energy—has been enlarged to include forms of potential energy or, beyond mechanics, the energy stored in an electromagnetic field. These other forms of energy can also be understood as powers that are 'active by definition'.

Insofar as the explanatory framework is successful in explaining the phenomena, and we have thus reason to accept the properties that it postulates, we are justified in accepting the powers which the framework introduces as active powers. This acceptance is not incompatible with the rationale underlying the basic distinction: that the power has been introduced as *active* within the successful explanatory framework, simply reflects that the power is introduced as the crucial element to explain changes of a certain kind. This is clearly so with the notion of energy: for energy was introduced as a 'potency' for exerting forces; and forces themselves were introduced—quasi by definition—as the factors responsible for changes in the motion of physical bodies.

I do not want to claim that the 'basic' distinction between activity and passivity, together with the two added modifications, already exhausts the distinction between activity and passivity. For instance, one might argue that the grammatical criterion mentioned earlier— that the power-manifestation is described by a verb with a causative element, used in the active voice—should function as an additional criterion, playing at least a subsidiary role when there is no clear verdict on the other criteria. I am rather sceptical about this, however. While I accept that fulfilment of the grammatical criterion can be an additional indication for a power's being active, if its results accord with the results reached by applying the other criteria, I do not think that we can use

---

external force, cannot be counted as external, as they have their explanatory role for the change only via the explanatory role of the interaction itself.

this criterion to decide the question on its own, if there is no clear result from applying these other criteria.

But, however this last issue is to be decided, for my overall argument it is sufficient to have shown that there are *some* active and *some* passive powers, and that consequently we can draw a distinction between the two which is not purely perspectival and therefore escapes the apparent paradox sketched at the beginning of this sub-section. It is true that our distinction is not altogether free from context-dependent factors. On the one hand it relies on the idea of different explanatory relevance, and depends, for particular powers, on what conditions we consider as 'normal' and which as 'extraordinary', and so on. On the other hand, in the case of causal interactions between particular objects, only the relative contributions of the objects involved in these interactions are relevant for the activity/passivity distinction. This degree of context-dependence, however, does not make the distinction useless for our general project of explaining substance-causation. For methods of picking out causes of a change from the bundle of preceding conditions notoriously rely on context-dependent considerations of just the same kind.[20] Only if the context-dependence had been complete, and the distinction had solely depended on the perspective adopted in the particular case, would we have been forced to renounce the idea of a general distinction between active and passive powers. But, as we have seen, this is not the case, for there are both clear instances of activity and passivity, and a standard for comparing which of two powers is more active. The general distinction can therefore be maintained.

8.1.2. *Irreducible substance-causation*

The distinction between active and passive powers that we have defended can be applied in a straightforward way to the explanation of substance-causation. When the active power of an object is manifested, issuing in an effect, the object itself is the cause of this effect because substance-causation consists in the manifestations of active (or 'causal') powers. This follows from what I consider as the core idea of designating some A as the cause of an effect B: namely, that A is the crucial factor responsible for the occurrence of the change. As established in the last sub-section, active powers are just those powers on whose manifestations the substance with its intrinsic properties is the crucial factor for the explanation of the change. As a factor's being crucial *tout court* normally corresponds to an appeal to this factor being crucial for the explanation of the change, we can conclude that when an active power is manifested, the substance possessing this power is the crucial factor responsible for the change, and thus the cause of the change produced. For example, when a magnet attracts a metallic object, and by the attraction the course of the object is changed, the magnet is the cause of the object's deviating from its original course. And when an unstable explosive explodes, it is itself the cause of the explosion.

---

[20] Cf. Hart and Honoré (1959), 32 ff.

Many philosophers will be prepared to concede that in some sense the magnet is the cause of the deviation, but argue that this statement must be analysed in a way that the 'real' cause is an event involving the object, or a fact about the object, or a property of the object. But I want to claim that such a reductive analysis of substance-causation is impossible. The object whose active power to bring about a change is manifested is the *irreducible* substance-cause of this change. In order to defend this claim I will now discuss the three different reductionist proposals that I have mentioned, and show that they will not work.

a) *Reducing substance-causation to event-causation.* Can causation by a substance, when understood as the exercise of an active power, be the same as causation by an event? By way of illustration, let us take a case already encountered earlier. A magnet is fastened inside a metallic box which isolates it from its environment by precluding interactions with objects outside the box. A small metallic ball is shot into the box at a certain angle, and on entering the box is attracted by the magnet and changes its direction. As we have claimed, the magnet is the cause of this deviation.

Now, which are the events to whose causal influence the causation of the ball's deviation by the magnet might be reduced? Four events come to mind: (1) that the ball is attracted by the magnet, (2) that it enters the box, (3) that the ball is set in motion, and (4) that the magnet has acquired its magnetic power.

Event (1), however, is just the event of the causal interaction between the magnet and the ball—that is, it is the event of the magnet manifesting its causal power, and thus the event of the magnet causing the ball to change its course! This rules out the possibility of a reductive analysis of causation by the magnet in terms of causation by this event, because this event is constituted by the magnet's playing its causal role.[21] This reductive analysis would only work if 'attracting' could be understood as something the magnet 'does' to the ball which is not itself a causing, and which in turn causes the deviation; but such an understanding is not possible, because there is no activity of 'attracting' which could be distinguished from the causing of the deviation.

Event (2), on the other hand, is not the same event as the causal interaction; and, in addition, it is itself an event-cause of the change. But nonetheless, causation by the magnet cannot be the same thing as causation by this event—basically for the reasons we encountered when discussing the failure of the reductionist analyses of power-ascriptions. In particular, event (2) can be the cause of the change even if the magnet itself is not, because the manifestation of its attracting power has been prevented by another factor, and the change is produced only via a 'wayward causal chain'. Thus, imagine that when the ball enters the box an extremely powerful blowing device, installed on the side of the box opposite to the magnet, at once begins to blow the ball towards the magnet, while the magnet itself loses its magnetic force. In this

---

[21] Cf. Byerly (1979), 65.

case, the event of the ball's entering the box is a cause of the change, while the magnet itself is not.

This last consideration also applies against the remaining candidates, events (3) and (4), which face the very same problem of deviant causal chains. We can therefore conclude that causation by a substance cannot be the same as causation by an event.

b) *Reducing substance-causation to fact-causation.* While the majority view restricts causal relata to events, philosophers such as Mellor have argued that the causal relata can also be facts or states of affairs.[22] If facts can be causes, this might help the reductionist in the following way. Facts are more fine-grained than events—possibly as fine-grained as propositions. If they are, we might be able to identify a *fact* that 'the magnet attracts the object' which does not include the fact 'that the object changes its course'; and we might then consider the first fact as a potential cause of the second.

Perhaps so. But I think that the whole approach of taking facts as causes should be resisted from the beginning, because it conflates the two distinct levels of causation and causal explanation. Following Strawson, I think that these two levels should be distinguished: causation is a relation 'in nature' that holds between things that exist and occur 'in the world'; while explanation is an 'intentional' or 'rational' relation holding between truths, propositions, or facts which are themselves not things 'in the world' but 'about' such things.[23] Of course, explanation and causation are closely related, and I have repeatedly made use of this connection in the preceding sections. I have even talked about objects and their properties as being 'crucial features in the explanation of an effect'. This way of talking is both natural and innocuous, as long as we remember that it is figurative. What is 'really' crucial for the explanation is *mentioning* the object or its properties; and what is crucial in the explanation are facts about the object's existence or that the object possesses a property. So, while accepting the close relation between the level of explanation and causation, where features of the one level are mirrored by features of the other, we should not think that both are one and the same. Consequently, we should reject the possibility of fact-causation, and, together with it, the second reductionist proposal.

c) *Reducing substance-causation to causation by powers.* Philosophers such as Mumford argue that powers themselves are causes,[24] and causation by powers appears to be a promising candidate for supplanting substance-causation because it evades all the problems connected with an attempted reduction of power-manifestations to other facts or events. For if a power is said to cause an event just if the event is the result of its manifestation, a theory of power-causation will be as realist and anti-reductionist about manifestations of powers as the substance-causation account that we have been devel-

---

[22] Mellor (1995), 8.
[23] Cf. Strawson (1985), 115.
[24] Mumford (1998), ch. 6.

oping. So, it will not be faced with difficulties like the problem of deviant causal chains, which have proved the undoing of the event-causal analysis.

However, as with regard to fact-causation, I have grave doubts that powers can, in principle, be causes of anything. The difficulties are due to the distinction between the level of causation and explanation that I have just been urging. Only particulars which are 'entities' on the first level can be causes of anything, but not those 'entities' that figure on the second. 'Entities' of the right kind are particular substances or events, and other particular things that exist or occur in the same way, such as amounts of stuff; while abstract 'entities'—if we suppose that such exist—appear only as entities on the explanatory level, and therefore cannot be causes. When one assumes that only particular events can be effects—as I do—then there is a further reason for thinking that abstract 'entities' cannot be causes, because it is difficult to conceive of any way in which these 'entities' could causally interact with particulars to cause effects in them.[25]

If properties are considered as universals, it is clear that they cannot be causes, on these criteria, for universals are abstract entities. (That properties thus conceived cannot be causes is even clearer, when one holds a nominalist view of properties and believes that abstract entitities do not exist at all.) However, there is one alternative view of properties: namely, trope theory—according to which, 'properties can be particulars'.[26] 'Abstract particulars' of this kind would be 'things' like the particular redness of a particular book—those 'things' that Mumford had wanted to identify as property-instances. If there were such 'abstract particulars' and the powers of individual objects were among them, this would open up the possibility that powers could be the right kind of 'entities' to be causes—namely, particulars—and that causation by powers could supplant causation by substances.

Nonetheless, I do not think that a reductive analysis of substance-causation along these lines is going to work. Partly, I am generally sceptical about trope theory. The idea of 'properties that are particulars' seems to involve a category-mistake. Also, trope theories seem to be faced with the following dilemma, depending on whether or not they assume general properties in addition to tropes. If they do, assuming tropes in addition to general properties seems to be a superfluous addition to one's ontology, for all the work which would be done by tropes could presumably also be done by general properties and events. But if trope theorists do not assume general properties, there is the old problem—pointed out by Bertrand Russell[27]—of how to explain that objects can have the same general properties: if there are no general properties, how can different objects have the same colour or form ? One possibility is that there are tropes resembling each other sufficiently for their possession to count as having the same

---

[25] This difficulty does not rule out that abstract entities can be causes of other abstract entities, as, for instance, in Mellor's fact-causation view (1995). However, such a view fails, because it collapses the causal level and the level of explanation.

[26] Cf. Campbell (1990), preface, xi.

[27] Russell (1911–12).

property F; but this explanation would require the general relation 'resemblance'. Additionally, this explanation presupposes that we can somehow pick out the right *respect* under which two tropes resemble each other—for example, as colours or as geometrical forms—and as this respect is determined by a general property, trope theorists have difficulties in explaining how this respect can be picked out.[28]

With regard to a treatment of powers as tropes there is even a further difficulty. Powers, as we have seen, are essentially directed at manifestations *of a certain kind*; that is, they are not directed at actual and particular manifestations. And it is difficult to see how the kind of manifestation at which a power is directed could be explained without already presupposing general properties. This difficulty makes it doubtful that a theory of powers will be workable without appeal to general properties.

Due to these difficulties for trope theories in general and trope theories of powers in particular, I will conclude that the attempted reduction of substance-causation to causation by properties, whether conceived of as general properties or tropes, is unpromising.

This completes our vindication of the claim that there is causation by inanimate substances, understood in terms of the manifestation of their active (or causal) powers, which is irreducible to causation in terms of events or to other alleged kinds of causation.

8.1.3. *Irreducible substance-causation as 'genuine' causation*

Even if most of the points I have been urging so far—that substances have active powers, that they can be called 'causes' of the effects of the manifestations of those powers, and that these manifestations are not reducible to purely event-causal processes—are granted, there will still be a lingering worry, among philosophers accustomed to the regularity theory of causation, concerning whether we really should call substances 'causes' in the same sense as events. Admittedly, these philosophers might say, there is something that the Humean 'mechanistic' picture, which construes objects as purely passive, has missed—but what it has missed is not a kind of causation distinct from event-causation, but a different phenomenon which ought to find itself another name, such as 'power manifestation'. I believe that such an answer expresses nothing more than an unfounded Humean prejudice about causation; but as this prejudice is so widespread it will be better to add some considerations concerning why substance-causation is causation in the same sense as is event-causation. I will try to argue that substance-causation must be regarded as a species of causation by showing that it has the characteristics traditionally connected with the notion of causation.

The core idea of 'causality' is 'derivativeness of an effect from its causes',[29] and though it is notoriously disputed what precisely is required for this 'derivativeness', there are some fundamental characteristics which have traditionally been connected

---

[28] Cf. Runggaldier and Kanzian (1998), 67.
[29] Anscombe (1971), 92.

with it. We must show that these characteristics are displayed by the relation between substance-cause and effect when we want to dispel remaining doubts about whether this relation is literally a *causal* relation. I will focus on four key characteristics, discussing one further condition that is often considered as part of the notion of causation.

(1) *Causes as necessary factors.* It is a widely accepted idea that a cause must be a *ceteris paribus* necessary factor for the occurrence of the effect—that in the situation in which the event occurred, it could not have occurred without the cause. Hume famously elevated this connection into his second definition of 'causation' in the *Enquiry* as a succession of one 'object' on another 'where if the first object had not been, the second never had existed'.[30] There are exceptions to this general connection in cases of causal overdetermination and of hypothetical substitute causes, which in the actual course of events are 'blocked' from causal influence by the actual cause. But these cases are only variants of the paradigmatic model of causation, where the cause is *ceteris paribus* necessary.

This first requirement on causal relations is satisfied in cases of substance-causation. When the effect is due to the manifestation of an active power of an object, then clearly this object must, *ceteris paribus*, exist if the effect is to occur: The deviation of the iron ball from its trajectory could not occur without the existence and presence of the magnet, if there are no other intervening factors present—that is, *ceteris paribus*. In this respect, substances are no worse candidates for being causes than events—the only difference being that in the case of objects their *existence* is a necessary condition, and in the case of events their *occurrence*.

(2) *Causation and causal explanation.* There is a crucial connection between causation and causal explanation of why the effect came about—philosophical recognition of which dates back at least to Aristotle's treatment of 'cause' in *Metaphysics Δ*. While Aristotle himself used 'cause' equivalently to 'explanatory feature',[31] thus equating mention of a cause with the giving of an explanation, modern philosophers have somewhat loosened this link, insofar as it is nowadays not usually claimed any more that *any* mention of the cause explains the effect. This is chiefly due to Davidson's arguments that the relation of explanation is intensional—it depends on how the factors involved are described—while the causal relation itself is extensional—its obtaining is independent from the descriptions chosen.[32] As Davidson pointed out, the eruption of a volcano can be both the cause of the destruction of a village and the event most discussed in the evening news, even though the information that the event most discussed in the evening news caused the destruction does not explain, on its own, this destruction. What is still

---

[30] Hume, *Enquiries*, 76.
[31] As becomes clear from his doctrine of the four causes, which correspond to four respects in which an effect can be explained, cf. *Metaphysics*, 1013a ff.
[32] Cf. Davidson (1963), 14; and (1967), 431.

widely accepted, however, is the weaker requirement that when A causes B there must be *some* descriptions of A and B under which B's occurrence can be explained by appeal to the factor A.[33]

Can substance-causes satisfy this requirement? At first glance it seems clear that they can. For instance, in the example we discussed earlier, mentioning the presence of a magnet explains satisfactorily why the iron ball changed its trajectory. Of course, not all descriptions of the substance will suffice for the explanation, but only descriptions which characterize it as a *powerful* substance. But this is no different to the case of event-causation, because—to reiterate Davidson's point—explanation is *generally* description-dependent,[34] in the case of causally related events as well as for other causally related entities.

However, there are two important arguments attempting to show that despite appearances, substance-causes do not satisfy the explanation requirement. The first argument focuses on the fact that when substances are described as powerful particulars, what is crucial to the explanation are powers of these substances. Such 'explanations' appealing to powers, it is claimed, are trivial because they just 'label' the phenomena which they proclaim to explain, without offering any real explanation. This is the historically influential *virtus dormitiva* objection against explanations in terms of powers. After our earlier presentation of the theory of powers, however, this objection can be easily dismissed. For powers are 'intrinsic' properties of objects, and thus explaining an effect by the manifestation of a power rules out external sources of this effect. Consequently, such an explanation is far from trivial, since it may well be false.[35] For example, in the case of a placebo, ascription of the power to bring about sleep would be wrong, and therefore the sleepiness of a person after ingestion of the placebo cannot be explained by a power of the placebo to bring about sleep.

Even when it is conceded that explanations in terms of powers have *some* explanatory force, one may still have the impression, though, that these explanations are only 'low-grade' compared to those explanations which tell us, in terms of an object's inner structure and the properties of its constituent parts, why the object behaves as it does.[36] Explaining the sleepiness of a person in terms of the power of a pill that he has ingested to produce sleepiness seems to be a much worse explanation than explaining it in terms of the chemical structure of the pill which was responsible for its

---

[33] Cf. Davidson's formulation of this requirement in (1967), 431.

[34] I suspect that McCann's criticism of agent-causation rests on a failure to keep this point in mind. McCann argues: 'A cause is supposed to…have some sort of explanatory priority with respect to the phenomenon to be explained. But this notion has no purchase with substances as such. *Qua* acting subject, I don't explain anything' (1998), 185. Well, that may be—but then, nothing explains anything else *per se*, and under descriptions such as 'magnet', or 'unstable explosive' substances have a good claim to explanatory relevance.

[35] Cf. Davidson (1987), 41.

[36] This view is voiced by Davidson (1987), 42, and (1993b), 302, when he argues that dependence of reasons-explanations on causal propensities makes these explanations low-grade in relation to 'hard science' explanations.

having this power, and so may appear to be only a 'promissory note' to be redeemed by an explanation of the second kind.[37]

This appearance—which is particularly strong when one accepts the causal conditional analysis of power-ascriptions—is, however, misleading, because it confuses two different questions: (a) why did the person become sleepy when she had taken the pill?, and (b) why did the pill produce the sleepiness or have the power to produce the sleepiness?[38] Question (a) is answered non-trivially by pointing out that the pill had the power to produce sleepiness, and question (b) is not because this question already presupposes that the pill possessed this power. But answering question (a) is sufficient for a causal explanation of the effect, because the explanandum in such an explanation is why the effect *occurred*, and question (b) concerns the *different* explanandum of how or why the effect was *produced* by its cause. As the causal conditional analysis of power-ascriptions is wrong, this further question may well have no answer, even though the effect itself can be explained. For example, when two electrons repel each other we can explain this effect by their electrical charge, but as this power of the electron lacks a base we cannot explain why or how the electrons have this power.

So, the *virtus dormitiva* objection against explanations in terms of substance-causes can be dismissed. The second objection, raised by Geert Keil, proceeds in a different direction. While accepting that explanations in terms of the powers of a substance have explanatory force, it denies that they constitute *causal* explanations. Instead, it claims, they are non-causal 'synchronic structural explanations' which explain only why one change in the subject caused another. What does the 'causal work', it is claimed, is not the powerful substance itself, but the event consisting of the substance entering into the specific situation and coming into contact with the other objects—for the existence of the substance on its own cannot cause anything.[39]

This kind of objection may have some plausibility so long as one accepts the causal conditional analysis of power-ascriptions. On this analysis, the 'real' causal work is done by the possession of the categorical base property in the specific situation, and no further causal explanation in terms of the substance and its powers is required. But we have already rejected this analysis and seen that powers are not reducible to categorical properties. Similarly, we can reject the argument that the powers-explanation is not a causal explanation because the real causal work is done by the event of the substance coming into contact. For as our discussion in Section 8.1.2 has made clear, a reduction of substance-causation to event-causation in this way is impossible. Consequently, there remains an irreducible explanatory contribution and a genuinely causal role of the powerful substance, on which a causal explanation of the effect by appeal to the powerful substance can be based.

---

[37] Cf. Quine (1974), 14.
[38] Cf. Mumford (1998), 138.
[39] Keil (2000), 309 f.

Once the irreducibility of power-manifestations is accepted, the second objection thus becomes implausible. Keil's own argument that only triggering causes—and thus only events—could be called 'causes', because they alone allow for *diachronic* causal explanations,[40] is also unconvincing. On the one hand there *is* a diachronic element involved in substance-causation, as the substance possesses the power before the manifestation. On the other hand, the possibility of simultaneous causation among events shows that diachronic explanation is not required even for event-causation. Keil's claim, therefore, amounts only to a refusal to *call* anything but triggering causes 'causes'. Understood as a stipulation for a new usage of the term, this refusal would be unexceptionable—but if intended to capture the normal meaning of 'cause' it has both the historically established meaning and ordinary usage against it. We can therefore reject the second objection against the possibility of causal explanations in terms of powerful substances along with the first.

(3) *Causation and temporal order.* There is continuing puzzlement about the possibility of backwards causation—which notion seems to involve a logical incoherence.[41] It appears absurd to think that something which occurred or began to exist only later than the effect could have caused this effect. As I share the misgivings about backwards causation, it seems clear to me that a cause cannot have come into existence or occurred later than its effect. This condition is clearly satisfied by substance-causes, because they can exert their powers and thereby cause effects only once they have come into existence.

(4) *Asymmetry of the causal relation.* As already noted, it is an important part of the idea of causation that causation has a direction, and that consequently, when A causes B, B does not thereby cause A. The directedness of causation has been expressed historically in the idea of a direction from activity to passivity, where activity is in the cause, while passivity is not in the effect, but in that which 'suffers' the effect.[42] As the difference between active and passive powers in our account of powers reflects this ancient distinction, the model of substance-causation which we have developed easily accounts for the directedness of causation.

(5) *Causes as sufficient factors.* In addition to characteristics (2) to (4), and either in addition to or as an alternative to (1), many philosophers have thought that causes must also be *ceteris paribus* sufficient factors for the effect.[43] This idea is intimately connected to the view that causes necessitate their effects. Given the presence of its cause, the effect, it appears, cannot but happen. If this is right, then there is a fundamental problem for substance-causation, for the existence of a powerful object usually does not suffice for a certain effect, but additionally there have to be

---

[40] Keil (2000), 310.
[41] Cf. Taylor (1966), 33 f.; Swinburne (1997), 86.
[42] Meixner (2001), 320.
[43] For example, Mill, *System of Logic*, book 3, ch. 5; Hart and Honoré (1959), 106 f.; and Hempel (1965), 349.

triggering events, or at least some contact with other objects, in order to produce the effect. On the assumption that *ceteris paribus* sufficiency is required, only these triggering events or the occurrence of the contact could count as causes.[44]

However, *ceteris paribus* sufficiency for the effect is not a convincing requirement on causes—if only because of the possibility of indeterministic causation among events which shows that not all causes necessitate their effects.[45] In order to accommodate this case, one might want to weaken the requirement in the following way: A can only be the cause of B if A is 'all that is required for B's occurrence'—that is, if A is a *ceteris paribus* necessary factor for B's occurrence and there are no other *ceteris paribus* necessary factors. In this case let us call A an 'exclusive necessary factor'. This weaker requirement would not rule out all substance-causes, because what is *ceteris paribus* necessary for radioactive decay or for unstable explosives to explode is only the existence of an object of the right kind. But the requirement would probably rule out most substance-causes, for the exercise of their powers requires the presence of an opportunity. Fortunately for substance-causation, this weaker requirement is also implausible, for in our normal causal explanations we uncontroversially consider factors as causes which are not exclusive necessary factors. For example, we accept that effects can be the product of *several* causes, and obviously not all these causes can be exclusive necessary factors.

The most that one could possibly require for causation with regard to sufficiency is something like the following: A cause must be a necessary *part* of a set of conditions which either jointly constitute an exclusive necessary factor or are jointly sufficient for the effect[46] (with included exceptions for causal overdetermination and hypothetical substitute causes). This requirement, however, can be satisfied not only by events, but also by powerful substances, because the existence of the powerful substance in conjunction with the opportunity or triggering-event is normally 'all that is required' for the effect, and none of the two factors can be cancelled. Neither can the substance cause the effect when there is no opportunity, nor is the opportunity sufficient when the substance either does not exist at all, or ceases to exist before producing the effect.

We can therefore conclude that substance-causation satisfies the traditional characteristics (1) through (4), and that, insofar as (5) is a plausible requirement on something counting as a cause, it can also be satisfied by substance-causes. Together with the evidence that we have already accumulated, this result should lay the lingering Humean worries about substance-causation to rest, and make it unavoidable to regard substance-causation as a 'genuine' bona fide kind of causation.

---

[44] Cf. Keil (2000), 309 f.
[45] Anscombe (1971), 101 ff.
[46] This requirement is a modification of Mackie's analysis of causes as INUS-conditions (1965), 414, where the main difference consists in turning the analysis into a disjunction and adding an 'INEN'-condition as a second disjunct.

8.2. Agent-causation by human beings

What remains to be done is to show how the general account of substance-causation—which we have elaborated for the case of inanimate substances—can be applied to the case of human agency. On my view, human agency in peripheral physical movements is a straightforward instance of the genus substance-causation for the special case where the causing substance is a human person, because, as I will argue, human abilities to perform physical actions are causal or active powers (Section 8.2.1). However, some philosophers, who accept that human beings can cause effects by doing something, object that they cannot cause the results of their own basic actions. I will try to show that this objection rests on an overly restrictive view of substance-causation that neglects important instances of 'direct' causation of effects in the field of inanimate substances (Section 8.2.2).

8.2.1. *Agent-causation and the causal powers of human beings*

Agent-causation can be explained by transferring the causal powers model of substance-causation that we have developed for inanimate substance-causes to the area where the relevant substances are human persons. Like the inanimate physical beings we have discussed, human persons are physical beings—biological substances—though they have characteristic features that no (or few) other substances of this kind possess.

The central features of the account of substance-causation remain the same. Agent-causation consists in exercises of active or causal powers of agents, and whether the power of an agent is active depends on basically the same considerations that have been elaborated in Section 8.1.1. The crucial question for deciding whether human agency can be explained on the basis of agent-causation is therefore the following: What are the active powers of human persons? Our project of explaining the characteristics of human agency in physical actions in terms of agent-causation will be successful only if the active powers of human persons are their abilities to perform physical actions—to move parts of their bodies and produce further effects by doing so.

To answer this question, let us first remind ourselves what qualifies a power as an active power of a substance. As we have seen, only powers whose manifestation necessarily involves a 'real' change can be either active or passive. For those powers, there are three central criteria for qualifying a power as active. It counts as active, first, when its manifestations are largely independent of specific external circumstances; second, in cases of interactions of several objects, when the object possessing the power is 'more' active than the other interacting objects; and third, when the power is already conceptually a power 'to produce effects', which has been introduced as part of a successful explanatory framework. What powers of human beings satisfy these requirements?

A first proposal would be the following. As human beings are biological organisms, the active powers of human beings are those powers of the biological organism that can be manifested under a wide range of external circumstances, or fulfil one of the other criteria. If this proposal is correct, then not only abilities to act will be active powers of human beings. For example, consider the tendency of the biological organism to lose its hair or its teeth as part of the normal process of biological decay—a tendency which can be manifested independently of any specific external circumstances once certain internal conditions are satisfied, and would therefore qualify as 'active' on the above criteria. Clearly, however, human beings do not act in losing their hair or teeth. Therefore, if the first proposal about the active powers of human beings goes through, there is little prospect of explaining what is specific about human agency and activity in terms of agent-causation.

However, this result can be avoided once we recognize that even though human beings are persons as well as biological organisms, there is a crucial distinction between being active *qua* person and being active *qua* biological organism.[47] For as we have seen, powers are intrinsic properties of substances, and whether a property is intrinsic to a substance depends on its connection to what the 'substance really is'. Depending on the kind of substance involved, this is either a connection to the internal physical or chemical structure that explains the possession of the features constituting the 'nominal essence' ascribed to the substance, or a connection to the features included in the 'nominal essence' (see Section 7.3). Which of the two connections is relevant depends on whether the inner structure is crucial to an understanding of the behaviour of objects with this 'nominal essence' *qua such objects*.

With regard to our understanding of biological organisms this is partly the case, for the inner physical structure is important insofar as it explains the characteristic behaviour of living beings; that is, deep-level microphysical structure will be relatively unimportant because it is not specific to living beings, while structure up from the level of cells will clearly be relevant. However, with regard to our concept of persons, neither the inner physical constitution nor the inner biological constitution is crucial for understanding the characteristic behaviour of them *qua persons*, and therefore properties must be connected to the concept of a person in order to count as an intrinsic property of this person. The relevant properties are those connected to the person's capacities for thought, emotions, and actions, because we understand the characteristic behaviour of persons in those terms. At the same time, these properties cannot be ascribed to the biological organism as such, but always depend on the identification of a person to whom we ascribe them. (For grammatical reasons, no belief or thought can be ascribed to my body, but only to me.)[48]

---

[47] This distinction is pointed out—without a background of substance-causality—by Karlsson (2002), 73 f., who traces it back to Thomas Aquinas, *Summa Theologiae*, IaIIae, Q.1, Art.1, where Aquinas distinguishes between 'human acts' resulting from choice, and 'acts of a man' that are done without deliberation.

[48] The distinction between doing something *qua* f and doing something *qua* g, where the criteria for 'doing' are different, will be worrying for those philosophers who believe that once a person is identical with a certain biological organism, Leibniz's law makes it unavoidable that anything it does *qua* person, it also does *qua* biological organism. However, this conclusion can be avoided by arguing that although a person is indeed a biological organism, the 'is' does not express strict identity, but some other relation—for example, the 'constitution' relation; cf. Wiggins (1980), ch. 1.

Consequently, we can distinguish between the powers of a biological organism as such and the powers of a person as such, even though human beings are biological organisms. This distinction implies a further distinction between what we, human agents, cause *qua* persons, and what we cause *qua* biological organisms. As we want to transfer the general model of substance-causation to the specific case of human agents, whom we primarily regard as persons, what is relevant for agent-causation is clearly the former—that is, what a person can cause *qua* person—rather than the latter. We can therefore reject the first proposal on what the active powers of human beings are, because it neglects the distinction we have drawn and focuses on the wrong kind of powers—namely, on those powers we possess *qua* biological organisms.

But which are those powers that we possess *qua* human persons? Davidson has proposed considering pro-attitudes of persons as their causal powers.[49] Pro-attitudes are intrinsic properties of persons, because they are obviously relevant to an understanding of the characteristic behaviour of human persons as such. Nevertheless, they are not *active* powers to produce change, for the simple reason that agents can desire things over which they have no influence, and that consequently, having a desire to X cannot be the same thing as having the active power to bring about X. A person who has lost the use of his right arm in an accident may desire that his right arm rises, but this does not mean that he has any influence on whether his arm rises or that his desire could be manifested in such a motion. Therefore, the range of desires does not circumscribe what an agent can bring about, nor what he can do 'on his own'. The same consideration applies against intentions as active powers, because we can intend to do things that we falsely believe we are able to do.

What circumscribes the range of what an agent can bring about are instead his abilities to act at will, insofar as the actions which are their manifestations necessarily involve 'real changes'—and these actions are, as we have seen, the physical actions of human beings. That these abilities are active powers becomes clear when we check their 'active character' on the criteria for active powers that we have elaborated. Abilities to move parts of one's body at will count as active because their manifestations are largely independent of external circumstances. The (external) opportunities for raising one's arm, shaking one's head, or moving one's foot, and so on, are extremely wide-ranging, covering most 'normal' situations for human beings when they are awake, and are absent only under extraordinary circumstances—for example, when the foot is stuck under a heavy suitcase. Under normal conditions it is only the internal circumstances of the agent—such as whether he intends to move his body—that are, next to his abilities to act, crucial to the explanation of the agent's movements and motions. Abilities to produce effects by interacting with other objects also count as active on the second criterion. Although I do not have the opportunity to open a book, move a table, or hang a painting on a wall in all normal situations, nevertheless, *when I*

---

[49] Davidson (1987), 41. In (1973), 63, he had proposed freedom of the will as a human causal power.

do so I am rightly considered to be the 'more' active part in the interaction—and the interaction is crucial for the occurrence of the change in the position of the objects. Both these results—with regard to bodily movements and with regard to interactions—are further strengthened by the consideration that the verbs which describe these activities are transitive verbs with a 'causative' element.

This shows that in general, abilities for physical action are active powers of human persons, and that in consequence, these persons are the agent-causes of the results of the manifestations of these powers. But are the two sets of physical actions performed by persons and of manifestations of active powers really *completely* coextensional? Two considerations, in particular, appear to exclude a complete overlap.

First, there are abilities to act, which, it seems, can be manifested only under specific circumstances. We have argued that the abilities to move parts of one's body at will are active because of the wide range of opportunities for their exercise, which makes their manifestation relatively independent of external circumstances. However, as we have seen when discussing deviant causal chains, there are abilities to act whose opportunities for exercise seem to be narrowly circumscribed. For example, when a person has an arm prosthesis where the severed nerve-connection is bridged by electrical wires which must be held together by another person, the first person's ability to move his arm can be exercised only under very narrowly circumscribed external circumstances.

Nevertheless, can we count those abilities as active powers of their possessors? I think we can, because there is a difference between conditions for exercise and conditions for possession of a power, and the former, not the latter, are relevant for the qualification of a power as active. Even though an object may possess the power to F only under narrowly circumscribed circumstances, we can still count the power to F as active if, so long as it is possessed, it can be exercised under normal circumstances—where the 'normal' circumstances which we consider are all circumstances under which the object possesses the power to F. This distinction between conditions for possession and conditions for exercise allows us to deal with the prosthesis case. The first person has the power to move his arm at will only when the second holds together the electrical wires. However, once those narrow conditions for the possession of the power are satisfied, he can exercise the power to move his arm under normal circumstances.

The second consideration concerns unintentional actions. The active powers of agents, which we have been discussing, are abilities to act *at will*, and this qualification connects these abilities to intentionality. The paradigm instances of doing X at will are cases of doing X intentionally, either because one has chosen to do so, or without prior choice. By contrast, doing X unintentionally—due to absent-mindedness, for example—appears to be a doubtful case of doing X *at will*. Consequently, our account of agent-causation as the manifestation of the active powers of human persons threatens to exclude purely unintentional actions—those actions that are not performed intentionally in *any* respect—and therefore threatens to offer only an incomplete picture of human agency.

However, although this consideration highlights an important point about active powers of human persons, the appearance that purely unintentional actions are no manifestations of those powers is fallacious. What is true is that the paradigm case of human agency is intentional agency. The primacy of intentional agency is expressed, on the level of conceptual dependences, by the fact that we could not have an idea of completely unintentional actions without having an idea of intentional agency, while the dependence does not hold conversely. Also, with regard to particular abilities to act there is a parallel primacy of intentional action. Possessing an ability to X implies that one can do X intentionally, while it is not necessary that one can do X unintentionally. The former implication stems primarily from our criteria for ability-ascriptions. We can say that an agent possesses the ability to move a part of his body only if he can do so (with some reliability) in response to being asked to do so, and his movement only counts as a 'response' to the request if it is intentional; and likewise for other abilities. That the possibility of doing X unintentionally is not required for possession of the ability to do X can be seen in cases where one has just learned a highly complex kind of action. For example, for the novice pianist, playing a very difficult piece of music requires attention and effort, and is therefore not something that he could do (purely) unintentionally.[50]

So, we can only do those kinds of things that we can also do intentionally—which is reflected by the fact that abilities to act are abilities to act *at will*. But this does not imply that unintentional actions cannot be manifestations of the *same* active powers as intentional actions. For that one does X intentionally means that one does it for a reason, and that one does X for a reason means that the performance of X is set within a larger pattern of actual or hypothetical behaviour or of mental states, as we shall see in Chapter 11. That one can do X intentionally means that the manifestation of the power to do X can occur within such a framework—and this possibility does not exclude that a manifestation of the very same power could also occur without such a framework.[51] Therefore, the fact that one can only do those things that one can also do intentionally is compatible with intentional actions being manifestations of the same active powers as unintentional actions.

Furthermore, we have good positive reasons to think that unintentional actions, as well as intentional actions, are manifestations of powers to act at will, because unintentional actions also involve the weaker sort of control by which one can directly change or stop the course of action once one becomes aware of what is happening. Thus, the second worry that the manifestations of active powers of a human agent do not cover all cases of human agency can also be rejected, and we can therefore

---

[50] The novice might do it unintentionally under one description, however. For example, when a piece is by Beethoven and he mistakenly believes it is by Mozart, he will not intentionally play a piece by Beethoven.

[51] It would only do so if an act of choice or an intention were among the necessary conditions for the power's exercise—that is, among the conditions constituting the 'occasion' of the exercise. But this is not the case. The phrase 'at will' in 'the power to move one's body at will' qualifies the exercise of the power—it tells us *what* the exercise of the power consists in—and does not spell out necessary conditions for the exercise.

conclude that the set of manifestations of active powers of human persons is indeed coextensional with the set of human physical actions.

8.2.2. Agent-causation and basic actions

There is, however, an alternative model of substance-causation and agent-causation, which, while also allowing for causal powers of agents, would not accept the claim that all physical actions are instances of agent-causings. The model rests on the idea that the 'basic conception' or prototype of not merely substance-causation, but of causation in general, is an interaction between two objects: an 'agent' and a 'patient', where the first object makes something happen by acting upon the second object.[52] Clear instances of this paradigm of interaction are the quotidian mechanical interactions between ourselves and other physical things. We cause a table to move by pushing it, we cause a door to open by pulling it, or we cause a table to collapse by placing a large weight on it.

The model of causation based on this paradigm of interaction differs in two crucial respects from the model of substance-causation which we have developed. First, while our model—as Hume's event-causal model—is based on a two-place causal relation between cause and effect, the former model has at its core a three-place relation between agent, patient, and effect. Second, this model distinguishes, in *all* cases of substance-causation, between causing X, on the one hand, and the 'mode of operation'[53] whereby the agent causes X, on the other hand, while our model leaves open the possibility that causing X and doing something to produce X may coincide. The second difference has an important consequence for the explanation of human agency in terms of agent-causation. While our model can accept that basic physical actions—actions consisting in moving parts of one's body directly—are instances of agent-causation, the alternative model rejects this claim, because in basic actions there is no 'mode of operation' distinguishable from bringing about the effect itself. Thus, for the latter model, not all human actions are instances of agent-causation.

Which of the two models is preferable? What speaks in favour of the latter model is that it often appears inappropriate to describe a basic physical action of raising one's arm as 'causing one's arm to rise'. In many cases such a description seems, at best, highly misleading, because it gives the impression that in order to raise his arm the agent did something else—for example, pulled a rope attached to it.

Nevertheless, as the following two considerations show, our model, according to which basic physical actions can also be considered as agent-causings, should be preferred. The first consideration is based on the observation that in the area of inanimate substance-causes there is not always a 'mode of operation' of the substance-cause whereby it causes the effect.[54] A case of this kind is our old case of a

---

[52] Rundle (2004), 61; Hacker (2007), ch. 3.
[53] The term is due to Brown (1968), 34 f.
[54] This possibility is also admitted by Hacker (2007), ch. 5.

magnet attracting an iron ball, causing it to change its trajectory. Here, the magnet does not do anything to the ball whereby it causes the change in the latter's trajectory. In particular, 'attracting' the ball is not a 'mode of operation' which could be distinguished from causing the change in the trajectory, but it is one and the same thing as causing this change. Nor is 'exerting magnetic force' a mode of operation, because it is not something that the magnet 'does' to the ball (or if it is something that it 'does' to the ball, it is nothing other than attracting it).[55] The magnet is therefore a substance-cause that lacks a 'mode of operation', which makes it difficult to understand why a 'mode of operation' should be necessary for human agent-causes. As we have hitherto proceeded on the assumption that substance-causation in both cases is basically the same kind of phenomenon, we would need some explanation for an alleged difference between the two with regard to direct causation—and I, for one, fail to see how such an explanation could be given.

The second consideration takes as its starting-point what I have called the 'core idea' of designating A as the cause of effect B—that A is the crucial factor responsible for the occurrence of B. This core idea is neutral with regard to direct or indirect causation, and does not introduce any requirement of a 'mode of operation' in the causing; for whether A is the crucial factor can be determined by appeal to the criteria developed in Section 8.1.1, and these criteria are silent about any modes of operations. For example, on these criteria an unstable explosive which explodes by itself counts as the substance-cause of the explosion, because it is the responsible factor for the explosion. It is no obstacle to this assessment that the unstable explosive has no 'mode of operation' in causing the explosion. Therefore, lack of a 'mode of operation' should not stand in the way of qualifying an agent as the cause of the results of his basic actions, either.

But when we accept that basic actions involve agent-causings, how can we then explain the linguistic 'oddity' involved in saying 'A caused his arm to rise', when A raises his arm directly? The correct answer to this query is of the same kind as the answer provided in Section 2.2, when dealing with the contention that cases of bodily movements might not generally be cases of bodily motions. We can accept that utterances of 'A caused his arm to rise' often imply that A did not raise his arm directly, while denying that this is due to the meaning of 'causing' itself rather than to a Gricean conversational implicature. As we have seen, these implicatures do not directly concern the truth or falsity of statements, but only whether utterances of these statements are inappropriate or misleading.

That this is indeed the right explanation of the linguistic oddity in question can be established by applying the 'cancelling' test—that is, by examining whether we can make the utterance 'A causes his arm to rise' appropriate by explicitly denying the normal expectations, and thereby removing the grounds for the misleading assump-

---

[55] Of course, it is true that the magnet causes the change in trajectory by exerting magnetic force. But this must not mislead us into thinking that the 'by'-clause in this statement expresses a mode of operation; instead, it expresses only an explanatory connection between the causing of the change and the magnetic force.

tions. This, however, would involve a lengthy investigation into the conversational expectations in talk about causation, which I cannot pursue here. I only want to point out that there are at least some cases where, even without cancelling, expressions such as 'causing', or one of its cognates—'producing', 'making', or 'bringing about'—can clearly be used to describe basic actions without any linguistic oddity. These are cases where basic actions involve exertion and effort—for example, when the tired marathon runner, who has already collapsed, scrambles to his feet again and by sheer will-power 'makes his aching legs move'. Here 'making move' describes a basic action, because 'by will-power' does not describe an action by which one moves one's legs. These cases provide us with sufficient reason to assume that describing basic actions as agent-causings is not false, but only potentially misleading.

I therefore believe that the charge of the alternative model of agent-causation can be countered, and that agents can be considered as the agent-causes of the results of their basic actions as well as of their non-basic actions.

8.3. The proposed account and the standard objections against agent-causation

A defence of our agent-causal account will be incomplete so long as we have not examined how the account fares with regard to the popular objections against agent-causation. Here I will focus on four objections which are both common among philosophers who attack agent-causation and which I regard as the most important ones: Broad's datability argument, the objection from the connection between causes and probability, the objection from the uniformity of causation, and Davidson's old worry about which explanatory paradigm could be connected with agent-causation.

8.3.1. Broad's datability objection

The most threatening argument against the possibility of irreducible agent-causation that does not already presuppose acceptance of a specific account of causation is the objection developed by C. D. Broad, which tries to show that causes must be datable in a way that only events can be. This argument has recently been revived and sharpened by Carl Ginet. Broad's original argument proceeds as follows:

> I see no *prima facie* objection to there being events that are not completely determined. But, insofar as an event *is* determined, an essential factor in its total cause must be other *events*. How can an event possibly be determined to happen at a certain date if its total cause contained no factor to which the notion of date has any application? And how can the notion of date have any application to anything that is not an event?[56]

---

[56] Broad (1952), 215.

Substituting 'caused' for 'determined' in order to remedy for Broad's exclusive focus on deterministic causation, the gist of his argument can be expressed as follows. The effects of causings—events, which are themselves datable—must have datable causes, because otherwise it would not be intelligible why the effects had to happen at a certain time; datability of the cause requires that the cause occurs at a certain moment, while persistence over a certain period of time is insufficient. As persons and substances persist only over periods of time, but do not occur at certain points in time, they cannot be causes.

Ginet's formulation of the objection shows more clearly what is at the core of this objection: namely, the perceived necessity of *contrastive* causal explanations. For Ginet, the agent-causalist position is incoherent, because an agent as cause cannot explain why the effect occurred at this moment rather than at another moment. This contrastive fact could be explained only by something that is datable in the same way the effect is datable itself; that is, by something which occurs. Even if one tries to supplement the agent-causal explanation by appeal to the reasons on which the agent acts, the lacuna in the explanation with regard to the precise timing is not filled up, because the reasons do not completely specify all details of the action.[57] This leaves the agent-causalist claiming that there is a cause which causes an effect at a certain moment, but that it is impossible to explain, by appeal to this cause, why the effect happened at exactly this time—and this conjunction, for Ginet, is inconsistent.

Broad's and Ginet's datability objection suffers from the fact that it was originally conceived—by Broad himself—for deterministic causation, where the idea of contrastive explanation has its natural place. For indeterministic causation, however, contrastive explanations of the features of the effect are not required. It is the characteristic of this kind of causation that another effect might have occurred under the very same circumstances. As the possibility of indeterministic causation is nowadays generally accepted, due to the acceptance of indeterminism in quantum physics, this rules out the possibility of directly inferring the impossibility of a causal relation between A and B from the fact that A does not provide us with a contrastive explanation of the features of B.[58]

However, even when we focus on deterministic causation only, the datability objection does not succeed.[59] For even if a contrastive explanation of why the effect happened exactly when it did is required, this does not mean that *all* true causes of the effect must, by themselves, provide us with such an explanation. It can be required only that knowledge of the *complete* set of factors that is sufficient for the occurrence of the effect enables us to provide such a contrastive explanation. That only this weaker requirement is plausible becomes clear when we think of effects which have two distinct event-causes, none of which is individually sufficient. For example, consider a

---

[57] Ginet (2002a), 215 ff.
[58] Cf. O'Connor (2000), 76.
[59] Mayr (2009), 49.

fall of stocks at the New York Stock Exchange that is caused both by bad data from the US real estate market and by news about the collapse of some Chinese enterprises, where each of these two factors would, on its own, have been counterbalanced by the Federal Bank's announcement of a cut in interest rates. In this scenario, while both factors are causes of the price drop, neither of them would, on its own, explain why the prices fell at precisely this time, but only together can they provide an explanation.

The weaker requirement can be satisfied by substance-causes as well as by event-causes. For there can be necessary conditions for the exercise of a power, whose fulfilment at a certain time explains why the effect of the manifestation of the power occurs at precisely that moment. Thus, substance-causation does not rule out that the precise timing of the effect can be contrastively explained by the complete set of factors which contributed to the occurrence of the effect. This allows us to reject the datability objection against agent-causation even for the deterministic case.

8.3.2. Causes and probability

While the first objection applied to substance-causation in general, there is a more specific worry about agent-causation that arises from the fact that the existence of an agent-cause does not make the occurrence of the effect more probable. Contrary to most powers of inanimate substances, human powers to act are not tendencies or dispositions to act, because they are two-way powers which we can, on their occasions for exercise, either exercise or refrain from exercising.[60] The fact that an agent exists as a powerful substance therefore does not, on its own, make it more probable that certain effects occur.

This will be seen as problematic when one believes that causes must affect the probabilities of their effects even before those effects occur.[61] Essentially the same point can be made in terms of prediction. Prediction of an event A on the basis of the existence or occurrence of B requires at least that B makes A more probable; and prediction is often considered as inseparably tied to causal explanation, so that the latter is only possible *post factum* if the effect could, in principle, have been predicted *ante factum*. Therefore, the failure of agent-causes to affect the probabilities of their effects *ante factum* seems to speak against the possibility of this form of causation.

But even if we grant that prediction and causal explanation are connected, the objection still fails because it presupposes an overly demanding form of prediction. The only form of prediction that can be reasonably required is that the effect can be predicted on the basis of knowledge of *all* the contributing factors, but not from each singly. That the stronger requirement makes no sense can be easily perceived from the fact that single factors which interact in the production of the effect jointly influence the probability of the effect, and the probability, given the interaction, can

---

[60] Kenny (1989), 66 f., 70. [61] Clarke (2003), 203 f.

differ starkly from the probability, given each factor singly. Thus, two medicines may carry a cancer risk of 10% each if taken singly, but 80% if taken in conjunction.

Agent-causes can fulfil the weaker requirement because—if set in a specific situation which comprises all the factors contributing to the effect—the agent's desires and abilities to act make certain courses of behaviour more probable than others. Therefore, the connection between causation and probability, if rightly understood, is no obstacle to accepting agent-causation.

8.3.3. The uniformity of causation

Some philosophers have found it worrying that there should be agent-causes as well as event-causes, because this would make causation a 'radically disunified phenomenon'.[62] These philosophers suppose that agent-causation and event-causation would work in two completely different ways, and it would therefore be doubtful how both could be instances of the same genus 'causation'. *Prima facie*, this objection can also be raised against the account of agent-causation which I have been developing, as the notion of powers on which it is based is a notion of properties which only substances, but not events, can possess—so that on my account, event-causation cannot function on the same model as agent-causation.

The most widespread attempt to answer this worry consists in trying to reduce one of the apparently disparate forms of causation to the other. Most philosophers, as we have seen, opt for a reduction of agent-causation in terms of event-causation—but, as we have argued, this project must be considered as a failure. There are also, however, a number of agent-causalists who argue for a reduction in the other direction—of event-causation in terms of agent-causation and substance-causation in general.[63]

An outright reduction of event-causation to substance-causation seems to be impossible, however, because the former is a weaker notion than the latter. The key respect in which it is weaker is that it is not 'process-specific'—that event A can cause B by any freak causal chain whatsoever, and still count as B's cause. Manifestations of powers, however, are incompatible with freak causal chains running from triggering events to the resulting effect—as we have seen when discussing deviant causal chain counter-examples to the reductive analyses of power-ascriptions. There is therefore little hope that the statement 'event A caused event B' could be analysed in terms of statements about substance-causation, because all statements of the latter kind would have logical implications that the purely event-causal statements do not have. Even the weaker claim that all instances of event-causation depend on instances of substance-causation—in the sense that there can only be an instance of the former if there is an instance of the latter—is unwarranted. Not all event-causings include manifestations of active powers, but there can be subsequent changes consisting only

---

[62] Clarke (2003), 208.
[63] This had already been proposed by Reid (1983), 523. Later, such a reduction was proposed by Byerly (1979), Swinburne (1997), and Lowe (2001) and (2002), 209 ff.

in the manifestations of passive powers, and we might still regard this sequence of changes as an instance of event-causation if these kinds of change are regularly correlated.

I think, therefore, that we have to accept that the concept 'cause' is not uniform, but has two distinct paradigms: of substance-causation and of event-causation. But this lack of uniformity does not turn 'causation' into a 'radically disunified phenomenon', because both paradigms hang together—for the event-causal paradigm, though irreducible to the substance-causal paradigm, is plausibly seen as deriving from this former paradigm. I think the right account of this derivation proceeds along the lines sketched by von Wright's manipulability view of event-causation, which derives the distinction between event-causes and effects from the 'distinction between things done and things brought about through action'.[64] For von Wright, the occurrence of A causes the occurrence of B if we bring about B by producing A, or if, assuming that we could produce A, we could thereby produce B. This account does not reduce event-causation to agent-causation, because we cannot explain the 'by'-relation in 'bringing about B by producing A' merely with elements from our theory of agent-causation. But if von Wright's account of event-causation is basically correct, then event-causation is inseparably connected to our active intervention in the course of nature—and this active intervention is nothing other than agent-causation. Therefore, we can consider both substance-causation and event-causation as having a common core, which 'unifies' the concept of causation.

8.3.4. Davidson's worry about agent-causation reconsidered

The last objection that I want to consider is Davidson's claim, from *Agency*, that talk about agent-causation lacks explanatory power. When we discussed this objection in Section 6.1 it became clear that Davidson's argument against the possibility of agent-causation is unconvincing, because it implicitly relies on the validity of the regularity theory of causation and on its connected paradigm of explanation: the covering-law model. We have seen that the first of these two assumptions is neither established nor unproblematic; and without this first assumption, the claim that the covering-law model of explanation is the only paradigm of causal explanation loses its basis. Therefore, Davidson fails to positively establish that agent-causation is impossible; but something remains from his argument: the challenge to agent-causal theories that they must show how agent-causal statements can have explanatory force.

With regard to substance-causation in inanimate substances, we implicitly answered this challenge in Section 8.1.3 when defending the claim that substance-causation meets the requirement of a connection between causation and causal explanation. We have argued that by describing the substance as a powerful particular with the power to produce the effect in question, we provide a causal explanation of the effect. When the

---

[64] Von Wright (1971), 73.

power in question is a disposition,[65] the explanation will even conform to the covering-law model of explanation, for it will be true that whenever a substance with this disposition is in such a situation, the effect occurs. When the power is a tendency, the effect will be explained as something likely to be brought about under the actual circumstances; and when it is a capacity it will be explained as something that the substance could bring about 'on its own'.

Obviously, the latter kinds of explanation tell us less than an explanation provided by the covering-law model, which shows why the effect *had to* happen; but nevertheless, they are informative explanations in their own right. First, they tell us *something* about why the effect occurred. This is clear when we consider the predictions which correspond to the explanations. Knowing what an object is likely to do or can do 'on its own' has genuine predictive value, and this value is obvious when the possible effects are highly dangerous and the predictions are vital for warning and taking counter-measures. Second, these explanations are not just 'deficient' forms of causal explanations, which will be 'filled out' and turned into explanations conforming to the covering-law model once we know all the relevant facts. For even independently from our theory of substance-causation, the possibility of indeterministic event-causation forces us to accept that for some effects there is no explanation of why these effects *had to* happen.

Basically, these same considerations also show that agent-causal statements do provide an explanation of why the effect occurred. However, for agent-causation an important modification is added to this picture, due to the impact of explanations of actions in terms of reasons and habits. Active powers of human agents themselves are neither dispositions nor tendencies to act, but capacities, because they are two-way powers which the agent can exercise or refrain from exercising. When the manifested power of an inanimate substance-cause is a capacity, the effect is explained only as something that the substance could produce 'on its own'—for example, in the case of an unstable explosive that explodes. In explanations of human actions, however, this 'mere' substance-causal explanation of the effect is more often than not supplemented by an explanation of the action in terms of motivating reasons, habits, and so on, of the agent. These further factors involve tendencies to act, because when an agent intends to act on a reason or has a habit to act in a certain way, there is an increased likelihood that given the right occasion, and given that he can act in a certain way, he will do so. This means that for most actions, once they are identified as manifestations of causal powers, they can be further explained as manifestations of those tendencies, and explanations in terms of tendencies are more informative than explanations in terms of capacities, because they present the effect as something that was likely to be produced, and not merely as something that could be produced.

---

[65] Even though the first criterion for active powers rules powers as active when they can be manifested under a wide range of external circumstances, it does not rule out that dispositions can be active powers, as long as their triggering conditions are primarily constituted by internal states of the substance.

That actions of human beings can be explained in this more informative way may create the impression that explanations in terms of abilities to act and the apparently more informative explanations in terms of motivating reasons or habits are rival explanations, and that the latter explanation is a better and preferable explanation of the effect by which we can circumvent agent-causal statements. Such a view, however, would be completely mistaken. Identifying an effect as agent-caused, and explaining an action in terms of reasons or habits, are not competing explanations for the same explanandum, but complementary explanations for different explananda. The agent-causal statement directly explains why the result of a physical action has happened, while the explanations in terms of reasons or habits primarily explain why the action was performed—that is, why the agent caused this effect. The latter's contribution to explaining the result of the action is only indirect, and always presupposes that this result is caused by the agent.

Explanations in terms of reasons and habits therefore cannot supplant agent-causal statements, but they supplement these statements by introducing a further explanatory element in terms of tendencies to act.[66] The relation between the active powers of human beings and those tendencies is best seen as a relation between 'lower-level' powers to produce physical change, and 'higher-level' powers which 'structure' the manifestations of these powers. (We will examine this relation further in Chapter 11.)

Davidson's worry about the possible explanatory force of agent-causal statements can thus be laid to rest, because these statements possess a dual explanatory impact. On the one hand, they present the result of the action as something that the agent could produce 'on his own', and thus provide the same kind of explanation that is generally provided by explanations in terms of capacities of substances. On the other hand, they 'open up' the way to explanations in terms of motivating reasons or habits, and corresponding tendencies to act. Even though the 'bare' agent-causal statements do not themselves contain these further explanations, they tell us that we can look for them, because the behaviour in question is at least a candidate for being explained in this way.

---

[66] Of course, this is not the only additional explanatory element introduced by reasons-explanations. They also make actions intelligible by showing how it seemed rational to the agent to perform them; cf. Chapter 11.

9

Are agent-causal powers reducible to microproperties?

After having shown that the agent-causal model that we have developed does not fall prey to the popular objections against agent-causation, there is one remaining worry about the possibility of human agent-causation that we need to address. Even when one accepts the claim that powers of substances are not reducible to categorical properties, there is another possible kind of reduction of powers that we have hitherto left aside. This is the possibility that the powers of composite substances might be completely reducible to the properties of their component parts and the way that the composite substance is made up from these parts. For some powers of composites such a reduction is both plausible and does not give rise to special worries. For example, the power to exert gravitational force derives from the mass of the object, and the mass of a composite object is, for macrophysical objects,[1] simply 'added up' from the masses of its (macrophysical) component parts. Consequently, the power of the composite object to exert gravitational force will be reducible to the powers of the component parts.

But in the case of the active powers of human persons that are manifested in agency, the possibility of such a reduction is deeply worrying, because these active powers are powers possessed by their bearers *qua* human persons. If these active powers could be completely reduced to the powers of the constituent neurophysiological parts of the biological organism, it seems that there would be no active role left to play for human persons as such, because their apparent activity would turn out to be 'nothing but' an activity of their constituent parts. In this case, human actions would still include activity of substances, but they would not include activity of the right kinds of substance—that is, of human agents. As we saw at the very beginning of our investigation, the idea of the latter activity is inseparably connected to our understanding of human agency, and so, it seems, if complete reduction is possible, our agent-causal model would after all turn out to be incapable of capturing the notion of human agency.

This general worry about the reducibility of active powers of human persons takes on different forms, depending on which kind of reducibility is in question. I will begin

---

[1] The mass of a composite substance is not always simply 'added up' from the masses of the component parts considered in isolation. Consider the mass of the nucleus of an atom in relation to the masses of the particles of which the nucleus consists.

by distinguishing five different degrees of dependence between the properties of a composite object and the properties of its component parts (Section 9.1). With regard to human abilities to act, the two most promising characterizations are those as systemic reducible properties or as systemic emergent properties. I will argue that human abilities to act can be subsumed most plausibly under the latter kind (Section 9.2). This result will lead to the further question of whether the manifestations of these powers involve 'downward' causation (Section 9.3).

9.1. Five degrees of dependence of the properties of composites

Properties of composite objects depend on the properties of their component parts in different degrees. Basically, we can distinguish between the five following degrees of dependence.

a) The dependence is strongest when a power is ascribed to a composite only because a component possesses the very same power. For instance, imagine a car with an built-in radio, which can emit the melody of the Bavarian Anthem. When we ascribe to the car as a whole the power to emit this melody, it is only 'by courtesy' of the power of the built-in radio to do so, to which the alleged power of the car can be completely reduced.

b) A slightly weaker form of dependence holds in the case of 'additive' properties of composite substances, which are 'added up' from the properties of the component parts. This means that the properties themselves or, in the case of powers, their manifestations can be presented as algebraic or vectorial[2] sums of the properties or manifestations of powers of the component parts taken singly. Analyses of properties of composites as 'sums' of the properties of the components are paradigm reductive explanations—a typical example being the 'reduction' of the additive property 'weight' of a macrophysical material object to the weights of its component parts.

Contrary to cases of dependence of kind a), in the case of 'additive' properties no part of the substance possesses the very same specific property as the composite substance itself. For example, no proper part of a composite material substance has the same mass as the composite substance itself. Thus, 'additive' properties are bona fide properties of the substances as wholes, ascriptions of which do genuine explanatory work. (Remember, for example, the explanation of gravitational attracting forces between two objects in terms of the masses of those objects.) Nevertheless, it is important to note that for 'additive' powers the component parts must possess the same general property—

---

[2] The paradigmatic case is the 'composition' of various mechanical forces on an object to the 'total' force which we calculate by vector addition. Cf. Mill, *System of Logic*, 428 f.

mass—as the composite object; thus, this general property cannot be a property which only objects of the same kind as the composite object can possess.

c) The third form of dependence, which is yet weaker than in the case of 'additive' properties, obtains in the case of 'systemic' reducible properties. 'Systemic' properties are properties that are possessed only by the whole composite object, while none of its parts possesses either the same specific property nor the same general property.[3] Standard systemic properties are the mental capacities of human beings which cannot be possessed by parts of the human organism, and structural properties of composite objects whose possession depends not only on the properties that the object's parts have themselves, but also on the arrangement of these parts within the object.[4] A typical structural property of the latter kind is the characteristic power of a thermostat.

With regard to systemic properties, one can adopt either a 'mechanistic' or an 'emergentist' view.[5] The properties for which the difference between these two views has been most extensively discussed are the mental properties of human beings. For a mechanist, these properties are completely reducible to properties of the parts of the organism and the relations holding among them—microproperties—while the emergentist considers these properties to be something novel and extra to the possession of the microproperties.

Complete reducibility has both an ontological and a corresponding epistemological aspect. Ontologically, it requires that the possession of the systemic power consists in nothing but the possession of the microproperties by the parts. To this corresponds, on the level of explanation, the possibility of a complete analysis of the possession of the systemic property in terms of the microproperties. I will focus on the latter aspect, because a reductive analysis of one property in terms of another is our only reason for thinking that possession of the former is wholly constituted by possession of the latter.

Providing a reductive analysis requires more than merely explaining why the composite object possesses the systemic property, given its microproperties. Consider the following case. Composite objects of kind A, which possess a certain highly complex internal structure S, all display a systemic property P, which is not displayed by any other kinds of object. As all objects possessing S also possess P, there is a nomic correlation[6] between S and P, which can be observed and then used to infer the possession of P from the possession of S, and in this way to explain why an object possesses P. This kind of explanation would not yet amount to a reductive analysis of P,

---

[3] Cf. Stephan (2002), 80 (with the proviso added by myself for general properties).
[4] My notion of 'structural' properties is more restricted than the notion used by O'Connor (1994), 93, as the latter also includes what I call additive properties.
[5] Since Broad (1925), 493, the terms 'emergent' and 'mechanist' are widely used for the distinction in question.
[6] In terms of Nagel's model of intertheoretical reduction, such nomic correlations comprise 'bridge laws' between higher-level and lower-level theories which connect the predicates of the two theoretical levels; cf. Nagel (1961), ch. 11.

because a nomic correlation can also hold when P is not reducible to S. This is clear from two types of case: (a) when the observed correlation is 'brute and unexplained',[7] especially when the two correlated properties are otherwise highly different, so that we cannot understand why objects with S should also possess P; and (b) when the possession of the systemic property P by the object influences the properties of the object's parts—i.e. when the latter's behaviour is different from their behaviour in other contexts, and this different behaviour could not be expected from the behaviour in the other contexts. In neither of these two kinds of case, the correlation between S and P shows that the possession of P consists in nothing but the possession of S, and therefore the obtaining of such a correlation does not imply that P is reducible to S.

What is required for a reductive analysis is, at a minimum, that there is not only a perceived nomic correlation between the systemic property and the microproperties, but that it can be explained why this nomic correlation holds—that is, that it can be explained why objects with microproperties of this kind must also have the correlated systemic property.[8] (This explanation must also be of a kind as not to exclude that the systemic property is reducible to those microproperties. For example, it must not present both properties as reducible, in different ways, to one common basis.) Such an explanation is possible only if we can deduce the specific correlation between the specific microproperties and systemic properties from more general principles—from general laws of science and composition principles, which apply to a wider range of objects than only objects of the very same kind or objects composed by them. This requires that we can infer the possession of P by the whole object from the following set of premises: (i) the properties of the component parts in isolation and in systems with less complexity than the one in question, (ii) general natural laws and laws that govern their behaviour in isolation and in systems with less complexity, and (iii) the arrangement of the parts within the substance.[9]

We will tentatively assume the possibility of a deduction of this kind as our criterion for the reducibility of systemic properties. Perhaps reducibility requires even more, but the criterion will be acceptable for our following discussion because it captures the key idea of the notion of reducibility that the systemic property must be due completely to the microproperties, while the microproperties must not themselves be influenced by the systemic property. A systemic property which satisfies this reducibility criterion is the characteristic power of a thermostat. That an object is a thermostat can be inferred once we know about the powers of its parts and how they are put together,

---

[7] Kim (1992), 126.

[8] As a consequence, Nagel's model of intertheoretical reduction is too permissive, because its conditions will also be satisfied by many emergent properties.

[9] This is a slightly elaborated form of Broad's famous criterion for irreducibility in terms of non-deducibility; cf. Broad (1925), 493; and Stephan (1992), 37.

and the behaviour of these parts can be explained by exactly the same general laws as when they are not conjoined within a thermostat.

d) Systemic properties for which a deduction of the kind just mentioned is impossible are 'emergent' properties. As long as they are correlated with microproperties of the object, we will call them 'emergent dependent properties'. These properties are novel or unpredictable in the sense that as long as we have not yet encountered objects whose structure has the same or a higher degree of complexity, we cannot, in principle, predict that there are properties of this kind, though their appearance can be predicted once we know with which microproperties they are correlated.

Some defenders of the claim that mental properties are emergent argue that emergence not only requires irreducibility to microproperties, but also requires that the emergent property is connected with a genuinely novel causal influence upon the microproperties. This type of influence is normally called 'downward causation'.[10] The latter requirement would exclude both epiphenomenal irreducible properties—if there are any—and properties which causally influence only other systemic properties from the range of emergent properties. For powers, the issue of downward causation has special importance, and we will defer discussion of this point until Section 9.3. For properties in general, however, the proposed requirement is overly restrictive, as the core idea of emergent properties is their irreducibility to microproperties, and this can be also exhibited by epiphenomenal emergent qualities.

Are there any systemic properties which we have positive reason to believe are emergent—or do we only lack, for some properties, reasons to consider them as reducible and therefore call them emergent 'by default'? In fact, there is an important range of properties which we have positive reason to regard as emergent—properties which involve holistic phenomena in one of the following two ways. (a) If the properties of the parts of the object on which the systemic property depends cannot be completely specified without reference to the whole object and its other parts; or (b) if the systemic properties themselves can be ascribed only holistically because their ascription is restricted by principles connecting them to other systemic properties and these principles do not guide—even indirectly—our ascriptions of the microproperties. In case (b), the individual systemic properties cannot be ascribed only on the basis of the microproperties of the parts, because their ascription depends on the ascription of the other systemic holistic properties.

In case (a), a deduction of the kind necessary for a reductive analysis is excluded, because the properties of the component parts within the object depend on the whole structure and therefore are not properties that these parts could possess in isolation or in less complex systems. In case (b), the possession of the systemic property does not depend only on the possession of microproperties by the parts, and is therefore not

---

[10] Cf. Sperry (1970), 586 ff.; and O'Connor (1994), 98. The underlying rationale is 'Alexander's Dictum' that nothing can be real when it has no causal influence.

reducible to them. (What might depend on the microproperties, however, is the possession of the whole set of interdependent systemic properties—but this dependence does not imply reducibility of any single systemic property from this set.)

The most important instance of an holistic phenomenon of kind (a) is quantum entanglement in physics, where the determinate spin state of a compound of two particles cannot be explained as the consequence of the spin states of the two components in isolation, because within the compound system the components are not in a spin state that they could individually be in if taken in isolation.[11] Instead, insofar as a spin state is ascribed to them at all, this state can be completely specified only by referring to the state of the other component,[12] and therefore is paradigmatically holistic in the sense of case (a). With regard to case (b), the most important example is propositional attitudes of human beings, if we accept Davidson's argument that there are holistic constraints of overall rationality and coherence on the ascriptions of such attitudes—constraints which are irrelevant for the ascription of the microproperties.[13] Since I accept this argument, I also accept that having a propositional attitude is an emergent property in the sense explained, because it depends not only on the microproperties of the parts of the agent's organism, but also on what other propositional attitudes he possesses.

e) The greatest degree of independence of systemic properties from microproperties obtains when the systemic properties are both emergent and not correlated with microproperties, but can be possessed independently from what microproperties the object possesses. We can call such properties 'emergent independent properties'. We can distinguish between two forms of independence: (i) synchronic independence, where the possession of the systemic property is independent of the possession of microproperties at the same time, and (ii) diachronic independence, where it is independent of even the microproperties which the parts have possessed previously.

As Paul Humphreys has shown, independence of kind (i) is possible in the special form that instances of the microproperties 'fuse' to produce the instance of the systemic property, thereby passing out of existence themselves.[14] In this case, lack of simultaneous instances of the microproperties and of the systemic property excludes the possibility of correlation. It is important to note, however, that this independence is compatible with diachronic dependence on microproperties, and it is indeed highly puzzling how—short of a miracle—emergent properties could be both synchronically and diachronically completely independent. Very probably, no properties of this latter kind can be instantiated in the course of nature.

---

[11] They are not in a 'pure state'. Cf. Maudlin (1998), 53; and Hüttemann (2005), 117.
[12] Cf. Humphreys (1997), 15. On the 'no-state mode' view, the particles within the compound system lack a spin state; cf. Maudlin (1998), 53 f.
[13] Davidson (1970a), 216 ff. Nor could the relevant holistic constraints for the ascription of propositional attitudes—especially internal coherence—be 'modelled' by neurophysiological correlations.
[14] Humphreys (1997), 10 ff.

9.2. The dependence of human powers on microproperties

To which of these different degrees are abilities to act at will—which we have identified as the active powers of human persons—dependent on the microproperties possessed by the parts of the human organism?

Dependence of kind (a) can be ruled out from the beginning, because no part of the human organism can have the power to move at will. Nor can human abilities to act at will plausibly be seen as additive properties. For additive powers, the behaviour in which the manifestation of the power consists is just a sum of the manifestations of the powers of the component parts taken together, and it must therefore be behaviour that could be exhibited by heaps or collections of the parts which are not put together to form a substance. Human abilities to act are not of this kind, because they are powers whose manifestation—human agency—can be displayed only by human beings, but not by heaps of the disconnected parts of their organisms. Therefore, human abilities to act must be systemic properties, and the question is only whether they are reducible or emergent systemic properties.

What would be required for a reductive analysis of an active power? As we have seen, a power is individuated by the following three criteria: what its manifestation consists in, what the conditions for the manifestation are, and how tightly the manifestation is linked to those conditions. A reductive analysis requires, at least, that we can deduce from the properties of the parts in isolation and within simpler systems, in conjunction with general laws and composition principles, the following statement (differing according to whether the power is a disposition, a tendency, or a capacity): that the characteristic manifestation must, will, or probably can, occur when the conditions for the manifestation of the power are satisfied. In the special case of human abilities to act at will, the specific manifestation—if our earlier arguments have been correct—is that certain motions of the body are produced 'at will'. A successful reductive analysis of these abilities must therefore explain how these motions can or will be produced 'according to the will' of the agent, on the basis of his microproperties.

The chief obstacle against providing such an analysis is clearly the qualification 'at will'. As already noted, this qualification connects the abilities to act to intentional agency; but it does not mean that all manifestations of those powers must be intentional actions. Instead, as we have argued in Section 8.2.1, these powers are also manifested in unintentional actions, where there is only the weaker connection to hypothetical intentions, that one can or will change one's course of action if one becomes aware of what is happening and intends not to act in this manner. In all cases, however, the qualification 'at will' is tied to actual or hypothetical intentions of the agent.

This introduces an holistic element into the possession of abilities to act at will, because both the possession and the lack of an intention to act in a specific way are holistic phenomena. What intentions can be ascribed to an agent depends on general holistic constraints of coherence and rationality, as intentions are propositional attitudes to which Davidson's argument about the holism of the mental applies. Unsurprisingly, this holistic element is an insurmountable obstacle against a reductive analysis of abilities to act 'at will'. For such an analysis would have to show not only how the relevant bodily motions can be produced, but also how these motions correspond to what the agent intends (or, at least, are not contrary to what he intends). The latter explanation would require that we can provide a reductive analysis of what it is to have a specific intention, in terms of the structure of the human organism, the properties of its parts (in isolation or within simpler systems), and general laws and composition principles. But an analysis of this kind cannot be offered, due to the holistic features of intentions that we have mentioned. This means that we also cannot provide a reductive analysis of correspondence to what the agent intends, which entails the failure of the overall attempt to reduce the ability to act *at will* to the microproperties of the human organism.

We can therefore conclude that abilities to act at will, in virtue of their holistic features, must be emergent systemic properties. This ensures for the agent himself—as such, and not just as an aggregate of his parts—a genuine 'role' in the production of the results of his basic actions. But does it already guarantee a genuinely *active* role of the agent as such?

9.3. Human powers and 'downward causation'

If we assume that there are epiphenomenal emergent properties, the possession of an emergent property does not guarantee *per se* an active role of its bearer. For active and passive powers, however, the claim that they might be epiphenomenal seems to be absurd. Such powers, *per se*, point towards the production or undergoing of changes, and therefore, it seems, must always be causally relevant.

However, there still remains a concern about whether any higher-level properties of composite objects—be they categorical properties or powers—can be causally relevant. In Section 1.1 we briefly encountered one form of this worry as a source of conflict between the commitment to the place of actions 'in the natural order' on the one hand, and the commitments to agential activity and reasons-explanations on the other. The most influential expression of this worry is Jaegwon Kim's argument about 'downward causation'. Presupposing the bottom-up picture of the world, Kim claims that any causal influence of higher-level phenomena would involve a downward causal influence on lower levels, which is impossible. We will begin by examining Kim's argument, which is based on causal closure principles (Section 9.3.1), and then address a related worry about causal overdetermination in human agency (Section 9.3.2).

9.3.1. Downward causation and causal closure

What underlies Kim's argument for the epiphenomenalism of higher-level properties is the view of reality as constituted by a hierarchy of different strata, from a fundamental level consisting only of fundamental particles upwards, through levels of progressively more complex phenomena involving composite objects. These higher-level phenomena, it is thought, arise from, and causally depend on, the processes at the fundamental level. Add to this picture of reality the two following assumptions: (i) that the fundamental level is 'causally closed'—it is governed by laws which allow only for causation by other phenomena at the same level—and (ii) that a higher-level phenomenon can be caused only by causing the lower-level processes from which it arises. The direct result is that all higher-level phenomena are really 'causally impotent', and that all 'real' causality occurs at the fundamental level.[15]

This basic line of thought seems to provide a powerful case for epiphenomenalism about higher-level properties, applicable both to reducible and to emergent dependent higher-level properties. If it were successful, the alleged active powers of human persons would turn out to be epiphenomenal, because they are higher-level properties. Consequently, they would only be sham active powers whose possession would not ensure any genuinely active role of the agent himself.

Kim's argument has been extensively discussed, and I cannot do justice to all its relevant features here. I will therefore focus only on the question of whether this argument is convincing in the particular case of human active powers.

My starting-point will be assumption (ii)—Kim's 'principle of downward causation'.[16] Intuitively, this principle is highly dubious. Why should causal relations between phenomena of the same level always involve causation of lower-level processes by higher-level phenomena? Furthermore, this principle, in its general form, has been successfully refuted by Humphreys, who used his notion of 'fusion' to do so. Where the higher-level property-instantiation is the fusion of several property-instantiations of the lower level, the latter have ceased to exist individually within the fusion. Therefore, it is possible that one fusion directly causes another fusion without causing the lower-level property-instantiations, because, as the latter need not exist individually when the fusion exists, there need not be any simultaneous corresponding lower-level instantiations via which the second fusion could be caused.[17] This shows that Kim's 'principle of downward causation' cannot generally be true.

However, Kim's principle might still be defended for a restricted field of application, where the lower-level property-instantiations exist simultaneously with the higher-level ones. This is the case for human actions. Even if we may be uncertain whether the instantiations at the fundamental level fuse and pass out of existence, at least at the macrophysical level, the parts of the human organism exist simultaneously with the human agent himself and have powers of their own. So, it can still be argued, following Kim, that phenomena at the level of human agency will be causally relevant only if they cause phenomena at the 'lower' level of the parts of the human organism.

---

[15] This general argument has been defended by Kim in a long series of papers from his (1989a) onwards.
[16] Kim (2000), 310.
[17] Humphreys (1997), 9 ff.

Even worse for the agent-causalist, it seems that Kim's principle is not even needed to establish that there must be downward causation in bodily movements, if these movements include agent-causation. For, as we have argued, what an agent causes are motions of parts of his body. These motions include phenomena on the lower level of neurophysiological processes, which have neurophysiological causes and effects themselves. For example, that my arm rises will include changes in the tensions of my arm-muscles, which in turn will cause new nervous signals to the brain. So, it seems, whenever the agent causes a bodily motion he will automatically also be causing neurophysiological phenomena, and so there will be downward causation from the level of agent-causation to the neurophysiological level.

Agent-causalists are therefore committed to downward causation—at least in a weak form. They are not committed to downward causation in the stronger form that there are events on the lower level of neurophysiological processes which are caused only by the agent. But they must assume that the powers of agents are causally relevant for producing events on the neurophysiological level. Without this assumption, the agent could not cause any physical effects, and his allegedly active powers would therefore be epiphenomenal.

Given that some form of downward causation is needed for bodily movements, the success of Kim's argument, when applied to human abilities to act, depends on whether we should accept his other premiss about causal closure. The specific kind of causal closure required for Kim's conclusion is closure of the neurophysiological level against causal interference from the level of human agency. The most important argument for accepting this kind of closure is based on the principle of the alleged causal closure of the physical realm. According to this latter principle, the physical realm is governed by laws which only allow for other physical phenomena to be causes of physical effects.[18] From this it would follow that higher-order mental entities could not contribute causally to the physical realm. Independently from the truth of this principle,[19] we can dismiss the relevance of this objection with regard to our agent-causal account, because this account neatly evades this particular problem. The principle relies on a picture of two separate levels of physical and mental entities, one of which must influence the course of events on the other level by inter-level interference. On the causal powers model of agent-causation, this picture is discarded, because the separation of two levels is transcended within the agent, who is a physical being possessing both mental properties and the power to directly influence the course of physical nature. As the agent himself is also a physical being, causation by him does not violate the principle of causal closure of the physical realm.

---

[18] Cf. Kim (1993). There is a weaker version of this principle according to which all physical effects have physical causes; but this version would clearly not suffice for demonstrating the impossibility of 'mental' influences into the physical realm; cf. Meixner (2002), 242 f.

[19] This principle is certainly not an established result of the natural sciences, because in their present state they are far from constituting a closed system of explanations; cf. Falkenburg (2006), 53. In particular, this principle is not implied by the physical conservation laws; cf. the discussion in Meixner (2002).

The principle of the causal closure of the physical realm is thus insufficient to exclude downward causation of events by the agent. What would be required for this would be a much stronger principle that all lower-level phenomena are causally closed off insofar as they cannot be causally influenced by entities from higher levels. A general principle of this kind would make not only emergent properties but all systemic properties of composite entities causally irrelevant for the behaviour of those entities' parts—for no systemic properties of a substance are possessed by the parts of the substance, and therefore they all appear only at the higher level of complexity on which the substance appears 'as a whole'. A general exclusion of the causal relevance of systemic properties would, however, be wildly implausible.

On the one hand, excluding *a priori* the causal relevance of systemic properties means excluding *a priori* a number of logically possible ways in which the behaviour of the components might be influenced by the object's systemic properties. For example, it is conceivable that the components in a system possessing a certain systemic property begin to display genuinely novel properties which are emergent in the sense explained earlier—properties which they lack in less complex composites or in isolation, and which cannot be deduced from their properties in the latter contexts. In such a case we can hardly avoid the conclusion that the possession of the systemic property is causally relevant to the behaviour of the properties of the parts,[20] and it would be absurd to rule out *a priori* that such cases exist.

On the other hand, general acceptance of causal closure of lower levels of phenomena would lead to a wholesale rejection of all our commonplace causal explanations of lower-level phenomena in terms of higher-level phenomena, and of the behaviour of components' parts in terms of the systemic properties of the composite substance. We would have to renounce all causal explanations of physical phenomena in terms of chemical phenomena, or of chemical phenomena in terms of biological phenomena—as these are typically seen as levels of increasing complexity. Also, we could no longer consider the switching on of a thermostat as the cause of its inbuilt heating device emitting heat—as the switching event concerns systemic properties of the thermostat—or the brain-fever of a human being as a cause of his arm's shivering. Nor could we continue to regard the experimental machinations of scientists as the causes of the microprocesses that ensue once the experimental set-up is in place. These results would be simply absurd, because these kinds of causal explanation are both perfectly working and reliable, and because they constitute one of the standard forms of causal explanations at our disposal. The absurdity of these results provides an extremely strong presumption against any general principle of causal closure of lower levels, because the costs implied by such a principle for our explanatory practices would be enormous.

To overcome this presumption we would need a very strong argument which shows that the rejection of the closure principles would clash with other deeply held

---

[20] Such cases are discussed by Gillett (2002), 114 ff.—who thinks, however, that the systemic emergent properties *non-causally* determine the lower-level properties.

assumptions central to our world-view; if there is simply a clash with some minor metaphysical principle we would instead regard this clash as a *reductio ad absurdum* of this principle. And I fail to see how a sufficiently strong argument showing the incompatibility with central assumptions could ever be offered; for the validation of a metaphysical principle that shows that lower-levels of reality must be causally closed would itself have to come from an explanatory practice which uses this principle. This is the very same kind of validation as that enjoyed by the myriad of causal statements connecting higher-level antecedents to lower-level effects, and so the principle of causal closure will not automatically take precedence. On the contrary, the enormous intuitive force of the former causal statements, and the fact that there is such an enormous range of successful explanatory practices involving these statements, will presumably force us to reject this principle in order to safeguard the latter practices.[21]

We can therefore reject Kim's argument as applied to the specific case of human agency, as it does not succeed in establishing that the agent cannot cause motions of parts of his body. As far as the alleged causal closure of the physical realm is concerned, agent-causation is not excluded by such closure, and general principles of causal closure of lower-level phenomena, which *would* exclude agent-causation, are wildly implausible.

9.3.2. Downward causation and causal overdetermination

Even if causal closure principles do not exclude downward causation in the case of human agency, our claim that the agent causes effects on the neurophysiological level may still appear problematic. The reason is that the neurophysiological phenomena which he causes will also have neurophysiological causes, of which we can even suppose that they are deterministic causes. Claiming that there is, in addition, an agent-cause of these phenomena, seems to introduce a problematic parallelism of both causings.

What is particularly problematic about this parallelism is the threat of causal and explanatory overdetermination, mentioned in Chapter 1. There would be two causal explanations of the same effect—the phenomena involved in the motion—one in terms of agent-causation, supplemented by a reasons-explanation, and another in terms of neurophysiological antecedents. Both explanations would be self-standing and, in a sense, complete, for it would suffice to know either of these explanations in order to understand why the effect has occurred.

If one accepts Kim's principle of explanatory exclusion that 'no event can be given more than one *complete* and *independent* explanation',[22] this result would be *ipso facto* unacceptable. The principle would force us either to reduce one of the two causal

---

[21] This line of thought follows Baker's arguments in 'Practical Realism' that successful explanatory practice should 'trump' metaphysical arguments in determining whether or not a property is causally relevant; cf. Baker (1993), 75 ff., and (1995) passim. A similar view is defended by Burge (1993).

[22] Kim (1989b), 258.

explanations to the other, or to reject one as false. And as the status of the neurophysiological explanation as a causal explanation of the effect is not in doubt, the only candidate for elimination or reduction is the agent-causal explanation.

The simple response to this argument is to reject its crucial premiss—the principle of explanatory exclusion—by pointing out that causal overdetermination of an effect by several sufficient causal factors is possible. But this response does not provide a satisfactory solution to our particular case, because we do not consider the case of human agency to be one of overdetermination. When both an agent and neurophysiological events within him cause (parts of) a bodily motion, we do not assume that they operate independently of each other, as it would be in the case of causal overdetermination.

In order to answer the threat of a parallelism involving overdetermination, we must explain the relation between the agent-cause and the neurophysiological processes, and show that while they are not independent of each other, their dependence does not imply reduction. A first attempt at explaining the relation between the two causal factors consists in claiming that what the agent causes directly is not the bodily motion but the neurophysiological events that lead to this motion.[23] But this attempt does not get us very far—for the identical problem as before also arises for these neurophysiological events, because they too have neurophysiological causes. Neither is it convincing to claim that the agent-cause is constituted by the neurophysiological processes and so the two causal factors are really one and the same. For if our argument about the irreducibility of human causal powers (in Section 9.2) is correct, the agent and his powers cannot be reduced to the neurophysiological properties of his parts and their manifestations.

Instead, the adequate way to characterize the relation between neurophysiological processes and agent-causation is in terms of necessary conditions. Even though agent-causation is not exhausted by neurophysiological processes, because it involves the manifestations of powers which are not reducible to powers of parts of the agent's organism, still the neurophysiological processes are necessary for the manifestation of human powers. The microstructure of the human organism and the powers of its parts that underlie these processes are part of the basis of the power, and knowledge of them allows us to explain, to an extent, why the agent possesses the power in question.[24]

For illustration, compare this case to the case of the power of water to dissolve sugar. When this power is manifested and sugar dissolves in a bowl of water, a process consisting of certain sequences of events occurs, in which water-molecules interact with the molecules making up the structure of the sugar-crystal. To the extent that we

---

[23] Chisholm (1966), 18 ff., 43 f.
[24] Alvarez and Hyman (1998), 232, even claim that we can explain why the substance has the power to F only to the extent that we can say what events occur when the substance Fs. This is not quite right, because there can be other factors which explain the possession of the power—for example, other emergent powers of the substance or powers of its parts.

can understand this process, we understand why water has this power, and which of the powers and categorical properties of the water molecules are relevant for this power and thus form its basis. The case is very similar with regard to human powers, with one crucial exception: that these powers are not reducible to powers of parts of the organism (see Section 9.2), while the power of water to dissolve sugar is presumably reducible to microproperties. But this difference between the two cases does not mean that the neurophysiological processes cannot contribute to an explanation of how the agent is able to act; it means only that these processes will not suffice for this explanation.

Explanations of effects in terms of the powerful agents that cause them and in terms of neurophysiological processes are therefore not competing, but complementary explanations.[25] As explanations they are independent of each other, in the sense that we can understand one kind of explanation even though we are completely unaware of the other kind. Thus, for long periods, people have been able to identify actions and explain them in terms of reasons, without having any notion of the nervous processes involved. The two explanations are also 'complete' in the sense that knowledge of either provides us with a satisfactory explanation of why the effect occurs. However, agent-causation and causation by neurophysiological processes are not in fact independent, but the latter is a necessary condition for the former. Nor are the two corresponding explanations complete explanations in the sense that either captures all the aspects of the production of the effect which requires explanation. The agent-causal explanation, even when enriched by a reasons-explanation, fails to tell us why the agent had the power, while neurophysiological explanation fails to tell us that the production constituted an action and can therefore be explained by reasons.

Only the second kind of independence and completeness, however, would suffice for causal overdetermination—and so we can reject the threatening picture of the agent and the neurophysiological processes causing the bodily motion each 'on their own'. The status of neurophysiological explanations as *bona fide* causal explanations therefore does not stand in the way of there being events that have both neurophysiological causes and agent-causes.[26]

---

[25] To use Alvarez and Hyman's phrase; (1998), 232.
[26] Bishop (2003), 239 f., raises a different objection: namely, that claiming both dependence of the emergent property on microproperties and a genuinely novel causal contribution by the property or its bearer, is inconsistent. Though agent-causal powers do depend on microproperties, this objection is unconvincing in their case, because as we have seen, there are no *sufficient* conditions for having an agent-causal power which could be spelled out in terms of microproperties. Equally, a related worry against downward causation—raised by Kim (2000), 318 f., and Cover and O'Leary-Hawthorne (1996), 60 ff., who argue that a conjunction of 'upward' determination and 'downward' causation would involve an impossible kind of 'self-causation'—is unconvincing. 'Self-causation' would only enter into the picture if the higher-order instantiation (or the agent) did cause the instantiation of its own neurophysiological basis (or the basis of the active power); and an agent-causalist is not committed to anything of this kind. In our theory, for instance, the agent causes a motion of his arm, which causing does not directly affect the neurophysiological bases of his powers.

We can therefore conclude that both arguments against the causal relevance of higher-order powers are unconvincing. There is thus no reason to believe that the active powers of human persons—their abilities to act—are only epiphenomenal and, for this reason, only sham powers which do not confer any genuinely active role on their bearers. Instead, given their status as irreducible and active powers of the agent, we can safely assume that in their exercise the agent himself is truly active.

9.4. Summary

Our defence of agent-causation against the threat of microreduction has formed the last part of our general answer to the worries about the conceptual possibility of agent-causation and the possible instantiation of agent-causal relations in the natural order. We have addressed these worries by explaining how agent-causation works in terms of the manifestations of active powers of human agents; and in the course of this explanation we have provided answers to three central questions which corresponded to the three standard objections against agent-causation.

(1) What does it mean to say that an agent caused an effect (if it does not mean that an event involving the agent caused the effect)?
(2) What more or what else does it mean to say that an agent directly caused an effect than simply to say that the agent performed a basic action with this result?
(3) How can agent-causation be instantiated in the natural order?

With regard to question (1) we have argued that human agents have active powers to move parts of their bodies, and that agent-causation consists in the exercise of those powers. As the notion of active powers has been explained not only for the case of human agents, the answer to question (1) also serves as an answer to question (2). That agent-causation as explained by the causal-powers model is compatible with the natural order has been shown by the following three considerations: (i) by demonstrating that our 'image of the world' must not only include categorical properties, but also powers as irreducible properties; (ii) by explaining how agent-causation is based on a sub-set of those powers—active powers; and (iii) by showing that these powers are not reducible to the microproperties of parts of the human organism. Taken together, (i) to (iii) make clear that agent-causation does not commit us to 'supernatural' phenomena, but only to things that we must anyway accept within a plausible picture of nature.

The apparent tensions between our original Theses 1 and 2 in Chapter 1—the Theses about agential activity and the status of actions as parts of the 'natural order'—have therefore evaporated together with the mysteriousness objection. For it has turned out that these tensions arise from a false and overly impoverished picture of nature: the event-causal, Humean, picture. On a plausible 'image of the world', there is no obstacle to agential activity being part of nature, because this image will in any case include powers and substance-causation, and agent-causation is simply the specific form which substance-causation takes when the substance is a human agent.

So, to the extent that it reconciles Theses 1 and 2, the agent-causalist approach has already been successful. What remains to be done is to show that the apparent tensions between this approach and the possibility of reasons-explanations for intentional actions—mentioned in Chapter 1—can also be dissolved. This requires an account of what it is to act for a reason.

There is a further reason why such an account is required. Traditional agent-causalists—in particular, libertarian ones—will complain that the account which I have developed hitherto allows only for a minimal form of agential control, but not for true self-determination or even 'ultimate control'. This complaint would be apt. I have, in the previous chapters, explained agent-causation merely in terms of the exercise of powers which are relatively independent of external circumstances, and substance-causation in this form does not, by itself, give the agent ultimate control over what he is doing—any more than it gives ultimate control to an unstable explosive over whether it will explode, or makes the explosive self-determined.

I think that presenting an account of 'ultimate control' is not something that can reasonably be required from our theory—both because the idea of ultimate control itself is so difficult to make sense of in the case of human beings, and because it is intimately connected to the problem of free will, with which we are not concerned here. But I accept that some account of self-determination is needed, for otherwise our agent-causal account would fail to capture the difference between human agency and the activity of other substances—such as unstable explosives—in full. What characterizes human agency is the ability to act for reasons, which is also a crucial part of self-determination. Can agent-causalists provide an account of this essential aspect of human agency?

10

Intentional agency and acting for reasons

So, let us turn to the task of showing how the agent-causal account we have been developing can accommodate agency for reasons and allow for reasons-explanations of human actions. As we have already solved the conflict between the first two commitments which are constitutive parts of our self-understanding as human agents—activity and our place in the natural order—we will have provided a complete answer to the problem of human agency once we have shown how agency for reasons can be integrated into our agent-causal account.

As we have seen in Chapter 1, there are two potential difficulties for agent-causal theories in accounting for agency for reasons. The first problem arises from Davidson's claim that what distinguishes reasons-explanations from *mere* rationalizations of actions is the obtaining of an event-causal link between some suitable mental event related to the motivating reason—the 'onslaught' of a desire, for example—and the agent's behaviour. As it is difficult to see how this event-causal element and the agent-causal element in action could be combined, this seems to leave us with a parallelism of both elements in the production of behaviour.[1] But if Davidson is right in his above claim about reasons-explanations, this parallelism entails that—absurdly—actions cannot themselves be explained by reasons-explanations if they are (or essentially involve) agent-causings.

The second difficulty arises with the assumption that agent-causation is a form of radical self-determination—for on this conception, agent-causation seems to be in conflict with determination by *any* other factors, including motivating reasons whose influence would compete with the agent's own radical control over his actions and decisions.

After our discussion, in the previous chapters, of the nature of agent-causation, we can be confident that the second difficulty will not arise with regard to our account. For this account does not construe agent-causation as automatically competing with other determining factors. Agent-causation has been explained as a manifestation of an active power, and such manifestations do not generally exclude the influence of other

---

[1] This was Clarke's view in (1993), for free actions.

factors. Instead, they even require the presence of some further factors—in particular of those factors which are relevant for the presence of an occasion for the exercise of the active power. If motivating reasons or their acceptance by the agent can be understood in terms of such factors, their influence will clearly not be at odds with the agent's causal influence.

The first difficulty, however—concerning the relation between the agent-causal and a supposed event-causal element in intentional action—, seems real enough. Therefore, our discussion throughout most of this chapter will focus on the following two questions. Does acting for a reason involve an event-causal connection between a mental antecedent and the action, and if so, does this lead to a problematic parallelism with the agent-causal element in action?

The first of these questions is very similar to the well-known question of whether reasons are causes. And indeed, when causalists have raised this latter question, and answered it in the affirmative, they have regularly regarded it as a question about whether mental events or mental states which motivate the action—desires and suitably connected beliefs—are potential causes of the action. On this conception, the general question of whether reasons can be causes was tacitly reduced to a particular kind of reasons—namely reasons connected with the agent's purposes or aims. Both kinds of mental state which the causalists were considering as potential causes—desires and beliefs about the desires' realizations—are directly connected to the agent's purpose in acting: the desire typically as a desire for the attainment of an aim, and the belief as a belief about how this aim might be achieved.

But these mental states are only indirectly connected to another group of reasons: those which consist in situations to which the agents respond in their actions. For example, assume that James crosses the street because John has been waving to him from the opposite side; then (part of) James' motivating reason for crossing is that John has been waving. Neither James' purpose in crossing the street—the purpose of meeting John—nor James' belief that by crossing the street he could do so immediately tells us this reason, because it does not follow from them that this was the situation to which James was reacting. He may have crossed the street with the same purpose and belief, while reacting to a quite different situation. He might, for example, have crossed the street because he knew that John always sat in front of a café in that place at that time of day. Also, conversely, James might have reacted to the same situation—to John's waving to him from the opposite side of the street—but acted with quite a different purpose. For example, John might have promised to wave to him when a shop on his side of the street, which James particularly wanted to visit, was open, and James' only purpose in crossing might have been to visit the shop. So, there is no one-to-one correlation between reasons in the 'situation' sense and reasons in the 'purpose' sense.

Motivating reasons in the 'situation' sense were typically ignored by causalists with respect to the question of whether reasons are causes of actions. I will follow suit, and in discussing the event-causal element in intentional action I will focus only on the connection between desires or pro-attitudes (and suitably related beliefs) and actions. The reason for this restriction is not only that the causalist discussion was likewise restricted;[2] but more importantly, the potential problem of a parallelism between the event-causal and the agent-causal element does not really arise with regard to reasons consisting in situations to which the agent reacts. Even if these situations should be event-causes of actions, they will most plausibly be so by providing occasions for the manifestations of active powers of the agent or by stimulating their exercise. This form of event-causal influence is neither incompatible with agent-causation, nor does it lead to the threatening parallelism which we have discussed; for what is event-caused, and thus explainable by citing the agent's reason, is the agent-causing—i.e. the action itself. I will therefore leave aside, for the following, the question of whether or not reasons of this kind are event-causes of the actions which are performed as responses to them.

So, presupposing a limited focus on reasons connected with purposes, how can we present an account of acting for a reason which is both compatible with the agent-causal position on agency and which avoids the threat of a problematic parallelism? To develop such an account, I will proceed as follows. I will begin by sketching the causalist arguments for the need to assume an event-causal element of this kind—the most influential of which is 'Davidson's challenge' (Section 10.1). Afterwards, I will consider whether an agent-causal theory could not, after all, adopt the causalist answer to this challenge. I will argue that although an agent-causal theory *could* indeed accept that when an agent acts for a reason his action is caused by a corresponding mental event, it still *should not* adopt the causalist view that such an element is constitutive for reasons-explanations, because, somewhat surprisingly, the causalist answer to Davidson's challenge is demonstrably false (Section 10.2). This result will motivate our search for alternative accounts of acting for a reason, and we will examine some unsuccessful non-causal theories (Section 10.3). The insights which these theories nevertheless contain will, in Chapter 11, provide the background for developing our own account of acting for a reason.

10.1. Davidson's challenge and the purported causal element in reasons-explanations

Today it is accepted by the majority of philosophers of action that the reasons for which an agent acts must be causally efficacious in producing his behaviour, and that reasons-explanations of actions must (also) be causal explanations if they are to be distinguished from mere rationalizations. Different arguments are advanced for this view:

(1) We can normally rephrase reasons-explanations without apparent change of content into formulations with recognizably causal idiom describing the connection

---

[2] An exception is Iorio (1998), who is, however, not a causalist in the traditional sense.

between reason and action.[3] For example, 'his belief *led* him to act, *resulted* in his action', or, concerning the 'onslaught' of a reason, 'the realization that his enemy was about to escape *produced* his foolhardy attack'.

(2) We can try to influence other people's actions as well as their emotions by influencing their evaluative or factual beliefs and their desires. While this can be easily explained if those beliefs and desires can be causally efficacious, it seems difficult to account for this fact if they play no causal role.[4]

(3) Reasons-explanations often support related counterfactuals in the same way as do causal statements.[5] For example, 'he bought a book because he wanted to read it' implies that, *ceteris paribus*, he would not have bought it had he not wanted to read it; and the same counterfactual conditional would be implied by 'his wanting to read the book caused him to buy it'.

We cannot dismiss these considerations simply by pointing out that, as argued in Chapter 4, motivating reasons are facts or propositions and, as such, not the right kind of objects to be causes—for the issue is not really one about the nature of these reasons. Even if motivating reasons themselves are not causes, coming to accept a reason, or realizing that one has a reason, are events, and as such, are potential event-causes of effects; and if their causal efficacy in producing behaviour should be required for the truth of the corresponding reasons-explanations, these explanations will plausibly contain a causal element. (Even though strictly speaking, desires and beliefs are, as attitudes, no possible event-causes, I will, for the sake of simplicity, continue with the loose but current practice of speaking of desires and beliefs as potential 'causes'.)

However, none of (1) to (3) are conclusive. With regard to (1), we can readily admit that the causal idiom suggests a causal relation between events connected with the desire or belief and the action. But first, not all such descriptions—such as 'results in'—need describe a causal relation between A and B, as they can also describe a 'manifestation relation'—that B is a manifestation of the power A—and we have seen that powers are not themselves causes. Second, the causal idiom is not applicable to all cases of actions performed for a reason, but only where we can pin-point one event or a conscious experience of the agent as an 'onslaught' of the belief or desire. Thus, 'his desire to see her caused him to run to the station' implies a strong and phenomenologically acute desire. But when a person routinely performs an intentional action, and when the pro-attitudes involved are longstanding and phenomenologically very weak attitudes which need not become conscious to the agent every time he performs an action of this kind, the causal idiom seems inappropriate. For example, when an agent brushes his teeth as he does every evening, he will supposedly do so for a reason—because, for example, he knows that brushing his teeth will reduce the risk of caries.

---

[3] Lanz (1993), 297; and Hornsby (1993), 287, fn. 7.
[4] Lanz (1993), 298.
[5] Hornsby (1993), 287, fn. 7.

Still, it would be inappropriate to say that 'his desire to reduce the risk of caries made him brush his teeth', when on that particular occasion he did not even explicitly think about this risk, for the causal idiom would suggest that the desire was somehow compulsive. So, while I accept that (1) makes it plausible to assume that *some* actions are caused by events which are related to the agent's motivating reasons—events, for example, which can be truly described as the agent's recognizing the reason, or feeling an acute pang of desire—this does not imply that *all* motivating reasons, or events connected to them, must be causally efficacious for the actions performed for these reasons.

Argument (2), on its own, is question-begging because it simply presupposes that influencing actions and emotions of others involves a *causal* influence on the action or the emotion. In some cases, our influence on other persons' behaviour is indeed plausibly seen as a causal influence—for example, when we forcibly prevent someone from doing what he wants. But this does not imply that the relation between an agent's reason for action and his action must also be causal, or that by influencing what reasons other persons have or recognize we must exercise a *causal* influence over their actions. Therefore, (2) lacks any independent force.

Lastly, (3) is inconclusive, because counterfactual dependence does not necessarily indicate a causal relation, but can also be the result of, for example, a logical connection or a common causal origin. Anti-causalists may well argue that the connection between the desire on which the agent acts and the action is logical rather than causal—at least for those many cases where our desires are phenomenologically very weak and there is no conscious experience identifiable as an 'onslaught' of desire. For, in these cases, our only clue to there being a pro-attitude of the agent, or an 'onslaught' of this pro-attitude, is that the agent has intentionally acted in that particular way.[6]

So, (1), (2) and (3), far from presenting a convincing case for the view that 'reasons must be causes', at best provide some grounds for assuming such a causal relation for a restricted sub-set of intentional actions. But why should we assume it for the rest?

To this question, the widely accepted answer is that Davidson's argument in *Actions, Reasons, and Causes* shows the necessity of a causal connection between motivating reasons and actions. Davidson did not really offer a positive argument to the effect that motivating reasons must be causes, but only raised a challenge for non-causal accounts of what it is to act for a reason. This challenge was directed primarily against non-causal theories according to which the sole point of reasons-explanations of action was to place the action within a wider pattern of desires, character-traits, and beliefs of the agent and a background of social practices.[7] If, for simplicity's sake, we concentrate only on desires and beliefs of the agent, all that is required for an agent to act for a reason, on such a view, is that he has a desire and a belief whose contents can be used as premisses of a practical syllogism with the conclusion that an action of this kind should

---

[6] This point was probably the core of the old Logical Connection Argument; cf. Hursthouse (2000), 85 f.
[7] Primarily, Davidson addresses Melden (1961).

be performed—for this guarantees that we can explain the action by setting it within a larger, recognizable pattern.

But, as Davidson has pointed out, this proposal does not suffice to explain acting for a reason; for an agent may simultaneously have several different reasons which would equally well make his action rationally intelligible, but may perform it for only one of those reasons.[8] Consider the following case. An officer commanding a regiment wants his side to win a crucial battle, and recognizes that the key to victory is to seize a certain hill from the enemy. However, due to his military training, whose lessons he has thoroughly taken to heart, he knows that even when a delay can cause the loss of the battle, he may not by himself take important decisions such as on how and when to attack, but may act only when he has been ordered to do so by his superior commander, and only in the way prescribed by the order. Fortunately, just at this moment the order to advance arrives, and the officer gives the signal to begin the attack on the hill. In this case, the reason for which he gives the signal is that he has been ordered to do so and wants to carry out his orders. But at the same time he has a further reason to give the signal—that he wants his side to win the battle, and seizing the hill is necessary for victory. Even though the latter reason would also make his action intelligible, *ex hypothesi* he does not act on it.

This shows that for an agent to act for a reason it does not suffice that this reason rationalizes his action, but there must be an extra element present. For Davidson, this extra element consists, famously, in a causal link between the reason for which the agent acts and his action.[9] The main force of this proposal lay not in Davidson's having offered a conclusive argument that such a link was needed, but in the fact that the mere request for an extra element, to distinguish having a reason from acting on a reason, was by itself a strong *ad hominem* argument against many anti-causalist philosophers of his time who had simply failed to address this distinction altogether.[10] Later anti-causalists, however, have tried to remedy this failure, and nowadays Davidson's consideration can at best be considered as a challenge which anti-causalists must meet—though it is, of course, far from clear that they can meet it, and causalists regularly claim that they fail to do so.[11]

10.2. Reacting to the challenge—why (surprisingly) causalism itself does not provide an answer

Given the agent-causal account which we have developed, how should we react to Davidson's challenge? In answering this question it is essential to keep separate three more specific questions: (a) the question of whether actions *can* be caused at all by prior

---

[8] Davidson (1963), 11 f.
[9] Davidson, loc. cit.
[10] An important exception being von Wright, as we will see below.
[11] For example, Mele (2003), 39 ff.

events, such as 'onslaughts' of beliefs and desires—i.e. the question whether, in principle, an agent-causalist *could* adopt Davidson's own solution; (b) whether actions *are* necessarily always so caused when the agent acts for a reason; and (c) whether the causal link between desire and action lies at the basis of the distinction between having a reason one does not act upon, and acting for this reason. The answer to (a), I believe, is 'yes'; the answer to (b) is 'probably not'; and the answer to (c) is 'clearly not', for Davidson's core claim is demonstrably false.

Let us consider the three questions in turn. If an action, as we have been arguing, is (or includes) the causing of an effect by the agent, can it then, in turn, itself be caused by a prior event such as an 'onslaught' of a desire ? There are two different reasons for which one may want to deny this possibility: either that the agent's causing an event is not itself an event, and that only events can be caused;[12] or, alternatively, that even if the agent-causing is an event, its internal structure excludes that it might be caused by something else,[13] or, at least, excludes that it might be caused by the 'onslaught' of a desire. With regard to the first argument, one might already want to deny the implicit premiss that only events can be caused; but it seems clear to me that what is caused must happen at a specific time,[14] and only events seem to possess the required 'datability' characteristic. So the relevant question with regard to the first argument is whether actions, understood as agent-causings, are themselves events.[15]

How one should answer this question depends on the concept of 'event' which is in play—for there is no neutral answer that fits all such concepts. If one takes a notion of 'event' with very coarse-grained concomitant identity criteria—such as the one advocated by Quine, who considers events to be segments of spacetime[16]—then indeed it would be problematic to think that actions could be events. For if they are events in this sense, it will be very hard to always keep them apart from the motions which are their results—which, for basic actions, will occupy the same place and segment of time. And this consequence would be very hard to accept,[17] because an action as a causing must be different from what is being caused—but how can it be different if it is the same event as the event that is caused?

So, I accept that actions cannot be events on Quine's spacetime segment view of events, or similarly coarse-grained conceptions of events; but this does not imply that actions

---

[12] Reid (1983), 524, thinks that actions are not events and cannot be caused. Alvarez and Hyman (1998), 219, and Lowe (2002), 205, also deny that actions are events, without, however, drawing the conclusion that they cannot be caused.

[13] O'Connor (2000), 52 f.

[14] At least what is caused within the natural order. For non-natural causes, I do not want to make this claim because, for example, Leibniz's view of God as the cause of a deterministic universe without temporal beginning appears to be consistent.

[15] The view that event-causings are not events, and for this reason, actions are neither, is defended by Bach (1980) and Stoecker (1993). If one follows this view one will accept the same result for agent-causings.

[16] Quine (1976), 260.

[17] Alvarez and Hyman (1998), 229, consider it an outright *reductio ad absurdum* of the claim that actions are events.

cannot be events in any sense, nor in the sense required for being potential effects of causings. For there are 'weaker' senses of events, connected with more fine-grained identity-criteria: for example, Kim's 'minimal' conceptions of events as instantiations of properties or relations by objects at a certain time.[18] Obviously, actions are instantiations of an (agent-)causal relation between agent-cause and effect, and, at least for basic actions, there is no reason to deny that they are datable,[19] as they happen at the same time as the bodily motions which are their results. Nor does classifying actions as events in this sense lead to the worrying result that bodily movements and bodily motions are the same events. For on Kim's 'minimal' conception of events, identity between events requires that the involved objects, properties and times are all identical, and this is not the case with regard to bodily movements and bodily motions. We should note, however, that plausible identity-conditions of actions must be slightly more coarse-grained than they would be on Kim's account. When, on a specific occasion, I run quickly, my running and my running quickly on this occasion are one and the same action. So, we must admit that at least adverbial qualifications of actions do not automatically change their identity; but this obviously does not make actions identical to their results.

We can thus conclude that actions can be considered as events in a 'weaker' sense, and events in this sense too possess the 'datability' characteristic required for being potential effects of causings. But might the inner structure of actions perhaps exclude that they are themselves caused, or, at least, caused by anything like 'onslaughts' of desires? Actions, understood as (essentially involving) agent-causings, are complex events with an internal structure of the form 'A causes B'. O'Connor has argued that in principle, a complex event with this internal structure cannot be directly caused by a further factor C, but only indirectly in either of the two following ways: if C causes A (the first constituent event of the complex event), or if C is what Dretske has called a 'structuring cause', providing the framework of circumstances in which A could produce B.[20] Structuring causes typically do this by providing a connection between two kinds of event, so that when an agent causes the first one, by doing so he causes the other. For example, the work of a mechanic who installs a door-bell is a structuring cause, because it establishes the connection between someone's pressing the bell and the bell's ringing.

If O'Connor is right, then an agent-causing event can, at least, not be caused by anything like an 'onslaught' of the agent's desire which leads to an action. For, on the first alternative possibility that O'Connor envisages, the agent-causing event cannot be caused, simply because the agent cannot literally be caused (only the birth of a person can be caused). And on the second alternative, the desires which the agent has at the

---

[18] Kim (1976), 159 f.
[19] For complex actions, finding a precise date for the 'causing' is much more difficult; cf. Alvarez and Hyman (1998), 244 f.
[20] Dretske (1988), ch. 2; and O'Connor (2000), 52 ff.

time of his action cannot cause the complex event either, for they do not establish connections between the agent and the results of his basic actions. What establishes such connections is, at best, something like surgery, by which an agent regains the use of a limb.

But are O'Connor's two alternatives the only ones how an agent-causing could itself be caused? No, because when the cause within the complex causing event is a substance, two further possibilities have to be added if our account of substance-causation in terms of causal powers is correct. It will also be possible that a further factor causes the complex event either by 'activating' the substance—for example, by transmitting energy to it so that it can cause the further change—or by bringing about an occasion for the exercise of the substance's power.[21] In both these cases—which have no parallel in the purely event-causal scenario—the further factor is the cause of the agent-causing event, and not just of the bodily motion caused by the agent.

Thus, there is no general obstacle against accepting that actions are events which can themselves be caused. Nor is there, in principle, any objection to identifying the conscious experiences of 'onslaughts' (or events outside the agent to which he consciously reacts) as causes of his actions when there are such identifiable events.[22] Only, as noted in Section 10.1, it seems that there are not always such events to be identified, and this makes it highly improbable that *every* action is caused by such an event which could be adequately described as the 'onslaught' of a desire.

More importantly still, Davidson's claim that it must be so caused in order to account for the difference between only having a reason for which one does not act and acting for that reason, is demonstrably false, even if we assume that all actions are caused by 'onslaughts' of desires. The reason for this falsity is not, as one might suppose, the problem of antecedential waywardness which the causalists have been unable to answer. This problem only prevents that what makes something an action, or an intentional action, is the event-causal link between antecedent mental event and behaviour. When we can already assume that something is an intentional action and that the agent has two reasons for this action, but acts on only one of the two reasons, then the problem of antecedential waywardness does not exclude that Davidson's answer to his own challenge might be true—that what makes it the case that the agent acts on one reason is that (an event connected to) this reason causes his action.[23]

---

[21] Cf. Harré and Madden (1975), 5, who implicitly identify as causes the stimulation of a suitable generative mechanism into action, or the clearing away of obstacles (which falls together with providing an occasion for the exercise of the power).

[22] On this point I agree with Anscombe (1957), § 11, who admits that there could be mental event-causes for intentional actions, while denying that this is what underlies acting for a reason.

[23] There are, however, cases of causal deviance which are relevant to Davidson's solution to his own challenge. For example, in case 4 at the beginning of Section 5.1, the nephew's desire to inherit his uncle's fortune causes the nephew's action of killing his uncle, even though the nephew does not kill his uncle in order to inherit the fortune. As these waywardness counter-examples against Davidson's proposal are rather complicated, I will focus on the simpler kind of counter-examples which I will be presenting immediately.

The problem which is fatal for Davidson's solution is, instead, the following. What the solution requires is that *only* the desire on which the agent acts is causally efficacious for the action—and this need not be the case. Even when the desire on which the agent acts causes the action, another desire which also rationalizes the action, but on which he does not act, may also cause the action.

In general terms, this possibility is due to two facts. On the one hand, as pointed out by Davidson, one and the same action can be described in different ways, so that we can enrich a description by an adverbial qualification without thereby forcibly changing the item described;[24] and on the other hand, when a certain occurrence has different aspects it may have several causes, all of which are responsible for a different aspect. For instance, assume that two forces are applied to an object—one of which pulls the object forward, while the other pulls it towards the left, with the result that the object moves forward towards the left. Then, the applications of both pulling forces are causes of the resulting event of the object's moving forward in this way, each being responsible for a different aspect of the motion.[25]

Due to these two facts, the following is possible. When an action has different aspects, different desires may be responsible for those aspects. For example, assume that a particular action is both an intentional F-ing, and also an action which is performed violently, brusquely, jerkily, or fluently. (The specific 'ways' in which actions are performed that I have in mind are all modifications by which the action is recognizably different from what it would be otherwise. For example, brusquely telling someone to get up is visibly different from kindly telling him to do so, because it involves, e.g., shouting at him.) Then it is quite possible that the agent may have, on the one hand, a desire to F on which he acts and which is responsible for his action being an intentional F-ing, and on the other hand, a further desire to G that is responsible for the specific way in which the action is performed—violently, brusquely, and so on. When, in such a case, we are justified in claiming that the first desire causes the (particular) action that is performed, then there is no reason to suppose that the second desire, which is responsible for the violence or brusqueness, does not also cause the particular action. As it is responsible for certain characteristics of this action, the performance of this particular action—which was a *brusque* F-ing, for example—depended on the agent's having this desire. If this is right, not only a desire on which the agent acts, but also a desire on which he does not act, can be a cause of his action. Then we need only pick out desires G with the right contents,

---

[24] For Davidson's logical analysis of action sentences, see his (1966), 119.
[25] This is a point which Davidson would also have to accept, for his account of causation requires only that cause and effect be related by a causal law under one description or other—cf. (1967)—and therefore it is possible that an event might be lawfully connected to a description of event A under description F, and to a description of event B under description G.

which, together with appropriate beliefs of the agent, rationalize the action, in order to generate counter-examples to refute Davidson's proposal.[26]

The following example will serve to illustrate this general possibility, and in developing it I will, for the sake of argument, assume that Davidson is right in ascribing a causal role to the desire on which the agent acts.

The basic set-up is the same as in the case of the officer commanding the attack on the hill, encountered in the previous section when presenting Davidson's challenge. As we have seen, the officer gives the signal to begin the attack only because he has been ordered to do so. Even though he also wants to win the battle and knows that seizing the hill is crucial for victory, he does not act for this reason, because he has thoroughly internalized the rules of military discipline. (Remember that without the order he would not have advanced, even if this would have meant that his side loses the battle.)

So, on Davidson's account, only the officer's desire to carry out his orders is a cause of his action. But we can well imagine that when the officer gives the signal, also his desire for victory manifests itself, because he does give the signal, full of verve, by vehemently brandishing his sword, while he would raise it only hesitantly if he lacked the desire to win, or thought the attack on the hill would not contribute to victory. As giving the signal by brandishing the sword is the same particular action as giving the signal by brandishing the sword vehemently, the officer's desire to win, being responsible for the vehemence of the brandishing, is as plausible a candidate for being a cause of the officer's action as is his desire to carry out his orders. In consequence, the desire fulfils Davidson's criterion for being the desire on which the officer acted—causal role and rationalizing function—even though the agent did not, *ex hypothesi*, act on this desire.

So, Davidson's introduction of a causal connection between action and desires does not answer his own challenge at all. This means that, somewhat ironically, we must look for a non-causal account to answer Davidson's challenge—the point of which had been to demonstrate the failure of precisely this type of account!

10.3. Some unsuccessful non-causal answers to Davidson's challenge

The non-causal analyses of acting for a reason that have been proposed in answer to Davidson's challenge can be roughly divided into three main types: (i) the approach which relies on the idea that it is ultimately a matter of the agent's own sincere assessment or understanding;[27] (ii) the strategy which claims that the *content* of the

---

[26] The counter-examples to Davidson's causalist solution to his own challenge thus ultimately arise from his own analysis of causation and action. The case would be different if, with Mellor (1995), we were to assume that facts, not events, are the effects of causings. But as we have argued, this latter view would rest on a failure to distinguish the level of causation from the level of causal explanation.

[27] This was the view proposed by von Wright (1963b), and as we shall see presently, was later modified.

agent's intention determines for which reason he acts;[28] and (iii) theories of teleological realism.[29] None of these approaches is completely satisfactory, but some of them contain elements which we will be able to re-use in the next chapter when developing our own account of acting for a reason.

Let us begin with the first kind of approach, which can best be discussed by following the different answers provided by von Wright—its chief proponent—to the question at issue. Originally, von Wright thought that the agent was the ultimate judge concerning the question for what reason he acted, and that, consequently[30] sincere verbal utterances of the agent were the ultimate criterion for deciding this issue. Later, however, as a consequence of his view that behaviour acquires its intentional character from being understood by the agent himself or by an outside observer as aiming at a certain result (see Section 1.2), he changed his mind. As with the question of how behaviour acquires its intentional character, the question of for which reason the agent acted could also not be separated, according to von Wright, from the act of understanding the action as having been performed for this reason. 'This means that the truth of the action explanation has no basis in facts other than the understanding itself of the action in the context of its reason.'[31] So, for the later von Wright, the connection between the action and the reason for which it is performed is established only by the act of understanding the action as having been performed for this reason.

This account has an important consequence for cases where the agent and an outsider disagree about the reason for which the agent has acted and the outsider finally manages to convince the agent of his view. On von Wright's theory, it does not make sense to distinguish, in these cases, between the agent's acquiring a new self-understanding and his coming to see his reasons correctly at last. For the connection between motivating reason and action—which is the basis for the truth of the reasons-explanation—is established only by the new understanding of the agent: it is not something that was there before, and of which the agent has 'only now' become aware. As a consequence, the 'truth' of reasons-explanations can be understood only in terms of a complete consensus of the agent and the observers of the action about the motivating reason.[32] Even without such consensus, however, different understandings could still be comparatively 'better' or 'worse', insofar as the story they tell about the agent may cohere more or less with the overall frame of the agent's biography.

---

[28] This approach was originally developed by Ginet (1990). More recent adherents include O'Connor (2000), 86, and Wallace (1999), 240 ff.

[29] The chief present-day exposition of this approach is Sehon's (2005). Another exponent is Wilson (1989), ch. 7. Stout's (1996) teleological behaviourism also shares important elements with teleological realism.

[30] Von Wright (1963b).

[31] Von Wright (1985), 21.

[32] Loc. cit.

I believe that there are three important truths about reasons-explanations that are rightly emphasized by von Wright's two accounts. First, it would be wrong to expect a plausible account of acting for reasons to provide us with a criterion yielding a *sharp* and generally applicable distinction between acting for one reason and acting for another. When we examine our normal practice of reasons-explanations, we recognize that this practice does not proceed on the implicit assumption that there is *always* a 'fact of the matter' about which reason the agent has acted on. Consider cases where the agent has a bundle of strong motives to do X, but it is not clear—even after thorough examination of his action, its circumstances, and his general character—on which of these motives he has acted. We do not have then to assume that our inability to decide this question rests on merely practical grounds—that is, that there is a fact of the matter which we are unable to establish only because we lack further evidence; for it may well be that we would not even know what kind of further evidence would decide the question. Instead, we should accept that in such cases our inability may stem from the fact that these cases are truly indeterminate, because the criteria for judging whether the agent acted on a particular reason have 'run out', without unequivocally determining an answer. Von Wright's positions allow for 'indeterminacy' cases of this kind, because the agent may not always himself provide a clear judgement about his reason, or there may be no consensus between the agent and the outside observer about the motivating reason.

Second, determining for which reason the agent has acted is clearly associated with the question of which reasons-explanation would fit best into—would provide the most coherent account of—the pattern of the agent's life story. Often, when we are faced with the question of whether the agent has acted, say, from a sense of duty or from personal vanity, we will be guided by our knowledge of the agent's general character and decide the question on its basis. It would, however, be wrong to assume that these considerations of overall coherence in the agent's life story are the only or even the primary criteria for determining on which reason the agent has acted. For an agent can occasionally act out of character, and these actions of his need not be unintentional. A man who is normally quite modest may be surprisingly proud about one of his own particular achievements, continuously boasting about it, while there is no reason discernible from his overall biography why he should be so proud of this achievement in particular. In such a case, the consideration of 'best fit' with his overall biography will not provide us with the right answer to the question of what reason he acts on.

Third, von Wright rightly gives a privileged place to the agent's own assessment of his motivating reason, whereas the causalist proposal did not obviously entail that the agent's own assessment should be privileged. In fact, we normally accept the agent's own judgement unless there is positive evidence to the contrary; and we will presently see why we are correct in giving the agent's own utterances this privileged role.

Where von Wright's account goes wrong, however, is in ascribing to the agent's utterances or understanding of his own action an *excessive* importance. His earlier proposal accorded to the agent's own sincere assessment a constitutive role for determining on which reason the agent has acted. And this is implausible, for the following considerations.

When von Wright, in his earlier proposal, talks about *sincere* verbal utterances of the agent about his motivation, this immediately raises the question of what 'sincerity' could mean here. If the agent's assessment is to be constitutive for determining for what reason the agent acted, what is it that the agent could be 'sincere' or 'insincere' about? Now, assume that this initial difficulty could be overcome by spelling out a notion of 'sincerity' which did not rely on truth, but instead, for example, relied on an absence of intention to deceive one's interlocutor. Then, von Wright's original account would still face the following difficulty. We believe that even when the agent has no intention to deceive us, we can sometimes overrule his own verdict, because he can be mistaken about his own intentions, or may have unconsciously been deceiving himself. Such unconscious self-deceptions—which are recognizable to outside observers—can happen, for instance, when an agent cannot face his responsibility for an action performed from particularly base motives which are too much at odds with his self-image. For example, imagine that Smith and Jones are both philosophers, and Jones, from envy, tells Smith that his books are no good, while successfully deceiving himself into thinking that he tells him only out of friendship, because 'someone must tell Smith how bad he is'. Here we would clearly allow some room for possible corrections of Jones' own assessment by other persons. But how could this possibility be allowed if the agent's motivating reason were to depend on the agent's own sincere assessment?

So, von Wright's first proposal, by according the agent's own judgement constitutive force, introduces a subjectivism about reasons-explanations which is incompatible with our normal conception of acting for reasons. His second proposal faces the same kind of problem. 'Truth' or 'correctness' of reasons-explanations, as we normally understand it, is not just a matter of consensus, but depends on the satisfaction of the criteria for acting on a reason. This satisfaction is an objective matter (even though, as we have mentioned, these criteria may not yield a clear verdict about the agent's reason in every case). Because it is an objective matter, we distinguish, logically, between acquiring a new self-understanding and coming to see one's reasons correctly—for the former change could itself be erroneous, involving a mistake about one's motivating reasons which had previously not been made. This logical distinction is one that von Wright's account is unable to draw.

We should therefore dismiss von Wright's accounts of what determines on which reason the agent has acted as overly subjectivist, because the agent's own judgement or self-understanding cannot play the constitutive role which von Wright thinks they do. But why, one may ask, should the agent's own assessments then be accorded a privileged role at all? To a large degree, this role stems from the fact that doing something intentionally requires that one 'knows what one is doing'[33]—or, at least,

---

[33] Cf. Hampshire (1959), 102.

what one is trying to do. With regard to many types of action, that a particular action falls under this type depends on the agent's pursuing a certain aim.[34] For example, actions such as signalling, voting in a general election, or reminding someone of a fact, all presuppose that what the agent does is aimed at a certain constitutive goal, such as drawing another person's attention to something, or contributing to determining who will be elected to parliament. Now, many of these types of action are not types of basic action. An agent does not signal 'just like that', but for example, by, waving his arm; and that the agent performs an act of signalling presupposes that this waving of his arm is aimed at drawing another person's attention. This means that when the agent intentionally signals, he must normally[35] know what aim he is pursuing with the more basic action by which he signals, which means that he knows the reason for which he performs this basic action. This point generally holds for the case of all intentionally performed non-basic actions of a type X, where doing X is connected to a certain aim, or, more generally, to a certain kind of motive. And it shows that whenever an agent does X intentionally, he can be relied on to know, for the more basic action by which he does X, for what reason he performs it.

This point accounts—at least to a considerable extent—for the importance that we assign to the agent's own verdict about his motivating reason.[36] However, there is one further crucial consideration, which we can discuss only after developing the account of acting for reasons which I will present in the next chapter.

Having examined von Wright's account, let us turn to the second non-causal strategy to meet Davidson's challenge, which claims that the content of the agent's intention, when he acts, determines the reason for which he acts. The basic idea is, simply, that an agent, when doing F intentionally, not merely intends to perform an action of a certain kind F, but intends to perform F for a certain reason, or in order to fulfil a certain desire of his. If this is true, then the agent's motivating reason can be 'read off' from the content of the concomitant intention. For the precise formulation of the intention's presumed content I will here follow Ginet, who claims that the intention must contain a demonstrative reference to the action which it accompanies—that is, that the agent must, concurrently with his doing F, intend *of* his F-ing, that by it he would achieve (or do) G.[37]

---

[34] This is the point—rightly stressed by von Wright (1971), 118 ff.—that understanding what the agent is doing often already involves recognizing the agent's aim. Cf. also Anscombe 1957 §47.

[35] There are, however, exceptional cases where an agent knows that he is signalling, but does not know by which basic action he actually does so.

[36] As Schroeder (2001), 165 f., rightly points out, there are also cases where the special evidential value of the agent's avowal is due to its being an expression of the very same desire as the action itself. For example, when I go to the kitchen to look for the newspaper and you ask me why I am going into the kitchen, my telling you my aim might itself be an expression of my desire to get the newspaper, because I might hope to persuade you to help me look for it. But such cases are rather exceptional.

[37] Cf. Ginet (2002b), 388. O'Connor slightly modifies this account in (2000), 86—adding the requirements that the agent has, antecedently to the action, desired to G and believed that by F-ing he could G, and that this desire persists during the performance of the action.

The proposal to answer Davidson's challenge by an appeal to *de re* intentions concomitant with the action can be given two different readings. On one reading, the proposal is true, but also, it seems, trivial, and will not really satisfy philosophers who accept Davidson's challenge as presenting a genuine problem which must be resolved. On the other reading, however, the proposal involves a substantial claim which is, I think, false.

In one sense, I think it is clearly true that when an agent does F for the reason that it leads to G-ing, he intends of his F-ing that by it he may G. This is due to the fact that doing F for the reason that it leads to G-ing and intending of one's F-ing that by it one may G are—when F is an action the agent performs—(almost) logically equivalent. But for precisely this reason, an answer to Davidson's challenge that consists only in substituting the second locution for the first is unlikely to satisfy those philosophers who believe that Davidson's challenge points out a real problem. Consider our earlier case of the general who orders the attack because he has been ordered to do so, and not because he wants to win the battle, even though he also has a desire to do so. Assume that we want to know what makes it the case that he acts for the one reason but not for the other. Telling us that this is the fact that he intends, by ordering the attack, to fulfil his duty will not be very enlightening: For, what makes it the case that the agent has this intention is just that this is the reason for which he acts.

This brings us to the second possible reading of Ginet's claim, on which this last point would be rejected. The second reading 'reifies' the agent's intention—by claiming either that it is encapsulated in a decision, or that it constitutes a distinct mental state on its own. In either case, the existence of the decision or the mental state with the right content could, in principle, be established in a different way than by establishing for what reason the agent acts. For example, when the agent makes a conscious decision he will be conscious of what it is that he decides to do—not merely to F, but to F in order thereby to G; and so, it can be truly explanatory, and free from circularity, to explain his acting because he wants to G in terms of the content of this decision.

However, when we present such a 'substantial' interpretation of Ginet's claim, which saves the claim from triviality, the claim becomes false. Very often it would simply be wrong to assume that agents have made a conscious decision or consciously entertain an intention when acting for a reason, or that the intentions they do consciously entertain have the content required for Ginet's solution. When agents lack such conscious decisions or intentions, the only grounds for ascribing to them an intention to do F in order thereby to G are either the fact that they act because they want to G, or, alternatively, exactly the same grounds as for judging that they act because they want to G. (And these grounds neither warrant ascribing to them a decision nor an intention as a distinct mental state on its own.) So, if Ginet's solution is meant as a *general* solution to Davidson's problem, and not merely one for cases where the agent has decided to F or consciously entertains an intention, it works only on the first reading. And, as we have seen, Ginet's proposal, so understood, does not provide an enlightening account of what distinguishes the reason for which the action was performed from other reasons favouring the same action, which the agent also had at the time of his action.

The last non-causal approach to Davidson's challenge which I want to examine in this section is the strategy of teleological realism, and I will focus on the version defended by Scott Sehon. On this account, the answer to the question for which reason the agent performed the action depends on the goal the agent's behaviour was directed at. Sehon does not believe that this notion of 'goal direction' can be reductively analysed, but he recognizes the need to provide an account of how we identify and justify explanations in terms of goals (teleological explanations) in order to give his proposal explanatory force.[38] Adopting Davidson's arguments that in ascribing propositional attitudes to an agent, we try to 'make sense' of him, looking for a theory that as far as possible 'finds him consistent, a believer of truths, and a lover of the good',[39] Sehon extends this rationale to answering the question at which goal the agent's behaviour is aimed. In answering this question, he claims, we rely on the following principle of rationality: 'Given two theories of an agent, it is unreasonable to believe the one according to which the agent is significantly less rational.'[40] This principle captures two expectations which are reflected in the following two maxims for finding a teleological explanation for an agent's ϕ-ing:

(I1) Find a ψ such that ϕ-ing is optimally appropriate for ψ-ing, given a viable theory of the agent's intentional states and circumstances.[41]

(I2) Find a ψ such that ψ-ing is the most valuable state of affairs towards which ϕ-ing could be directed, given a viable theory of the agent's intentional states and circumstances.[42]

So, according to Sehon, in order to determine the aim which the agent was pursuing by his action, we have to consider both optimal appropriateness of the behaviour for reaching the aim, and the relative value of the aim—both subjectively, for the agent, and for us, because the aims must also have 'rhyme and reason' for the observer—and, presumably, to reach a reflective equilibrium between these two considerations.

I believe that Sehon's account contains a considerable kernel of truth, and, as we shall see, my own proposal will incorporate some of his insights. Nevertheless, it is not fully satisfactory, because fulfilment of the two criteria contained in (I1) and (I2) is neither necessary nor sufficient to determine for which reason the agent acted; and as a consequence, there are important groups of cases for which (I1) and (I2) yield the wrong results. I now want to discuss three relevant kinds of case which show that the fulfilment of (I1) and (I2), respectively, is not necessary, and that even the fulfilment of both is sometimes not enough for doing ϕ in order to ψ.

---

[38] Such an account provides what Sehon calls an 'epistemology of teleological explanation'; (2005), 137.
[39] Davidson (1970a), 222. [40] Sehon (2005), 139.
[41] Sehon (2005), 146. [42] Sehon (2005), 147.

Let us begin with (I1). Is optimal appropriateness of one's action—given one's beliefs—for a certain aim really required for acting for that aim? As (I1) is an expression of Sehon's rationality principle, this would presuppose that rational agents are generally 'maximizers' about means to their ends—that is, that given a certain aim they will always choose the way which, they believe, best guarantees reaching one's aim. But in many cases, rational agents will, arguably, be 'satisficers' rather than 'maximizers'—that is, they will 'set a threshold level of fulfilment and choose the first course of action of those coming to mind that one expects to meet this level'.[43] Agents can be satisficers both with regard to the amount of utility to achieve and with regard to the means which they take for an adopted end. Once they have hit upon a means to this end that does not involve overly great sacrifices and holds a reasonable promise of success, they may choose this means without continuing to search for a possibly existing more efficient means. This method does not seem irrational if the threshold for what they accept as 'not overly great sacrifices' is sufficiently low and the threshold for 'reasonable promise of success' is sufficiently high. But even if it should be irrational, it is certainly a method which people standardly apply in deciding what to do and which we therefore have to take into account when determining which aims they are pursuing. Thus, optimal appropriateness of one's action for a pre-set aim cannot be required for acting in order to reach that aim, because the agent may be content with settling for less appropriate means.[44]

But what about (I2)? Assuming that an action is equally appropriate for several possible aims, is the aim for which the agent acts then necessarily the one which is most valuable, given the agent's intentional states and the circumstances? No, because an action can be performed for more than one reason, and not all these reasons need to have the same importance for the agent. Consider, for example, the case of an agent who has promised to visit a friend who is in hospital, and assume that he would like to see his friend also independently of his promise. We can well imagine that both the agent's desire to fulfil his promise and his independent desire to see his friend would by themselves be sufficient reasons for his visit, and that, consequently, when the agent visits his friend on Saturday afternoon, he does so both because he wants to keeps his promise and because he wants to see him. All of this would be quite compatible with the agent's valuing one of these aims higher than the other. The agent may, for instance, believe that keeping one's promises is more important than seeing one's friends. This shows that there are cases where the agent (also) acts for an aim, which, given his pro-attitudes and beliefs, is not the most valuable one for him.

The two criteria—of optimal appropriateness of the action for an aim and of highest relative value of the aim—do not even jointly provide sufficient conditions for determining the agent's motivating reason. An action may be optimally appropriate

---

[43] Gauthier (1986), 184.
[44] Not even optimal appropriateness given the agent's beliefs is required, for it may follow from the agent's beliefs that there is a better means, though he may still fail to realize this, cf. below.

for reaching an aim which the agent values highly, and the agent may, due to stupidity or a failure of rationality, still not perform the action in order to reach that aim. Examples of this kind are cases where the agent has beliefs from which it would follow that the action is optimally appropriate for the aim, but has not drawn this inference because he has failed to 'put two and two together'. For examples, James—a business executive—may have long desired to watch Xavi play in a football game; and as he well knows, Xavi plays for FC Barcelona, whose home stadium is Camp Nou. One day, James is invited to participate in a business hospitality trip to Camp Nou to watch a game. However, completely absorbed in talking shop with his business colleagues, he fails to realize that he could now watch Xavi, even though he has neither lost interest in watching the player nor forgotten that Xavi is playing with FC Barcelona (if someone were to explicitly ask James where Xavi plays, he could still give the right answer). In this case, James' action of going to the stadium was, given his own beliefs, optimally appropriate for an aim which he valued very highly—watching Xavi play. Nevertheless, he did not go to the stadium in order to do so, because, occupied as he was, he failed to put together the various informations at his disposal, and did not realize that by going to the stadium he could do what he valued highly. This shows that even if the criteria implicit in (I1) and (I2) are satisfied, this still does not guarantee that the agent acts in order to fulfil the aim selected by these criteria.

For these reasons, I do not think that Sehon's account is ultimately successful. But, given that the causalist answer to Davidson's challenge has also failed, how can we then explain the difference between the reason on which one acts, and a reason which would also favour the action one performs but for which one does not act? The answer to this question, in my view, is the following. The fact that an agent is acting for one reason rather than another is, in essence, the fact that the agent is following a standard of success provided by this reason rather than by the other reason.

11
Understanding human agency

In this chapter we will turn to the task of developing the promised account of acting for a reason in terms of following a standard of success. We will see that this latter notion is very similar to the Wittgensteinian notion of rule-following, and we will show that the offered account of acting for a reason is not a covertly event-causalist one (Section 11.1). The account will also allow us to explain how the 'rationalizing' element of reasons-explanations is intrinsically connected to the explanatory element, so that reasons-explanations truly explain actions *by* making them intelligible. These considerations will complete our unified model of human action, which will finally allow us to answer the problem of human agency (Section 11.2).

11.1. Acting for a reason as following a standard of success

The basic assumption underlying my account is that the factors which determine for what reason an agent acts cannot be divorced from the criteria on which we rely to determine the agent's motivating reason, but are intimately and insolubly related—though not identical—to them. This means that ultimately it is our everyday practice of ascribing motivating reasons which will provide us with an answer to Davidson's challenge—if anything will. And, it is crucial to notice, this will not merely be an answer to the epistemological question of how we can determine for what reason an agent has acted, but will also be an answer to the constitutive or metaphysical question about what makes it true that the agent acts for one reason and not for another.

The central point of this assumption can be best illustrated by comparing the strategy for answering the constitutive question which relies on this assumption, with the strategy followed by Davidson in the 1960s.[1] For Davidson, the epistemological criteria that we use for determining for which reason an agent has acted are the considerations of rationality and overall coherence among his mental states that are generally relevant for the interpretative enterprise of 'making sense of the agent'. What makes the reasons-explanation true, however, is something completely different: the obtaining

---

[1] Later, the situation changed when Davidson introduced reliance on psychological laws in reasons-explanations—which, however, applied only to the particular agent specifically; cf. (1976), 273 f.

of an event-causal link between reason and action, which for Davidson must be based on a strict causal law. Due to the anomalousness of the mental, this law must be phrased in purely physical terms, and it is extremely difficult to see how the epistemological criteria, which concern mental phenomena, could provide even indirect evidence for the existence of such a connecting law.

The main source of this difficulty is that, given Davidson's general views on causation, we need some reason to assume that a strict law holds in order to be confident that a causal statement is true.[2] In some cases, as Davidson himself argues, observed rough regularities—which will normally be all we have to go upon—can already justify the assumption that there is a strict covering law—for example, when we observe that stones being thrown against window-panes regularly lead to the latter's breaking. However, in the case of reasons-explanations, which also involve rough regularities in the agent's behaviour, we cannot justify our confidence in the existence of a strict covering law in this way. For when the observed rough regularities already connect physical descriptions of the events involved, as in the window-breaking case, our confidence is based on the assumption that the observed correlations may, by modification and refinement, be eventually transformed into a strict law, or, conversely, be derived from such a law. But, if Davidson's anomalousness thesis is true, we cannot make a parallel assumption in the case of rough mental–physical or mental–mental regularities, because we already know that they can *never* be turned into strict laws. Thus, considerations about the agent's rationality and internal coherence— which concern only rough regularities between the agent's mental states, so described, or between them and the agent's behaviour—cannot give us any reason, even indirectly, to believe that a strict law holds.[3] This means that they do not really provide us with a reason to think that the fact which supposedly makes the reasons-explanation true—the existence of the event-causal connection—obtains. So for Davidson, it seems, the epistemological criteria used for assessing whether the reasons-explanation is true, and the fact which makes this explanation true, are entirely divorced.[4]

On the assumption on which I shall proceed, such a radical divorce is not possible. Instead, the facts relevant to the truth of the reasons-explanation statement that 'the agent acted because he wanted to F' are the same facts as those we try to determine in our everyday practice of reasons-explanations in order to settle the question of what reason the agent has acted on. The truth-conditions and the epistemic criteria for statements about agents' reasons, we can say, go hand in hand—though they are not identical,

---

[2] Even though we need not already know the precise formulation of the law. Cf. Davidson (1967), 170.
[3] In (1970a), 219, Davidson addressed this problem by arguing that in some cases generalizations give us reasons to believe that there exists a strict law which, however, can be stated only in another vocabulary (heteronomic generalizations). But even in this case our confidence must ultimately be based on the expectation that the strict laws will explain, together with adequate bridging laws, the rough generalizations—and this is something we cannot expect when the generalizations involve descriptions in mental terms, due to the anomalousness of the mental.
[4] For the criticism of this consequence of Davidson's account, see Stoutland (1985), 51 f.

because the epistemic criteria may not suffice to establish conclusively whether or not these conditions are fulfilled.[5] But if, *per impossibile*, we could establish *all* the facts relevant within our everyday practice, there would be no further fact not internally or 'logically' related to these facts, or that could not be 'read off' from them, that would be pertinent to the truth of the reasons-explanation statement.

The reason for attributing this importance to the epistemic criteria is that I consider this to be the natural fall-back position when we lack a plausible alternative account of what makes reasons-explanations true. Any account which were to introduce a factor unconnected to the epistemic criteria as the 'truth-maker' of a reasons-explanation would still have to be assessed for its adequacy by examining whether it conforms to our pre-theoretical verdicts on motivating reasons. If there are cases where it does not conform, these cases will constitute counter-examples refuting the proposed account. The relevant pre-theoretical verdicts, however, will reflect our epistemological criteria which we normally use to decide these cases. Therefore, the most straightforward way of developing an account which is sure to not be faulted for non-conformity with one's pre-theoretical verdicts is to take facts as truth-conditions which are internally related to the epistemic criteria. And, in the absence of a positive argument that some additional truth-maker is required, the principle of parsimony in theory-building requires us to include *only* these facts in the account.

The relevant epistemic criteria in the case of reasons-explanations, as I shall argue, are all concerned with the presence of a particular kind of structure of the agent's behaviour, its concomitant feelings, steps in practical deliberation, and beliefs. This is the characteristic structure of taking something as one's 'standard of success and failure', or 'of correctness and incorrectness'. The facts that we are trying to establish, when examining the question for what reason the agent has acted, are all facts which are constitutive aspects of following such a standard. According to my initial assumption, following a standard of success will therefore itself be constitutive for acting for a reason.

This crucial point about the connection between the apparently 'merely' epistemological question about on what evidence we rely to find out the agent's motivating reason and the constitutive question about what determines his motivating reason, must be kept in mind during the course of the following investigation.

11.1.1. Acting for a reason and the structure of behaviour

In what respect is the structure or pattern of behaviour relevant to the question of the reason for which the agent has acted? In the previous chapter we mentioned the possibility that considerations about which explanations 'fit best' into the pattern of the agent's overall life-story are relevant for correctness of reasons-explanations. But these

---

[5] This is true, in particular, for facts about the intentional states of other persons. *Pace* behaviourism, the behavioural evidence that we have often does not unequivocally determine whether or not an agent has an intentional state of kind X.

were only considerations about how the action *as a whole* is set within a larger pattern or structure. What we have hitherto ignored is the fact that instances of activity themselves *display* characteristic structures which contain crucial clues about the agent's motivating reasons.

To develop this latter idea we can take our cue from von Wright's remark that intention is not a mental state accompanying an action, but lies 'in the behaviour'—in its specific pattern or 'physiognomy'.[6] Intentional behaviour displays a certain characteristic structure of 'purposefulness' which distinguishes it not only from mechanical behaviour, but also from aimless behaviour such as idle lingering. This special structure has been the object of teleological explanations,[7] which have been rivals of event-causal theories in the field of reasons-explanations, and have insisted that instead of depending on a certain etiology, the purposeful character of the behaviour depends on its being a teleologically guided process.[8]

We will take this idea as our point of departure, from which, by subsequent modifications, our own account will be developed. As the teleological guidance account is primarily an account of what it is to act with a certain aim or purpose, we will begin our examination with actions performed in order to reach a certain aim or purpose, and then extend the account to provide a general answer to Davidson's challenge.

Teleological guidance is usually explained in terms of negative feedback mechanisms[9]—a notion encountered in Chapter 5, where we discussed the failed causalist attempts to solve the problem of antecedential waywardness. Now, however, our focus has shifted from analysing the nature of action—which we have explained by appeal to agent-causation—to analysing agency for reasons, or intentional action. For the latter analysis, we can thus already presuppose the notion of action, and need not present an account of the teleological guidance required for acting with a certain goal in terms of non-actional feedback processes. Instead, we can focus directly on feedback processes by which the agent actively controls features of his environment or his own properties.

In feedback processes of this kind, the agent, when pursuing a certain goal, must be able and willing to react sensitively to changes in the environment which threaten the attainment of this goal or make it otherwise necessary to adopt different means for attaining his goal. His reaction consists in taking corrective measures and performing actions conducive to overcoming obstacles, or else taking the means to his end which are necessary under the new circumstances. That is, the process not only involves the agent's doing what he thinks is necessary to achieve the aim, but also that he tries again when he has failed, that he acts to circumvent obstacles which he

---

[6] Von Wright (1969), 32.
[7] 'Teleological explanations' in this sense—explanations of processes as exhibiting certain patterns—are only a subgroup of what are normally called teleological explanations, for the latter include all kinds of 'in-order-to' explanations.
[8] Cf. Collins (1987), ch. vi.
[9] Cf. Nagel (1953), Collins (1987), and Woodfield (1976), ch. 11.

perceives, corrects his movements when they deviate from the route to the proposed aim, and so on. I will call this pattern in an agent's activity its 'teleological structure'.[10]

From the teleological structure of intentional behaviour, one can regularly 'read off' the aim pursued by this behaviour. For example, when the agent makes several attempts to obtain something, and we do not antecedently know what it is he is trying to obtain, we can determine his aim by looking at how he reacts to changes, what changes in his behaviour intelligible as 'corrective measures' occur, when he stops his attempts, and so on, and ask ourselves which aim of the agent makes most sense of this pattern. And once we have settled on a candidate aim—say A—we can check this assessment by examining how the agent reacts to obstacles to obtaining A, whether he tries again, whether he stops when he has obtained A, and so on.[11]

'Reading off' the agent's aim in this way is of crucial importance for explaining agency for reasons. This is illustrated by the fact that if the conditions for a teleological structure are fulfilled and we discern such a pattern in the agent's behaviour, we cannot (except for some additional considerations discussed below) avoid describing the behaviour as being performed in order to achieve the aim we can 'read off' from this pattern. In particular, we shall have to do so even if the agent's own explicit avowals about his intentions or the general context of the agent's overall behaviour—the criteria proposed by the accounts discussed in Section 10.3—suggest another aim.

If there are discrepancies between an aim F suggested by the teleological structure of behaviour and the aim suggested by the latter two considerations, this may lead us to conclude (a) that the agent has wrong beliefs about the necessary means or the situation in general, (b) that his avowal is insincere, (c) that he has fundamentally changed his preferences and values, or (d) that he has an intention of which he is unaware. The striking thing is that, apart from alternative (a), the discrepancies will not lead us to revise our claim that the agent acted with aim F, but will lead us to make one of the assumptions (b), (c), or (d), which demonstrates that we regard the teleological structure of behaviour as more directly relevant to determining the agent's purpose than fulfilment of the other two criteria—important though they are.

To illustrate this point, consider the following two examples. First, assume that we have a virtuous and disinterested nephew, of whom we can reliably assume (i) that he is strictly honest, and (ii) that he has never been interested in the money of his rich aunt. However, when he once visits his aunt, who is very sick, his conversation continuously wanders back to the matter of her will. He is particularly nice and even servile, and keeps talking about the pieces of her furniture that would 'fit so nicely into my own appartment', and so on. In short, his behaviour clearly displays the purposeful structure of behaviour aimed at securing his inclusion in his aunt's will. Now assume that when we ask the nephew whether he was so nice to his aunt for this pecuniary motive, he

---

[10] An alternative term, used by Woodfield (1976), is 'plasticity' of behaviour.
[11] Of course, such a complicated procedure is not always required. Many activities already have, to use von Wright's phrase, a 'physiognomy' which we recognize at once as the physiognomy of 'being aimed at X'.

denies this with full sincerity; and assume also that neither before nor after this event is he particularly interested in money matters. In this case, we would probably accept that he had no *conscious* intention of trying to be included in his aunt's will; but despite the contrary evidence regarding his overall life-story and his honest avowal of his intentions, we will still claim that he behaved as he did in order to secure the inheritance, even though this intention was unconscious.

The second example is one where the agent's aim can, in an even more literal sense, be 'read off' his behaviour. An assassin has been hired to lie in wait for a person wearing a black coat who will pass at a particular thoroughfare, and to shoot him. Assume that we see the killer adjusting his gun, and following constantly, with the sights of his gun, the movements of a man wearing a grey coat—each time trying to aim at him when he stands still, but refraining from shooting when the man moves out of focus. In this case, when the killer eventually fires and his shot hits the man, we will be forced to conclude that in firing, he intended to kill the man wearing the grey coat, even though he has been paid to kill a man wearing a black coat, and even if, with every appearance of sincerity, he asserts that he had planned to shoot the man in the black coat. We would infer that the assassin was either unable to correctly distinguish the colours black and grey, that he did not really intend to do what he had been hired to do, or that he had forgotten what it was. Again, the evidence from the observable teleological structure of his behaviour proves to be stronger than evidence provided by the agent's utterances or by how his behaviour fits best into the overall system of his aims and preferences. So, we can conclude, as a first step, (i) that the teleological structure of the agent's behaviour is crucial for determining for which reason he acts, and (ii) that in this respect it is more important than the agent's own verdict and the consideration of 'best fit' with the agent's overall life-story.

The kind of teleological structure which we have described is an essential part of what it is to take something as one's standard of success. From our observation of his corrective movements we can infer that there is a standard by which—at least implicitly—he assesses his behaviour and considers himself—in cases of non-conformity of his behaviour to this standard—to have 'made a mistake'; and similarly, from our observation of his repeated attempts and adaptive responses to obstacles, we can infer that he takes himself to have hitherto 'failed to succeed'. The standard of success which we ascribe to the agent in these cases is, roughly, 'getting X', when X is the aim that he is pursuing. For all we have said so far, when only looking at the teleological structure itself, both the ascribed standard and the agent's self-assessment might be completely implicit, and do not yet presuppose any conscious corresponding self-assessment on the agent's part. But, as we shall see, following a standard of success, and acting with a certain aim, normally must also involve a proneness to such conscious self-assessments.

However, there is more to taking something as one's standard of success than the presence of a teleological structure of the kind described above. There are three essential aspects which are crucial additional factors in determining the agent's motivating reasons. We will examine these factors in more detail after we have discussed one important respect in which we must modify our first account of how the teleological structure determines the agent's aim.

(a) The required modification concerns the question of sensitivity *to which factors* is relevant for determining the teleological structure of the behaviour and the aim which can be 'read off' from the structure. In our original presentation we discussed sensitivity towards obstacles and untoward changes in the environment. However, it is quite possible that an agent is mistaken about obstacles or about the appropriate ways to circumvent them; and he may fail to realize that he has already succeeded in reaching his aim.

In trying to determine the teleological structure of the behaviour, it will obviously make a considerable difference whether we take—as our foil for determining both whether the behaviour is systematically sensitive to changes in the environment at all, and to which changes it is so sensitive—the facts about the agent's environment as they actually obtain, or the agent's perceptions of those facts. The first alternative will often lead to a false verdict about the agent's aim. When an agent does not recognize that he has failed to capture his friend's attention by waving his arms, we cannot conclude from the fact that he stops waving that he has not been waving his arms in order to capture his friend's attention. So, the agent's perceptions of, and beliefs about, the circumstances must be relevant for determining the teleological structure.

However, concluding from this that it is these perceptions and beliefs rather than the circumstances themselves which are relevant seems to conflict with the normativist account of the nature of motivating reasons defended in Chapter 4—according to which, the agent's reasons are normative and non-normative facts, as they are seen by the agent. This conflict is avoided, however, when we recognize that what the agent's behaviour is sensitive to are not, strictly speaking, his perceptions and beliefs themselves, but the circumstances *as he perceives them* or as he believes them to be.

We can therefore modify our initial teleological guidance model of acting with a certain aim, as follows: The teleological structure of the agent's behaviour, to be determined on the basis of the relevant circumstances as they are perceived and believed to obtain by the agent, is crucial in determining the agent's aims and purposes.

(b) The teleological structure of one's actual behaviour is, however, not the only factor which determines the agent's motivating reason; nor is it, often, the only fact we try to establish when we want to discover this reason. Often, actual behaviour does not display a teleological structure, because the agent encounters no obstacles and reaches his aim at the first attempt. In these cases, our ascriptions of aims rely on our confidence that certain counterfactual conditionals about what the agent would do if obstacles arose are true, and that the hypothetical behaviour he would display would have an adequate teleological structure. Similarly, hypothetical teleological structure can be appealed to in cases where the agent fails to reach his aim because of a false belief about the conduciveness of his action to this aim and has no means of correcting his error.

Consider the case where an agent manages, without any difficulty, to obtain a drink by opening a fridge and finding a bottle of wine inside. When we now state that he has opened the fridge in order to obtain a drink, we commit ourselves to the claim that in addition to the statement that he has actually opened the fridge and obtained a drink, the following counterfactual statements are true: that, *ceteris paribus*, had the fridge been empty, the agent would have gone into the cellar to look for wine, or done something else conducive to obtaining a drink, if possible; that, *ceteris paribus*, had someone told him that the fridge was empty or had his host given him a drink before he reached the fridge, he would not have attempted to open the door in the first place, and so on.

(c) Actual and hypothetical teleological structures of behaviour do not yet exhaust the notion of following a standard of success, however; nor are they the only factors which (constitutively) determine the agent's motivating reason. That there must be further factors becomes clear, for instance, in cases where a teleological structure is either compatible with several different aims that the agent might be pursuing, or even positively suggests a wrong aim, because the agent who is pursuing an aim is not willing to pursue it at any price. In abstract terms, cases of this kind have the following structure. An agent, while doing x in order to y, has another aim that he values still higher, doing z; but does not perform x in order to z. Nevertheless, the higher-valued aim of doing z influences the structure of the behaviour by restricting the agent's pursuit of the aim of doing y. This prevents us from correctly 'reading off' his real aim from the structure of his behaviour or from the hypothetical behaviour we can confidently ascribe to him, because the teleological structure falsely suggests doing z as the agent's aim, or is, at least, equally compatible with this aim.[12]

Consider the following example. Burglar A visits a town in order to inspect some houses he intends to burgle on a later occasion. However, A has to spend the whole time dodging detective B, who is close on his tracks, in such a way that each time, before A can even begin to inspect a house, he has to disappear from the scene as fast as possible. In this case, A's actual behaviour will indeed display a teleological structure— but only with regard to the aim of not being caught by B, and not with regard to the aim with which he, *ex hypothesi*, visited the town: to inspect some sites for new burglaries. For A never had the chance to do things which are manifestly goal-directed at inspecting houses. Thus, his real aim will not be evident in the teleological structure

---

[12] Another case of this kind is due to Woodfield (1976), 158.

of his actual behaviour at all—even though he clearly came to the town not in order to avoid being caught by B, but in order to inspect these sites.[13]

The hypothetical teleological structure of behaviour can also be misleading with regard to the agent's aim. Suppose that our burglar A is lurking in the dark shadow of a house-entrance, waiting for a passer-by in order to rob him. Assume that A's reason for hiding in the shadow is only that the passer-by will not see him until he attacks, not that A might be better able to escape if detective B should arrive. Unfortunately for A, however, nobody comes along, and so after a while, A gives up and leaves. Then, the following two counterfactuals were true of A while he was lurking in the house-entrance: (i) if B came along, A would slip away; (ii) if a passer-by appeared and B came along, A would slip away. These two counterfactuals suggest that A was lurking in the shadow in order to be able to slip away from B (rather than in order to make an unexpected attack on a passing victim), and so the teleological structure of A's hypothetical behaviour either points to the wrong aim 'escaping from B' or is, at least, ambiguous as to whether it points at 'escaping from B' or at 'attacking an unsuspecting victim' as the agent's aim. However, *ex hypothesi*, A's aim in hiding in the house-entrance was only the second, not the first one.[14]

Generalizing from these examples, we can draw the following conclusion. When an agent, while performing an action with aim y, has a further, unconnected aim z, which has an even higher importance for him than y, but for which he does not perform this particular action, his actual and hypothetical behaviour will often display a teleological structure (also) pointing towards this further aim. Consequently, an account of 'acting for a reason' which is based solely on the teleological structure of behaviour will yield recognizably false verdicts, or no clear verdicts, about the agent's motivating reason(s) in these cases.

To deal with those cases we must rely on some further considerations which are also relevant to 'taking something as a standard of success'. If the success of doing x depends, for the agent, on attaining y, then if y has not been attained, the agent will consider his doing x as a failure, and there will be the typical displays of 'failure behaviour' which show that the agent is dissatisfied,[15] or, in the contrary case, displays of 'success behaviour'.

---

[13] This difficulty cannot be solved by appealing to A's hypothetical behaviour either—for though it is true that A would begin to inspect the houses if B were not following in his tracks, it would be question-begging to rely on this particular counterfactual at this point, when we want to decide whether 'escaping B' or 'inspecting houses' is the aim A pursued in visiting the town.

[14] Therefore, even if we assume that we could read off A's true aim—attacking an unsuspecting victim—from his actual or hypothetical behaviour, the teleological structure by itself would still provide us with equal or even better reason to believe that the action was also performed for a further reason—being able to escape—for which it was, in fact, not performed.

[15] Cf. Wittgenstein, *Philosophical Investigations*, § 54, where he reminds us of the characteristic behaviour of a person correcting a mistake.

These displays do not themselves belong to the teleological process, because they are not conducive to the aim pursued, but only express satisfaction or dissatisfaction. But they provide crucial evidence about the agent's purpose. Swearing angrily, signs of being downcast, verbal assessments of failure, and so on, versus signs of feeling elated or content and being in a celebratory mood, are all relevant criteria on which we rely to determine whether the agent has reached his aim or has failed to do so. Thus, A's manifestations of frustration when he leaves the town show us that he has not achieved the aim of his visit, even though he has managed not to be caught by B. This kind of success and failure behaviour is evidence as important, for determining what the agent is aiming at, as the evidence about the teleological structure of the behaviour itself. As with the latter criterion, both actual and hypothetical success and failure behaviour are to be taken into account, and it is the circumstances as they are believed to be by the agent that are relevant for determining with what the agent is satisfied or dissatisfied.

While the display of success and failure behaviour by the agent provides the evidence on which we judge that he is following a certain standard of success, it is not strictly what determines the truth of our judgement. The truth of the judgement depends on the presence of the feelings of satisfaction or dissatisfaction on the agent's part; and that the agent is feeling satisfied or dissatisfied is the fact for which the agent's success and failure behaviour is the relevant, though not always conclusive, evidence. For while these feelings typically manifest themselves in behaviour of this kind, they need not always do so; for example, the agent may consciously suppress such behaviour in order to deceive others about his aims. At the same time, we must also be careful not to assume that 'success feelings' have always similar phenomenological characteristics or that they must always be feelings of happiness or joy, and likewise for feelings of dissatisfaction. An agent can feel unhappy about achieving what he had intended to achieve; for example, if he was only fulfilling a painful duty. Then the only success feeling of the agent may be a half-hearted or even bitter feeling of 'having done it' or 'being finished'.

The importance of 'success and failure feelings' in determining the agent's motivating reason cannot only be perceived from our practice of reasons-explanation, where success and failure behaviour provides us with important evidence. It is also, for systematic reasons, to be expected that something like this must supplement the teleological structure, if we compare the case of reasons-explanations of human actions with teleological explanations in biology. In the latter case, we normally ascribe an aim not merely on the basis of observed teleological structure, but only when we can in addition identify how the behaviour contributes to the plant's or animal's biological 'well-being', or satisfies one of its biological needs. In the case of human beings, actions are performed not only to fulfil biological needs or to further the agent's 'well-being', so a strictly corresponding criterion cannot be used. But it is very plausible that there must be some analogous element in this case too, and 'success and failure feelings' are a functional analogue of 'well-being', which suitably allows for the wide variety of aims which human beings pursue.

(d) There is yet another crucial aspect of following a standard of success, on which we often rely in order to determine an agent's motivating reason. The cases discussed in (c) are not the only ones where the teleological structure fails to deliver the right verdict about the agent's motivating reason. There is a second kind of case, where the agent pursues an intermediate goal y only because he thinks it is conducive to a yet higher-valued goal z. In these cases, the agent has 'multi-layered' systems of aims—that is, he does x in order to y (y being the intermediary aim), while he intends to y in order to z (z being the overall aim). In cases with this structure, neither the teleological structure of the agent's behaviour nor his success or failure feelings will always provide us with the right answer to the question of why the agent did x, because they suggest that he acted only in order to do the thing most conducive for z.[16]

Consider the following case. James is fumbling at the door of the fridge, and he tries to open the door in order to get a bottle of wine which he believes is inside—because he wants to get drunk. Even though, *ex hypothesi*, acquiring the bottle is James' real 'intermediate' aim in trying to open the door, the teleological structure of his actual or hypothetical behaviour will not correctly reflect this intermediate aim. For imagine that while James is trying to open the door, someone presents him with an alcoholic beverage—a bottle of whisky, say—that is even more effective with regard to James's overall aim of getting drunk. Then, James will take the bottle of whisky and desist from trying to open the door. So, the teleological structure (actual and hypothetical) of his behaviour does not point towards the correct intermediate aim of getting a bottle of wine, but, as one can easily see, towards the aim of obtaining the drink most effective for getting drunk (which need not be to obtain a bottle of wine). This is hardly surprising, because for James, the value of obtaining the bottle of wine depends on its conduciveness to getting drunk, and therefore, once he realizes a better way to do so, he will, if he is rational, prefer this better way.

One might object that by examining the teleological structure of James' behaviour in more detail, we might still be able to distinguish whether he has the intermediate aim of obtaining the bottle of wine, or whether his aim is simply to obtain a drink most effective for getting drunk. Distinguishing between the two cases, one might want to argue, is possible by looking at the following counterfactual conditional which will only hold of James in the first case but not in the second case: namely, that if he did not think that obtaining the bottle of wine was his best chance of getting drunk, he would not try to open the door of the fridge. Only because he has this belief, one might think, James has the intermediate aim of obtaining the bottle of wine—otherwise he would

---

[16] A different case of this kind is used by Woodfield (1976), 158, to argue that teleological structure is not sufficient for selecting the agent's aim, but that a causal role of the desire on which he acts is also required. This further conclusion is unwarranted, if the arguments which I offer here are successful.

either have another intermediate aim, such as obtaining a bottle of whisky, or simply aim at obtaining the drink most effective for getting drunk. But this is not true. James need not believe that obtaining the bottle of wine is the best, or in the circumstances the only, means of getting drunk. Obtaining a bottle of wine may just have been the first thing he thought of when thinking about how to get drunk. If it was, this will explain why he has the intermediate aim of getting a bottle of wine, but it will not change anything about the teleological structure of his behaviour pointing towards the aim of obtaining the drink that is most effective for getting drunk.

Nor will we get the correct result by examining the agent's success and failure feelings. When James obtains a bottle of whisky instead of the bottle of wine he was originally looking for, he will not be disappointed and feel that he has not got what he wanted, but will rather be over-satisfied because he has done even better than expected. For him, the value of obtaining a bottle of wine depended hierarchically on the value of his overall aim of getting drunk. This latter aim provided the 'point' of the former, and when he has reached something that is even more conducive to the latter aim, the agent will hardly feel that he has failed, but rather that he has over-achieved.

Therefore, the combination of teleological structure and feelings of success or failure will not produce the right result about the intermediate aim for which the agent really tried to open the door of the fridge, which was to obtain a bottle of wine. In order to deal with cases of this kind, we must appeal to yet a further dimension of how the agent's purpose guides the agent's activity.

When an agent acts with a certain aim, he takes this aim to make requirements on him which will structure his ensuing behaviour insofar as he allows himself to be guided by them. These requirements are normative for the agent in the sense that he assesses his own behaviour as to success or failure with regard to whether he has acted in accordance with them. We have already discussed some important aspects of this guidance with respect to the teleological structure of behaviour and the connection to the agent's success or failure feelings. Another crucial aspect of guidance expresses itself in individual or joint practical deliberation about what to do, before or during the action, and in *ex post* justifications of his actions. In practical deliberation, the purpose provides the premiss in the agent's deliberation, from which he proceeds to the conclusion that he should act in this way; and after the action it is to this aim that he appeals in justifying his action (as far as he is sincere). The first of these two aspects is especially important for us here, because the second consideration, due to the possibility of self-deceptive *ex post* rationalizations, cannot on its own provide a constitutive criterion to determine the agent's aim.

It will hardly be surprising that the course of the agent's practical deliberation is also relevant for determining his aim—and in fact, this was already implicit in our earlier characterization of reasons-explanations in Chapter 4, where we connected their rationalizing function to 'retracing' the course of the agent's deliberation. Nor does the appeal to the course of the agent's deliberation introduce a completely new or independent consideration with regard to the two factors which we have already discussed here: teleological structure and success or failure feelings.

For the agent's using a justifying premiss connected to the purpose in his deliberation to arrive at the conclusion that he should act in the way that he does is, so to speak, the 'reverse side of the coin' with regard to teleological structure and success or failure feelings, in two crucial respects. First, while success and failure feelings as well as corrective behaviour and repeated attempts embody a *simultaneous* or *retrospective* assessment of (a part of) the action as a success or a failure, use of the corresponding premiss in practical deliberation shows that the agent *prospectively* takes the purpose to provide the point of his action—the standard by which it is to be assessed. And second, in cases where the agent has explicitly thought through the steps which he takes in order to achieve his aim, the observable teleological structure will, on the observable 'outside', mirror the structure of his practical deliberation, which will provide its 'internal' counterpart. How the two structures mirror one another becomes clear when we remind ourselves of the different aspects of the teleological structure: taking the steps thought necessary to achieve the aim, repeating one's attempts, circumventing obstacles, and so on. Each of these steps could be justified in practical deliberation as a means of attaining one's aim.

The parallel between teleological structure and forms of justification in practical deliberation helps us to understand better the following points about following a standard of success which have already arisen in our discussion but have not yet been adequately explained. (1) How in multi-layered systems of aims, the higher aim provides the 'point' of the intermediate aim. This mirrors the way in which, in practical reasoning, the conclusion of a practical syllogism depends on the (major) evaluative premiss corresponding to the ultimate aim. (2) How following a 'standard of success' is truly a normative notion. In connection with the teleological structure, we have already mentioned that corrective behaviour, etc., shows that the agent, at least implicitly, assesses his behaviour for conformity to a certain standard. The very thin notion of normativity required for merely implicit assessment becomes much more substantial once we recognize that the agent himself, when his action is accompanied by practical deliberation, explicitly takes his aim to (partially) justify his behaviour, believing that pursuing this aim requires of him a certain kind of behaviour. (3) How following a standard of success is connected to a proneness to conscious self-assessments of one's behaviour as successful or not successful. This follows both from the role of success and failure feelings discussed in (c), and from the connection between following a standard of success and possibly explicit practical deliberation discussed here.

Given this connection, whether something is the aim which the agent pursues by his action also depends on whether it provides the justifying premiss from which, in his practical deliberation, he has proceeded to the conclusion that he should act in this way. The premiss correlated to the purpose which the agent uses in his practical deliberation will be a value-judgement ascribing a desirability characteristic to acting in a certain way, if our arguments in Chapter 4 are correct. (If no detailed explicit practical deliberation actually takes place, it is sufficient that the agent implicitly uses the premiss, or would use it were he to go through explicit practical reasoning.)

By taking this additional factor into account, we can deal with the cases of 'intermediate aims'. In these cases we have a multi-layered hierarchical structure of purposes, which is reflected, in the agent's practical reasoning, in series of practical syllogisms. For instance, in our original case of the agent who tries to open the door of the fridge in order to obtain a bottle of wine because he wants to get drunk, the premiss from which he has reasoned that he should open the door of the fridge is that he should obtain a bottle of wine, which was, in turn, derived from the premiss that it would be—*pro tanto*—a good idea to get drunk. Even though there might have been better ways of getting drunk than with a bottle of wine—e.g. with a bottle of whisky—the premiss from which the agent actually derived the conclusion that he should open the door of the fridge was that he should obtain a bottle of wine, not the premiss that he should obtain a bottle of whisky. Therefore, by rightly tracking the process of practical reasoning on the agent's part—insofar as this is possible—we will be able to determine on which intermediate aim he was acting.

We must, however, add a note of caution here. Very often we can only track the course of practical deliberation indirectly by deriving it from the teleological structure of the behaviour and success and failure feelings of the agent. In this case, as far as our epistemic criteria are concerned, the structure of practical reasoning cannot provide independent evidence about the agent's purpose. While this restricts the range of fruitful applicability of the epistemic criterion, it clearly does not reduce it to zero, for there remain many cases where the practical reasoning is explicit, and we can establish its course independently from establishing the teleological structure of the agent's behaviour and his success or failure feelings.

Let us take stock. We have argued that what determines what aim the agent pursues by his action is the 'standard of success' that the agent is following in his action. The epistemic criteria upon which our judgement about the agent's aim or purpose is based all pertain to establishing those facts which are constitutive for the agent's following such a standard. The relevant facts which we have been considering so far are:

(1) teleological structure of the (actual or hypothetical) behaviour;
(2) (actual and hypothetical) success and failure feelings;
(3) (actually or hypothetically) making use of the aim as a premiss in the practical deliberation leading to the action

(where all three factors are determined on the basis of the circumstances as perceived or believed to obtain by the agent).

So, what an agent takes as the 'standard of success' of his action depends roughly on the obtaining of the welter of actual and counterfactual truths satisfying criteria (1), (2), and (3). That there are three different criteria raises the question of how they are interrelated, and whether all of them must be satisfied in each case. In the paradigm case of intentional action there will be facts satisfying all three criteria—that is, the agent will display teleological behaviour, success and failure feelings, and practical deliberation satisfying criteria (1), (2), and (3), and all these facts will point towards the same aim of the agent. From what we have said so far, this is hardly surprising, because (1) and (2) embody the agent's simultaneous or retrospective assessment of his behaviour as success or failure, while (3) embodies his prospective assessment—and in the normal case, these assessments go together.

But not in every case will there be facts pertaining to all three criteria. Consider cases where the agent's intention is unconscious. Here, the agent may lack success or failure feelings, and it may not be true that he would have such feelings if he succeeded or failed in achieving his aim. Also, he may not go through explicit deliberation, and it might even be the case that were he to go through such deliberation he would be at a loss to say from which justifying premiss he is to proceed in deciding what to do, because he is himself unaware of, or uncertain about, his aim. What is present in such cases is only the (actual or hypothetical) teleological structure of the agent's behaviour.

This suggests that of the three criteria discussed, criterion (1) plays a special role compared with criteria (2) and (3), because there must always be some (actual or hypothetical) teleological structure of the agent's behaviour which is relevant to determining the agent's aim, while the same point does not hold with respect to (2) and (3). Of course, as we have seen, the aim suggested by the teleological structure of behaviour can be 'corrected' by criteria (2) and (3), as in cases (c) and (d) discussed above; and so the teleological structure need not always be one pointing to the agent's aim. But when there are no facts pertaining to (2) and (3)—as can be the case for some unconscious intentions—the agent's aim is solely determined by criterion (1). The same point does not hold vice versa. If there is no (actual or hypothetical) teleological structure whatsoever, the agent does not act in order to attain an aim, even though he may, for instance, have a success feeling when he reaches this alleged aim. Therefore, at least as far as our ascription of an aim is concerned, (1) provides something like a defeasible criterion, which determines the agent's aim in the absence of other factors, but which can be 'corrected' in the described ways by (2) and (3), in the group of cases discussed in (c) and (d).

Though (1), (2), and (3) are the main facts that we try to establish, in our everyday practice, when trying to decide which aim an agent was pursuing, I do not want to claim that they constitute an exhaustive list of all relevant facts which we take into account; nor do I believe that such an exhaustive list can be offered. But this impossibility does not present a problem for the proposed explanation of 'acting with an aim' as 'taking something as the standard of success for one's action', as long as we can plausibly assume that all the other criteria relevant for determining the agent's aim also pertain to following a standard of success.

If we cannot offer an exhaustive list, this shows only that the notion of 'following a standard of success' cannot be reductively analysed, in terms of necessary and sufficient conditions, by a combination of categorical statements and counterfactual conditionals.

But a truly reductive account of 'following a standard of success' cannot, in any case, plausibly be expected. This notion is an essentially normative notion—if only because normative considerations are relevant for determining which conditionals are to be included in the welter of conditionals connected to (1), (2), and (3); for example, for deciding what behaviour is to count as 'corrective'. Therefore, the notion cannot plausibly be analysed in purely non-normative terms, while any analysis in normative terms is ultimately bound to be circular. This is the same as with the Wittgensteinian notion of rule-following—and, as I will argue in the next section, taking something as one's standard of success is, in important respects, very similar to rule-following, understood in this way.

Before we can address this issue, however, we must return to the list of criteria determining the motivating reason. Following our discussion in Section 10.3, the question arises about what role the proposed criteria we have discussed there—the agent's self-ascription, and the 'best fit' into the pattern of the agent's overall life-story—play for deciding the question for which reason the agent has acted. They obviously provide important hints upon which we rely, in everyday life, to answer this question, but are they also 'constitutive' criteria like (1), (2), and (3)?

We have already seen why it would be problematic to treat them thus. With regard to self-ascriptions the problem is, on the one hand, that these ascriptions would have to be sincere and that this presupposes something about which the agent is sincere; on the other hand, there is the problem of possible self-deception. The difficulty with according constitutive force to the 'best fit' consideration is that agents can, on occasion, radically change their behaviour or act out of character. So we can hardly regard these two considerations as providing constitutive criteria—but how can we then explain why they possess special evidential weight?

Our proposed account offers an answer to this question. The special role of the agent's own avowals about his intentions is explained by the fact that following a standard of success involves—at least in normal cases—that the agent knows which standard he is following. Leaving cases of unconscious intentions aside, at least implicit knowledge of this standard is required for several of the constitutive conditions of acting with a purpose that we have discussed. For example, with regard to condition (1), when an agent ceases his attempts after reaching his aim, he normally does this because he knows that he has got what he wanted, which usually requires that he knows what this is; and with regard to condition (3), when actual practical deliberation has taken place, the agent can be expected to know which premisses he has used in arriving at his conclusions. But the special authority of avowals has its limits; for the knowledge may be only implicit, and may not always reach the conscious level, especially for quasi-mechanical activities which the agent has thoroughly internalized.

The importance of fitting the agent's action into an overall pattern of a consistent 'life-story' stems from the following two facts. First, the patterns of intentional actions with their characteristic structure do not stand in isolation, but are in turn embedded into even larger structures which can cover considerable life-spans of the agent. For example, when an agent pursues a large overall project—such as an expedition to the

North Pole, which occupies years of his life—his activities during this period will be structured by this overall project. Many of these activities will be embedded in a multi-layered system of ends, as described earlier, and therefore their specific aims will have to be assessed on the background of this overall system.

Second, knowledge of the general pattern of the agent's behaviour is often the grounds on which we assess the truth of the counterfactual conditionals connected with criteria (1), (2), and (3), when we either have no other evidence concerning the matter, or we think it unnecessary to look for such evidence. Imagine, for example, that an agent is trying to open the fridge, but fails, and we know that on all the prior occasions when he has gone to the fridge he has either taken out a bottle of wine or, when there has been no wine inside the fridge, has started to look elsewhere for a bottle of wine. In this case we will assume that, on this occasion, the counterfactual conditionals required for the satisfaction of (1) with regard to teleological behaviour aimed at obtaining wine are true of the agent. So, 'fit' of a reason within the agent's overall life-story is indeed connected to important evidence about the fulfilment of the constitutive criteria (1), (2), and (3). But the evidence which this 'fit' provides is only indirect, and loses its importance once we can, in this particular case, establish by more direct means whether criteria (1), (2), and (3) are fulfilled. Therefore, we cannot regard 'fit' within the agent's overall story as a constitutive criterion for determining the agent's motivating reason.

To conclude this sub-section, I want to turn to the question of how the account of acting with an aim, in terms of following a standard of success, developed so far, can be extended to other cases of acting for a reason. Acting with a certain purpose can be generally analysed along the lines proposed here, but performing an action without pursuing a further aim lying beyond it seems to pose a problem, because here we cannot directly apply the model of pursuing an aim that we have developed.

Nevertheless, I believe that even these cases can be explained on the 'following a standard' model—though in many cases, especially when actions are performed for moral reasons, it will be more appropriate to speak of a 'standard of correctness' rather than 'of success'. For instance, when James visits his sick aunt because he believes he has a moral duty to do so, doing his duty can hardly be considered as an aim which James pursues. But it still provides a standard with which James compares his behaviour for conformity, so that when his actions in his own perception fail to match the standard, he will correct them. For instance, when he has been told that his aunt will not survive his visit and he believes it to be morally more important to save her life than to visit her, he will cancel his planned visit. And obviously, there is also a form of success or failure feeling, which in the moral case is roughly a good or bad conscience. As the notion of following a 'standard of correctness' captures these features, without suggesting that there is an aim which the agent pursues, we can adequately describe acting for moral reasons by this notion.

For other cases of intentional actions performed without further aims, we can use the same basic strategy—although speaking of a 'standard of correctness' in cases where the agent does not act for moral reasons might give the false impression that the agent must believe his action to be right or justified overall. This is obviously not required, for agents can intentionally do things they know to be wrong. But as long as we keep in mind that the relevant sense of 'following a standard' is just the one we have explained for the case of 'following a standard of success', which does not include any judgement on the agent's part that his action is best overall, there will be no harm in describing these cases as instances of 'following a standard of correctness' which is provided by the reason for which one acts.[17]

11.1.2. *Acting for a reason, rule-following, and (once again) the apparent need for a causal connection*

So far I have tried to show that what determines an agent's reason for acting is whether he is following a standard of success provided by this reason. However, even if one concedes this point, one might still object that it is not really the agent's following a standard of success which makes it true that he acts for this reason. For, one might argue, the agent's following such a standard is in turn reducible to other facts, which will ultimately provide the 'truth-makers' for reasons-explanations. Here I want to address these worries about reducibility by relating the notion of following a standard to a Wittgensteinian, non-causalist notion of rule-following. Afterwards, I will turn to the question of whether the account which I have been developing—even if no reduction is possible—may at least presuppose an event-causal connection between desire and action.

As I have already stated, I take the notion of 'following a standard of success' to be an irreducibly normative notion that cannot be reductively analysed by the welter of categorical statements and counterfactual conditionals which are connected to the satisfaction of criteria (1), (2), and (3). This is the same as in the case of rule-following on the Wittgensteinian understanding, which also cannot be completely analysed in non-normative terms. In particular, as Wittgenstein has shown, rule-following cannot be analysed in terms of the possession of an inner 'mental picture' of what one must do,[18] but always presupposes a certain practice of application. *Pari passu*, we can say that following a standard of success cannot simply be analysed in terms of the agent's having a mental state with a representation of the standard which then causes his actions—and this means that it cannot be analysed in the way in which causalists traditionally want to analyse acting for a reason.

As an intrinsically normative activity, following a standard of success shares not only this feature of rule-following, but there are several other characteristics that these phenomena have in common. Both phenomena imply at least a weak form of normativity,

---

[17] There is a certain variety in the ways in which a motivating reason can provide the standard which the agent is following in his action. This variety corresponds to the different kinds of reasons-explanations of action: for example, 'in-response-to', 'in-conformity-to', and 'teleological reasons'; cf. Stoutland (2001), 84.

[18] Cf. Wittgenstein, *Philosophical Investigations*, §§ 138 ff.

involving the possibility of conformity, mistakes, and correction, and of a certain importance or weight being attributed to conformity. Furthermore, the criteria for following a standard of success and rule-following are to a large extent the same—as is shown by a brief comparison of the criteria for following an aim, which we have just elaborated, and the criteria—proposed by Wittgenstein in *Philosophical Investigations*, § 54—for determining by which rules a game is played. Rule-following involves the same teleological patterns of behaviour, failure and success behaviour, and appeal to the rule in determining what to do.

These shared characteristics provide some grounds for considering following a standard of success—and therefore, acting for a reason—as a minimal form of rule-following. This seems especially tempting when we have in mind the 'minimal' form of rule-following which Wittgenstein uses in some places of the *Philosophical Investigations*.[19] The main obstacle to regarding acting for reasons *per se* as a form of rule-following proper is, I think, the kind of inherent generality of rules, which following a standard of success lacks.[20] Nothing can be a rule unless, in principle, it can be applied on a plurality of different occasions by different persons. This is what, we might say, distinguishes rules from specific commands to particular addressees. The standard of success connected with a purpose, however, lacks this characteristic because it may be 'too particularist' or a 'one-time affair'. Nothing need follow about what I or someone else should do on any other occasion when I, for instance, act for a completely inconsequential aim which I have only on one particular occasion—for example, when I try to catch a fly out of boredom.[21] Of course, some purposes *may* involve general standards such as a purpose to live up to an ideal, but this is not necessary.

While it is true that standards of success may be 'too particularist' for following such a standard to count as rule-following, we should note that the difference here is one of degree, rather than categorical. For even the standard of success one is following in acting for a reason is applicable to a plurality of occasions, though its scope may be very restricted. The standard is, in principle, repeatedly applicable not only interpersonally, because other persons may share the agent's aim and pursue it jointly with him, but also in the case of individual action. For it is in principle possible, even for trivial aims, that I fail to obtain what I want, despite repeated attempts, and every new attempt is a new case of applying the same standard, as long as I am still pursuing the aim. This implicit generality of the standard becomes the more recognizable, the more extensive the project of pursuing the aim is—that is, if it includes either a series of sub-steps to be

---

[19] For example, Wittgenstein, *Philosophical Investigations*, § 83, where the people playing with the ball and 'making up the rules as they go along' are not following rules in a strict sense.

[20] Other characteristics which have been proposed for rules, and which standards of success do not seem to generally possess, are the involvement of rule-expressions and second-order exclusionary reasons not to act on countervailing reasons to behave differently; cf. Raz (1975), 141.

[21] *Pace* Stoutland (2007), 90 f., who thinks that the reason on which the agent acts is determined by the maxim of his action. Maxims—at least on the Kantian version which Stoutland uses—are inherently general, at least for the person herself—cf. Kant, *Critique of Practical Reason*, AA 35—and so Stoutland's solution would exclude 'one-time affair' reasons.

performed one after the other, or the regularly repeated performance of one kind of action. For example, consider an aim such as keeping one's teeth free from caries, which (presumably) requires that one brushes one's teeth every evening. Here, pursuing the aim will include that one 'makes it a rule for himself' to brush one's teeth every evening (unless this would be bad for one's teeth).

Rule-following therefore remains a very fruitful model of comparison for acting for a reason, which highlights the inherent normativity of the latter. Nevertheless, describing acting for a reason as being, *per se*, a case of rule-following proper would still be misleading, because it would make it appear as if by acting for a reason we necessarily committed ourselves to a general rule.

To conclude our discussion of agency for reasons, we have to address the question of how the account that I have proposed—acting for a reason as following a standard of success—relates to causalist accounts of intentional agency. As I have already stated, I think that the notion of following a standard of success contains an irreducibly normative residue, and that consequently it cannot be reduced to purely non-normative facts. But a causalist might accept this non-reducibility claim and still argue that acting for reason A at least presupposes, as a necessary condition, a causal connection between some mental state suitably connected to A and the action. If this claim were true, this would not rehabilitate Davidson's answer to his own challenge, for we have seen in Section 10.2 that such a causal link cannot be the essential factor which distinguishes the motivating reason from other reasons which the agent had, but on which he did not act. However, it would vindicate the claim that every intentional action presupposes some mental event—presumably an 'onslaught' of a desire—as its cause. As I have argued in Section 10.1, I do not think that this claim is plausible. Therefore, I had better show that my account of acting for a reason does not itself introduce such an event-causal connection.

To begin with, clearly our explanation of the different components of the notion of 'following a standard' has not explicitly referred to the causal etiology of the action in terms of mental antecedents. But does our account implicitly rely on causal mechanisms? Of course, several causal mechanisms—in particular, in the agent's nervous system—must function properly for the agent to be able to follow a standard of success. But in giving an explanation of his behaviour in terms of the standard he was following, we are not talking about these causal mechanisms. We are not concerned with how the agent's bodily motions are produced by his nervous mechanism, but with the teleological pattern of his behaviour, its connection to the agent's deliberation, success and failure behaviour, and so on. We are, so to speak, on a different level of explanation—and the causalist claim about a necessary event-causal connection is only interesting, or controversial, if this alleged causal connection somehow 'shows up' on the level of reasons-explanations.

However, one might argue that my account introduces just such an event-causal connection on the level of reasons-explanations, in one of the following two ways. First, by its appeal to hypothetical behaviour, hypothetical feelings of success or failure and hypothetical deliberation in criteria (1), (2), and (3). The welter of counterfactuals required for the satisfaction of the criteria, one might claim, will need a truth-maker, and the truth-maker can only be a causal connection between a mental state of the agent and his action (or the whole complex consisting of action, success and failure feeling, and deliberation).

But such an argument would not be successful. Though it is true that causal statements support counterfactual conditionals, they do not support conditionals of the required kind: 'X caused my raising my hand' supports 'without X I would not have raised my hand'. Although the truth of this counterfactual conditional (substituting 'desire to Y' for 'X') is also required for acting for a reason, the counterfactual conditionals needed for satisfaction of criteria (1), (2), and (3) are, for the most part, quite different. They are, for instance, 'if, according to the agent's beliefs, Y-ing had been necessary for A-ing, and not X-ing, he would have Y-ed instead of X-ed'. Counterfactuals of this kind are not supported by the statement 'the desire to A caused the X-ing'.[22]

One might object that while one-track event-causation may fail to do the trick, sustaining causation of the action by a desire will yield the needed counterfactuals. Perhaps so—but on what grounds should we assume that a certain mental state, such as a desire, will be the sustaining cause of the action? Why should we believe that for the whole welter of counterfactuals and of actual truths satisfying criteria (1), (2), and (3) there must be one mental state whose causal impact is their common truth-maker and which can be identified as this desire?

There is an obvious alternative candidate for the truth-maker of the counterfactual conditionals in question: the agent's possession of a complex disposition or tendency to behave in the way described by criteria (1), (2), and (3). This complex tendency will be possessed by the agent as long as he acts for the motivating reason in question, and an action which he performs for this reason will itself be a manifestation of this tendency. As we have argued at length in Chapter 7, manifestations of tendencies are not reducible to event-causation.[23] Of course, this does not exclude that such manifestations can *also* involve event-causal processes; consider the complicated event-causal process which evolves when a piece of sugar dissolves in water. But this possibility by itself does not help the causalist here, given the dialectical position, for he would still have to show that the manifestation *must* include an event-causal link of the kind that he envisages—event-causation by a desire. His main argument for accepting this link has been Davidson's challenge, and as a manifestation account allows us to answer Davidson's challenge without positing such a link, his central argument for his key claim no longer works.

---

[22] Cf. Sehon (2005), 159.
[23] Nor are the manifestations caused by the tendencies in question; for the arguments that we have presented in Section 8.1.2, to show that active powers are not causes of their manifestations, apply, as one can easily see, to any other power as well.

So, there is no need to assume that desires must be (sustaining) causes of actions motivated by these desires. But, one might argue, my account of acting for a reason relies on event-causal links in a second and quite different way—particularly if we follow the suggestion in the last paragraph to understand intentional actions as manifestations of complex tendencies. The tendencies in question are, *inter alia*, tendencies to react in certain ways to external or internal situations, and when the intentional action in question is the manifestation of such a tendency, the situation to which the agent has reacted can be seen as the event-cause of the action. In this case, it may be argued, the situation can be identified as the 'onslaught' of the agent's desire, which will suffice to vindicate the causalist claim that the action is, loosely speaking, caused by the desire on which the agent acts.

There is much to be said in response to this proposal, and I will focus only on what I consider to be its central difficulty. In cases where we react to situations, the relevant event-causes will primarily be reasons in the 'situation' sense rather than the 'purpose' sense, taking up the distinction noted at the beginning of Chapter 10. As stated there, I have no quarrel with the claim that reasons in the 'situation' sense are event-causes of actions. Maybe they are even event-causes in all cases of intentional actions. But, it is crucial to notice, this does not directly yield the causalist claim—for remember that this was a claim about reasons in the 'purpose' sense, and included that there must be a *mental* event which causes the action. The situation to which one reacts, however, need not be a mental event, but can also be something external, such as another person waving on the other side of the street. Causalists will probably reply that even in this case the agent will have to be aware of this situation, and his noticing the situation or becoming aware of it will provide the mental event we are seeking; in fact, 'noticing events' of this kind seem to be one of the items that Davidson had in mind when talking about 'onslaughts' of desires.[24]

However, even an appeal to 'noticing events' will not get the causalist what he wants. The main problem is that even when we suppose there must always be a separate 'noticing event', this event cannot always plausibly figure as an 'onslaught' of the motivating desire. The relevant noticing events need not be directly tied to any desires, but can be quite independent from them, in the following two respects. First, noticing the situation, to which I later respond by doing something, does not presuppose that I already have a desire to which noticing this situation is pertinent. For example, when I notice that you are waving at me from across the street, I may not have a desire to meet you—though I may acquire the desire afterwards, when I begin to think about your waving at me and about what I should do in response. Second, as noted at the beginning of Chapter 10, there is no one-to-one correlation between reasons in the 'situation' sense and reasons in the 'purpose' or 'desire' sense, and therefore there is no one-to-one correlation between reasons in the latter sense and

---

[24] Cf. Davidson (1963), 12 f.

noticing a situation. Noticing a situation to which one reacts in one's action is compatible with many different purposes one may have in acting. (Remember that when James crosses the street in response to John's waving at him, he may have either the purpose of meeting John or of visiting the shop). This point obviously also holds when the relevant desires are only acquired after the noticing event. So, a noticing event can occur before the agent has the desire on which he later acts, and need not determine which desire he will acquire or on which desire he will act. But when the noticing event is independent of the motivating desire in these two respects, there seems to be no point whatsoever in calling it the desire's 'onslaught', and this undermines the general idea that when the noticing event causes the action, we can, *ipso facto*, qualify the desire as the action's cause in a loose sense. So, even if we accept that intentional actions are always caused by some reason in the 'situation' sense, this does not commit us to the causalist claim that it must also be caused by some reason in the 'purpose' or 'desire' sense.

For these reasons, the proposed account of acting for a reason in terms of following a standard of success does not even implicitly commit to us to an event-causal link between the motivating desire and the action. However, the causalist might still have one lingering worry. Perhaps assuming an event-causal link of the kind envisaged is not required for answering the *constitutive* question, of what makes it the case that the agent acted for this reason rather than for another reason. But is there not the further question of *why* the agent acted for this reason rather than for the other reason, which we can answer only by positing an event-causal link of the proposed kind?

I agree that this further question is important for most cases from which Davidson's challenge acquires its force, because there are alternative desires on which the agent might have acted. It is far from clear, however, why the answer to this new question must be to posit a causal link of the proposed kind. There are obvious alternatives to this—for example, appealing to the agent's character traits—which manifest themselves in his assigning more weight to one consideration than the other.[25] But whatever the correct answer to the causalist's further query is going to look like, it is clear that the causalist will need some further argument for his conclusion that an event-causal link is required, because our answer to Davidson's challenge does not by itself imply that the correct answer to the new question must be the causalist's answer. So, even with regard to the causalist's further question, our account of what it is to act for a reason does not commit us to an event-causal link between motivating desire and action.

I therefore conclude that the account of acting for a reason defended here does not presuppose that for all intentional actions there is an event-causal link between a pro-attitude and the action. Motivating reasons are neither event-causes themselves, nor must they necessarily be related to such causes. If anything, reasons should be seen,

---

[25] For an explanation in terms of character traits, see Schueler (2003), sec. 3.2.

in Aristotle's terminology, not only as 'final' but also 'formal' causes, because they provide actions with their 'form'[26] or internal structure.

11.2. Putting it all together

We now have at hand all the different elements required for an account of human agency which integrates all the three basic commitments constitutive of our self-understanding as human agents. All that now needs to be done is to put these parts together and show how they are interrelated.

Before doing so, let us briefly reiterate, on the one hand, which truths either included in or following from the three basic commitments must be accommodated by our account, and on the other hand, which elements for an account of human agency we have actually assembled. The truths about agency which must be accommodated are as follows.

(1) Human actions are displays of human activity (Thesis 1).
(2) Human actions are part of the 'natural order' (Thesis 2). From this general claim we can plausibly derive two more particular requirements:
  (2a) Human activity must be something that can occur in the natural order (from (1)).
  (2b) Given the findings of biology and neurophysiology, agential activity cannot be completely independent of neurophysiological and biological processes.
(3) Intentional actions are amenable to reasons-explanations (Thesis 3). As our considerations in Section 1.1 have shown, there are two particular claims contained in (3):
  (3a) Reasons-explanations are rationalizations (that is the distinguishing characteristic which makes them *reasons*-explanations).
  (3b) Reasons-explanations are genuine explanations—not *mere* rationalizations.

The elements which we have for an account of human agency are the following:

(1★) Actions involve agent-causings (Chapter 8).
(1★★) The active powers of human persons which are manifested in action are emergent systemic properties—that is, they are ascribable only to the agent himself and not to his parts, and are not reducible to microproperties; they are not merely epiphenomenal properties (Chapter 9).
(2★) Agent-causation is a type of substance-causation, understood as the manifestation of an active power; on any plausible account of the 'natural order',

---

[26] Cf. Thomas Aquinas, *Summa Theologiae*, I.II., 9, 1. Also, Buchheim (2006), 132 ff., exploits the idea that reasons are connected to 'forms' of action.

(2★★) When an agent's active power is manifested, the obtaining of certain neurophysiological processes in the agent's organism is a necessary condition for this manifestation (Section 9.3.2).

(3★) When an agent acts for a reason, he follows a standard of success or correctness provided by this reason (Section 11.1).

When we begin to compare these different elements, we easily see that (1) can be accounted for by (1★) and (1★★), while (2), (2a), and (2b) are accounted for by (2★) and (2★★).

The agent-causal role of the agent guarantees a genuinely active role of the agent himself in the action, given that the causal powers in whose manifestation the action consists must be ascribed to the agent himself and possess genuine causal relevance. At the same time, there is no problem in fitting agential activity, explained as the manifestation of active powers of the agent, into the 'natural order', once an implausible and overly impoverished picture of nature—the Humean event-causalist view of nature—has been abandoned. Active powers form a sub-group of powers; and powers, on any plausible account of nature that respects our commitment to power-explanations, will have to be admitted as genuine properties which are not reducible to categorical properties (the main overall result of Chapter 8). Also, even though (1★★) prevents a reduction of the agent's active powers to his microproperties, (2★★) guarantees that these powers remain anchored in neurophysiological and biological processes, in accordance with both the findings and the commitments of the biological sciences.

But what about the relation between (3), (3a), and (3b) on the one hand, and (3★) on the other? It is a chief merit of the account of acting for a reason in terms of following a standard of success that it is able to explain how (3a) and (3b) are interrelated, and how reasons-explanations can play both those roles.

When we understand acting for a reason as following a standard of success as presented in Section 11.1, it must be the function of reasons-explanations to locate the action within the structure constituted by the agent's behaviour, emotional responses, thoughts, and practical reasoning which is constitutive for following the relevant standard of success. This structure is essentially one within which it is possible to assess behaviour as successful/correct or unsuccessful/incorrect, and behaviour can be justified or criticized according to whether or not it is in accord with the standard which one is following. (For convenience, I will call a structure of this kind a 'normative practice'.) As we saw in Section 11.1, in the paradigm case of intentional agency, the agent consciously locates himself within this practice by justifying or criticizing his behaviour accordingly in his practical deliberation. This feature of potential assessment accounts for the rationalizing function of reasons-explanations; for within such a normative practice, this assessment can have genuine justifying force. Once I show that what I did was done in order to reach the aim I was pursuing, I have not only explained what I have done, but also (partly) justified it.[27] The original situation, from which the rationalizing function of reasons-explanations derives, is the situation in which two persons both take part in the same normative practice—which means, with regard to our specific case, that they both pursue the same aim.

Of course, the rationalizing force that reasons-explanations generally possess is much weaker than the truly justifying force which reasons-explanations have in this kind of situation; for the author of the reasons-explanation, or his interlocutors, need not share the agent's aim, and so will not be participating in the same normative practice. But even when the author does not actually partake in the normative practice, he still knows what it is like to be engaged in such a practice, and how, within these practices, actions can be justified. Because he could in principle imagine himself taking part in the normative practice in which the agent is engaged, and justifying his action in the way that the agent is doing now, finding out the standard which the agent is following enables him to see some point in the agent's behaviour. He can understand that as long as one considers only the framework of this particular normative practice, the agent is (partly) justified in doing what he does, although from a more encompassing perspective this may not be the case. (I will call both the truly justifying force that reasons-explanations have within the normative practice, and the derived rationalizing force they have without, the 'rationalizing-justificatory function of reasons-explanations'.)

At the same time, the fact that reasons-explanations locate the agent's action within a structure of the described kind ensures that they are not *mere* rationalizations of behaviour; for it implies that by giving a reasons-explanation, the speaker commits himself to the claim that there is a corresponding structure. This claim can be false even if the speaker has succeeded in seeing some point in the agent's behaviour by which he can make sense of it; for the speaker may not have observed the whole of the relevant structure, and from the behaviour he has observed, may have falsely conjectured as to what the rest of the structure is like, because the particular item of behaviour he has observed could be embedded equally well in different structures. Then, his original reasons-explanation can be falsified by further evidence about what the structure is really like. Alternatively, the speaker may have made false assumptions about the agent's relevant hypothetical behaviour, which might also have led him to a false judgement about the structure into which the observed behaviour was to be embedded.

The intrinsic connection between the structural and the normative aspect of following a standard of success explains the simultaneously rationalizing-justificatory and explanatory function of reasons-explanations. Consider a reasons-explanation of one particular attempt to obtain F by doing G. The rationalizing-justificatory function of this reasons-explanation stems from presenting the attempt of G-ing as being set within a normative practice inside which it can be justified as an instance of following the

---

[27] Even within this practice I may fail to justify my behaviour completely, if, for instance, I have chosen a very bad and inefficient way of achieving my aim.

standard of success connected to the agent's aim of obtaining F. The explanatory function is quite similar to the function of explanations in terms of dispositions or tendencies. A certain item of behaviour is explained as the manifestation of one of the dispositions connected with the welter of material and counterfactual conditionals which are responsible for the characteristic structure of intentional agency. Since this characteristic structure is constitutive for following a standard of success, seeing what the structure is like is inseparably connected to seeing the action as set within this kind of normative practice, and thus to seeing a point of the action. For this reason, the explanatory value is inseparably tied to the rationalizing-justificatory function, and vice versa; and we can truly say that reasons-explanations explain actions by making them rationally intelligible.

Well, not quite 'inseparably'. For the connection between rationalization and explanation can break down for certain observers who adopt a purely 'apersonal' or 'objective' stance towards the agent's behaviour. As previously stated, the rationalizing-justificatory function of the explanation presupposes that the observer is able to imagine that he is engaged in the same normative practice as the agent is engaged in at the moment. On certain occasions, however, this may either be impossible for the observer, or he may not care to do so. The agent's purpose may be too shocking or alien to be truly intelligible to him; for example, a person who observes the purposeful actions of a mad and particularly brutal killer may just be unable to imagine how he could himself ever pursue such an aim. Alternatively, the observer may be a highly manipulative person who does not see other people as pursuing 'a good', but instead as 'driven' by their desires, character traits, and stimuli. Such a person does not consider the behaviour of other persons as a response to perceived reasons, nor something for which the question of justification—at least in a limited framework—would arise. Instead, he regards it like a 'mechanism' which can be 'steered' by applying the right kind of stimuli.

In both cases, the observer will ignore the rationalizing aspect of reasons-explanations, and rely only on the structure of the agent's behaviour in order to predict his behaviour or to influence it. The resulting kind of explanation will then, in principle, be no different from ordinary disposition or tendency explanations of the behaviour of inanimate substances or animals; and the stance adopted with regard to these agents will not, in principle, be different from the stance adopted vis-à-vis inanimate substances or animals. They will be seen either as a potential source of danger, such as an unstable explosive, or as something to be manipulated, such as the objects with which the scientist experiments in the laboratory.

We can thus distinguish two different stances which we can adopt in explaining human actions:[28] a 'personal' stance, by which explaining the agent's behaviour is intrinsically connected to a rationalizing and (partly) justifying enterprise, and an

---

[28] This distinction is different, one should note, from the one famously drawn by Strawson in his (1962) between personal and objective attitudes.

'objective' or 'apersonal' stance, where we are concerned only with the structure of the agent's behaviour which is connected with his acting for a reason, and do not care about 'understanding' his action as performed for a perceived good. In a clear sense, the second stance is a degenerate form of the first stance, and its existence is parasitic on the existence of the first stance—for the structure and the normative practice of following a standard of success are inherently related, and the second stance severs this connection.

Therefore, by adopting the account presented in Section 11.1, of acting for reasons, we can explain how, in the normal case, reasons-explanations have both a rationalizing and an explanatory function, thereby doing justice to both (3a) and (3b). But does this account of acting for reasons also fit within the account of agency provided by (1★) to (2★★)? In particular, is this account of acting for reasons compatible with the view of actions as agent-causings?

That it is so compatible follows straightforwardly from the inherent connection between following a standard of success and its constituent structure. The relevant structure in one's behaviour is, at least partly, a structure among the manifestations of one's active powers. For as we have seen, acting for a reason depends both on how one does behave in the action-situation and how one would react in a range of counterfactual situations, and these reactions are generally not mere reflexes, but actions. (As the structure also involves emotions and thoughts, however, the manifestations of powers other than the agent's active powers are also involved.) Agency for reasons thus 'structures'—for the limited time where the agent is being guided by a particular reason—the manifestations of certain active powers, connecting them to certain situations. Consequently, having an aim or a motivating reason involves a complex power to act in certain ways in specific situations. This power is not a disposition, but only a tendency, because one need not always show the specified reactions in order to count as acting for a reason.

It is important to see that this power is not itself a power for physical change, nor is it among the active powers of human beings which circumscribe the range of what the agent can bring about. What the agent can do in different situations depends only on his pre-existing abilities to act. The agent's having an aim does not add anything to those powers, nor could it 'take over' from an ability to act if this ability were to be lost. Therefore, any manifestation of the specific power involved in acting for a reason must, at the same time, also involve a manifestation of another power of the agent—especially an ability to act.

Construing the relationship between agency for reasons and agent-causation in this way shows how both can be combined within a unified account of agency. On the 'structuring' model of agency for reasons, reasons-explanations will not be in conflict with agent-causal statements, but, in an obvious way, will supplement them while depending on them for their application, because the powers relevant for agency for reasons in particular are 'superimposed' on the pre-existing active powers of the agent. Our account also evades the threat of explanatory overdetermination between neurophysiological explanations and reasons-explanations. For, as we saw in Chapter 9, this problem can be averted with regard to the relation between agent-causation and neurophysiological processes. Since reasons-explanations appear on the same explanatory level as, and in combination with, agent-causal explanations, there is no reason to assume that the same solution—construing neurophysiological processes as necessary conditions for agency for reasons—could not be applied to them as well.

We can thus conclude that the model of acting for reasons that we have defended successfully completes our unified account of human agency, and shows how the apparent tensions between agency for reasons, agential control, and the place of human actions in the 'natural order' can be satisfactorily dissolved. To conclude our account, there is only one final task to fulfil, which, in Section 2.2, I promised to eventually address.

From Section 2.2. onwards we explicitly restricted our examination to performances in order to bring key issues in the dispute between intentionalism, agent-causalism, and event-causalism into better focus. This restriction means that although we have now successfully developed an account of the nature of human agency in performances, we do not yet know how this account relates to other actions. What, we may ask, makes them actions as well, though they do not involve agent-causation?

The answer is as follows. What connects these other actions to performances and makes them actions is that they too can be performed intentionally. At first glance this may appear circular—but really, it is not. On the account of acting for reasons that I have defended, this implies a certain kind of integration of the item in question into the structure of behaviour, concomitant feelings, and thoughts, which is constitutive for following a standard of success. This requirement is substantially stronger than the condition that the agent must have a reason for the item in question, which would also hold in the case of many desires and beliefs; in addition there must be the described teleological structure as well as the connection to 'success and behaviour feelings' and practical deliberation. When something fulfils this additional requirement it is sufficiently similar to the standard case of agency, which involves agent-causation, to also qualify it as an action.

If this is correct, it is only further proof of the explanatory resources of the proposed combination of the agent-causal approach with an account of agency for reasons in terms of following a standard of success. For by providing solutions to the apparent tensions between the three basic commitments involved in our self-understanding as human agents—to agential activity, the place of human actions in the 'natural order', and to reasons-explanations—this combination has answered the problem of human agency and provided the basis for a successful account of human agency, which does full justice to all three of these commitments.

References

Adams, F. and Mele, A. (1989). 'The Role of Intention in Intentional Action', *Canadian Journal of Philosophy*, 19: 511 ff.
Alston, William (1986). 'An Action-Plan Interpretation of Purposive Explanations of Actions', *Theory and Decision*, 20: 275 ff.
Alvarez, Maria (2001). 'Letting Happen, Omissions, and Causation', *Grazer Philosophische Studien*, 61: 63 ff.
——(2009). 'How Many Kinds of Reasons?', *Philosophical Explorations*, 12(2): 181 ff.
——and Hyman, John (1998). 'Agents and their Actions', *Philosophy*, 73: 219 ff.
Ammereller, Erich (2005). 'Die Gründe des Handelnden', in E. Ammereller and W. Vossenkuhl (eds.), *Rationale Motivation*. Paderborn: Mentis.
Anscombe, Elizabeth (1957). *Intention*. First edn. Oxford: Blackwell.
——(1971). 'Causality and Determination', reprinted in E. Sosa and M. Tooley (eds.) *Causation*. Oxford: Oxford University Press, 1993.
Aristotle (1995). *Physik, Philosophische Schriften Band 6*, transl. and ed. H. G. Zekl. Hamburg: Meiner.
——(2002). *Nicomachean Ethics*, transl. and ed. C. Rowe and S. Broadie. Oxford: Oxford University Press.
——(2003). *Metaphysik*, transl. and ed. H. G. Zekl. Würzburg: Königshausen & Neumann.
Armstrong, David (1968). *A Materialist Theory of the Mind*. London: Routledge.
——(1997). *A World of States of Affairs*. Cambridge: Cambridge University Press.
Aronson, J. (1971). 'On the Grammar of "Cause"', *Synthese*, 22: 414 ff.
Audi, Robert (1986). 'Acting for Reasons', reprinted in A. Mele (ed.), *The Philosophy of Action*. Oxford: Oxford University Press, 1997.
——(1989). *Practical Reasoning*. London: Routledge.
Ayer, Alfred (1973). *The Central Questions of Philosophy*. London: Weidenfeld.
Bach, Kent (1978). 'A Representational Theory of Action', *Philosophical Studies*, 34: 361 ff.
——(1980). 'Actions are Not Events', *Mind*, 89: 114 ff.
Baker, Lynn R. (1993). 'Metaphysics and Mental Causation', in J. Heil and A. Mele (eds.), *Mental Causation*. Oxford: Oxford University Press.
——(1995). *Explaining Attitudes*. Cambridge: Cambridge University Press.
Bennett, Daniel (1965). 'Action, Reason, and Purpose', *Journal of Philosophy*, 62: 85 ff.
Bennett, M. R. and Hacker, Peter M. (2003). *Philosophical Foundations of Neuroscience*. Malden, MA: Wiley-Blackwell.
Bishop, John (1981). 'Peacocke on Intentional Explanation', *Analysis*, 41: 92 ff.
——(1983). 'Agent Causation', *Mind*, 92: 61 ff.
——(1985). 'Causal Deviancy and Multiple Intentions: A Reply to James Montmarquet', *Analysis*, 45: 163 ff.
——(1986). 'Is Agent-Causality a Conceptual Primitive', *Synthese*, 67: 225 ff.

Bishop, John (1989). *Natural Agency: An Essay on the Causal Theory of Action.* Cambridge: Cambridge University Press.

——(2003). 'Prospects for a Naturalist Libertarianism: O'Connor's Persons and Causes', *Philosophy and Phenomenological Research*, 66: 228 ff.

Bittner, Rüdiger (2001). *Doing Things for Reasons.* Oxford: Oxford University Press.

Blakemore, S. J. and Decety, J. (2001). 'From the Perception of Action to the Understanding of Intention', *Natural Review Neuroscience*, 2: 561 ff.

Block, Ned (1980). 'Introduction: What is Physicalism?', in Block (ed.), *Readings in the Philosophy of Psychology.* Vol. 1. London: Methuen.

Brand, Myles (1984). *Intending and Acting: Toward a Naturalized Action Theory*, Cambridge, MA: MIT Press.

——(1989). 'Proximate Causes of Action', *Philosophical Perspectives*, 3: 424 ff.

Bratman, Michael (1984). 'Two Faces of Intention', reprinted in A. Mele (ed.), *The Philosophy of Action.* Oxford: Oxford University Press, 1997.

——(1987). *Intentions, Plans, and Practical Reason.* Cambridge, MA: Harvard University Press.

——(1996). 'Identification, Decision, and Treating as a Reason', *Philosophical Topics*, 24: 1 ff.

——(2000). 'Reflection, Planning and Temporally Extended Agency', *The Philosophical Review*, 109: 35 ff.

——(2001). 'Two Problems about Human Agency', *Proceedings of the Aristotelian Society*, 101: 309 ff.

——(2002). 'Hierarchy, Circularity, and Double Reduction', in S. Buss and L. Overton (eds.), *Contours of Agency: Essays on Themes from Harry Frankfurt.* Cambridge, MA: MIT Press.

——(2003). 'Autonomy and Hierarchy', in E. F. Paul, F. D. Miller, and J. Paul (eds.), *Autonomy.* Cambridge: Cambridge University Press.

——(2005). 'Planning Agency, Autonomous Agency', in J. C. Taylor (ed.), *Personal Autonomy: New Essays on Personal Autonomy and its Role in Contemporary Moral Philosophy.* Cambridge: Cambridge University Press.

Broad, C. D. (1925). 'Mechanism and Emergentism', reprinted in J. Kim and E. Sosa (eds.) *Metaphysics: An Anthology.* Oxford: Blackwell, 1999.

——(1952). 'Determinism, Indeterminism, and Libertarianism', in C. D. Broad, *Ethics and the History of Philosophy.* London: Routledge & Kegan Paul.

Brown, D. G. (1968). *Action.* Toronto: University of Toronto Press.

Buchheim, Thomas (2006). *Unser Verlangen nach Freiheit: Kein Traum, sondern Drama mit Zukunft.* Hamburg: Meiner.

Burge, Tyler (1993). 'Mind–Body Causation and Explanatory Practice', in J. Heil and A. Mele (eds.), *Mental Causation.* Oxford: Oxford University Press.

Byerly, Henry (1979). 'Substantial Causes and Nomic Determination', *Philosophy of Science*, 46: 57 ff.

Campbell, C. A. (1951). 'Is "Freewill" a Pseudo-Problem?', *Mind*, 60: 441 ff.

Campbell, K. (1990). *Abstract Particulars.* Oxford: Blackwell.

Carnap, Rudolf (1953). 'Testability and Meaning', in H. Feigl and M. Brodbeck (eds.), *Readings in the Philosophy of Science.* New York: Appleton-Century-Crofts.

Cartwright, Nancy (1989). *Nature's Capacities and their Measurement.* Oxford: Oxford University Press.

——(1997). 'Where the Laws of Nature Come From', *Dialectica*, 51: 65 ff.

Chang, Ruth (2004). 'Can Desires Provide Reasons for Action?', in J. Wallace *et al.* (eds.), *Reasons and Value: Themes from the Moral Philosophy of Joseph Raz*. Oxford: Oxford University Press.

Chisholm, Roderick (1958). 'Responsibility and Avoidability', in S. Hook (ed.), *Determinism and Freedom in the Age of Modern Physics*. New York: New York University Press.

——(1966). 'Freedom and Action', in K. Lehrer (ed.), *Freedom and Determinism*. New York: Random House.

——(1969). 'Some Puzzles about Agency', in K. Lambert (ed.), *The Logical Way of Doing Things*. New Haven, CT: Yale University Press.

——(1976). *Person and Object. A Metaphysical Study*. London: Allen and Unwin.

——(1978). 'Comments and Replies', *Philosophia*, 7: 597 ff.

——(1995). 'Agents, Causes and Events: the Problem of Free Will', in O'Connor (ed.), *Agents, Causes and Events: Essays on Determinism and Free Will*. New York: Oxford University Press.

Churchland, Paul M. (1970). 'The Logical Character of Action-Explanations', *Philosophical Review*, 79: 214 ff.

——(1981). 'Eliminative Materialism and the Propositional Attitudes', *Journal of Philosophy*, 78: 67 ff.

Churchland, Patricia S. (1986). *Neurophilosophy. Toward a Unified Science of the Mind-Brain*. Cambridge, MA: MIT Press.

Clarke, Randolph (1993). 'Towards a Credible Agent-causal Account of Free Will', reprinted in T. O'Connor (ed.), *Agents, Causes and Events: Essays on Determinism and Free Will*. New York: Oxford University Press, 1995.

——(1996). 'Agent Causation and Event Causation in the Production of Free Action', *Philosophical Topics*, 24: 19 ff.

——(2000). 'Modest Libertarianism', *Philosophical Perspectives*, 14: 21 ff.

——(2003). *Libertarian Accounts of Free Will*. Oxford: Oxford University Press.

Collins, Arthur (1987). *The Nature of Mental Things*. Notre Dame, IN: University of Notre Dame Press.

——(1997). 'The Psychological Reality of Reasons', *Ratio*, 10(2): 108 ff.

Cover, J. A. and O'Leary-Hawthorne, J. (1996). 'Free Agency and Materialism', in J. Jordan and D. Howard-Snyder (eds.). *Faith, Freedom, and Rationality: Philosophy of Religion Today*. Lanham, MD: Rowman and Littlefield.

Crane, Tim (ed.) (1996). *Dispositions. A Debate*. London and New York: Routledge.

Cross, Troy (2005). 'What is a Disposition?', *Synthèse*, 144: 321 ff.

Cuypers, Stefaan (1998). 'Robust Activity, Event-Causation, and Agent-Causation', in J. Bransen and S. Cuypers (eds.), *Human Action, Deliberation and Causation*. Dordrecht: Kluwer.

Dancy, Jonathan (2000). *Practical Reality*. Oxford: Clarendon Press.

——(2003). 'Replies', *Philosophy and Phenomenological Research*, 67: 468 ff.

Danto, Arthur (1965). 'Basic Actions', reprinted in A. White (ed.), *The Philosophy of Action*. Oxford: Oxford University Press, 1968.

Darwall, Stephen (1983). *Impartial Reasons*. Ithaca, NY: Cornell University Press.

Davidson, Donald (1963). 'Actions, Reasons, and Causes', reprinted in Davidson (1980).

——(1966). 'The Logical Analysis of Action Sentences', reprinted in Davidson (1980).

——(1967). 'Causal Relations', reprinted in Davidson (1980).

——(1970a). 'Mental Events', reprinted in Davidson (1980).

Davidson, Donald (1970b). 'How is Weakness of the Will Possible?', reprinted in Davidson (1980).
——(1971a). 'Agency', reprinted in Davidson (1980).
——(1971b). 'Psychology as Philosophy', reprinted in Davidson (1980).
——(1973a). 'Freedom to Act', reprinted in Davidson (1980).
——(1973b). 'Radical Interpretation', reprinted in Davidson (1984).
——(1976). 'Hempel on Explaining Actions', reprinted in Davidson (1980).
——(1978). 'Intention', reprinted in Davidson (1980).
——(1980). *Essays on Actions and Events*. Oxford: Oxford University Press.
——(1984). *Inquiries into Truth and Interpretation*. Oxford: Oxford University Press.
——(1987). 'Problems in the Explanation of Action', in P. Pettit, R. Sylvan, and J. Norman (eds.), *Metaphysics and Morality: Essays in Honour of J. J. C. Smart*. Oxford: Blackwell.
——(1990). 'Representation and Interpretation', in M. Said, W. Newton-Smith, R. Viale, and K. Wilkes (eds.), *Modelling the Mind*. Oxford: Oxford University Press.
——(1993a). 'Thinking Causes', in J. Heil and A. Mele (eds.), *Mental Causation*. Oxford: Oxford University Press.
——(1993b). 'Replies to Stoecker', in R. Stoecker (ed.), *Reflecting Davidson: Donald Davidson Responding to an International Forum of Philosophers*. Berlin and New York: de Gruyter.
Descartes, René (1982). *Principia Philosophiae. Oeuvres de Descartes VIII–1*, ed. C. Adam and P. Tannery. Paris: Librairie Philosophique J. Vrin.
Donagan, Alan (1987). *Choice: The Essential Element in Human Action*. London and New York: Routledge & Kegan Paul.
Dretske, Fred (1988). *Explaining Behavior*. Bradford, MA: MIT Press.
Edgley, R. (1965). 'Practical Reason', reprinted in J. Raz (ed.), *Practical Reasoning*. Oxford Oxford University Press, 1978.
Ehring, D. (1986). 'The Transference Theory of Causation', *Synthèse*, 67: 249 ff.
Ellis, Brian (2001). *Scientific Essentialism*. Cambridge: Cambridge University Press.
Enç, Berent (2003). *How We Act: Causes, Reasons, and Intentions*. Oxford: Oxford University Press.
——(2004). 'Causal Theories of Intentional Behavior and Wayward Causal Chains', *Behavior and Philosophy*, 32: 149 ff.
Falkenburg, Brigitte (2006). 'Was heißt es, determiniert zu sein? Grenzen der naturwissenschaftlichen Erklärung', in D. Sturma (ed.), *Philosophie und Neurowissenschaften*. Frankfurt am Main: Suhrkamp.
Fischer, John Martin (1994). *The Metaphysics of Free Will*. Oxford: Blackwell.
Frankfurt, Harry (1969). 'Alternate Possibilities and Moral Responsibility', *Journal of Philosophy*, 66: 829 ff.
——(1971). 'Freedom of the Will and the Concept of a Person', reprinted in G. Watson (ed.), *Free Will*, first edn. Oxford: Oxford University Press, 1982.
——(1975). 'Three Concepts of Free Action', reprinted in Frankfurt (1988a).
——(1977). 'Identification and Externality', reprinted in Frankfurt (1988a).
——(1978). 'The Problem of Action', reprinted in A. Mele (ed.), *The Philosophy of Action*, Oxford: Oxford University Press, 1997.
——(1987). 'Identification and Wholeheartedness', reprinted in Frankfurt (1988a).
——(1988a). *The Importance of What we Care About*. Cambridge: Cambridge University Press.
——(1988b). 'The Importance of What we Care About', in Frankfurt (1988a).

—— (1992). 'The Faintest Passion', reprinted in Frankfurt (1999).
—— (1993). 'Autonomy, Necessity, and Love', reprinted in Frankfurt (1999).
—— (1999). *Necessity, Volition, and Love*. Cambridge: Cambridge University Press.
—— (2002). 'Replies', in S. Buss and L. Overton (eds.), *Contours of Agency: Essays on Themes from Harry Frankfurt*. Cambridge, MA: MIT Press.
—— (2004). 'Disengaging Reason', in J. Wallace *et al.* (eds.), *Reasons and Value: Themes from the Moral Philosophy of Joseph Raz*. Oxford: Oxford University Press.
—— (2006). *Taking Ourselves Seriously. Getting it Right*, ed. Debra Satz. Stanford: Stanford University Press.
Frith, C. D., Blakemore, S.-J., and Wolpert, D. M. (2000). 'Explaining the Symptoms of Schizophrenia: Abnormalities in the Awareness of Actions', *Brain Research Reviews*, 31: 357 ff.
Gauthier, David (1986). *Morals by Agreement*. Oxford: Clarendon Press.
Gibbard, Allan (1990). *Wise Choices, Apt Feelings*. Cambridge, MA: Harvard University Press.
Gillett, Carl (2002). 'The Varieties of Emergence: Their Purposes, Obligations and Importance', *Grazer Philosophische Studien*, 65: 95 ff.
Ginet, Carl (1990). *On Action*. Cambridge: Cambridge University Press.
—— (2002a). 'Freedom, Responsibility and Agency', in R. Kane (ed.), *Free Will*. Oxford: Blackwell.
—— (2002b). 'Reasons Explanations of Action: Causalist versus Noncausalist Accounts', in R. Kane (ed.), *The Oxford Handbook of Free Will*. Oxford: Oxford University Press.
Goldman, Alvin (1970). *A Theory of Human Action*. Princeton, NJ: Princeton University Press.
Goodman, Nelson (1955). *Fact, Fiction and Forecast*. First edn. Cambridge, MA: Harvard University Press.
Greenwood, John (1989). 'Agency, Causality, and Meaning', *Journal for the Theory of Social Behaviour*, 18: 95 ff.
Grice, Paul (1975). 'Logic and Conversation', reprinted in Grice (1989).
—— (1981). 'Presupposition and Conversational Implicature', reprinted in Grice (1989).
—— (1989). *Studies in the Ways of Words*. Cambridge, MA: Harvard University Press.
Gustafson, D. (1987). *Intention and Agency*. Dordrecht and Boston: Reidel.
Hacker, Peter (2007). *Human Nature: The Categorial Framework*. Oxford and Malden, MA: Blackwell.
Hampshire, Stuart (1959). *Thought and Action*. New edn. London: Chatto and Windus, 1982.
Handbuch der philosophischen Grundbegriffe, Studienausgabe, eds. H. Krings, H. M. Baumgartner, and C. Wild. München: Kösel, 1973 ff.
Harman, Gilbert (1976). 'Practical Reasoning', reprinted in A. Mele (ed.), *The Philosophy of Action*. Oxford: Oxford University Press, 1997.
—— (1993). 'Desired Desires', in R. G. Fry and C. W. Morris (eds.), *Value Welfare and Morality*. Cambridge: Cambridge University Press.
Harré, Rom (2001). 'Active Powers and Powerful Actors', *Philosophy*, 48 (suppl.): 91 ff.
—— and Madden, E. H. (1975). *Causal Powers: A Theory of Natural Necessity*. Oxford: Blackwell.
Hart, H. L. A. and Honoré, T. (1959). *Causation in the Law*. First edn. Oxford: Clarendon Press.
Hawthorne, J. and Manley, D. (2005). 'Stephen Mumford: Dispositions', *Noûs*, 39: 179 ff.
Heil, J. (2003). *From an Ontological Point of View*. Oxford: Clarendon Press.
—— (2005). 'Dispositions', *Synthése*, 144: 343 ff.
Hempel, Carl (1965). *Aspects of Scientific Explanation*. New York: Free Press.

Hobbes, Thomas (1991). *Leviathan*, ed. Richard Tuck. Cambridge: Cambridge University Press.
——(1997). *Elemente der Philosophie. Erste Abteilung: Der Körper*, transl. and ed. K. Schuhman. Hamburg: Meiner.
Honderich, Ted (1993). *How Free Are You? The Determinism Problem*. Oxford and New York: Oxford University Press.
Hornsby, Jennifer (1980). *Actions*. London: Routledge & Kegan Paul.
——(1993). 'Agency and Causal Explanation', reprinted in A. Mele (ed.), *The Philosophy of Action*. Oxford: Oxford University Press, 1997.
——(2004). 'Agency and Actions', in John Hyman and Helen Steward (eds.), *Agency and Action*. Cambridge: Cambridge University Press.
Hume, David (1974). *Enquiries concerning Human Understanding and Concerning the Principles of Morals*, reprinted from the 1777 edition, ed. L. Selby-Bigge and P. Nidditch, third edn. Oxford: Clarendon Press.
——(1978). *A Treatise of Human Nature*, ed. L. Selby-Bigge and P. Nidditch, second edn. Oxford: Clarendon Press.
Humphreys, Paul (1997). 'How Properties Emerge', *Philosophy of Science*, 64: 1 ff.
Hursthouse, Rosalind (2000). 'Intention', in R. Teichmann (ed.), *Logic, Cause and Action: Essays in Honour of Elizabeth Anscombe*. Cambridge: Cambridge University Press.
Hüttemann, Andreas (2005). 'Explanation, Emergence, and Quantum Entanglement', *Philosophy of Science*, 72: 114 ff.
Hyman, John (1999). 'How Knowledge Works', *Philosophical Quarterly*, 49: 433 ff.
Iorio, Marco (1998). *Echte Gründe, echte Vernunft. Über Handlungen, ihre Erklärung und Begründung*. Dresden: Dresden University Press.
Jackson, Frank (1998). *From Metaphysics to Ethics: A Defence of Conceptual Analysis*. Oxford: Oxford University Press.
James, William (1890). *Principles of Psychology*, reprinted. New York: Dover, 1950.
Jeannerod, Marc (1997). *The Cognitive Neuroscience of Action*. Oxford: Blackwell.
——(2003). 'Consciousness of Action and Self-Consciousness: A Cognitive Neuroscience Approach', in J. Roessler and N. Eilan (eds.), *Agency and Self-Awareness*. Oxford: Clarendon Press.
Kane, Robert (1996). *The Significance of Free Will*. New York: Oxford University Press.
Kant, Immanuel (1961). *Kritik der praktischen Vernunft*, ed. Joachim Kopper. Stuttgart: Reclam.
——(1996). *Kritik der reinen Vernunft*, ed. Ingeborg Heidemann. Stuttgart: Reclam.
Karlsson, Mikael (2002). 'Agency and Patiency: Back to Nature?', *Philosophical Explorations*, 5: 59 ff.
Keil, Geert (2000). *Handeln und Verursachen*. Frankfurt am Main: Klostermann.
Kenny, Anthony (1963). *Action, Emotion and the Will*. London: Routledge & Kegan Paul.
——(1975). *Freedom, Will and Power*. Oxford: Blackwell.
——(1989). *The Metaphysics of Mind*. Oxford: Clarendon Press.
Kim, Jaegwon (1976). 'Events as Property Exemplifications', in M. Brand and D. Walton (eds.), *Action Theory*. Dordrecht: Springer.
——(1989a). 'The Myth of Nonreductive Materialism', *Proceedings and Addresses of the American Philosophical Association*, 63: 31 ff.
——(1989b). 'Mechanism, Purpose, and Explanatory Exclusion', reprinted in A. Mele (ed.), *The Philosophy of Action*. Oxford: Oxford University Press, 1997.

——(1992). '"Downward Causation" and Emergence', in A. Beckermann, H. Flohr, and J. Kim (eds.), *Emergence or Reduction? Essays on the Prospects of Nonreductive Physicalism*. Berlin and New York: de Gruyter.

——(1993). 'The Non-Reductivist's Trouble with Mental Causation', in J. Heil and A. Mele (eds.), *Mental Causation*. Oxford: Oxford University Press, 1997.

——(1998). *Mind in a Physical World*. Cambridge, MA: MIT Press.

——(2000). 'Making Sense of Downward Causation', in P. Andersen, C. Emmeche, N. Finnemann, and P. Christiansen (eds.), *Downward Causation. Minds, Bodies and Matter*. Aarhus: Aarhus University Press.

Korsgaard, Christine (1996). *The Sources of Normativity*, ed. Onora O'Neill. Cambridge: Cambridge University Press.

Kripke, Saul (1980). *Naming and Necessity*. Cambridge, MA: Harvard University Press.

Kusser, Anna (2000). 'Zwei-Stufen-Theorie und praktische Überlegung', in M. Betzler and B. Guckes (eds.), *Autonomes Handeln. Beiträge zur Philosophie Harry G. Frankfurts*. Berlin: Akademie-Verlag.

Lakoff, George (1965). 'On the Nature of Syntactic Irregularity', in *Mathematical Linguistics and Automatic Translation*, ed. A. Oettinger (report no. NSF-16 to the National Science Foundation). Cambridge, MA: Harvard University Computation Laboratory.

Lanz, Peter (1993). 'The Explanatory Force of Action Explanations', in R. Stoecker (ed.), *Reflecting Davidson: Donald Davidson Responding to an International Forum of Philosophers*. Berlin and New York: de Gruyter.

Lewis, David (1973). 'Causation', reprinted in J. Kim and E. Sosa (eds.), *Metaphysics: An Anthology*. Oxford: Blackwell, 1999.

——(1979). 'Counterfactual Dependence and Time's Arrow', reprinted in Lewis, *Philosophical Papers*, vol. 2. Oxford: Clarendon Press, 1986.

——(1997). 'Finkish Dispositions', *Philosophical Quarterly*, 47: 143 ff.

Libet, Benjamin (1985). 'Unconscious Cerebral Initiative and the Role of Conscious Will in Voluntary Action', *Behavioral Brain Sciences*, 8: 529 ff.

Locke, John (1975). *An Essay Concerning Human Understanding*, ed. P. Nidditch. Oxford: Clarendon Press.

Lowe, Jonathan (2001). 'Event Causation and Agent Causation', *Grazer Philosophische Studien*, 61: 1 ff.

——(2002). *A Survey of Metaphysics*. Oxford: Oxford University Press.

——(2006). *The Four-Category Ontology*. Oxford: Clarendon Press.

Mackie, J. L. (1965). 'Causes and Conditions', reprinted in J. Kim and E. Sosa (eds.), *Metaphysics: An Anthology*. Oxford: Blackwell, 1999.

Malcolm, Norman (1968). 'The Conceivability of Mechanism', reprinted in G. Watson (ed.), *Free Will*, first edn. Oxford: Oxford University Press, 1982.

Malebranche, Nicholas (1982). *The Search after Truth*, transl. and ed. T. Lennon and P. Olscamp. Cambridge: Cambridge University Press, 1982.

Marcel, Anthony (2003). 'The Sense of Agency: Awareness and Ownership of Action', in J. Roessler and N. Eilan (eds.), *Agency and Self-Awareness*. Oxford: Clarendon Press.

Martin, C. B. (1994). 'Dispositions and Conditionals', *Philosophical Quarterly*, 44: 1 ff.

Maudlin, Tim (1998). 'Part and Whole in Quantum Mechanics', in E. Castellani (ed.), *Interpreting Bodies*. Princeton, NJ: Princeton University Press.

McCann, Hugh (1998). *The Works of Agency: On Human Action, Will, and Freedom*. Ithaca, NY: Cornell University Press.

Mayr, Erasmus (2009). 'Akteurskausalität und das Datiertheitsproblem', *Erwägen Wissen Ethik*, 20 (1): 48 ff.

McDowell, John (1981). 'Non-Cognitivism and Rule Following', reprinted in A. Crary and R. Read (eds.), *The New Wittgenstein*. London and New York: Routledge, 2000.

——(1985). 'Functionalism and Anomalous Monism', in E. LePore and B. McLaughlin (eds.), *Actions and Events: Perspectives on the Philosophy of Donald Davidson*. Oxford: Blackwell.

Meixner, Uwe (2001). *Theorie der Kausalität*. Paderborn: Mentis.

——(2002). 'How to Reconcile Non-Physical Causation with the Physical Conservation Laws', in C. U. Moulines and K.-G. Niebergall (eds.), *Argument und Analyse*. Paderborn: Mentis.

Melden, A. I. (1961). *Free Action*. London: Routledge & Kegan Paul.

Mele, Alfred (1987). 'Intentional Action and Wayward Causal Chains: The Problem of Tertiary Waywardness', *Philosophical Studies*, 51: 55 ff.

——(1992). *Springs of Action: Understanding Intentional Behaviour*. New York: Oxford University Press.

——(1995). *Autonomous Agents: From Self-Control to Autonomy*. New York: Oxford University Press.

——(2000). 'Goal-Directed Action: Teleological Explanations, Causal Theories, and Deviance', *Philosophical Perspectives*, 14: 279 ff.

——(2003). *Motivation and Agency*. Oxford: Oxford University Press.

——(2005). 'Agnostic Autonomism Revisited', in J. C. Taylor (ed.), *Personal Autonomy: New Essays on Personal Autonomy and its Role in Contemporary Moral Philosophy*. Cambridge: Cambridge University Press.

——(2006a). 'Practical Mistakes and Intentional Actions', *American Philosophical Quarterly*, 43: 249 ff.

——(2006b). *Free Will and Luck*. Oxford: Oxford University Press.

——and Moser, Paul (1994). 'Intentional Action', reprinted in A. Mele (ed.), *The Philosophy of Action*. Oxford: Oxford University Press, 1997.

Mellor, D. H. (1974). 'In Defence of Dispositions', *Philosophical Review*, 83: 157 ff.

——(1995). *The Facts of Causation*. London and New York: Routledge.

Mill, John Stuart (1879). *System of Logic*, tenth edn. London: Longmans, Green.

Mitchell, Dorothy (1982). 'Deviant Causal Chains', *American Philosophical Quarterly*, 19: 351 ff.

Molnar, George (2003). *Powers: A Study in Metaphysics*, ed. S. Mumford. Oxford: Oxford University Press.

Montmarquet, James (1982). 'Causal Deviancy and Multiple Intentions', *Analysis*, 42: 106 ff.

——(1986). 'Prosthesis and Pre-emption', *Analysis*, 46: 147 ff.

Moran, Richard (2002). 'Frankfurt on Identification', in S. Buss and L. Overton (eds.), *Contours of Agency: Essays on Themes from Harry Frankfurt*. Cambridge, MA: MIT Press.

Morton, Adam (1975). 'Because he Thought he had Insulted Him', *Journal of Philosophy*, 72: 5 ff.

Moya, Carlos (1990). *The Philosophy of Action: An Introduction*. Cambridge: Polity Press.

Mumford, Stephen (1998). *Dispositions*. Oxford: Oxford University Press.

Nadler, Steven (2000). 'Malebranche on Causation', in Nadler (ed.), *The Cambrige Companion to Malebranche*. Cambridge and New York: Cambridge University Press.

Nagel, Ernest (1953). 'Teleological Explanations and Teleological Systems', reprinted in H. Feigl and M. Brodbeck (eds.), *Readings in the Philosophy of Science*. New York: Appleton-Century-Crofts.
——(1961). *The Structure of Science*. New York: Harcourt, Brace & World.
Nagel, Thomas (1978). *The Possibility of Altruism*. Princeton, NJ: Princeton University Press.
——(1986). *The View from Nowhere*. New York: Oxford University Press.
Nida-Rümelin, Julian (2005). *Über menschliche Freiheit*. Stuttgart: Reclam.
O'Connor, Timothy (1994). 'Emergent Properties', *American Philosophical Quarterly*, 31: 91 ff.
——(1995). 'Agent Causation', in O'Connor (ed.), *Agents, Causes and Events: Essays on Determinism and Free Will*. New York: Oxford University Press.
——(2000). *Persons and Causes: The Metaphysics of Free Will*. Oxford and New York: Oxford University Press.
O'Shaughnessy, B. (1973). 'Trying (as the Mental "Pineal Gland")', *Journal of Philosophy*, 70: 365 ff.
Pacherie, E., Green, M., and Bayne, T. (2006). 'Phenomenology and Delusion: Who Put the "Alien" in Alien Control?', *Consciousness and Cognition*, 15: 566 ff.
Peacocke, Christopher (1979a). 'Deviant Causal Chains', *Midwest Studies in Philosophy*, 4: 123 ff.
——(1979b). *Holistic Explanation, Action, Space, Interpretation*. Oxford: Clarendon Press.
Pears, David (1975). 'The Appropriate Causation of Intentional Basic Actions', *Critica*, 7: 39 ff.
Pereboom, Derk (2001). *Living Without Free Will*. Cambridge: Cambridge University Press.
Perner, Josef (2003). 'Dual Control and the Causal Theory of Action: The Case of Non-intentional Action', in J. Roessler and N. Eilan (eds.), *Agency and Self-Awareness*. Oxford: Clarendon Press.
Pettit, P. and Smith, M. (1990). 'Backgrounding Desire', *The Philosophical Review*, 99: 565 ff.
Pollock, J.L. (1976). *Subjunctive Reasoning*. Dordrecht: Reidel.
Popper, Karl (1972). *Objective Knowledge: An Evolutionary Approach*. Oxford: Clarendon Press.
Prichard, H.A. (1949). *Moral Obligation*. Oxford: Clarendon Press.
Prior, Elizabeth (1985). *Dispositions*. Aberdeen: Aberdeen University Press.
——and Pargetter, R. and Jackson, F. (1982). 'Three Theses about Dispositions', *American Philosophical Quarterly*, 19: 251 ff.
Proust, Joelle (2003). 'Perceiving Intentions', in J. Roessler and N. Eilan (eds.), *Agency and Self-Awareness*. Oxford: Clarendon Press.
Quante, Michael (2000). 'The Things we Do for Love. Zur Weiterentwicklung von Frankfurts Analyse personaler Autonomie', in M. Betzler and B. Guckes (eds.), *Autonomes Handeln. Beiträge zur Philosophie Harry G. Frankfurts*. Berlin: Akademie-Verlag.
Quine, Willard Van Orman (1960). *Word and Object*, first edn. Cambridge, MA: Wiley.
——(1961). *From a Logical Point of View*, second edn. Cambridge, MA: Harvard University Press.
——(1969). 'Natural Kinds', reprinted in J. Kim and E. Sosa (eds.), *Metaphysics: An Anthology*. Oxford: Blackwell, 1999.
——(1974). *The Roots of Reference*. LaSalle, IL: Open Court.
——(1976). 'On Multiplying Entities', in Quine, *The Ways of Paradox and Other Essays*. Cambridge, MA: Harvard University Press.
——(1985). 'Events and Reification', in E. LePore and B. McLaughlin (eds.), *Actions and Events: Perspectives on the Philosophy of Donald Davidson*. Oxford: Blackwell.

Raz, Joseph (1975). 'Reasons for Actions, Decisions and Norms', reprinted in Raz (ed.), *Practical Reasoning*. Oxford: Oxford University Press, 1978.
——(1978). 'Introduction', in Raz (ed.), *Practical Reasoning*. Oxford: Oxford University Press.
——(1999). *Engaging Reason*. Oxford: Oxford University Press.
Reichenbach, Hans (1956). *The Direction of Time*. Berkeley and Los Angeles: University of California Press.
Reid, Thomas (1983). *Philosophical Works*, eighth edn., ed. W. Hamilton. Edinburgh: 1895; reprinted, with an introduction by H. Bracken, second edn. Hildesheim: Olms.
Rives, Bradley (2005). 'Why Dispositions are (Still) Distinct from their Bases and Causally Impotent', *American Philosophical Quarterly*, 42: 19 ff.
Roessler, J. and Eilan, N. (eds.) (2003). 'Agency and Self-Awareness: Mechanisms and Epistemology', in Roessler and Eilan (eds.), *Agency and Self-Awareness*. Oxford: Clarendon Press.
Rowe, William (1995). 'Two Concepts of Freedom', reprinted in T. O'Connor (ed.), *Agents, Causes and Events: Essays on Determinism and Free Will*. New York: Oxford University Press, 1995.
Rundle, Bede (2004). *Why there is Something rather than Nothing*. Oxford: Clarendon Press.
Runggaldier, E. and Kanzian, C. (1998). *Grundprobleme der Analytischen Ontologie*. Paderborn: Schöningh.
Russell, Bertrand (1911–12). 'On the Relation of Universals and Particulars', *Proceedings of the Aristotelian Society*, 12: 1 ff.
Ryle, Gilbert (1990). *The Concept of Mind*. Repr. Harmondsworth: Penguin.
Salmon, Wesley (1973). 'Causality: Production and Propagation', reprinted in E. Sosa and M. Tooley (eds.), *Causation*. Oxford: Oxford University Press, 1993.
Scanlon, Michael (1998). *What We Owe to Each Other*. Cambridge, MA: Belknap Press of Harvard University Press.
——(2002). 'Reasons and Passions', in S. Buss and L. Overton (eds.), *Contours of Agency: Essays on Themes from Harry Frankfurt*. Cambridge: MIT Press.
Schroeder, Severin (2001). 'Are Reasons Causes?: A Wittgensteinian Response to Davidson', in Schroeder (ed.), *Wittgenstein and Contemporary Philosophy of Mind*. Basingstoke: Palgrave.
Schroeter, François (2004). 'Endorsement and Autonomous Agency', *Philosophy and Phenomenological Research*, 69: 633 ff.
Schueler, G. F. (2003). *Reasons and Purposes: Human Rationality and the Teleological Explanation of Action*. Oxford: Oxford University Press.
Searle, John (1983). *Intentionality*. Cambridge: Cambridge University Press.
——(1984). *Minds, Brains, and Science*. Cambridge, MA: Harvard University Press.
——(2001). *Rationality in Action*. Cambridge, MA, and London: MIT Press.
Sehon, Scott (1997). 'Deviant Causal Chains and the Irreducibility of Teleological Explanation', *Pacific Philosophical Quarterly*, 78: 195 ff.
——(2005). *Teleological Realism: Mind, Agency, and Explanation*. Cambridge, MA: MIT Press.
Sellars, Wilfred (1962). 'Philosophy and the Scientific Image of Man', reprinted in Sellars, *Science, Perception and Reality*. London: Routledge & Kegan Paul, 1963.
——(1966). 'Fatalism and Determinism', in K. Lehrer (ed.), *Freedom and Determinism*. New York: Random House.
Shope, Robert (1991). 'Non-Deviant Causal Chains', *Journal of Philosophical Research*, 16: 251 ff.
Smith, A. D. (1977). 'Dispositional Properties', *Mind*, 86: 439 ff.

Smith, Michael (1987). 'The Humean Theory of Motivation', *Mind*, 96: 36 ff.
Sosa, E. and Tooley, M. (1993). 'Introduction', in Sosa and Tooley (eds.), *Causation*. Oxford: Oxford University Press,1993.
Sperry, Roger (1970). 'An Objective Approach to Subjective Experience', *Psychological Review*, 77: 585 ff.
Stephan, Achim (1992). 'Emergence: A Systematic View on its Historical Facets', in A. Beckermann, H. Flohr, and J. Kim (eds.), *Emergence or Reduction? Essays on the Prospects of Non-reductive Physicalism*. Berlin and New York: de Gruyter.
—— (2002). 'Emergentism, Irreducibility and Downward Causation', *Grazer Philosophische Studien*, 62: 77 ff.
Steward, Helen (1997). *The Ontology of Mind: Events, Processes, and States*. Oxford: Clarendon Press.
Stoecker, Ralf (1993). 'Reasons, Actions, and their Relationship', in Stoecker (ed.), *Donald Davidson Responding to an International Forum of Philosophers*. Berlin and New York: de Gruyter.
—— (2001). 'Agents in Action', *Grazer Philosophische Studien*, 61: 21 ff.
—— (2003). 'Climbers, Pigs and Wiggled Ears: The Problem of Waywardness in Action Theory', in S. Walter and H. D. Heckmann (eds.), *Physicalism and Mental Causation: The Metaphysics of Mind and Action*. Exeter: Imprint Academic.
Stout, Rowland (1996). *Things that Happen Because They Should*. Oxford: Oxford University Press.
—— (2005). *Action*. Chesham: McGill-Queen's University Press.
Stoutland, Frederick (1976a). 'The Causation of Behavior', in J. Hintikka (ed.), 'Essays on Wittgenstein in Honour of G. H. von Wright', *Acta Philosophica Fennica*, 28: 286 ff.
—— (1976b). 'The Causal Theory of Action', in J. Manninen and R. Tuomela (eds.), *Essays on Explanation and Understanding*. Dordrecht: Reidel.
—— (1985). 'Davidson on Intentional Behaviour', in E. LePore and B. McLaughlin (eds.), *Actions and Events: Perspectives on the Philosophy of Donald Davidson*. Oxford: Blackwell.
—— (1989). 'Von Wright's Theory of Action', in P. A. Schilpp and L. E. Hahn (eds.), *The Philosophy of Georg Henrik von Wright*. La Salle, IL: Open Court.
—— (1998). 'The Real Reasons', in J. Bransen and S. Cuypers (eds.), *Human Action, Deliberation and Causation*. Dordrecht: Kluwer.
—— (2001). 'Responsive Action and the Belief-Desire Model', *Grazer Philosophische Studien*, 61: 82 ff.
—— (2007). 'Reasons for Action and Psychological States', in A. Leist (ed.), *Action in Context*. Berlin and New York: de Gruyter.
Strawson, Galen (1989). *The Secret Connexion: Causation, Realism, and David Hume*. Oxford: Clarendon Press.
Strawson, Peter (1959). *Individuals*. London: Methuen.
—— (1962). 'Freedom and Resentment', reprinted in G. Watson (ed.), *Free Will*, first edn. Oxford: Oxford University Press 1982.
—— (1985). 'Causation and Explanation', in B. Vermazen and J. Hintikka (eds.), *Essays on Davidson. Actions and Events*. Oxford: Clarendon Press.
Swinburne, Richard (1997). 'The Irreducibility of Causation', *Dialectica*, 51: 79 ff.
Taylor, Richard (1958). 'Determinism and the Theory of Agency', in S. Hook (ed.), *Determinism and Freedom in the Age of Modern Physics*. New York: New York University Press.
—— (1966). *Action and Purpose*. Englewood Cliffs, NJ: Prentice-Hall.
—— (1982). 'Agent and Patient: Is There a Distinction?', *Erkenntnis*, 18: 223 ff.

Tenenbaum, Sergio (2007). *Appearances of the Good: An Essay on the Nature of Practical Reason*. Cambridge: Cambridge University Press.
Thalberg, Irving (1969). 'Constituents and Causes of Emotion and Action', *Philosophical Quarterly*, 23: 2 ff.
——(1976). 'How does Agent Causality Work?', in M. Brand and D. Walton (eds.), *Action Theory*. Dordrecht: Springer.
——(1984). 'Do Our Intentions Cause Our Intentional Actions', *American Philosophical Quarterly*, 21: 249 ff.
Thayer, H. S. (ed.) (1953). *Newton's Philosophy of Nature*. New York: Hafner.
Thomas Aquinas (1988). *Summa Theologiae*. Milan: Editiones Paulinae.
Thorp, John (1980). *Free Will: A Defence against Neurophysiological Determinism*. London: Routledge & Kegan Paul.
Tooley, Michael (1990). 'The Nature of Causation: A Singularist Account', reprinted in J. Kim and E. Sosa (eds.), *Metaphysics: An Anthology*. Oxford: Blackwell, 1999.
Van Fraasen, Bas C. (1980). *The Scientific Image*. Oxford: Clarendon Press.
Van Inwagen, Peter (1983). *An Essay on Free Will*. Oxford: Clarendon Press.
——(2002). 'Free Will Remains a Mystery', in R. Kane (ed.), *The Oxford Handbook of Free Will*. Oxford: Oxford University Press.
Velleman, David (1992). 'What Happens When Someone Acts?', *Mind*, 101: 461 ff.
von Wright, Georg Henrik (1963a). *Norm and Action: A Logical Enquiry*. London: Routledge & Kegan Paul.
——(1963b). *The Varieties of Goodness*. London: Routledge & Kegan Paul.
——(1968). 'General Theory of Action', *Acta Philosophica Fennica*, 21.
——(1969). 'On the So-called Practical Inference', reprinted in von Wright, *Practical Reason*. Oxford: Blackwell, 1983.
——(1971). *Explanation and Understanding*. London: Routledge & Kegan Paul.
——(1974). *Causality and Determinism*. New York: Columbia University Press.
——(1980). 'Freedom and Determination', *Acta Philosophica Fennica*, 30(1).
——(1983). *Practical Reason*. Oxford: Blackwell.
——(1985). 'Of Human Freedom', reprinted in von Wright, *In the Shadow of Descartes*. Dordrecht: Kluwer, 1998.
——(1989). 'A Reply to My Critics', in P. A. Schilpp and L. E. Hahn (eds.), *The Philosophy of Georg Henrik von Wright*. La Salle, IL: Open Court.
Vossenkuhl, Wilhelm (2006). *Die Möglichkeit des Guten. Ethik im 21. Jahrhundert*. München: Beck.
Walde, Bettina (2006). *Willensfreiheit und Hirnforschung: Das Freiheitsmodell des epistemischen Libertarismus*. Paderborn: Mentis.
Wallace, R. J. (1990). 'How to Argue about Practical Reason', *Mind*, 99: 355 ff.
——(1999). 'Three Conceptions of Rational Agency', *Ethical Theory and Moral Practice*, 2: 217 ff.
——(2003). 'Explanation, Deliberations, and Reasons', *Philosophy and Phenomenological Research*, 67: 427 ff.
Watson, Gary (1975). 'Free Agency', reprinted in Watson (ed.), *Free Will*, first edn. Oxford: Oxford University Press, 1982.
——(1977). 'Scepticism about Weakness of the Will', *The Philosophical Review*, 86: 316 ff.
——(1987). 'Free Action and Free Will', *Mind*, 94: 145 ff.

——(2003). 'The Work of the Will', reprinted in Watson, *Agency and Answerability: Collected Essays*. Oxford: Clarendon Press, 2004.

Wedgwood, Ralph (2006). 'The Normative Force of Reasoning', *Noûs*, 40: 660 ff.

Wegner, Daniel (2002). *The Illusion of Conscious Will*. Cambridge, MA, and London: MIT Press.

——and Wheatley, T. (1999). 'Apparent Mental Causation: Sources of the Experience of Will', *American Psychologist*, 54: 480 ff.

White, Alan (1968). 'Introduction', in White (ed.), *The Philosophy of Action*. Oxford: Oxford University Press, 1968.

Wiggins, David (1980). *Sameness and Substance*. Cambridge, MA: Harvard University Press.

Williams, Bernard (1979). 'Internal and External Reasons', reprinted in Williams, *Moral Luck*. Cambridge: Cambridge University Press, 1981.

Wilson, George M. (1989). *The Intentionality of Human Action*, revised edn. Stanford: Stanford University Press.

Wittgenstein, Ludwig (1993). *Tractatus Logico-Philosophicus. Werkausgabe Band I*, ninth edn. Frankfurt a.M.: Suhrkamp.

Wolf, Susan (1990). *Freedom within Reason*. Oxford: Oxford University Press.

Woodfield, Andrew (1976). *Teleology*. Cambridge: Cambridge University Press.

Yaffe, Gideon (2004). *Manifest Activity: Thomas Reid's Theory of Action*. Oxford: Clarendon Press.

Index

abilities to act
   'on-off' abilities 120, 130
action-schemata 125–6
addict 47–8, 51–3, 62–3, 72, 75, 87, 89
afferent image 123–4
akrasia 49–51, 64, 76, 78–9, 97, 124, 136
alienation 47–52, 54–5, 58–60, 62–5, 68–80, 82, 87–90, 96–9, 101
Alvarez, M. 4, 15 fn. 22, 20 fn. 46, 31 fn. 18, 43, 83 fn. 27, 143 fn. 5, 149, 150 fn. 23, 245 fn. 24, 246 fn. 25, 255 fn. 12, 256 fn. 19
Ammereller, E. 84 fn. 35, 86 fn. 44, 92 fn. 56
Anarchic Hand 48, 125–6
Anscombe, E. 4, 6 fn. 3, 20 fn. 45, 67, 147, 154 fn. 37, 213 fn. 29, 218 fn. 45, 257 fn. 22, 263 fn. 34
appearance of the good 99–101
Aquinas 220 fn. 47, 291 fn. 26
Aristotle 40, 166, 199 fn. 1, 214, 291

Bach, K. 109 fn. 20, 123 fn. 56, 128 fn. 67, 255 fn. 15
base property 179 fn. 24, 183–5, 216
basic action 29–30, 33, 39, 106, 121 fn. 51, 125–6, 129, 133, 139, 146, 149–150, 160, 219, 224–6, 240, 247, 255–7, 263
belief
   as background condition 95
   content of 84, 86, 92, 94, 99
   evaluative 84, 92, 98–9, 252
Bishop, J. 15 fn. 22, 28 fn. 9, 43, 107 fn. 10, 108 fn. 14, 109 fn. 19, 110 fn. 24, 112–14, 116 fn. 36, 118 fn. 43, 127–130, 150 fn. 24, 246 fn. 26
Bishop's requirement 113–14, 127, 130
Bittner, R. 84
'bottom up' picture of the world 9, 11–12, 16, 43, 240
Brand, M. 17 fn. 30, 106, 108 fn. 12, 114 fn. 29, 115–116, 178
Bratman, M. 20 fn. 44, 39 fn. 38, 47, 54 fn. 22, 69, 71 fn. 4, 73, 77–82, 90
Broad, C.D. 226–7, 235 fn. 5, 236 fn. 9
Buchheim, T. 291 fn. 26

Cartwright, N. 162 fn. 62, 173–4, 182 fn. 31
categorical property 160, 163–6, 169, 175–7, 180–7, 189, 191, 196–7, 216, 233, 240, 246–7, 292

causation
   and necessary conditions 214
   deterministic 41, 158, 227–8, 244
   direction of 156–9, 217
   immediate/proximate 108, 114–17, 121, 178
   indeterministic 41–2, 218, 227, 231
   nomological theory of 149–150
   observability of 153–4
   regularity theory of 145–9, 151–2, 156–7, 159, 213, 230
   simultaneous 108, 115, 117, 156 fn. 42, 157–159, 217
   sustaining causation 109, 116, 121–130, 140, 288
causative element 154, 202–3, 208, 222
Chisholm, R. 13 fn. 20, 15, 40 fn. 42, 41–2, 105 fn. 4, 143 fn. 5, 151 fn. 29, 245 fn. 23
Churchland, P.M. 11 fn. 15, 17
Churchland, P.S. 17, 129 fn. 69
Clarke, R. 12 fn. 18, 41, 143 fn. 5, 228 fn. 61, 229 fn. 62, 249 fn. 1
closure, causal 16 fn. 28, 240, 242–4
cognitivism 83
Collins, A. 84 fn. 35, 94 fn. 61, 95 fn. 63, 271 fn. 8
composites 40, 187, 233–5, 240–1, 243
conceptual analysis 110–11
consequence *(technical sense)* 27–28, 106
contrastive explanation 227–8
control
   counterfactual element of 32–3
   ultimate 5, 248

Dancy, J. 9 fn. 12, 83 fn. 27, 84–6, 93–5
datability objection 226–8
Davidson, D. 9 fn. 12, 12, 16 fn. 26, 17, 20–1, 28–30, 38–9, 70–2, 77, 83 fn. 29, 85 fn. 38, 104 fn. 2, 105 fn. 5, 106 fn. 8, 114–15, 137–9, 143, 145–7, 149–152, 156, 160 fn. 57, 181 fn. 27, 184 fn. 39, 214–15, 221, 226, 230, 232, 238, 240, 249, 251, 253–5, 257–9, 263–5, 267–9, 271, 287–290
Davidson's challenge 251–4, 259, 263–5, 267–8, 271, 288, 290
de dicto desire 65–68, 81
Descartes, R. 154 fn. 39, 199–200
desirability characteristic 17 fn. 31, 280
desire
   in the directed-attention sense 100–1

312 INDEX

deviance, causal, *see* waywardness
dispositions 124, 131, 137–140, 144, 161–6, 170–2, 175–180, 182, 186 fn. 42, 188, 200, 203, 206, 228, 231, 239, 288, 294–5
disposition-ascriptions/dispositional statements
  conditional analyses of 170–180, 216
  inference-ticket view of 166, 170
  reducibility of, *see* power-ascriptions
downward causation 234, 237, 240–6
Δύναμις 166

efferent image 123–4
eliminative materialism 16–17
emergence 235–241, 243, 245 fn. 24, 246 fn. 26, 291
'emerging scientific picture of the world' 16, 43, 143
Enc, B. 104 fn. 1, 109 fn. 21, 121 fn. 51, 130–3, 135
Ἐνέργεια 166
epiphenomenalism 12 fn. 16, 181–2, 237, 240–2, 247, 291
essence, nominal 192, 195–6, 220
essence, real 145, 169, 188–196
evolution 131, 133, 135 fn. 88
experiment
  controlled 173–4, 186
  randomized 173–4, 186, 196
explanation
  causal 10–11, 146, 149–152, 156, 176, 211, 214–18, 227–8, 230–1, 243–6, 251
  factive vs. non-factive 93
explanatory value 114, 142–3, 149, 294
explosive, unstable 163, 167–8, 206, 209, 215 fn. 34, 218, 225, 231, 248, 294
externalism about reasons 84
externality of desires, *see* alienation

feedback systems 109, 122–130, 135–6, 140, 271
finkishness 171, 177–9
formal cause 291
Frankfurt , H. 3, 42 fn. 54, 46–64, 69–72, 74–7, 97 fn. 68, 102, 109 fn. 20, 115 fn. 31, 121
functionalism 111–13, 176, 181–2
fusion 241

goal 123, 125, 134, 263, 265, 271, 275, 278
Goldman, A. 20 fn. 46, 30 fn. 13, 107, 151 fn. 26, 178
Grice, P. 35, 225

habits 231–2
Hacker, P. 4, 8 fn. 6, 122 fn. 53, 224 fn. 52
Harré, R. 108 fn. 18, 143 fn. 5, 153 fn. 33, 154 fn. 36, 166, 178 fn. 21, 188–191, 199 fn. 1, 200 fn. 7, 201 fn. 11, 203 fn. 13, 204, 206 fn. 17, 257 fn. 21

Hempel, C. 11 fn. 15, 148 fn. 18, 149, 217 fn. 43
hierarchical model of the will 46, 52–64 , 77
higher-order desires and volitions 53–7, 61–3
Hobbes, T. 37–8, 46–7, 52–3, 147
holism 237–240
Hornsby, J. 16 fn. 27, 29 fn. 11, 39 fn. 37, 44 fn. 62, 80 fn. 25, 143 fn. 2, 252 fn. 3
Hume, D. 9, 37, 47, 65, 142, 144–9, 152–7, 160, 164, 166–8, 170, 214, 224
Humphreys, P. 238, 241
Hydraulic model 47, 65
Hyman, J. 4, 15 fn. 22, 20 fn. 46, 43, 84 fn. 36, 86 fn. 46, 93, 143 fn. 5, 149, 150 fn. 23, 245 fn. 24, 246 fn. 25, 255 fn. 12, 256 fn. 19

identity-condition
  for actions 20–1
  for events 256
  for instantiations 183–4
implicature, conversational 35–6, 225
incompatibilism 24 fn. 2, 41–2
informativity principle 35
intentionalism 5, 18–19, 29–32, 296
intervention / manipulation view of causation 159, 230
Iorio, M. 83 fn. 31, 84, 86, 251 fn. 2

Jeannerod, M. 8 fn. 5, 125 fn. 59, 126 fn. 64, 127 fn. 65
judgement, evaluative 55 fn. 26, 63–4, 90–1, 96, 99, 101

Kant, I. 115, 286 fn. 21
Keil, G. 108 fn. 12, 216–18
Kenny, A. 4, 27 fn. 4, 28 fn. 8, 43 fn. 61, 108 fn. 11, 162 fn. 62, 175 fn. 12, 206 fn. 18, 228 fn. 60
Kim, J. 10 fn. 13, 12 fn. 16, 16 fn. 28, 182 fn. 28, 236 fn. 7, 240–242, 244, 246 fn. 26, 256
Korsgaard, C. 55 fn. 25, 57 fn. 32

Leibniz, G.W. 220 fn. 48, 255 fn. 14
Lewis, D. 158 fn. 52, 178–180
Libet's experiment 8 fn. 5
Locke, J. 37 fn. 31, 40 fn. 48, 79, 166, 199–202
Lowe, J. 41, 143 fn. 5, 165 fn. 68, 187 fn. 43, 229 fn. 63, 255 fn. 12

Madden, E.H. 108 fn. 18, 143 fn. 5, 153 fn. 33, 154 fn. 36, 166, 178 fn. 21, 188–191, 199 fn. 1, 200 fn. 7, 201 fn. 11, 203 fn. 13, 204, 257 fn. 21
Malebranche, N. 147, 199 fn. 4
Martin, C.B. 171–2, 177–8, 182 fn. 31
McDowell, J. 10 fn. 14, 47 fn. 1

INDEX   313

Mele, A. 21 fn. 48, 39 fn. 40, 41 fn. 52, 42 fn. 55, 106 fn. 7, 108 fn. 13, 109 fn. 20, 116, 123 fn. 56, 124 fn. 58, 129 fn. 71, 254 fn. 11
Mellor, D. 157 fn. 44, 160, 166, 211, 212 fn. 25, 259 fn. 26
microproperties, reducibility to 16, 233–240, 246–7, 291–2
microstructure 186, 245
Milgram experiments 78–79
Mill, J.S. 37 fn. 31, 148, 217 fn. 43, 234 fn. 2
mode of operation 224–5
Molnar, G. 157 fn. 44, 163 fn. 63, 170 fn. 2, 171 fn. 6, 172 fn. 8, 178 fn. 19, 185 fn. 41, 186 fn. 42, 187 fn. 44, 189 fn. 48, 194 fn. 56
Müller-Lyer illusion 101
Mumford, S. 164 fn. 66, 182–5, 211–12, 216 fn. 38

Nagel, E. 122 fn. 54, 235 fn. 6, 236 fn. 8, 271 fn. 9
Nagel, T. 9 fn. 11, 98
natural order 2–3, 5–6, 14–15, 19, 22, 24–6, 127, 142–5, 240, 247, 249, 255 fn. 14, 291–2, 296
naturalization 43, 103, 112, 114 fn. 29
necessity
 conceptual 188, 190–1
 epistemic 190–1
 natural 169, 188–197
Newton, I. 199, 200 fn. 5
Nida-Rümelin, J. 58 fn. 34
non-basic action 29–30, 106, 139 fn. 99, 146, 159, 226, 263

O'Connor, T. 15, 16 fn. 25, 41, 42 fn. 56, 143 fn. 5, 150 fn. 24, 227 fn. 58, 235 fn. 4, 237 fn. 10, 255 fn. 13, 256–7, 260 fn. 28, 263 fn. 37
occasion for exercise of a power 162–3, 200, 205–6, 223 fn. 51, 228, 250–1, 257
opportunity for exercise of a power 206, 218, 221–2
overdetermination
 causal 33, 148, 182 fn. 28, 214, 218, 240, 244–6
 explanatory 10–11, 296

Peacocke, C. 108–9, 117–9, 127–8
performance *(technical sense)* 23, 27–30, 32–3, 296
personal identity
 Lockean conception of 79
power-ascriptions
 (conceptual) irreducibility of 170–180, 197
 experimental testing of 172–4, 186
powers
 active 40–1, 145, 160, 198–210, 213–14, 217–224, 229, 231–3, 239, 241–2, 246 fn. 26, 247, 249–251, 288 fn. 23, 291–2, 295

categorical bases of 176, 179 fn. 24, 183–7, 216
causal 108 fn. 18, 109, 131, 137–9, 145–6, 159–161, 176, 182, 200, 206 fn. 17, 209, 213, 219–221, 224, 231, 242, 245, 257, 292
determinate 161–2, 164
generic 161–3
intrinsicality of (internality of) 170, 176, 178–9, 186 fn. 42, 189–191, 194–6, 204, 209, 215, 220–1
manifestation / realization of 109, 130–1, 133–4, 160–7, 170–2, 174, 176–8, 180, 186 fn. 42, 188, 190–1, 195–6, 199–200, 202–6, 208–224, 228–232, 234, 239, 245, 247, 249, 251–2, 288–9, 291–2, 294–5
ontological irreducibility of 145, 160, 181–7, 197, 217
passive 198–9, 202–209, 217, 230, 240
realism about 165–8, 176
pro-attitude 38, 47, 137, 221, 251–3, 266, 290
problem of free will 6, 13–14, 24, 41–3, 52, 54 fn. 21, 248
problem of human agency 2, 4–5, 13–14, 17, 19, 23–6, 43, 52, 54 fn. 21, 103, 141–2, 249, 268, 296
process, causal
 Aristotelian conception of 130, 133–4, 137
 Russellian conception of 133
properties
 dualist view of 187
 emergent 16, 234–243, 245 fn. 24, 246 fn. 26, 291
 monism about 182–3, 185, 187
 systemic 234–240, 243, 291
proximate intention 21 fn. 48, 39, 124–5
psychologism about reasons 83, 86–8, 92
purpose 131–2, 250–1, 271–2, 274, 277, 279–281, 283–4, 286, 289–290, 294

Quine, W.V.O. 110 fn. 22, 175, 176 fn. 14, 184 fn. 39, 190, 216 fn. 37, 255

rationalization 9–12, 38, 85, 249, 251, 279, 291, 293–4
rationalizing function
 objective vs. subjective 71–3
 of reasons-explanations 9–10, 17, 69–70, 279, 292–3
Raz, J. 4, 6 fn. 3, 17 fn. 32, 20 fn. 42, 74 fn. 9, 75 fn. 13, 83 fn. 27, 84 fn. 35, 86 fn. 46, 89 fn. 52, 96 fn. 66, 97–8, 286 fn. 20
reasons
 as causes 12, 249–254, 287–291
 justifying/normative 83, 85–6
 motivating 83–95, 231–2, 249–250, 252–3, 260–3, 266, 268, 270–1, 274–8, 283–5, 287–8, 290, 295

reduction, *see* microproperties, power-ascriptions, powers
Reid, T. 40–1, 143 fn. 5, 200–2, 229 fn. 63, 255 fn. 12
result of action *(technical sense)* 23, 27–30, 32–4, 36, 39, 104, 106, 121 fn. 51, 126, 129, 132, 137–9, 149–150, 160, 219, 225–6, 232, 255–7
rule-following 268, 283, 285–7
Rundle, B. 39 fn. 41, 191 fn. 53, 224 fn. 52
Russell, B. 133, 165 fn. 68, 212
Ryle, G. 38 fn. 32, 161–2, 166, 168, 170, 175

Scanlon, T. 50, 74 fn. 8, 98 fn. 72, 100
Searle, J. 9 fn. 9, 16 fn. 27, 39 fn. 37, 105 fn. 6, 115, 124 fn. 58, 142–3
Sehon, S. 117 fn. 39, 119, 260 fn. 29, 265–6, 288 fn. 22
self-assessment 273, 280
self-reflective attitude 77–80
Sellars, W. 24 fn. 3, 159 fn. 55
sensitivity 108, 117–121, 130, 134–6, 140, 274
Smith, M. 66 fn. 55, 83 fn. 27, 99 fn. 73
standard model 2–3, 12 fn. 18, 17, 37–9, 42–7
Stoecker, R. 70 fn. 3, 109 fn. 21, 131, 133, 137–9, 255 fn. 15
Stout, R. 109 fn. 21, 130–1, 133–8, 260 fn. 29
Stoutland, F. 18 fn. 35, 20 fn. 43, 31 fn. 16, 32 fn. 19, 33 fn. 20, 34, 36, 44 fn. 63, 84 fn. 35, 86 fn. 46, 93 fn. 58, 269 fn. 4, 285 fn. 17, 286 fn. 21
Strawson, G. 147 fn. 9, 148 fn. 16
Strawson, P. 114 fn. 28, 153–5, 193, 211
substance-causation 3, 144–6, 160, 169, 176, 182, 198, 209–219, 221, 224–5, 228–231, 247, 291–2
syllogism, practical 17–18, 38, 66, 70–2, 94, 253, 280–1

Taylor, R. 15 fn. 22, 41 fn. 50, 43, 143 fn. 5, 149, 151 fn. 29, 157, 217 fn. 41

teleological explanation 2, 18–19, 134–6, 265, 271, 277
teleological structure 272–282, 286–7, 296
Tenenbaum, S. 99 fn. 75
Thalberg, I. 16 fn. 27, 109 fn. 20, 151–2
Thomas, *see* Aquinas
token-token identity 16, 181–3, 185, 187
treating a desire as reason-giving 3, 47, 69–80, 82, 87–91, 96, 102
tropes 159 fn. 54, 183 fn. 34, 212–13
type-type identity 181

unintentional actions 20–1, 106, 125–6, 222–3, 239, 261

valuational system 63–4
values 63, 272
Van Inwagen, P. 24 fn. 1, 42 fn. 54
Velleman, D. 9 fn. 10, 47, 58, 60 fn. 39, 65–8, 76, 81
virtus dormitiva objection 215–16
volition 37–40, 53–8, 61–3, 71, 77
Von Wright, G.H. 4, 18 fn. 35, 19, 27–8, 30–4, 36, 43 fn. 61, 84, 143–4, 159, 230, 254 fn. 10, 259 fn. 27, 260–3, 271, 272 fn. 11
Vossenkuhl, W. 43 fn. 60

Wallace, J. 83 fn. 30, 85 fn. 40, 92 fn. 56, 260 fn. 28
Watson, G. 46, 48 fn. 4, 54–5, 57 fn. 33, 58, 63–5, 76, 87–8, 97, 99
waywardness
  antecedential 104, 106, 108, 110, 113, 116, 119–121, 140, 257, 271
  consequential 106
wholeheartedness 50 fn. 12, 51
Williams, B. 92–3, 95
Wittgenstein, L. 4, 35, 193 fn. 55, 268, 276 fn. 15, 283, 285–6

x-complete cause 178–180

The manufacturer's authorised representative in the EU for product safety is
Oxford University Press España S.A. of el Parque Empresarial San Fernando de
Henares, Avenida de Castilla, 2 – 28830 Madrid (www.oup.es/en or product.
safety@oup.com). OUP España S.A. also acts as importer into Spain of products
made by the manufacturer.

www.ingramcontent.com/pod-product-compliance
Lightning Source LLC
Chambersburg PA
CBHW071157040326
40611CB00080B/1798